# Hollywood FINANCIAL Directory

Published
Annually

Volume No. **3**

· · · · · · · · · · · · · · · · · · · · · · · · · · · · · · · · ·

▼

COPYRIGHT NOTICE

▼

TRADEMARK

Phone 310.315.4815 or
800.815.0503 (outside California)
Fax: 310.315.4816
· · · · · · · · · · · · · · · · ·

ISBN 1-878989-54-5

**HOLLYWOOD CREATIVE DIRECTORY**
3000 W. Olympic Blvd. • Suite 2525 • Santa Monica, CA 90404

# CONTENTS

*(\* next to a listing denotes a new entry or new title)*

▼

## *Hollywood Creative Directory* Staff

LINDA THURMAN — *Managing Editor*

RACHAEL R. BERRY — *Director of Administration*

JENNIFER BESAND — *Business Manager*

D.V. LAWRENCE — *Director of Marketing & Advertising*

GEORGE SMITH — *Director of Operations*

S.M. SMITH, CINDY CASAMA — *Research*

letter ....from The Editor

Dear Readers:

**Welcome to the new improved *Hollywood Financial Directory*.**

You'll find even more accurate, up-to-date information inside the new look designed by graphic artist, Dotti Albertine, who also created the new logo for our publishing company, the *Hollywood Creative Directory, Inc.*

On February 20th, we moved down the hall into a new office suite in the Lantana Center which will allow our growing staff to serve you better. Our phone and fax numbers remain the same.

To keep pace with the cost of operations and manufacturing without raising the price of our directories, *we are accepting display advertising.* Call for a rate card.

This year also marks the introduction of the *Hollywood Interactive Entertainment Directory.* We now offer six distinct directories focusing on different segments of the industry. Look for information and order form on the color pages.

Thank you to our readers and the companies and executives listed in the following pages. You make the *Hollywood Financial Directory* an integral part of our exciting industry.

Here's to great entertainment!

Very truly yours,

Linda Thurman
Managing Editor

# PLEASE DO NOT COPY THIS BOOK

We offer **REWARDS** on information of illegal photocopying or distribution of any of our books. Please call our office. *Your identity will be protected.*

# 310.315.4815

· · · · · · · · · · · · · · · · · · · · · · · · · · · · · · · · · · · · · · · · · · ·

To obtain multiple copies or subscriptions, call about our volume discounts!

# Hollywood AGENTS & MANAGERS Directory (HAD)

★ 3,200 Names of agents, managers & casting directors

★ Over 1,025 talent & literary agencies & managers across the nation

★ Addresses, phone & fax numbers, current titles

★ Published twice a year — February & August

*"I'm on the phone with hundreds of agents on a daily basis. The* **Hollywood Agents & Managers Directory** *is a constant resource for me."*
— **Danielle Portnoy, Brillstein-Grey Entertainment**

This is a directory that no one in the industry should be without whether you are a producer or casting director trying to locate talent or talent seeking representation. Included in the listings are representatives of actors, comedians, dancers, voice-over artists, models, composers, songwriters, directors, producers, writers, below-the-line talent, and photographers. Plus a bonus section of film and television casting directors. (160 pages)

## — PUBLISHED EACH FEBRUARY • AUGUST —

1 YEAR SUBSCRIPTION (ASUB1) _____ $75 + TAX/SHIPPING
2 YEAR SUBSCRIPTION (ASUB2) _____ $140 + TAX/SHIPPING
SINGLE ISSUES(HAD)_____ $45 + TAX/SHIPPING

Call **310.315.4815 • 800.815.0503** (outside California)

# Hollywood DISTRIBUTORS Directory

## (HDD)

- ★ 559 domestic & foreign distributors
- ★ 1,940 names & titles of sales, acquisitions, public relations & marketing staffs
- ★ Cable & syndicated television
- ★ Pay-per-view television
- ★ Addresses, phone & fax numbers and recent releases
- ★ Published every January

*"The **Hollywood Distributors Directory** is as valuable a resource as my Mac. Nowadays, producers need to wear a lot of hats. One of those hats is distribution. It's important to know who those players are, both domestically and abroad."*
**— George Paige, Producer**

If you're an independent producer seeking financing or distribution for your next film or series, the first step is the *Hollywood Distributors Directory*. This reliable and comprehensive directory will make film and television distribution accessible to you. Placing your project is much easier when you know who to contact. With extensive lists of public relation companies, sales and marketing staffs, and foreign and domestic distribution companies, this book is an invaluable complement to the *Hollywood Creative Directory*. *(125 pages)*

## — PUBLISHED EACH JANUARY —

**SINGLE ISSUES (HDD)** _____ **$45 + TAX/SHIPPING**

Call **310.315.4815 • 800.815.0503** (outside California)

# Hollywood INTERACTIVE ENTERTAINMENT Directory (HID)

★ Title Developers

★ Publishers

★ Platform Companies

★ Interactive TV

★ Includes games, business applications, education, & on-line services

*"In a dynamic, emerging industry like interactive media, it is essential to have the most up to date information on who's doing what and the* **Hollywood Interactive Entertainment Directory** *is the* <u>*only real source*</u>."
— **Scott Lahman, Development Executive, Activision**

The interactive community is fast becoming an important part of Hollywood. Want to turn your movie into a game? How about turning your game into a movie? Writers, actors, musicians, composers will all find this directory helpful when seeking employment opportunities. Become familiar with the future. Get interactive. (100 pages)

## — PUBLISHED EACH JANUARY —

**SINGLE ISSUES (HID)** _____ **$45 + TAX/SHIPPING**

Call **310.315.4815** • **800.815.0503** (outside California)

# Hollywood CREATIVE Directory (HCD)

## "The Film and Television Industry Bible"

- ★ Over 5,750 names
- ★ Producers - studio & network executives - writers - directors
- ★ Over 1,650 production companies, studios & networks
- ★ Includes addresses, phone & fax numbers - produced credits - staff & titles
- ★ Also companies with studio deals
- ★ Updated three times a year: March-July-November

"...*invaluable*...it's the largest group of producers I've gotten in a room at the same time..." — **Tim Daly (Wings), actor/producer**

Looking for a producer? Better make sure this book is an integral part of your library. The *Hollywood Creative Directory* gives complete up-to-date information on the status of current Hollywood production executives. If you are a writer looking to send query letters, the *Hollywood Creative Directory* will give you names and titles of development executives and story editors. Living and working within the fast paced movie an television industry requires keeping up with the changes. The *Hollywood Creative Directory* is *the* source for the Hollywood low-down. (175 pages)

## — PUBLISHED EACH MARCH • JULY • NOVEMBER —

| | |
|---|---|
| I YEAR SUBSCRIPTION (CSUBI) _____ | $105 + TAX/SHIPPING |
| 2 YEAR SUBSCRIPTION (CSUB2) _____ | $198 + TAX/SHIPPING |
| SINGLE ISSUES (HCD) _____ | $45 + TAX/SHIPPING |

Call **310.315.4815** • **800.815.0503** (outside California)

# Hollywood MOVIE MUSIC Directory ♫ ♫

## (HMD)

★ Music supervisors, composers, lyricists, music executives

★ Clearance & licensing, music libraries

★ Music production, publishers and A&R staffs

★ Over 1,625 names

★ Over 885 companies

★ Published every May

*"When I'm looking to hire a music supervisor, I use the* **Hollywood Movie Music Directory** *as my guide."* — **Carl Schurtz, composer**

What would a car chase be without the music? Whether you're selling your Oscar winning song or looking for music for your project, the *Hollywood Movie Music Directory* will satisfy all your needs. It's a priceless resource if you are a music executive at a major studio or a small independent — or want to find out who is. If you have music or need music, put this directory in your book collection. (115 pages)

## — PUBLISHED EACH MAY —

**SINGLE ISSUES (HMD)** _____ **$45 +TAX/SHIPPING**

Call **310.315.4815** • **800.815.0503** (outside California)

# Hollywood QUICKPHONE Directory (HQD)

## Now Available in Subscription Form

★ Includes all the company names from the Hollywood Creative Directory, the Hollywood Agents & Managers Directory and the Hollywood Distributors Directory

★ Over 3,000 company phone numbers listed alphabetically

★ Easy-to-read format

*"My life as an agent would be over without the Hollywood Quickphone Directory."*
— **Michael Lewis, Literary Agent, Shapiro-Lichtman Agency**

It fits in a briefcase. It fits in a purse. It fits in a glove compartment. It fits in a budget. If you spend time running around town you don't want to be without this compact directory. It's the information age and the most valuable information is a phone number. For quick access to 3,000 entertainment company phone numbers, pick up a copy of the *Hollywood Quickphone Directory*. (60 pages)

## — PUBLISHED EACH MARCH-JULY-NOVEMBER —

1 YEAR SUBSCRIPTION(QSUB1) _____ $35 + TAX/SHIPPING
2 YEAR SUBSCRIPTION (QSUB2) _____ $65 + TAX/SHIPPING
SINGLE ISSUES (HQD) _____ $15 + TAX/SHIPPING

Call **310.315.4815** • **800.815.0503** (outside California)

**MAILING LISTS** *ON LABELS & MAILMERGE SOFTWARE*

Mr. & Mrs. Jane Doe
9000 Z Lane
Star City, UT
91602

## REACH EVERYONE IN HOLLYWOOD
## WITHOUT HAVING TO TYPE A SINGLE ADDRESS LABEL!

### LABELS & MAILMERGE SOFTWARE FOR:

*Hollywood Creative Directory (HCD)*
*Hollywood Agents/Managers Directory (HAD)*
*Hollywood Distributors Directory (HDD)*
*Hollywood Financial Directory (HFD)*
*Hollywood Movie Music Directory (HMD)*
*Hollywood Interactive Entertainment Directory (HID)*

| DISCOUNTS | |
|---|---|
| Any 2 Lists | 15% OFF |
| Any 3 Lists | 20% OFF |
| Any 4 Lists | 25% OFF |
| All 6 Lists | 30% OFF |

### LABEL SPECIFICATIONS

Avery Laserjet labels, 3-up, 30 per page, 1 x 2-5/8" per label. Can be sorted by Last Name, Company, Address, City, Zip.

### DISC SPECIFICATIONS FOR MAILMERGE SOFTWARE

ASCII, Text File, delimited by quotation mrks. Comes in a 3.5" High Density Disc (1.44MB). Works best with Microsoft Word. ONLY WORKS ON IBM OR IBM COMPATIBLE SYSTEMS.

| TITLE | HCD | HAD | HDD | HFD | HID | HMD |
|---|---|---|---|---|---|---|
| **LABELS (ONE TIME)** | $350 | $250 | $225 | $200 | $175 | $175 |
| **Labels Subscription** | | | | | | |
| (HCD 3-A-Year/HAD 2-A-Year) | $600 | $425 | — | — | — | — |
| **Disc (one Time)** | $550 | $350 | $325 | $300 | $275 | $275 |
| **Disc Subscription** | | | | | | |
| (HCD 3-A-Year/HAD2-A-Year) | $700 | $500 | — | — | — | — |

## TO ORDER CALL:
## 310-315-4815 or 800-815-0503 (outside California).
### California residents must pay 8.25% sales tax. Prices include shipping.

# HCD CLASSIFIED ADS
## Below-the-Line

★ For as little as $1.00 per word, reach over 5,000 potential employers

★ Includes credits, phone numbers, union affiliations, job category

★ High exposure for 4 months

*"I was a little skeptical about advertising, but my ad in the* **Hollywood Creative Directory** *led to an immediate job on a feature film."* — **Baqi Kopelman, gaffer**

It's no secret that everyone in the entertainment industry uses the *Hollywood Creative Directory* several times a day. Producers, directors, production managers, agents, casting directors are all among the subscribers to these informative books. When choosing a place to advertise, it is important to consider the many potential publications for your advertising dollar. One of the most proven ways to get results from advertising is to place your ad in front of people who are your target customers. Take advantage of this outstanding marketing opportunity by running an ad in the HCD classifieds.

## SAMPLE JOB CATEGORIES:

**Animal Handlers/Trainers • Art Directors • Assistant Art Directors
Assistant Location Managers • Assistant Sound Editors • Best Boys
Boom Operators • Camera Operators • Casting Associates • ETC.**

## COST — $1 PER WORD.

Your name, phone number and job category are complimentary. Compose your own ad. If you have any questions, or are unsure which job category to use, give us a call at **310-315-4815**. Place your ad in 3 consecutive issues of the *Hollywood Creative Directory* and get the 4th ad **FREE**.

## DEADLINES:

**FEBRUARY 10th** _____ For the **MARCH** issue
**JUNE 10th** _____ For the **JULY** issue
**OCTOBER 10th** _____ For the **NOVEMBER** issue

Call **310.315.4815** • **800.815.0503** (outside California)

# Hollywood EXECUTIVE LIBRARY

## (HEL)

SAVE $125.00!!!!!

▼ **INCLUDES:**

★ One-Year-Subscription to the *Hollywood Creative Directory*

★ One-Year-Subscription to the *Hollywood Agents & Managers Directory*

★ One-Year-Subscription to the *Hollywood Quickphone Directory*

★ The *Hollywood Distributors Directory*

★ The *Hollywood Financial Directory*

★ The *Hollywood Movie Music Directory*

★ The *Hollywood Interactive Entertainment Directory*

Be smart. Be informed. Save money. Have all of Hollywood right at your fingertips at a special discounted price. The *Hollywood Executive Library* is a complete set of all our subscriptions and titles. Be ahead of the game with your up-to-date knowledge of the ever changing scene. Makes an impressive gift.

**A COMPLETE SET OF OUR BOOKS FOR ONE OR TWO YEARS**

**1 YEAR SUBSCRIPTION (HEL1)** _____ **$325 + TAX/SHIPPING**
**2 YEAR SUBSCRIPTION (HEL2)** _____ **$600 + TAX/SHIPPING**

Call **310.315.4815 • 800.815.0503** (outside California)

# PRICE SCHEDULE

Order by Phone, FAX or Mail by Using VISA/MC or AMEX

| TITLES | ITEM | PRICE | CA TAX | U.S. SHIP |
|---|---|---|---|---|
| Hollywood Executive Library (1year) | HEL1 | $325.00 | $26.81 | $42.00 |
| Hollywood Executive Library (2 year) | HEL2 | $600.00 | $49.5 | $84.00 |
| Hollywood Creative Dir (single issue) | HCD | 45.00 | 3.71 | 3.50 |
| HCD 1-Year Subscription (Saves you 30%) | CSUB1 | 105.00 | 8.66 | 10.50 |
| HCD 2-Year Subscription (Saves you 33%) | CSUB2 | 198.00 | 17.33 | 21.00 |
| Hollywood Agents/Managers Directory | HAD | 45.00 | 3.71 | 3.50 |
| HAD 1-Year Subscription (Saves you 17%) | ASUB1 | 75.00 | 6.19 | 7.00 |
| HAD 2-Year Subscription ( Saves you 23%) | ASUB2 | 140.00 | 11.55 | 14.00 |
| Hollywood Distributors Directory | HDD | 45.00 | 3.71 | 3.50 |
| Hollywood Financial Directory | HFD | 45.00 | 3.71 | 3.50 |
| Hollywood Interactive Entertainment Dir. | HID | 45.00 | 3.71 | 3.50 |
| Hollywood Movie Music Directory | HMD | 45.00 | 3.71 | 3.50 |
| Hollywood Quickphone Directory | HQD | 15.00 | 1.24 | 3.50 |
| Hollywood Quickphone Dir. (1 year) | QSUB1 | 35.00 | 2.89 | 10.50 |
| Hollywood Quickphone Dir. (2 year) | QSUB2 | 65.00 | 5.36 | 21.00 |

PRICES SUBJECT TO CHANGE WITHOUT NOTICE. ALL SALES ARE FINAL.

## CHECK OR MONEY ORDER TO:
**HOLLYWOOD CREATIVE DIRECTORY**
3000 W. Olympic Bvd., Suite 2413
Santa Monica, CA 90404-5041

## CREDIT CARD ORDERS:
**Phone:** 310-315-4815 or 800-815-0503 (outside California)
**FAX:** 310-315-4816 • **E-MAIL:** hcd@vine.org

## CANADA & FOREIGN:
Sent Airmail. Payable in U.S. Dollars or on funds drawn on a U.S. Bank. **Canada:** Multiply U.S. Shipping X 2.
**Foreign:** Multiply U.S. Shipping X 4.

## U.S. ORDERS:
Sent UPS Ground (Allow 3 days in CA and 5-10 out-of-state)
Please enclose proper tax and shipping.

# ORDER FORM

**ALL ORDERS MUST BE PRE-PAID**
Credit Card Orders are by Mail, FAX or Phone

| TITLES | ITEM | PRICE | QUANT | TOTAL |
|---|---|---|---|---|
| Hollywood Executive Library (1 year) | HEL1 | $325.00 | | |
| Hollywood Executive Library (2 year) | HEL2 | $600.00 | | |
| Hollywood Creative Dir. (single issue) | HCD | 45.00 | | |
| HCD 1-Year Subscription (Saves you 30%) | CSUB1 | 105.00 | | |
| HCD 2-Year Subscription (Saves you 33%) | CSUB2 | 198.00 | | |
| Hollywood Agents/Managers Directory | HAD | 45.00 | | |
| HAD 1-Year Subscription (Saves you 17%) | ASUB1 | 75.00 | | |
| HAD 2-Year Subscription ( Saves you 23%) | ASUB2 | 140.00 | | |
| Hollywood Distributors Directory | HDD | 45.00 | | |
| Hollywood Financial Directory | HFD | 45.00 | | |
| Hollywood Interactive Entertainment Dir. | HID | 45.00 | | |
| Hollywood Movie Music Directory | HMD | 45.00 | | |
| Hollywood Quickphone Directory | HQD | 15.00 | | |
| Hollywood Quickphone Dir. (1 year) | QSUB1 | 35.00 | | |
| Hollywood Quickphone Dir. (2 year) | QSUB2 | 65.00 | | |

SUBTOTAL
CA RES. ADD 8.25% TAX
ADD $3.50 Shipping per Book
TOTAL ENCLOSED

☐ VISA ☐ MC ☐ AMEX

Cardholder Name

Card Number _____ Expiration

Signature

Name

Company _____ Telephone

Street Address _____ (U.P.S. does not deliver to post office boxes.)

City _____ State _____ Zip

# SECTION A.

## Companies and Their Staff

# SECTION A.
# COMPANIES AND STAFF

**21ST CENTURY FILM CORP**.....................................................310-552-1383
    Fax:.............................................................310-552-1405
1925 Century Park East, Ste. 340
Los Angeles, CA 90067
Type: Motion Picture Production
    Ron Durkin............................................................Trustee
    Maryellen Sebold.......................................................Trustee
    *Andrea Miller.........................VP, International Sales & Administration

**40 ACRES & A MULE FILMWORKS INC**....................................718-624-3703
124 Dekalb Ave.
Brooklyn, NY 11217
Type: Motion Picture Production
    Spike Lee..........................................................President
    Vanda Simon.......................................................Comptroller

**A&E TELEVISION NETWORKS**.............................................212-661-4500
    Fax:.............................................................212-983-4370
235 E. 45th St.
New York, NY 10017
Type: Television Production
    *Nickolas Davatzes...............................................President/CEO
    *Seymour H. Lesser.............................................Exec. VP, CFO
    *Dan Davids......................Sr. VP, General Mgr., The History Channel
    *Scott Richardson.........................VP, Public Affairs & Communications
    *Joseph Warren..........................VP, Corporate Business Development
    *Mary Ann Zimmer.....................VP, Business Affairs & General Counsel

**A-PIX ENTERTAINMENT**...................................................212-764-7171
    Fax:.............................................................212-575-6578
500 Fifth Ave., 46th Floor
New York, NY 10010
Type: Distribution
    Robert Baruc.......................................................President

**ABC CABLE & INTL. BROADCAST GROUP**.................................212-456-7777
77 W. 66th St.
New York, NY 10025
    **New div. at CapCities/ABC Inc.
Type: Television Production + Distribution
    Herbert A. Granath.................................................President
    *John Healy.........................Exec. VP, ABC/Pres., ABC Intl. Operations
    Richard Spinner.............................Pres., ABC European Operations
    *Joseph Y. Abrams...........................Pres., ABC Distribution Company

**ABC ENTERTAINMENT**...........................310-557-7777/212-456-7777
    Fax:.............................................................310-557-7160
2040 Ave. of the Stars
Los Angeles, CA 90067-4785
    **ALSO: 77 W. 66th St., New York, NY 10023
Type: Television Production
    Ronald B. Sunderland.........................Exec. VP, Business Affairs/Contracts
    Michael C. Lang......................Sr. VP, Business Affairs, Broadcast Ops.
    John Wolters..................................Sr. VP, East Coast Operations
    Christine Hikawa.......................VP, Broadcast Standards & Practices
    Alan Rowan...............................VP-Asst. Controller, West Coast

**ABC PRODUCTIONS** .................................................... **310-557-6860**
　Fax:............................................................. 310-557-6021
　2020 Ave. of the Stars, 5th Fl.
　Los Angeles, CA 90067
　Type: Television Production
　Brandon Stoddard ............................................... President
　Amy Adelson ......................................... Sr. VP, Creative Affairs
　Michael Ross ......................................... Sr. VP, Business Affairs
　Ada Goldberg......................................... VP, Business & Legal Affairs
　John Schwartz ............................................ VP, Finance & Admin.

**\*AEI - ATCHITY ENT. INTL.** ................................... **213-932-0407**
　Fax:............................................................. 213-932-0321
　9601 Wilshire Blvd., Ste. 1202
　Beverly Hills, CA 90210
　Type: Motion Picture Production + Television Production
　\*Kenneth Atchity ............................................ Executive Producer

**AON ENTERTAINMENT LTD. INS. SERVICES** .................... **818-506-1500/212-661-5700**
　Fax:......................................................... 818-509-7565/212-661-7262
　10 Universal City Plaza, Ste. 2200
　Universal City, CA 91608-1002
　\*\*ALSO: 711 3rd Ave. 18th fl. New York, NY 10017
　Type: General Insurance
　\*Frank A. Powers ................................................ President
　\*Guy DeMarco ..................................... Sr. VP, General Manager (LA)
　Eric Gemballa......................................... Sr. VP, Underwriting
　\*Sandee Howle ..................................... VP, General Manager (NY)
　Richard Parkinson ............................................ VP, Underwriting

**ABOUT FACE PRODS.** ......................................... **310-278-6886/212-431-8616**
　Fax:......................................................... 310-450-5668/212-431-9144
　1341 Ocean Ave., Ste. 437
　Santa Monica, CA 90401
　\*\*ALSO: 211 W. Broadway, New York, NY 10013
　Type: Motion Picture Production
　\*Nicholas Hondrogen ............................................ Producer/Owner
　\*George Bennett ............................................ Business Affairs

**ABRAHAM & COMPANY, DAVID.** ............................... **\*203-222-1919**
　320 Post Road W.
　Westport, CT 06880
　\*\*TV/Cable/Radio
　Type: Financial Consulting
　David Abraham ................................................ President
　Lisa A. Broderick........................... Managing Dir., Technology Consulting
　Thomas E. Millitzer ..................... Managing Dir., Communications Brokerage

**\*ACTIVE ENTERTAINMENT.** ................................... **303-368-4336**
　Fax:............................................................. 303-985-3950
　821 State St., #205
　Santa Barbara, CA 80202
　Type: Motion Picture Production + Distribution
　\*Kenneth Badish ................................................ President
　\*Laura Halloway............................................ Vice President

**ACTOR'S EQUITY ASSOCIATION (A.E.A.)** .................... **213-462-2334/212-869-8530**
　6430 Sunset Blvd., Ste. 700
　Hollywood, CA 90028
　\*\*ALSO: 165 W 46 St. NY 10036/203 N Wabash, Chi. IL 60601
　Type: Guild/Union
　Alan Eisenberg.................................................. Exec. Secretary
　Jacqueline Veglie.................................................. Controller
　Gloria Crespo ............................. Bonding Secretary, Eastern Region (NY)
　Kathey Wilson ............................. Bonding Secretary, Western Region (LA)
　Margaret Kielley ..................... Bonding Secretary, Midwestern Region (Chicago)

**ADMEDIA CORPORATE ADVISORS INC.** ...................................... 212-759-1870
   Fax:................................................................... 212-888-4960
   866 Third Ave., 26th Fl.
   New York, NY 10022-6221
   Type:  Financial Consulting
    *Robert Garrett ............................................................. President

**ALBRIGHT, YEE & SCHIMT** ............................................... 213-626-2000
   Fax:................................................................... 213-626-2661
   333 S. Grand, 28th Fl.
   Los Angeles, CA 90071
   **Music contracts
   Type:  Entertainment Law
   Clifton Albright .......................................................... Partner
   Lucien Schimt ........................................................... Partner
   Derek Yee................................................................ Partner

**ALLIANCE COMMUNICATIONS** ............................... 310-275-5501/416-967-1174
   Fax:................................................................... 310-275-5502
   301 N. Canon Dr., Ste. 318
   Beverly Hills, CA 90210
   Type:  Motion Picture Production + Television Production
   *Robert Lantos ......................................................... Chairman/CEO (Toronto)
   Gord Haines ............................................................ Chief Operating Officer
   Rick Miller............................................................. Chief Financial Officer
   *George Burger.......................................... Exec. VP, Corporate Development
   *Kelly Smith ............................................... Sr. VP, Business Affairs
   John Robinson .......................................... VP, Legal Affairs (Toronto)

**\*ALPERIN, ESQ., HOWARD K.** ............................................... 310-314-1140
   Fax:................................................................... 310-314-1136
   c/o Gillin & Alperin
   2828 Donald Douglas Loop N., 2nd Fl.
   Santa Monica, CA 90405
   Type:  Entertainment Law
   *Howard K. Alperin ..................................................... Attorney
   *Philip H. Gillin ........................................................ Attorney

**AMSOUTH BANK, N.A.** ....................................................... 205-307-4118
   Fax:................................................................... 205-581-7479
   P.O. Box 11007
   Birmingham, AL 35288
   Type:  Banking
   Douglas F. Elliott....................................... Commercial Loan Officer

**\*AMBLIN ENTERTAINMENT** ................................................. 818-777-4600
   100 Universal Plaza, Bung. 477
   Universal City, CA 91608
   Type:  Motion Picture Production + Television Production
   *Steven Spielberg ....................................... Director-Executive Producer
   *Walter Parkes ........................................ President, Amblin Entertainment

**AMERICAN BUSINESS INS. BROKERS LA, INC./ACORDIA** ..................... 818-377-3800
   Fax:................................................................... 818-377-3899
   15760 Ventura Blvd., 14th Floor
   Encino, CA 91436-3095
   Type:  General Insurance
   Steve Abram............................................... VP, Communication & Ent.
   Paul Jones................................................. VP, MP & TV Div.

**AMERICAN FIRST RUN STUDIOS** . . . . . . . . . . . . . . . . . . . . . . . . . . . . . . . . . . . . . . . **818-981-4950**
    Fax:. . . . . . . . . . . . . . . . . . . . . . . . . . . . . . . . . . . . . . . . . . . . . . . . . . . . . . . . . 818-501-6224
    14225 Ventura Blvd.
    Sherman Oaks, CA 91423
    **Motion Picture/TV production & distribution
    Type:  Motion Picture Production + Television Production
    Max Keller . . . . . . . . . . . . . . . . . . . . . . . . . . . . . . . . . . . . . . . . . . . . . . . . . . Chairman
    Micheline Keller . . . . . . . . . . . . . . . . . . . . . . . . . . . . . . . . . . . . . . . . . . . . President
    *Brian Ton . . . . . . . . . . . . . . . . . . . . . . . . . . . . . . . . . . . . . . . VP, Business Affairs

**AMERICAN PLAYHOUSE** . . . . . . . . . . . . . . . . . . . . . . . . . . . . . . . . . . . . . . . . **212-757-4300**
    Fax:. . . . . . . . . . . . . . . . . . . . . . . . . . . . . . . . . . . . . . . . . . . . . . . . . . . . . . . . . 212-333-7552
    1776 Broadway, 9th Fl.
    New York, NY 10019-1990
    Type:  Motion Picture Production + Television Production
    Ward B. Chamberlin . . . . . . . . . . . . . . . . . . . . . . . . . . . . . . . . . . . . . . . Chairman
    Lindsay Law. . . . . . . . . . . . . . . . . . . . . . . . . . . . . . . . . . . . . . . . . . . . . . President
    Barbara Ludlum . . . . . . . . . . . . . . . . . . . . . . . . . . . . . . . . Asst. Treasurer-Controller
    Sandra Schulberg . . . . . . . . . . . . . . . . . . . . . . . . . . . . . . . . . Sr. Vice President
    *Timothy Brennan . . . . . . . . . . . . . . . . . . . . . . . . . . . . . . . . . . . . . . . . VP/CFO
    Roberta Lynn Tross . . . . . . . . . . . . . . . . . . . . . . . . . . . . . VP, Business/Legal Affairs

**AMERICAN SPECIALTY UNDERWRITERS (ASU)** . . . . . . . . . . . . . . . . . **310-789-1930/800-809-5080**
    Fax:. . . . . . . . . . . . . . . . . . . . . . . . . . . . . . . . . . . . . . . . . . . . . . . . . . . . . . . . . 310-789-1935
    1925 Century Park East, Ste. 1350
    Los Angeles, CA 90067
    **Contingency Risks / Offices: Boston, Atlanta & London
    Type:  General Insurance
    Edward A. Dipple . . . . . . . . . . . . . . . . . . . . . . . . . . . . . . . . . . . . . . President
    Candace Hallett . . . . . . . . . . . . . . . . . . . . . . . . . . . . . . . . . . . . . VP, Operations
    Valerie J. Evans . . . . . . . . . . . . . . . . . . . . . . . . . . . . . . . . . Marketing Director
    Jeff Gerber . . . . . . . . . . . . . . . . . . . . . . . . . . . . . . . . . . . Mgr., Entertainment Risks

**ANGELIKA FILMS** . . . . . . . . . . . . . . . . . . . . . . . . . . . . . . . . . . . . . . . . . . . . . . **212-274-1990**
    Fax:. . . . . . . . . . . . . . . . . . . . . . . . . . . . . . . . . . . . . . . . . . . . . . . . . . . . . . . . . 212-966-4957
    110 Greene St., Ste. 1102
    New York, NY 10012
    Type:  Motion Picture Production
    Joseph J.M. Saleh. . . . . . . . . . . . . . . . . . . . . . . . . . . . . . . . . . . . . . . President
    Alex Massis . . . . . . . . . . . . . . . . . . . . . . . . . . . . . . . . . Exec. VP, Intl. Affairs
    Rafael Guadalupe. . . . . . . . . . . . . . . . . . . . . . . . . . . . . . . . VP, Business Affairs

**\*ARAMA ENTERTAINMENT** . . . . . . . . . . . . . . . . . . . . . . . . . . . . . . . . . . . . . . **818-788-6400**
    Fax:. . . . . . . . . . . . . . . . . . . . . . . . . . . . . . . . . . . . . . . . . . . . . . . . . . . . . . . . . 818-990-9344
    16250 Ventura Blvd., Ste. 345
    Encino, CA 91436
    Type:  Motion Picture Production
    *Shimon Arama . . . . . . . . . . . . . . . . . . . . . . . . . . . . . . . President/Chairman
    *Avi Levy . . . . . . . . . . . . . . . . . . . . . . . . . . . . . . . . . VP, Production Finance
    *Michael Marshall . . . . . . . . . . . . . . . . . . . . . . . . . . . . . . . VP, Business Affairs

**ARMSTRONG, HIRSCH, JACKOWAY, TYERMAN & WERTHEIMER** . . . . . . . . . . . . . **310-553-0305**
  Fax: . . . . . . . . . . . . . . . . . . . . . . . . . . . . . . . . . . . . . . . . . . . . . . . . . . . . . . . . . . 310-553-5036
  1888 Century Park East, Ste. 1800
  Los Angeles, CA 90067
Type:  Entertainment Law
  *Susan C. Adamson . . . . . . . . . . . . . . . . . . . . . . . . . . . . . . . . . . . . . . . Partner
  *Allan L. Alexander . . . . . . . . . . . . . . . . . . . . . . . . . . . . . . . . . . . . . Partner
  Arthur Armstrong. . . . . . . . . . . . . . . . . . . . . . . . . . . . . . . . . . . . . . . Partner
  *Karl R. Austen. . . . . . . . . . . . . . . . . . . . . . . . . . . . . . . . . . . . . . . . Partner
  *Joseph D'Onofrio . . . . . . . . . . . . . . . . . . . . . . . . . . . . . . . . . . . . . Partner
  *Alan J. Epstein . . . . . . . . . . . . . . . . . . . . . . . . . . . . . . . . . . . . . . . Partner
  *J. Gunnar Erickson . . . . . . . . . . . . . . . . . . . . . . . . . . . . . . . . . . . Partner
  *Andrew L. Galker . . . . . . . . . . . . . . . . . . . . . . . . . . . . . . . . . . . . . Partner
  *Robert S. Getman . . . . . . . . . . . . . . . . . . . . . . . . . . . . . . . . . . . . Partner
  *George T. Hayum . . . . . . . . . . . . . . . . . . . . . . . . . . . . . . . . . . . . Partner
  Barry Hirsch. . . . . . . . . . . . . . . . . . . . . . . . . . . . . . . . . . . . . . . . . . Partner
  James Jackoway. . . . . . . . . . . . . . . . . . . . . . . . . . . . . . . . . . . . . . Partner
  *Jonathan D. Kaufelt . . . . . . . . . . . . . . . . . . . . . . . . . . . . . . . . . . Partner
  *James C. Mandelbaum . . . . . . . . . . . . . . . . . . . . . . . . . . . . . . . Partner
  *Marcy S. Morris . . . . . . . . . . . . . . . . . . . . . . . . . . . . . . . . . . . . . Partner
  *Geoffry W. Oblath . . . . . . . . . . . . . . . . . . . . . . . . . . . . . . . . . . Partner
  *Elizabeth M. Pongracic. . . . . . . . . . . . . . . . . . . . . . . . . . . . . . . Partner
  *Robert L. Stulberg. . . . . . . . . . . . . . . . . . . . . . . . . . . . . . . . . . . Partner
  Barry Tyerman . . . . . . . . . . . . . . . . . . . . . . . . . . . . . . . . . . . . . . . Partner
  *Robert S. Wallerstein . . . . . . . . . . . . . . . . . . . . . . . . . . . . . . . . Partner
  *Eric C. Weissler . . . . . . . . . . . . . . . . . . . . . . . . . . . . . . . . . . . . Partner
  Alan Wertheimer . . . . . . . . . . . . . . . . . . . . . . . . . . . . . . . . . . . . Partner
  *Ronald J. Bass . . . . . . . . . . . . . . . . . . . . . . . . . . . . . . . . . Of Counsel
  *Geraldine S. Hemmerling . . . . . . . . . . . . . . . . . . . . . . . . Of Counsel

**\*ARTISTS FINANCIAL MANAGEMENT, LTD.** . . . . . . . . . . . . . . . . . . . . . . . . . . **310-246-0600**
  Fax: . . . . . . . . . . . . . . . . . . . . . . . . . . . . . . . . . . . . . . . . . . . . . . . . . . . . . . . . 310-246-0695
  8899 Beverly Blvd., #808
  Los Angeles, CA 90048
Type:  Business Management
  *Roger Haber . . . . . . . . . . . . . . . . . . . . . . . . . . . . . . . . . . . . President
  *Carrie Kirshman . . . . . . . . . . . . . . . . . . . . . . . . . . . . Vice President

**ARTISTS LEGAL & ACCOUNTING ASSISTANCE** . . . . . . . . . . . . . . . . . . . . . . . **512-476-4458**
  P.O. Box 2577
  Austin, TX 78768
  **Pro bono legal & acctg. services to low income artists
Type:  Entertainment Law
  Anne Gilliam . . . . . . . . . . . . . . . . . . . . . . . . . . . . . . . . . Exec. Director

**ASHERSON & KLEIN** . . . . . . . . . . . . . . . . . . . . . . . . . . . . . . . . . . . . . . . . **310-247-6070**
  Fax: . . . . . . . . . . . . . . . . . . . . . . . . . . . . . . . . . . . . . . . . . . . . . . . . . . 310-278-8454
  9150 Wilshire Blvd., Ste. 201
  Beverly Hills, CA 90212
  **Unable to confirm by press time
Type:  Entertainment Law
  Neville Asherson . . . . . . . . . . . . . . . . . . . . . . . . . . . . . . . . . Attorney

**ASHLEY & FRISBY** . . . . . . . . . . . . . . . . . . . . . . . . . . . . . . . . . . . . . . . . **310-858-8330**
  Fax: . . . . . . . . . . . . . . . . . . . . . . . . . . . . . . . . . . . . . . . . . . . . . . . . 310-859-9339
  280 S. Beverly Dr., Ste. 402
  Beverly Hills, CA 90212-3900
Type:  Entertainment Law
  Stephen Ashley . . . . . . . . . . . . . . . . . . . . . . . . . . . Managing Partner
  Michael Frisby . . . . . . . . . . . . . . . . . . . . . . . . . . . . . . . . . . Partner

**\*ATKINSON ESQ., HEATHER R.** ........................................... **818-881-4463**
    Fax: ....................................................................... 818-881-3786
    18401 Burbank Blvd., Ste. 212
    Tarzana, CA 91356
    \*\*Personalized & interactive client services;film & music
Type: Entertainment Law
    \*Heather R. Atkinson ........................................................ Attorney

**AUGUST ENTERTAINMENT** ............................................... **213-658-8888**
    Fax: ....................................................................... 213-658-7654
    838 N. Fairfax Ave.
    Los Angeles, CA 90046
Type: Motion Picture Production + Television Production
    Gregory Cascante ..................................................... President-CEO
    Elizabeth V. Davis .................................................. Sr. VP, Finance

**AUSTIN PRODS., BRUCE.** ............................................... **818-842-0820**
    Fax: ....................................................................... 818-842-6653
    727 N. Victory Blvd.
    Burbank, CA 91502
Type: Motion Picture Production + Television Production
    \*Bruce Austin ............................................................. CEO
    Robert Francke ................................................... VP, Operations

**AVENUE PICTURES** ..................................................... **310-996-6800**
    Fax: ....................................................................... 310-473-4376
    11111 Santa Monica Blvd., Ste. 2110
    Los Angeles, CA 90025
Type: Motion Picture Production + Television Production
    Cary Brokaw ........................................................ Chairman-CEO
    \*Randy Robinson ............................................. President of Television
    Sheri Halfon ...................................... Sr. VP-CFO (310-006-6815)
    Judy Geletko ...................................... Controller (310-996-6818)
    \*Corey Silverstein ............................................... Office Manager

**BDO SEIDMAN** ......................................................... **310-557-0300**
    Fax: ....................................................................... 310-557-1777
    1900 Ave. of the Stars, 11th Fl.
    Los Angeles, CA 90067
    \*\*Acctg & Consultants TV-Actors-Writers-MP
Type: Business Management
    Mike Lichner .......................................... Partner In Charge, Ent. Ind. Group
    \*Herb Klein ......................................................... Audit Partner
    \*Ed Mahoney ......................................................... Tax Partner

**BALTIMORE PICTURES** ................................................. **213-956-4140**
    Fax: ....................................................................... 213-956-1043
    c/o Paramount Pictures
    5555 Melrose Ave., DeMille Bldg.
    Los Angeles, CA 90038
Type: Motion Picture Production + Television Production
    \*Barry Levinson ......................................................... President
    Amy Solan ..................................................... CFO/Business Affairs

**BAMBERGER BUSINESS MGMT.** ......................................... **310-446-2780**
    Fax: ....................................................................... 310-466-2787
    10866 Wilshire Blvd., Ste. 1000
    Los Angeles, CA 90024-4303
    \*\*Unable to confirm by press time
Type: Business Management
    Henry J. Bamberger ....................................................... Owner

**BANK OF AMERICA, ENT. & MEDIA IND. GROUP** ............................ **213-228-3446**
   Fax: ............................................................ 213-228-3145
   c/o Division 5777
   555 S. Flower St.
   Los Angeles, CA 90071
   Type:  Production Financing + Banking
   Laura Calhoun ................................................ Sr. VP, Ent. & Media Industry Grp.


**\*BANK OF AMERICA, NT&SA** ...................................... **310-785-6050**
   Fax: ............................................................ 310-785-6100
   c/o Century City Comm. Bank Ent.
   2049 Century Park East
   Los Angeles, CA 90067
   Type:  Production Financing + Banking
   *Steve Ryan ..................................................... Regional Sr. Vice President
   *Scott Aney ...................................................... VP, Relationship Mgr.
   *Sheryl Bond .................................................... VP, Credit Risk Mgr.
   *Fred Denitz .................................................... VP, Regional Marketing Officer


**BANK OF CALIFORNIA, THE** ................................................. **213-243-3092**
   Fax: ............................................................ 213-629-0147
   550 S. Hope St., 5th Fl.
   Los Angeles, CA 90071
   **Motion Pictures & Television
   Type:  Production Financing + Production Co-Financing
   Anna Bagdasarian .............................................. VP, Mgr. Ent. Specialty Unit
   Peter M. Graham II ............................................ Vice President (213-243-3093)


**BANK OF MONTREAL** ......................................................... **212-605-1424**
   Fax: ............................................................ 212-605-1648
   430 Park Ave.
   New York, NY 10022
   Type:  Banking
   Yvonne Bos ..................................................... Managing Director
   *Michael Andres ................................................. Director
   *Rene Encarnacion .............................................. Director
   *Allegra Griffiths ............................................... Director
   *Karen Klapper ................................................. Director
   Gretchen Shugart ............................................... Director
   Patrick Sullivan ................................................ Director


**BANNER ASSOCS., BOB.** ..................................................... **310-557-1800**
   Fax: ............................................................ 310-557-1880
   10350 Santa Monica Blvd. #290
   Los Angeles, CA 90025
   Type:  Television Production + Distribution
   Bob Banner ..................................................... President
   Chuck Banner ................................................... VP, Admin. & Prod.


**BANQUE PARIBAS** ........................................................... **310-551-7300**
   Fax: ............................................................ 310-556-8759
   2029 Century Park East, Ste. 3900
   Los Angeles, CA 90067
   Type:  Production Financing + Banking + Financial Consulting
   Michael Mendelsohn ............................................ Group Vice President
   Doug Hansen ................................................... Vice President
   Jean-Yves Fillion ............................................... Vice President


**BARAB, VAUGHAN & KLINE** ............................................... **310-276-1122**
   Fax: ............................................................ 310-276-3374
   9606 Santa Monica Blvd., Ste. 250
   Beverly Hills, CA 90210
   **Contracts & Litigation
   Type:  Entertainment Law
   Konrad L. Trope ............................................... Attorney

**BARON LAW OFFICE, STEPHEN** . . . . . . . . . . . . **310-260-6060**
Fax:. . . . . . . . . . . . . . . . . . . . . . . . . . . . . . . 310-260-6061
1299 Ocean Ave., Ste. 312
Santa Monica, CA 90401-1110
Type: Entertainment Law + Production Co-Financing
Stephen Baron . . . . . . . . . . . . . . . . . . . . . . Owner-Partner

**BARR FILMS**. . . . . . . . . . . . . . . . . **818-338-7878/800-234-7878**
Fax:. . . . . . . . . . . . . . . . . . . . . . . . . . . . . . . 818-814-2672
12801 Schabarum Ave.
Irwindale, CA 91706
\*\*Videos for schools & libraries.
Type: Video Production
Alex Bell . . . . . . . . . . . . . . . . . . . . . . . . . . . President
\*Dave Moore. . . . . . . . . . . . . . . . . Chief Financial Officer

**BAYWATCH PRODUCTION CO.**. . . . . . . . . . . . **310-302-9164**
Fax:. . . . . . . . . . . . . . . . . . . . . . . . . . . . . . . 310-302-9190
5433 Beethoven St.
Los Angeles, CA 90066
\*\*Syndication and MOW's.
Type: Television Production
Michael Berk . . . . . . . . . . . . . . . . . . Executive Producer
Gregory J. Bonann. . . . . . . . . . . . . . . Executive Producer
David Hasselhoff. . . . . . . . . . . . . . . . Executive Producer
Doug Schwartz. . . . . . . . . . . . . . . . . . Executive Producer

**BEACON PICTURES** . . . . . . . . . . . . . . . . . **213-850-2651**
Fax:. . . . . . . . . . . . . . . . . . . . . . . . . . . . . . . 213-850-2613
c/o Warner-Hollywood Studios
1041 N. Formosa Ave.
Hollywood, CA 90046-6798
Type: Motion Picture Production + Television Production
Armyan Bernstein . . . . . . . . . . . . . . . . . . . . Chairman
Cindy McWethey . . . . . . . . . . . . . . . . . . . . Controller
Phil Altmann . . . . . . . . . . . . . . . . . . . . . . Accounting
Thomas Bliss . . . . . . . . . . . VP, Production/Business Affairs
Debbie Von Arx. . . . . . . . . . . . . . . . . . . Legal Affairs

**BEDKER, LONDON & KOSSOW** . . . . . . . . . . **212-541-7070**
Fax:. . . . . . . . . . . . . . . . . . . . . . . . . . . . . . . 212-541-7080
1841 Broadway, Ste. 600
New York, NY 10023
\*\*Music
Type: Entertainment Law + Business Management
Mortimer Becker . . . . . . . . . . . . . . . . . . . . . Partner
Dan Kossow . . . . . . . . . . . . . . . . . . . . . . . . Partner

**BEHR & ROBINSON** . . . . . . . . . . . . . . . . . **310-556-9200**
Fax:. . . . . . . . . . . . . . . . . . . . . . . . . . . . . . . 310-556-9229
2049 Century Park East, Ste. 2690
Los Angeles, CA 90067
Type: Entertainment Law
Joel Behr. . . . . . . . . . . . . . . . . . . . . . . . . . . Partner
Peter Robinson . . . . . . . . . . . . . . . . . . . . . . Partner
Howard Abramson. . . . . . . . . . . . . . . . . . . Associate
Dennis Cline. . . . . . . . . . . . . . . . . . . . . . . Associate
\*Jonathan L. Handel . . . . . . . . . . . . . . . . . . Associate
\*Christopher Tricarico . . . . . . . . . . . . . . . . . Associate

**BELDOCK LEVINE & HOFFMAN** . . . . . . . . . . . . . . . . . . . . . . . . . . . . . . . . . . . . . **212-490-0400**
   Fax: . . . . . . . . . . . . . . . . . . . . . . . . . . . . . . . . . . . . . . . . . . . . . . . 212-557-0565
   c/o Elliot L. Hoffman
   99 Park Ave., Ste. 1600
   New York, NY 10016-1503
   \*\*Motion Pictures, Television
   Type:  Entertainment Law + Business Management
   Jeff Greenberg . . . . . . . . . . . . . . . . . . . . . . . . . . . . . . . . . . . . Attorney
   Elliot L. Hoffman . . . . . . . . . . . . . . . . . . . . . . . . . . . . . . . . . Attorney
   Brian E. Maas . . . . . . . . . . . . . . . . . . . . . . . . . . . . . . . . . . . . Attorney
   Peter S. Matorin . . . . . . . . . . . . . . . . . . . . . . . . . . . . . . . . . . Attorney
   Melvin E. Wulf . . . . . . . . . . . . . . . . . . . . . . . . . . . . . . . . . . . Attorney

**BELL ASSOCIATES, DAVE** . . . . . . . . . . . . . . . . . . . . . . . . . . . . . . . . . . . **213-851-7801**
   Fax: . . . . . . . . . . . . . . . . . . . . . . . . . . . . . . . . . . . . . . . . . 213-851-9349
   3211 Cahuenga Blvd. West
   Hollywood, CA 90068
   Type:  Motion Picture Production + Television Production
   Cynthia Shapiro . . . . . . . . . . . . . . . . . . . . . . . . . . . . . VP, Business Affairs

**BERGER, KAHN, SHAFTON, MOSS, FIGLER, SIMON & GLADSTONE** . . . . . . . . . . . **310-821-9000**
   Fax: . . . . . . . . . . . . . . . . . . . . . . . . . . . . . . . . . . . . . . . . . 310-578-6178
   4215 Glencoe Ave., 2nd fl.
   Marina del Rey, CA 90292
   Type:  Entertainment Law + Business Management + Financial Consulting + General Insurance
   Craig Simon . . . . . . . . . . . . . . . . . . . . . . . . . . . . . . . . . Managing Partner
   Leon Gladstone . . . . . . . . . . . . . . . . . . . . . . . . . . . . . . . . . Attorney
   David A. Helfant . . . . . . . . . . . . . . . . . . . . . . . . . . . . . . . . Attorney
   Chuck Kahn . . . . . . . . . . . . . . . . . . . . . . . . . . . . . . . . . . . . Attorney
   \*Jason Kay . . . . . . . . . . . . . . . . . . . . . . . . . . . . . . . . . . . . Attorney
   \*Joseph Koenig . . . . . . . . . . . . . . . . . . . . . . . . . . . . . . . . . Attorney
   \*Hillary Meisels . . . . . . . . . . . . . . . . . . . . . . . . . . . . . . . . . Attorney

**BERGGREN, ARTHUR T.** . . . . . . . . . . . . . . . . . . . . . . . . . . . . . . . . . . . **310-392-3088**
   Fax: . . . . . . . . . . . . . . . . . . . . . . . . . . . . . . . . . . . . . . . . . 310-392-0931
   169 Pier Ave., Penthouse
   Santa Monica, CA 90405-5311
   \*\*Music
   Type:  Entertainment Law
   Arthur Berggren . . . . . . . . . . . . . . . . . . . . . . . . . . . . . . . . . Attorney
   \*Ruth Johnson . . . . . . . . . . . . . . . . . . . . . . . . . . . . . . Office Manager

**BERKE, JEFF** . . . . . . . . . . . . . . . . . . . . . . . . . . . . . . . . . . . . . . . . **310-312-0221**
   Fax: . . . . . . . . . . . . . . . . . . . . . . . . . . . . . . . . . . . . . . . . . 310-478-3020
   11766 Wilshire Blvd., Ste. 550
   Los Angeles, CA 90025
   Type:  Entertainment Law
   Jeff Berke . . . . . . . . . . . . . . . . . . . . . . . . . . . . . . . . . . . . . . Attorney

**\*BERKOVER & CO., CPA, ROSALYN** . . . . . . . . . . . . . . . . . . . . . . . . . . . . **310-446-2026**
   Fax: . . . . . . . . . . . . . . . . . . . . . . . . . . . . . . . . . . . . . . . . . 310-474-9916
   10866 Wilshire Blvd., Ste. 1200
   Los Angeles, CA 90024-4336
   \*\*Income taxes & tax planning; Trusts & Estates
   Type:  Business Management + Financial Consulting + Business Affairs
   \*Rosalyn Berkover . . . . . . . . . . . . . . . . . . . . . . . . . . . . . . . . Principal

**BERLIN, ANN LURIE, FIDDLEHEADS, LTD.** . . . . . . . . . . . . . . . . . . . . . . . **212-713-0890**
   350 W. 57th St., Ste. 11A
   New York, NY 10019-3758
   \*\*Small Business Entrepreneurs, Actors, Writers, MP & TV
   Type:  Business Management
   Ann Lurie Berlin . . . . . . . . . . . . . . . . . . . . . . . . . . . . . . . . . Principal

**BERNSTEIN, FOX, GOLDBERG & LICKER** . . . . . . . . . . . . . . . . . . . . . . . . . . . . . . . . . . . . **310-277-3373**
    Fax: . . . . . . . . . . . . . . . . . . . . . . . . . . . . . . . . . . . . . . . . . . . . . . . . . . . . . . . . . . . 310-785-9035
    1875 Century Park East., Ste. 1300
    Los Angeles, CA 90067
    Type: Business Management
    *Arnold Bernstein . . . . . . . . . . . . . . . . . . . . . . . . . . . . . . . . . . . . . . . . . . Partner/CPA
    Martin Fox . . . . . . . . . . . . . . . . . . . . . . . . . . . . . . . . . . . . . . . . . . . . . . . . Partner/CPA
    *Robert Goldberg . . . . . . . . . . . . . . . . . . . . . . . . . . . . . . . . . . . . . . . . . Partner/CPA
    Martin Licker . . . . . . . . . . . . . . . . . . . . . . . . . . . . . . . . . . . . . . . . . . . . . Partner/CPA

**BETZER FILMS INC., JUST** . . . . . . . . . . . . . . . . . . . . . . . . . . . . . . . . . . . . . . . . . . **310-657-1086**
    Fax: . . . . . . . . . . . . . . . . . . . . . . . . . . . . . . . . . . . . . . . . . . . . . . . . . . . . . . . . . . . 310-657-6457
    c/o Panorama Film Intl.
    1100 Alta Loma Rd., Ste. 808
    Los Angeles, CA 90069
    Type: Motion Picture Production + Distribution + Production Financing + Production Co-Financing
    Just Betzer . . . . . . . . . . . . . . . . . . . . . . . . . . . . . . . . . . . . . . . . . . . . . . . President-CEO
    David Hutchinson . . . . . . . . . . . . . . . . . . . . . . . . . . . . . . . . . VP, Legal/Business Affairs

**BIENSTOCK & CLARK** . . . . . . . . . . . . . . . . . . . . . . . . . . . . . . . . . . . . . . . . . . . . **310-314-8660**
    Fax: . . . . . . . . . . . . . . . . . . . . . . . . . . . . . . . . . . . . . . . . . . . . . . . . . . . . . . . . . . . 310-314-8662
    3340 Ocean Park Blvd., Ste. 3075
    Santa Monica, CA 90405
    **Motion Pictures, Television, Music
    Type: Entertainment Law + Legal Affairs
    Terry Bienstock . . . . . . . . . . . . . . . . . . . . . . . . . . . . . . . . . . . . . . . . . . . . . Partner
    Roger Clark . . . . . . . . . . . . . . . . . . . . . . . . . . . . . . . . . . . . . . . . . . . . . . . . Partner

**\*BIG SKY ENTERTAINMENT** . . . . . . . . . . . . . . . . . . . . . . . . . . . . . . . . . . . . . . . **805-297-4253**
    27422 Laurel Glen Circle
    Valencia, CA 91354
    Type: Motion Picture Production + Television Production + Video Production
    *Todd A. Miller . . . . . . . . . . . . . . . . . . . . . . . . . . . . . . . . . . . . . Chief Executive Officer
    *Matt Kleinman . . . . . . . . . . . . . . . . . . . . . . . . . . . . . . . . . . . . . . . . . . . . President
    *Aaron Kleinman . . . . . . . . . . . . . . . . . . . . . . . . . . . . . . . . . . . . . Business Affairs
    *Glen A. Smith . . . . . . . . . . . . . . . . . . . . . . . . . . . . . . . . . . . . . . . . Legal Affairs

**\*BLACK & WHITE TELEVISION, INC.** . . . . . . . . . . . . . . . . . . . . . . . . . . . . . . . **213-467-8822**
    Fax: . . . . . . . . . . . . . . . . . . . . . . . . . . . . . . . . . . . . . . . . . . . . . . . . . . . . . . . . . . . 213-939-4685
    P.O. Box 761428
    Los Angeles, CA 90076
    Type: Motion Picture Production + Television Production
    *Paris Barclay . . . . . . . . . . . . . . . . . . . . . . . . . . . . . . . . . . . . . . . . . . . President
    *Joel Hinman . . . . . . . . . . . . . . . . . . . . . . . . . . . . . . . . . . . . . . . Vice President
    *Joseph Kelly . . . . . . . . . . . . . . . . . . . . . . . . . . . . . . . . . . . . . . . Business Manager

**BLACK ENTERTAINMENT TV** . . . . . . . . . . . . . . . . . . . . . . . . . . . . **202-608-2000/818-566-9948**
    Fax: . . . . . . . . . . . . . . . . . . . . . . . . . . . . . . . . . . . . . . . . . . . . . . . . . . . . . . . . . . . 818-566-1655
    c/o 1 BET Plaza
    1900 West Place
    N.E. Washington, DC 20018-1211
    **ALSO: 2801 W. Olive Ave., Burbank, CA 91505
    Type: Television Production
    Andre Barnwell . . . . . . . . . . . . . . . . . . . . . . . . . . . Dir., Finance & Operations, West Coast
    *Aubrey Clarke . . . . . . . . . . . . . . . . . . . . . . . . . . . . . . . . . . . . . . Finance Coordinator

**BLACKMAN, A. LEE** . . . . . . . . . . . . . . . . . . . . . . . . . . . . . . . . . . . . . . . . . . . . **310-260-5070**
    Fax: . . . . . . . . . . . . . . . . . . . . . . . . . . . . . . . . . . . . . . . . . . . . . . . . . . . . . . . . . . . 310-260-5080
    1299 Ocean Ave. #310
    Santa Monica, CA 90401
    Type: Entertainment Law
    A. Lee Blackman . . . . . . . . . . . . . . . . . . . . . . . . . . . . . . . . . . . . . . . . . . . . Attorney

**BLACKWELL, THE LAW OFFICES OF WILLIAM W.**...........................310-447-6181
    12304 Santa Monica Blvd., Ste 300
    West Los Angeles, CA 90025
    \*\*Music, Screenwriters
    Type: Entertainment Law
    William Blackwell ............................................. Attorney

**BLANC, WILLIAMS, JOHNSTON & KRONSTADT**.............................310-552-2500
    Fax:............................................................310-552-1191
    1900 Ave. of the Stars, 17th Fl.
    Los Angeles, CA 90067-4403
    Type: Entertainment Law
    \*Ronald L. Blanc .............................................. Attorney
    Samuel J. Fox ................................................. Attorney
    Dawn Weekes Glenn ........................................... Attorney
    Sam Mandel ................................................... Attorney
    Harley J. Williams ............................................. Attorney

**BLAU, EDWARD** .............................................**310-556-8468**
    Fax:............................................................310-282-0579
    10100 Santa Monica Blvd., Ste. 250
    Los Angeles, CA 90067
    \*\*all related industry areas
    Type: Entertainment Law
    Edward Blau................................................... Attorney

**\*BLOCKBUSTER ENTERTAINMENT GROUP** ........................**212-258-6000**
    Fax:............................................................212-258-6175
    1515 Broadway
    New York, NY 10036
    Type: Distribution
    \*Steven R. Berrard ......................................... President/CEO
    \*Mathew Blank ................................... CEO, Showtime Networks Inc.
    \*Nelson Schwab III............................. Chairman, Paramount Parks
    \*George D. Johnson, Jr..................... President, Retail Operations, Blockbuster
    \*Thomas W. Hawkins........................... Exec. VP, Legal & Finance
    \*J. Ronald Castell ................. Sr. VP, Prgrmg.,Blockbuster/Exec. VP, Spelling Ent

**BLOOM DEKOM HERGOTT & COOK**..................................**310-859-6800**
    Fax:............................................................310-859-2788
    150 S. Rodeo Dr., 3rd Fl.
    Beverly Hills, CA 90212
    \*\*Motion Pictures, Television, Music
    Type: Entertainment Law
    Stephen D. Barnes .............................................. Partner
    Jacob A. Bloom ................................................ Partner
    Leigh C. Brecheen ............................................. Partner
    Stephen B. Breimer ............................................ Partner
    Steven L. Brookman ........................................... Partner
    Melanie K. Cook ............................................... Partner
    Peter J. Dekom................................................. Partner
    John D. Diemer ................................................ Partner
    Lawrence H. Greaves............................................ Partner
    Candice S. Hanson ............................................. Partner
    Alan S. Hergott ............................................... Partner
    Thomas F. Hunter .............................................. Partner
    Tina J. Kahn .................................................. Partner
    Deborah L. Klein .............................................. Partner
    John S. LaViolette ............................................. Partner
    Stuart M. Rosenthal ........................................... Partner
    \*Robyn L. Roth................................................ Partner
    Lary C. Simpson .............................................. Partner
    \*Richard D. Thompson.......................................... Partner
    \*David B. Feldman ............................................ Associate
    \*Josh B. Grode ............................................... Associate
    \*Robert D. Offer.............................................. Associate
    \*Roger L. Patton .............................................. Associate

**BLUE RIDER PICTURES** . . . . . . . . . . . . . . . . . . . . . . . . . . . . . . . . . . . . . . . **310-314-8246**
Fax:. . . . . . . . . . . . . . . . . . . . . . . . . . . . . . . . . . . . . . . . . . . . . . . . . . . . . . . 310-581-4352
2800 28th St., Ste. 109
Santa Monica, CA 90405
Type: Motion Picture Production + Distribution
Jeff Geoffray . . . . . . . . . . . . . . . . . . . . . . . . . . . . . . . . . . . . . . . Chief Financial Officer
Walter Josten . . . . . . . . . . . . . . . . . . . . . . . . . . . . . . . . . . . . . . Chief Operating Officer

**BOCHCO PRODS., STEVEN** . . . . . . . . . . . . . . . . . . . . . . . . . . . . . . . **310-369-2400**
Fax:. . . . . . . . . . . . . . . . . . . . . . . . . . . . . . . . . . . . . . . . . . . . . . . . . . . . . . . 310-369-3941
10201 W. Pico Blvd.
Los Angeles, CA 90035
Type: Television Production
Steven Bochco . . . . . . . . . . . . . . . . . . . . . . . . . . . . . . . . . . . . . . . . . . Chairman-CEO
Dayna Flanagan . . . . . . . . . . . . . . . . . . . . . . . . . . . . . . . . . . President, Production
Franklin B. Rohner. . . . . . . . . . . . . . . . . . . . . . . . . . . . . . . . . . . . . President-CFO
Arnold Shane . . . . . . . . . . . . . . . . . . . . . . . . . . . . . . . . Sr. VP, Business Affairs
Barbara Kroells . . . . . . . . . . . . . . . . . . . . . . . . . . . . . . . . VP, Administration
James A. Roach . . . . . . . . . . . . . . . . . . . . . . . . . . . . . . . . . . . . VP, Finance

**\*BOHBOT ENTERTAINMENT** . . . . . . . . . . . . . . . . . . . . . . . . . . . . **212-213-2700**
Fax:. . . . . . . . . . . . . . . . . . . . . . . . . . . . . . . . . . . . . . . . . . . . . . . . . . . . . 212-685-6488
41 Madison Ave.
New York, NY 10010
\*\*Media Planning & buying; licensing & merchandising
Type: Distribution
\*Allen J. Bohbot . . . . . . . . . . . . . . . . . . . . . . . . . . . . . . . . . . . . . . . . . . . . . CEO
\*Ralph Sorrentino . . . . . . . . . . . . . . . . . . . . . . . . . . . . . . . . . . President & COO
\*Robin Silverman . . . . . . . . . . . . . . . . . . . . . . . . . . . . . . Exec. VP, Operations
\*Joanne Staikopoulos . . . . . . . . . . . . . . . Exec. VP, Worldwide Finance & Admin.
\*Tami Morachnick . . . . . . . . . . . . . . . . . . . . . . VP, Legal & Business Affairs
\*Mike Piccininni . . . . . . . . . . . . . . . . . . . . . . . . . . . . . . . . . . VP/Controller
\*Susan Danziger . . . . . . . . . . . . . . . . . . . . . . . Manager, Legal & Business Affairs

**BORTMAN, DAVID ATTORNEY AT LAW** . . . . . . . . . . . . . . . . . . . **310-201-6500**
Fax:. . . . . . . . . . . . . . . . . . . . . . . . . . . . . . . . . . . . . . . . . . . . . . . . . . . . . 310-277-7787
2049 Century Park East, Ste. 1800
Los Angeles, CA 90067
Type: Entertainment Law
David Bortman. . . . . . . . . . . . . . . . . . . . . . . . . . . . . . . . . . . . . . . . . . . . Attorney

**BOZ PRODUCTIONS** . . . . . . . . . . . . . . . . . . . . . . . . . . . . . . . . . . . . . **213-876-3232**
Fax:. . . . . . . . . . . . . . . . . . . . . . . . . . . . . . . . . . . . . . . . . . . . . . . . . . . . . 213-876-3231
7612 Fountain Ave.
Los Angeles, CA 90046-4008
Type: Motion Picture Production
Brian Curran. . . . . . . . . . . . . . . . . . . . . . . . . . . . . . . . . . . VP, Business Affairs

**BRAUN PRODUCTIONS, DAVID** . . . . . . . . . . . . . . . . . . . . . . . . . . . **310-453-0089**
Fax:. . . . . . . . . . . . . . . . . . . . . . . . . . . . . . . . . . . . . . . . . . . . . . . . . . . . . 310-829-2148
2530 Wilshire Blvd., 3rd Fl.
Santa Monica, CA 90403
Type: Motion Picture Production + Television Production
Doug Guarino. . . . . . . . . . . . . . . . . . . . . . . . . . . . . . . . . . Vice President-CFO

**BRAVERMAN, CODRON & CO.** . . . . . . . . . . . . . . . . . . . . . . . . . . . . **310-278-5850**
Fax:. . . . . . . . . . . . . . . . . . . . . . . . . . . . . . . . . . . . . . . . . . . . . . . . . . . . . 310-271-7065
c/o Curtis Abramson
233 S. Beverly Dr.
Beverly Hills, CA 90212
\*\*Motion Pictures & Music
Type: Business Management + Financial Consulting
Curtis Abramson . . . . . . . . . . . . . . . . . . . . . . . . . . . . . . . . . . . . . . . . . Partner
Irving Codron. . . . . . . . . . . . . . . . . . . . . . . . . . . . . . . . . . . . . . . . . . . Partner

**BRITISH CONNECTION** . . . . . . . . . . . . . . . . . . . . . . . . . . . . . . . . . . . . **818-997-3755**
    Fax:. . . . . . . . . . . . . . . . . . . . . . . . . . . . . . . . . . . . . . . . . . . . 818-787-8713
    14411 Kittridge St., Ste. 255
    Van Nuys, CA 91405
    Type:  Production Financing + Production Co-Financing + Distribution
    Judy Hevenly . . . . . . . . . . . . . . . . . . . . . . . . . . . . . . . . . . . . . . . . Owner

**BROOKSFILMS, LTD.** . . . . . . . . . . . . . . . . . . . . . . . . . . . . . . . . . . **310-369-1375**
    Fax:. . . . . . . . . . . . . . . . . . . . . . . . . . . . . . . . . . . . . . . . . . . . 310-369-3366
    c/o 20th Century Fox Film Corp.
    10201 W. Pico Blvd., Bldg. 215
    Los Angeles, CA 90035
    Type:  Motion Picture Production
    Leah Zappy . . . . . . . . . . . . . . . . . . . . . . . . . . . . . . . . . . VP, Administration

**BROWNING, JACOBSON & KLEIN** . . . . . . . . . . . . . . . . . . . . . . . . **310-247-8777**
    Fax:. . . . . . . . . . . . . . . . . . . . . . . . . . . . . . . . . . . . . . . . . . . . 310-247-1827
    9595 Wilshire Blvd., Ste. 601
    Beverly Hills, CA 90212
    Type:  Entertainment Law
    Kenneth L. Browning. . . . . . . . . . . . . . . . . . . . . . . . . . . . . . . . . Partner
    William P. Jacobson. . . . . . . . . . . . . . . . . . . . . . . . . . . . . . . . . Partner
    Philip I. Klein. . . . . . . . . . . . . . . . . . . . . . . . . . . . . . . . . . . . . Partner
    \*Shep Rosenman. . . . . . . . . . . . . . . . . . . . . . . . . . . . . . . . . Attorney

**BUCHALTER, NEMER, FIELDS & YOUNGER.** . . . . . . . . . . . . . . . . . **213-891-1700**
    Fax:. . . . . . . . . . . . . . . . . . . . . . . . . . . . . . . . . . . . . . . . . . . . 310-551-0233
    601 S. Figueroa St., Ste. 2400
    Los Angeles, CA 90017-5704
    \*\*Telex: 687 485, Answbk: BNYFYLSA
    Type:  Entertainment Law
    Sol Rosenthal . . . . . . . . . . . . . . . . . . . . . . . . . . . . . . . . . . . . Attorney
    Gary Stamler . . . . . . . . . . . . . . . . . . . . . . . . . . . . . . . . . . . . Attorney

**BUCKEYE COMMUNICATIONS** . . . . . . . . . . . . . . . . . . . . . . . . . . . **212-888-9115**
    Fax:. . . . . . . . . . . . . . . . . . . . . . . . . . . . . . . . . . . . . . . . . . . . 212-888-9399
    425 Park Ave., 27th Fl.
    New York, NY 10022
    Type:  Motion Picture Production + Television Production + Video Production + Production Financing
    Stanley F. Buchthal . . . . . . . . . . . . . . . . . . . . . . . . . . . . . . . . . Chairman
    Cheryl Miller Houser. . . . . . . . . . . . . . . . . . . . . . . . . . . . . . VP, Entertainment

**BUDGETS BY DESIGN** . . . . . . . . . . . . . . . . . . . . . . . . . . . . . . . . . **213-654-6231**
    Fax:. . . . . . . . . . . . . . . . . . . . . . . . . . . . . . . . . . . . . . . . . . . . 213-654-5483
    8153 Amor Rd.
    Los Angeles, CA 90046
    \*\*Budgets for Feature & TV Production
    Type:  Financial Consulting
    \*Yudi Bennett. . . . . . . . . . . . . . . . . . . . . . . . . . . . . . . . . . . Co-Owner
    \*Robert Schneider. . . . . . . . . . . . . . . . . . . . . . . . . . . . . . . . Co-Owner

**BUENA VISTA HOME VIDEO** . . . . . . . . . . . . . . . . . . . . . . . . . . . . **818-560-1000**
    500 S. Buena Vista St.
    Burbank, CA 91521
    Type:  Video Production
    \*David C. Hendler . . . . . . . . . . . . . . . . . . . . . . Sr. VP, Worldwide Finance & Admin.
    \*Craig Kornblau . . . . . . . . . . . . . . . . . . . . . . . . . . Sr. VP, Worldwide Operations
    John J. Reagan . . . . . . . . . . . . . . . . . . . . . . . . . . Sr. VP, Business/Legal Affairs
    \*Judy Denenholz. . . . . . . . . . . . . . . . . . . . . . . . . . VP, Television/Legal Affairs
    Dennis Dort . . . . . . . . . . . . . . . . . . . . . . . . . . . . . VP, Business/Legal Affairs
    Chris Menosky. . . . . . . . . . . . . . . . . . . . . . . . . . . . VP, Intl. Admin./Operations
    \*Greg Probert . . . . . . . . . . . . . . . . . . . . . . Sr. VP, Intl. Finance & Administration
    Diana C. Rivera . . . . . . . . . . . . . . . . . . . . . . . . . . . . . VP, Intl. Operations

**BUENA VISTA INTERNATIONAL** . . . . . . . . . . . . . . . . . . . . . . . . . . . . . . . . . . . . . . . **818-560-1000**
　　500 S. Buena Vista St.
　　Burbank, CA 91521
　　Type: Distribution
　　Lawrence Kaplan . . . . . . . . . . . . . . . . . . . . . . . . . . . . . . . . . . . . . . . Sr. VP/General Manager
　　Ann Mather . . . . . . . . . . . . . . . . . . . . . . . . . . . . . . . . . . . . . VP, Finance Administration

**BUENA VISTA PICTS. DISTRIB.** . . . . . . . . . . . . . . . . . . . . . . . . . . . . . . . . . . . . **818-567-5000**
　　Fax: . . . . . . . . . . . . . . . . . . . . . . . . . . . . . . . . . . . . . . . . . . . . . . . . . . . . . . 818-972-9448
　　3900 W. Alameda Ave., Ste. 2400
　　Burbank, CA 91505
　　Type: Distribution
　　Robert Cunningham . . . . . . . . . . . . . . . . . . . . . . . . . . . . . . . . . Vice President-Gen. Coun.
　　*Deborah Morrison . . . . . . . . . . . . . . . . . . . . . . . . . . . . . . . . . . . . . . . . . . . VP, Finance

**BUENA VISTA TELEVISION** . . . . . . . . . . . . . . . . . . . . . . . . . . . . . . . . . . . . . . . . **818-560-1000**
　　Fax: . . . . . . . . . . . . . . . . . . . . . . . . . . . . . . . . . . . . . . . . . . . . . . . . . . . . . . 818-563-2601
　　c/o Walt Disney Studios
　　500 S. Buena Vista, Team Disney Bldg.
　　Burbank, CA 91521-0424
　　Type: Television Production + Distribution
　　Kenneth D. Werner . . . . . . . . . . . . . . . . . . . . . . . . . . . . . . . . . Sr. VP, Business Affairs
　　Andrew Lewis . . . . . . . . . . . . . . . . . . . . . . . . . . . . VP, Finance & Planning (818-560-2073)

**\*BURRUD PRODUCTIONS, BILL** . . . . . . . . . . . . . . . . . . . . . . . . . . . . . . . . . . . **714-846-7174**
　　Fax: . . . . . . . . . . . . . . . . . . . . . . . . . . . . . . . . . . . . . . . . . . . . . . . . . . . . . . 714-846-4814
　　16902 Bolsa Chica St., Ste. 203
　　Huntington Beach, CA 92649
　　Type: Television Production + Video Production + Distribution
　　*John Burrud . . . . . . . . . . . . . . . . . . . . . . . . . . . . . . . . . . . . . . . . . . . . . . . President
　　*Jennifer Sexton . . . . . . . . . . . . . . . . . . . . . . . . . . . . . . . . . . . . . . . . Financial Officer

**BUSINESS MANAGEMENT OFFICE, THE** . . . . . . . . . . . . . . . . . . . . . . . . . . . . **818-509-1811**
　　Fax: . . . . . . . . . . . . . . . . . . . . . . . . . . . . . . . . . . . . . . . . . . . . . . . . . . . . . . 818-509-2915
　　4605 Lankershim Blvd., Ste. 325
　　North Hollywood, CA 91602
　　**Financial Planning, Income Taxes - all forms of ent.
　　Type: Business Management
　　Nancy Arntzen . . . . . . . . . . . . . . . . . . . . . . . . . . . . . . . . . . . . . Enrolled Agent, F.P.P.
　　David Arntzen . . . . . . . . . . . . . . . . . . . . . . . . . . . . . . . Enrolled Agent, C.F.P., Owner

**C.M. MANAGEMENT** . . . . . . . . . . . . . . . . . . . . . . . . . . . . . . . . . . . . . . . . . . . . . **818-704-7800**
　　Fax: . . . . . . . . . . . . . . . . . . . . . . . . . . . . . . . . . . . . . . . . . . . . . . . . . . . . . . 818-704-0185
　　7957 Nita Ave.
　　Canoga Park, CA 91304
　　**Music
　　Type: Business Management
　　Craig Miller . . . . . . . . . . . . . . . . . . . . . . . . . . . . . . . . . . . . . . . . . . . . . . . . . . Owner
　　Ralph Mitchel . . . . . . . . . . . . . . . . . . . . . . . . . . . . . . . . . . . . . . . . . . . . . Associate
　　*Isabel Miller . . . . . . . . . . . . . . . . . . . . . . . . . . . . . . . . . . . . . . . . . . . . Office Mgr.

**CBS ENTERTAINMENT** . . . . . . . . . . . . . . . . . . . . . . . . . . . . . . . . . . . . . . . . . . **213-852-2345**
　　7800 Beverly Blvd.
　　Los Angeles, CA 90036-2188
　　**Financial fax: 213-852-2161
　　Type: Television Production
　　Deborah Barak-Milgrom . . . . . . . . . . . . . . . . . . . . . . . . . . . . . Deputy West Coast Counsel
　　Susan Holliday . . . . . . . . . . . . . . . . . . . . . . . . . . . Deputy Gen. Counsel West Coast-Asst. Sec.
　　*Ellen Oran Kaden . . . . . . . . . . . . . . . . . . . . . . . . . . . Exec. VP-General Counsel-Secretary
　　*Peter W. Keegan . . . . . . . . . . . . . . . . . . . . . . . . . . . . . . . . . . . . . . Exec. VP, Finance
　　Martin Franks . . . . . . . . . . . . . . . . . . . . . . . . . . . . . . . . . . . . . . . Sr. Vice President
　　William B. Klein . . . . . . . . . . . . . . . . . . . . . . . . . . . . . . . . Sr. VP, Business Affairs
　　*Gary McCarthy . . . . . . . . . . . . . . . . . . . . . . . . . . . . . . . . . . . . . . . . . . VP, Finance

**CABIN FEVER ENTERTAINMENT**..........................................203-863-5200
   Fax:...........................................................203-863-5258
   100 W. Putnam Ave.
   Greenwich, CT 06830
   Type: Distribution
   Thomas A. Molito......................................................President
   Andrew Chapin...............................................VP, Administration
   Susan Steele...........................................Contract Administrator

**CALIFORNIA UNITED BANK**.............................................310-475-3603
   Fax:...........................................................310-475-9082
   10880 Wilshire Blvd., Ste. 1200
   Los Angeles, CA 90024
   **Motion Pictures, TV, Music, BM & related ent. ind. srvc
   Type: Banking
   Melanie Krinsky...................Sr. VP-Mgr., Ent. Div. (310-475-2342)
   Joanna Lucceshi.........................................Sr. Vice President
   Carole Bakshi.......................................VP, Entertainment Div.
   *Susan Dudas.......................................VP, Entertainment Div.
   Lori Graf...........................................VP, Entertainment Div.
   *Mandie Rush.......................................VP, Entertainment Div.

**CANNELL PRODS. INC., STEPHEN J.**......................................213-465-5800
   7083 Hollywood Blvd.
   Los Angeles, CA 90028
   Type: Television Production
   *Kim LeMasters.......................................................President
   *Joseph C. Kaczorowski................Sr. VP-Chief Financial Officer, Cannell Studios
   *Howard D. Kurtzman.........................................Sr. VP, Business Affairs
   *Carla Carmichael..................................VP, Budgeting/Estimating
   *Andrew Hubsch.......................................................VP/Controller

**CANNON PICTURES**.....................................................310-772-7764
   Fax:...........................................................310-843-0919
   8200 Wilshire Blvd.
   Beverly Hills, CA 90211
   Type: Motion Picture Production
   Christopher Pearce..................................................President-CEO
   Richard Inoyue...........................................................VP-CFO

**\*CAPELL, COYNE & CO.**...............................................310-553-0310
   Fax:...........................................................310-553-4023
   1875 Century Park East, Ste. 2250
   Los Angeles, CA 90067
   Type: Business Management + Production Accounting
   *David Capell.......................................................President
   *Stephen Coyne....................................................Partner/CPA
   *Victor Rose...........................................Production Accounting
   *Paul Kleinbaum..........................................................CPA
   *Jon Weiner..............................................................CPA

**CAPELLA FILMS INC.**.................................................310-247-4700
   Fax:...........................................................310-247-4701
   9242 Beverly Blvd., Ste. 280
   Beverly Hills, CA 90210-3710
   Type: Motion Picture Production
   Willi Baer.........................................................Co-chairman
   Rolf Deyhle.......................................................Co-chairman
   *Mark Seiler.....................................................President/CEO

**CARLTON, ROSANNE** ...................................................... **310-854-6621**
    Fax:................................................................310-854-6002
    8500 Melrose Ave., Ste. 208
    West Hollywood, CA 90069
    **CPA - Actors - Producers - Radio
    Type: Business Management
    Rosanne Carlton............................................. Certified Public Accountant

**CAROLCO PICTURES** ...................................................... **310-859-8800**
    Fax:................................................................310-657-1629
    8800 Sunset Blvd.
    Los Angeles, CA 90069-2105
    Type: Motion Picture Production
    Mario Kassar ..................................................... Chairman of the Board
    Robert Goldsmith............................................ Sr. VP-General Counsel
    Karen Taylor ............................................................. Sr. VP, Finance
    Lewis Weakland............................................ Sr. VP, Business Affairs/Features

**CAROLINA BARNES CAPITAL INC.** ...................................... **212-593-1313**
    Fax:................................................................212-593-1349
    300 Park Ave.
    New York, NY 10022
    **Full service investment & merchant banking firm.
    Type: Financial Consulting + Banking
    Frank E. Barnes III.......................................................President
    William A. Merritt, Jr. .............................................. General Counsel
    Kerry A. McMahon ........................................... Dir., Corporate Finance
    *Marylew H. Redd ............................................ Dir., Private Placements
    April Masnica.................................................... Mgr., Operations
    *Eric M. McAllister ................................................... Associate

**CARSEY-WERNER CO., THE** .............................................. **818-760-5598**
    Fax:................................................................818-760-5974
    4024 Radford Ave., Bldg. 3
    Studio City, CA 91604
    Type: Television Production + Distribution + Motion Picture Production
    Marcy Carsey.......................................... Owner-Executive Producer
    Tom Werner............................................ Owner-Executive Producer
    Stuart Glickman ......................................... Vice Chairman-CEO
    Caryn Mandabach ..............................................President
    Bob Dubelko ............................................................ Sr. VP-CFO
    *Dirk W. van de Bunt......................................... Sr. VP, Business Affairs
    *Diane Chavez ................................................... VP, Legal Affairs
    Bob Christison .................................................... VP, Operations
    *Bret Sarnoff.................................................... VP, Conroller
    Elizabeth Whelpley .............................................. VP, Business Affairs
    *Nina Bass .................................................. Dir., Human Resources
    *Laura Black................................... Dir., Admin. Affairs for M.Carsey/T.Werner
    *Rochelle Gerson ................................................ Dir., Business Affairs
    Suzanne Habbershaw................................... Assoc. Dir., Business Affairs
    *Gabriela Marino-Park .................................. Mgr., Production Accounting
    *Toni McCalmont ............................................... Mgr., Accounting

**CARTHAY CIRCLE PICTURES & MGMT.** ................................... **310-657-5454**
    Fax:................................................................310-657-8783
    213 S. Stanley Dr.
    Beverly Hills, CA 90211
    Type: Motion Picture Production + Television Production
    William Blaylock .............................................................. Partner
    Sarah Jackson.............................................................. Partner
    *Paul Canterna .......................................................... Associate

**CASSANDRA GROUP INC., THE** ............................... 617-437-0217/212-966-5760
    Fax: ................................................ 617-437-0606/212-966-5693
    715 Boylston St., 4th Fl.
    Boston, MA 02116-2612
    **Inv. mgmt. for those in the arts.
    Type: Financial Consulting
    Mr. Dana C. Giacchetto ..................................................... President


**CASTLE ROCK ENTERTAINMENT** .......................................... 310-285-2300
    Fax: ............................................................... 310-205-2759
    335 N. Maple Dr., Ste. 135
    Beverly Hills, CA 90210-3867
    Type: Motion Picture Production + Television Production
    Alan Horn ................................................................. Chairman-CEO
    Rob Reiner ................................................................... No title
    Glenn Padnick .......................................... Pres., Castle Rock Television Inc.
    Andrew Scheinman ............................................................ No title
    Martin Shafer ........................................... Pres., Castle Rock Pictures Inc.
    *Liz Glotzer ........................................ Pres., Production, Castle Rock Pict.
    *Massimo Graziosi ............................... President, Castle Rock International
    Sue Fickenscher ................................................... Chief Financial Officer
    *Greg Paul .................................................... Chief Operating Officer
    *Robin Green .................................... Sr. VP, Castle Rock Television Inc.
    Jeffrey Stott .................................................... Sr. VP, Production Mgmt.
    Jess Wittenberg ............................................ Sr. VP, Business/Legal Affairs
    Julia Bingham .................................................... VP, Legal Affairs
    David Goodman ................................................... VP, Business Affairs
    *Alison Harstedt ............................................... VP, Production Mgmt.
    *Rich Klubeck .................................................... VP, Legal Affairs
    Carlos Perez ..................................................... VP, Administration
    *John Barry .................................................. International Controller
    *Sergio Gallozzi ......................................... Accounting, CR International
    *Al Haferkamp ....................................................... Dir., Finance
    *Robin Hoggan-Egbinger ............................................ Dir., Accounting
    *Ken Low ........................................... Dir., Business & Legal Affairs
    Jan Streimer .................................................. Dir., Human Resources
    *Dana George ................................................. Marketing Administrator
    *Ron Harrell ...................................................... Jr. Accountant
    *Lori Koravos ................................................ Production Contoller
    *Ami Krell ................................................. Purchasing Coordinator
    *Filip Dawana .................................................. Accounts Payable


**CAVELLA, CATHERINE A.** ....................................... 310-552-2425
    1801 Century Park East, 24th Fl.
    Los Angeles, CA 90067
    **Music
    Type: Entertainment Law
    Catherine A. Cavella ......................................................... Attorney


**CELEBRITY HOME ENT.** ........................................ 818-595-0666
    Fax: ............................................................... 818-716-0168
    22025 Ventura Blvd. #200
    Woodland Hills, CA 91364
    Type: Video Production
    Noel Bloom ................................................................. Chairman
    Cheryl Jordan ..................................................... Chief Financial Officer
    Andrew Stern ..................................................... Chief Executive Officer


**CHANCELLOR ENTERTAINMENT** ....................................... 310-474-4521
    Fax: ............................................................... 310-470-9273
    10600 Holman Ave., Ste. 1
    Los Angeles, CA 90024
    Type: Motion Picture Production + Television Production
    Robert P. Marcucci ........................................................ President-CEO
    *Colleen Malone Engel ...................................................... Office Manager

**CHECK ENTERTAINMENT** ................................................. **213-650-7227**
    Fax: ................................................................. 213-650-7237
    7906 Santa Monica Blvd., Ste. 217
    Los Angeles, CA 90046
    Type: Motion Picture Production + Television Production
    David Gabai ............................................... VP, Business Affairs

**CHEMICAL BANK, ENT. IND. GROUP** ....................................... **310-788-5600**
    Fax: ................................................................. 310-788-5628
    c/o Chemical Bank NY Corp. - USA
    1800 Century Park East, Ste. 400
    Los Angeles, CA 90067
    **Motion Pictures
    Type: Production Financing
    John Miller .................................................. Managing Director

**CHRYSTIE & BERLE** ...................................................... **310-788-7700**
    Fax: ................................................................. 310-201-0436
    1925 Century Park East, 22nd Fl.
    Los Angeles, CA 90067-2723
    **Motion Pictures
    Type: Entertainment Law + Business Affairs + Legal Affairs + Production Financing
    Stephen Chrystie ..................................................... Partner
    Elihu M. Berle ....................................................... Partner

**CHUBB INSURANCE CO.** ................................................... **213-658-6500**
    Fax: ................................................................. 213-658-6027
    6500 Wilshire Blvd., 9th fl.
    Los Angeles, CA 90048
    Type: General Insurance
    Bill Mitchell ....................................... Branch Mgr.-Sr. Vice President
    *Wendy Diaz ...................................... Sr. Entertainment Underwriter
    *David Fike ............................................... Mgr., Entertainment
    *Paula Mannion ................................... Chubb Wholesale Division

**\*CINE GRANDE CORPORATION** ............................................ **310-358-2240**
    Fax: ................................................................. 310-659-0071
    554 Norwich Dr.
    Los Angeles, CA 90048
    Type: Motion Picture Production
    *Silvio Muraglia ........................................... Chairman-CEO
    *Daniel J. Sladek ................................. Gen. Partner-Pres., Prod.
    *Suzanne C. Martin ......................... Assoc. Dir., Business Affairs

**CINEMA LINE FILMS CORP.** ............................................... **310-271-4200**
    Fax: ................................................................. 310-271-8200
    150 S. Rodeo Dr., Ste. 120
    Beverly Hills, CA 90212-2775
    Type: Motion Picture Production
    Verna Harrah ........................................................ Co-chairman
    Carole Little ........................................................ Co-chairman
    Leonard Rabinowitz .................................................. Co-chairman

**CINEMA SEVEN PRODS.** ................................................... **212-315-1060**
    Fax: ................................................................. 212-315-1085
    c/o Carnegie Hall
    154 W. 57th St., Ste. 112
    New York, NY 10019
    Type: Motion Picture Production
    Lea Blackman ...................................................... Exec. Accountant
    Chantal Ribeiro ..................................................... Prod. Exec.

**CINEQUANON PICTURES INTL. INC.** . . . . . . . . . . . . . . . . . . . . . . . . . . . . . . . . . . . . . . . .**213-658-6043**
    Fax:. . . . . . . . . . . . . . . . . . . . . . . . . . . . . . . . . . . . . . . . . . . . . . . . . . . . . . . . . . . 213-658-6087
    8489 W. Third St.
    Los Angeles, CA 90048
    Type:  Motion Picture Production
    *Daniel Sales. . . . . . . . . . . . . . . . . . . . . . . . . . . . . . . . . . . . . . . . . . . . . . . . . President
    *Jennifer Peckham . . . . . . . . . . . . . . . . . . . . . . . . . . . . . . . . . . . . . . . . . . . . Exec. VP
    *Stacey Kivel . . . . . . . . . . . . . . . . . . . . . . . . . . . . . . Dir., Acquisitions & Legal Affairs
    *George Marinos . . . . . . . . . . . . . . . . . . . . . . . . . . . . . . . . . . . . . Dir. Business Affairs

**\*CINERGI PICTURES ENTERTAINMENT INC.** . . . . . . . . . . . . . . . . . . . . . . . . . . . . .**310-315-6000**
    Fax:. . . . . . . . . . . . . . . . . . . . . . . . . . . . . . . . . . . . . . . . . . . . . . . . . . . . . . . . . 310-828-0443
    2308 Broadway
    Santa Monica, CA 90404-2916
    Type:  Motion Picture Production
    *Andrew Vajna . . . . . . . . . . . . . . . . . . . . . . . . . . . . . . . . . . . . . . . . . . . . President
    *Warren Braverman . . . . . . . . . . . . . . . . . . . . . . . . . . . . . . . . . . . . . . . . . CFO
    *Dianne Caplan Lebovits . . . . . . . . . . . . . . . . . . . . . . . . . . . . . . General Counsel
    *Randolph Paul. . . . . . . . . . . . . . . . . . . . . . . . . . . . . . . . . Sr. VP, Business Affairs
    *Erick Feitshans . . . . . . . . . . . . . . . . . . . . . . . . . . . . . . . . . . . . . . . VP, Legal
    *Barbara Green . . . . . . . . . . . . . . . . . . . . . . . . . . . . . . . . . . . . . . . VP, Finance

**CINETEL FILMS** . . . . . . . . . . . . . . . . . . . . . . . . . . . . . . . . . . . . . . . . . . . . . .**213-654-4000**
    Fax:. . . . . . . . . . . . . . . . . . . . . . . . . . . . . . . . . . . . . . . . . . . . . . . . . . . . . . . . . 213-650-6400
    8255 Sunset Blvd.
    Los Angeles, CA 90046
    Type:  Motion Picture Production
    Nick Gorenc. . . . . . . . . . . . . . . . . . . . . . . . . . . . . . . . . . . . Chief Financial Officer
    Steve Gregoropoulos . . . . . . . . . . . . . . . . . . . . . . . . . . . . . . . . . VP, Legal Affairs

**CINEVILLE INC.** . . . . . . . . . . . . . . . . . . . . . . . . . . . . . . . . . . . . . . . . . . . .**310-394-4699**
    Fax:. . . . . . . . . . . . . . . . . . . . . . . . . . . . . . . . . . . . . . . . . . . . . . . . . . . . . . . . . 310-394-3052
    225 Santa Monica Blvd., 7th Floor
    Santa Monica, CA 90401
    Type:  Motion Picture Production + Video Production
    Robert Strauss . . . . . . . . . . . . . . . . . . . . . . . . . . . . . . . . . . . VP, Business Affairs

**\*CINEWORLD PICTURES, LTD.** . . . . . . . . . . . . . . . . . . . . . . . . . . . . .**213-467-2225/818-789-6015**
    Fax:. . . . . . . . . . . . . . . . . . . . . . . . . . . . . . . . . . . . . . . 213-467-2225/818-789-1341
    15720 Ventura Blvd., #306
    Encino, CA 91436
    Type:  Production Financing + Financial Consulting + Production Co-Financing
    *Joseph Solomon . . . . . . . . . . . . . . . . . . . . . . . . . . . . . . . . . . . . . . President

**CITADEL ENTERTAINMENT, L.P.** . . . . . . . . . . . . . . . . . . . . . . . . . . . . . . . . . . .**310-477-5112**
    Fax:. . . . . . . . . . . . . . . . . . . . . . . . . . . . . . . . . . . . . . . . . . . . . . . . . . . . . . . . . 310-312-9781
    11340 W. Olympic Blvd., Ste. 100
    Los Angeles, CA 90064-1611
    Type:  Motion Picture Production + Television Production
    David R. Ginsburg. . . . . . . . . . . . . . . . . . . . . . . . . . . . . . . . . . . . . . . President
    Richard A. Maltin . . . . . . . . . . . . . . . . . . . . . . . . . . . . . . . . . Chief Financial Officer
    Anne Morea . . . . . . . . . . . . . . . . . . . . . . . . . . . . . . . . . . . . . VP, Business Affairs

**CITY NATIONAL BANK - ENT. DIV.** . . . . . . . . . . . . . . . . . . . . . . . . . . . . . . . . . . .**310-888-6200**
    400 N. Roxbury Dr., 4th Fl.
    Beverly Hills, CA 90210
    **Motion Pictures
    Type:  Production Financing + Banking
    Martha Henderson . . . . . . . . . . . . . . . . . . . . . . . . . . . . . . . . . Exec. Vice President
    Mary Yoel . . . . . . . . . . . . . . . . . . . . . . . . . . . . . . . . . . . . Sr. VP-Asst. Mgr., Ent. Div.

**CLARK PRODS., DICK** . . . . . . . . . . . . . . . . . . . . . . . . . . . . . . . . . . . . . . . . . . . . . . **818-841-3003**
   Fax: . . . . . . . . . . . . . . . . . . . . . . . . . . . . . . . . . . . . . . . . . . . . . . . . . . . . . 818-954-8609
   3003 W. Olive Ave.
   Burbank, CA 91505-4590
   Type:  Television Production + Motion Picture Production
   Dick Clark . . . . . . . . . . . . . . . . . . . . . . . . . . . . . . . . . . . . . . . . . . . . . . . . Chairman-CEO
   Francis C. La Maina . . . . . . . . . . . . . . . . . . . . . . . . . . . . . . . . . . . . . . . President-COO
   Ken Ferguson . . . . . . . . . . . . . . . . . . . . . . . . . . . . . . . . . . . . . . . . . . CFO-VP, Finance
   Aviva Bergman . . . . . . . . . . . . . . . . . . . . . . . . . . . . . . . . . . . . Sr. VP, Business Affairs
   Bob Chuck . . . . . . . . . . . . . . . . . . . . . . . . . . . . . . . . . . . . . . . VP, Special Projects
   Bryan Thompson . . . . . . . . . . . . . . . . . . . . . . . . . . . . . . . . . . . . . . . . . . . Controller
   Michael Compton . . . . . . . . . . . . . . . . . . . . . . . . . . . . . . . . . . . Mgr., Business Affairs

**CODIKOW & CARROLL** . . . . . . . . . . . . . . . . . . . . . . . . . . . . . . . . . . . . . . . . . **310-271-0241**
   Fax: . . . . . . . . . . . . . . . . . . . . . . . . . . . . . . . . . . . . . . . . . . . . . . . . . . . . . 310-271-0775
   9113 Sunset Blvd.
   Los Angeles, CA 90069
   Type:  Entertainment Law
   Rosemary Carroll . . . . . . . . . . . . . . . . . . . . . . . . . . . . . . . . . . . . . . . . . . . . Attorney
   David Codikow . . . . . . . . . . . . . . . . . . . . . . . . . . . . . . . . . . . . . . . . . . . . . Attorney
   *Stacy Fass . . . . . . . . . . . . . . . . . . . . . . . . . . . . . . . . . . . . . . . . . . . . . . . . Attorney
   *Richard Gelles . . . . . . . . . . . . . . . . . . . . . . . . . . . . . . . . . . . . . . . . . . . . . Attorney
   *Janine Natter . . . . . . . . . . . . . . . . . . . . . . . . . . . . . . . . . . . . . . . . . . . . . Attorney

**COHEN & LUCKENBACHER** . . . . . . . . . . . . . . . . . . . . . . . . . . . . . . . . . . . . **213-938-5000**
   Fax: . . . . . . . . . . . . . . . . . . . . . . . . . . . . . . . . . . . . . . . . . . . . . . . . . . . . . 213-936-6354
   740 N. La Brea Ave., 2nd Fl.
   Los Angeles, CA 90038-3339
   Type:  Entertainment Law
   Martin Cohen . . . . . . . . . . . . . . . . . . . . . . . . . . . . . . . . . . . . . . . . . . . . . . Attorney
   Evan Cohen . . . . . . . . . . . . . . . . . . . . . . . . . . . . . . . . . . . . . . . . . . . . . . . Attorney
   *Frank Luckenbacher . . . . . . . . . . . . . . . . . . . . . . . . . . . . . . . . . . . . . . . . . Attorney

**COHEN, ALLAN S.** . . . . . . . . . . . . . . . . . . . . . . . . . . . . . . . . . . . . . . . . . . . . **213-385-3071**
   Fax: . . . . . . . . . . . . . . . . . . . . . . . . . . . . . . . . . . . . . . . . . . . . . . . . . . . . . 213-385-1108
   3424 Wilshire Blvd., Ste. 1100
   Los Angeles, CA 90010
   Type:  Entertainment Law
   Allan S Cohen . . . . . . . . . . . . . . . . . . . . . . . . . . . . . . . . . . . . . . . . . . . . . . Attorney

**COLOSSAL PICTURES** . . . . . . . . . . . . . . . . . . . . . . . . . . . **415-550-8772/415-252-6620**
   Fax: . . . . . . . . . . . . . . . . . . . . . . . . . . . . . . . . . . . . . 415-824-0389/415-864-1349
   2800 Third St.
   San Francisco, CA 94107
   Type:  Motion Picture Production + Television Production
   Drew Takahashi . . . . . . . . . . . . . . . . . . . . . . . . . . . . . . . . . . . . . . . . . . . . Chairman
   Warren Franklin . . . . . . . . . . . . . . . . . . . . . . . . . . . . . . . . . Chief Operating Officer
   Mark Jacobsen . . . . . . . . . . . . . . . . . . . . . . . . . . . . . . . . . . . . . . . General Counsel
   Terry Thurlow . . . . . . . . . . . . . . . . . . . . . . . . . . . . . . . . . . . . . . . . . Dir., Finance

**COLUMBIA PICTS. TELEVISION** . . . . . . . . . . . . . . . . . . . . . . . . . . . . . . . . . **310-202-1234**
   Fax: . . . . . . . . . . . . . . . . . . . . . . . . . . . . . . . . . . . . . . . . . . . . . . . . . . . . . 310-202-3721
   9336 W. Washington Blvd.
   Culver City, CA 90232
   Type:  Television Production
   Don Loughery . . . . . . . . . . . . . . . . . . . . . . . . . . . . . . . . . . . Exec. VP, Business Affairs
   *Sander Schwartz . . . . . . . . . . . . . . . . . . . . . . . . . . . . . . . . . Sr. VP, Business Affairs
   *Joanne Mazzo . . . . . . . . . . . . . . . . . . . . . . . . . . . . . . . . . . . . . VP, Business Affairs

**COLUMBIA PICTURES** . . . . . . . . . . . . . . . . . . . . . . . . . . . . . . . . . . . . . . . . . . . **310-280-8000**
    Fax: . . . . . . . . . . . . . . . . . . . . . . . . . . . . . . . . . . . . . . . . . . . . . . . . . 310-280-1883
    10202 W. Washington Blvd.
    Culver City, CA 90232-3195
    Type: Motion Picture Production
    Lisa Henson . . . . . . . . . . . . . . . . . . . . . . . . . . . . . . . . . . . . . . . . . . . . . President
    Robin Russell . . . . . . . . . . . . . . . . . . . . . . . . . . . . . . . . Exec. VP, Business Affairs
    Alan Kreiger . . . . . . . . . . . . . . . . . . . . . . . . . . . . . . . . . . Sr. VP, Business Affairs
    \*Bryan Lee . . . . . . . . . . . . . . . . . . . . . . . . . . . . . . . . . . . . . . Sr. Vice President
    Roger Toll . . . . . . . . . . . . . . . . . . . . . . . . . . . . . . . . . . . . Sr. VP, Legal Affairs
    Darrell Walker . . . . . . . . . . . . . . . . . . . . . . . . . . . . . . . . Sr. VP, Business Affairs
    \*Deb Bruenell . . . . . . . . . . . . . . . . . . . . . . . . . . . . . . . . . . . VP, Legal Affairs
    Thomas Stack . . . . . . . . . . . . . . . . . . . . . VP, Business Affairs Contract Administration
    \*Reid Sullivan . . . . . . . . . . . . . . . . . . . . . . . . . . . . . . . . . . . . . . VP, Operations
    \*Mark Wyman . . . . . . . . . . . . . . . . . . . . . . . . . . . . . . . . . . . . VP, Legal Affairs

**COLUMBIA TRISTAR HOME VIDEO** . . . . . . . . . . . . . . . . . . . . . . . . . . . . . **310-280-8000**
    Fax: . . . . . . . . . . . . . . . . . . . . . . . . . . . . . . . . . . . . . . . . . . . . . . . . . 310-280-2037
    10202 W. Washington Ave.
    Culver City, CA 90232
    Type: Distribution
    \*Peter Schlessel . . . . . . . . . . . . . . . . . . . . . . . . Sr. VP, Business Affairs (x 4452)
    \*Adrian Alperovich . . . . . . . . . . . . . . . . . . . . . . Dir., Business Affairs (x4186)
    \*Joyce Webster . . . . . . . . . . . . . . . . . . . . . . . . . Dir., Business Affairs (x 4533)

**\*COLUMBIA TRISTAR MOTION PICTURE COMPANIES** . . . . . . . . . . . . . . . . . . . . **310-280-8000**
    Fax: . . . . . . . . . . . . . . . . . . . . . . . . . . . . . . . . . . . . . . . . . . . . . . . . . 310-280-1883
    10202 W. Washington Blvd.
    Culver City, CA 90232
    Type: Motion Picture Production
    \*Mark Canton . . . . . . . . . . . . . . . . . . . . . . . . . . . . . . . . . . . . . . . . Chairman
    \*Fred Bernstein . . . . . . . . . . . . . . . . . . . . . . . . . . . . . . . . . . . . . . President
    \*Sheldon Rabinowitz . . . . . . . . . . . . . . . . . . . . . . . . . . . . . Exec. VP, Finance

**COLUMBIA TRISTAR TV DISTRIBUTION** . . . . . . . . . . . . . . . . . . . . . . . . . . **310-280-8000**
    10202 W. Washington Blvd.
    Culver City, CA 90232
    Type: Distribution
    Barry Thurston . . . . . . . . . . . . . . . . . . . . . . . . . . . . . . . . . . . . . . . President
    Richard Frankie . . . . . . . . . . . . . . . . . . . . . . . . . . . . Sr. VP, Business Affairs

**\*COLUMBIA TRISTAR TELEVISION** . . . . . . . . . . . . . . . . . . . . . . . . . . . . . **310-202-1234**
    9336 W. Washington Blvd.
    Culver City, CA 90232
    Type: Television Production
    \*Jon Feltheimer . . . . . . . . . . . . . . . . . . . . . . . . . . . . . . . . . . . . . President
    \*Andrew J. Kaplan . . . . . . . . . . . . . . . . . . . . . . . . . . . Sr. Exec. Vice President

**COMEDY CENTRAL** . . . . . . . . . . . . . . . . . . . . . . . . . . . . . . . . . . . . . . . **212-767-8600**
    Fax: . . . . . . . . . . . . . . . . . . . . . . . . . . . . . . . . . . . . . . . . . . . . . . . . . 212-767-8592
    1775 Broadway, 10th Floor
    New York, NY 10019
    Type: Television Production
    Robert M. Kreek . . . . . . . . . . . . . . . . . . . . . . . . . . . . . . . . . . . President-CEO
    Sarah Miller . . . . . . . . . . . . . . . . . . . . . . . . . . Exec. VP, Operations & Finance
    Steven Paul Mark . . . . . . . . . . . . . . . . . . . . . . . Sr. VP, Legal/Business Affairs
    Joan Aceste . . . . . . . . . . . . . . . . . . . . . . . . . . . . VP, Legal/Business Affairs
    John Cucci . . . . . . . . . . . . . . . . . . . . . . . . . . . . . . . . . . . . . VP-Controller
    Molly Kramer . . . . . . . . . . . . . . . . . . . . . . . . . Dir., Budget & Financial Planning
    Patty Newburger . . . . . . . . . . . . . . . . . . . . . . . . . . . . . Dir., Corporate Affairs
    Chris Pergola . . . . . . . . . . . . . . . . . . . . . . . . . . . . . . Dir., General Accounting

**COMMUNICATION FOR TRANSFORMATION**..............................310-285-8018
    Fax:.................................................................310-477-0653
  11718 Barrington Ct., Ste. 340
  Los Angeles, CA 90049
  Type: Production Financing
  Deborah Tennison ............................................. President


**\*COMPLETE FILM CORP.**.................................................310-315-4767
    Fax:.................................................................310-315-4768
  3000 W. Olympic Blvd., Ste. 1432
  Santa Monica, CA 90404
  Type: Completion Bond
  \*Martin Fink ................................................ President


**CONCORDE/NEW HORIZONS CORP.**........................................310-820-6733
    Fax:.................................................................310-207-6816
  11600 San Vicente Blvd.
  Los Angeles, CA 90049
  Type: Motion Picture Production
  \*Roger Corman.............................................. President
  \*Cheryl Parnell................................................ Exec. VP
  \*Julie Corman ............................................ Vice President
  \*Goly Jamshidi .......................................... VP, Finance
  \*Edward Reilly, Jr.................................. VP, Business/Legal Affairs


**COPLAN, DANIEL J.**.....................................................310-822-5037
    Fax:.................................................................310-823-4325
  330 Washington St., Ste. 400
  Marina del Rey, CA 90292
  \*\*Motion Pictures & Distribution
  Type: Entertainment Law
  Daniel J. Coplan.............................................. Attorney


**CORBER, BRIAN LEE** ....................................................818-786-7133
    Fax:.................................................................818-785-6495
  P.O. Box 44212
  Panorama City, CA 91412-0212
  \*\*Artists - Writers - Directors - Composers - Musicians
  Type: Entertainment Law + Legal Affairs + Business Affairs
  Brian Lee Corber .............................................. Attorney


**COUDERT BROS.**.........................................................213-688-9088
    Fax:.................................................................213-689-4467
  1055 W. 7th St., 20th Fl.
  Los Angeles, CA 90017
  Type: Entertainment Law + Business Management
  Richard Garzilli ............................................... Partner
  Robert Jesuele ............................................... Associate


**COULTER & SANDS, INC.**.................................................212-742-9850
    Fax:.................................................................212-742-0671
  56 Beaver St., Ste. 801
  New York, NY 10004-2436
  Type: Completion Bond + General Insurance
  Debra Kozee................................................. President
  Julie Coulter ............................................. Vice President

**COUNTRYMAN & MCDANIEL** . . . . . . . . . . . . . . . . . . . . . . . . . . . . . . . . . . . . . . . . **213-487-0347**
    Fax: . . . . . . . . . . . . . . . . . . . . . . . . . . . . . . . . . . . . . . . . . . . . . . . . . . . . . . . 213-487-0453
    3435 Wilshire Blvd., Ste. 2612
    Los Angeles, CA 90010
    \*\*Music - Estate planning and maritime, bus. agreements
    Type: Entertainment Law + Business Management
    Byron C. Countryman . . . . . . . . . . . . . . . . . . . . . . . . . . . . . . . . . . . . . . . . Partner
    Michael S. McDaniel . . . . . . . . . . . . . . . . . . . . . . . . . . . . . . . . . . . . . . . . Partner
    \*Stephen L. Bucklin . . . . . . . . . . . . . . . . . . . . . . . . . . . . . . . . . . . . . . . . Associate

**\*CRAMER COMPANY, THE** . . . . . . . . . . . . . . . . . . . . . . . . . . . . . . . . . . . . . . . . **213-877-0150**
    Fax: . . . . . . . . . . . . . . . . . . . . . . . . . . . . . . . . . . . . . . . . . . . . . . . . . . . . . . . 213-877-0159
    4605 Lankershim Blvd., Ste. 617
    North Hollywood, CA 91602
    Type: Television Production
    \*Douglas S. Cramer . . . . . . . . . . . . . . . . . . . . . . . . . . . . . . . . . . . . . . . . President
    \*Ruth Boubel . . . . . . . . . . . . . . . . . . . . . . . . . . . . . . . . Exec. VP, Business Affairs
    \*Jodi Broitman . . . . . . . . . . . . . . . . . . . . . . . . . . . . . . . . . Asst. to the President

**CREATIVE ROAD CORP.** . . . . . . . . . . . . . . . . . . . . . . . . . . . . . . . . . . . . . . . . **213-658-7224**
    Fax: . . . . . . . . . . . . . . . . . . . . . . . . . . . . . . . . . . . . . . . . . . . . . . . . . . . . . . . 213-658-7228
    8222 Melrose Ave.
    Los Angeles, CA 90046
    Type: Motion Picture Production + Television Production
    \*T.J. Castronovo . . . . . . . . . . . . . . . . . . . . . . . . . . . . . . . . . . . . . . . . President
    Raymond Rappa . . . . . . . . . . . . . . . . . . . . . . . . . . . . . . . . . VP, Business Affairs

**CRESTAR BANK** . . . . . . . . . . . . . . . . . . . . . . . . . . . . . . . . . . . . . . . . **804-782-5000**
    Fax: . . . . . . . . . . . . . . . . . . . . . . . . . . . . . . . . . . . . . . . . . . . . . . . . . . . . . . . 804-782-5413
    919 E. Main St., P.O. Box 26665
    Richmond, VA 23261-6548
    Type: Financial Consulting + Banking
    J. Eric Millham . . . . . . . . . . . . . . . . . . . . . . . . . . . . . . . . . . . . . . . . Vice President
    Thomas C. Palmer . . . . . . . . . . . . . . . . . . . . . . . . . . . . . . . . . . . . . . Vice President

**CROWN INTL. PICTURES.** . . . . . . . . . . . . . . . . . . . . . . . . . . . . . . . . . . . **310-657-6700**
    Fax: . . . . . . . . . . . . . . . . . . . . . . . . . . . . . . . . . . . . . . . . . . . . . . . . . . . . . . . 310-657-4489
    8701 Wilshire Blvd.
    Beverly Hills, CA 90211
    Type: Motion Picture Production
    Mark Tenser . . . . . . . . . . . . . . . . . . . . . . . . . . . . . . . . . . . . . . President-CEO
    \*Jim Boyd . . . . . . . . . . . . . . . . . . . . . . . . . . . VP, Finance & Administration
    \*Scott Schwimer . . . . . . . . . . . . . . . Sr. VP, Business Affairs/Legal Affairs & Personnel

**CULVER STUDIOS, THE** . . . . . . . . . . . . . . . . . . . . . . . . . . . . . . . . . . . . **310-202-1234**
    Fax: . . . . . . . . . . . . . . . . . . . . . . . . . . . . . . . . . . . . . . . . . . . . . . . . . . . . . . . 310-202-3272
    9336 W. Washington Blvd.
    Culver City, CA 90232-2600
    Type: Motion Picture Production + Television Production
    Jan Kelly . . . . . . . . . . . . . . . . . . . . . . . . . . . . . . . . . . . . . . . . VP, Operations

**DIC ENTERTAINMENT** . . . . . . . . . . . . . . . . . . . . . . . . . . . . . . . . . . . . **818-955-5400**
    Fax: . . . . . . . . . . . . . . . . . . . . . . . . . . . . . . . . . . . . . . . . . . . . . . . . . . . . . . . 818-955-5696
    303 N. Glenoaks Blvd.
    Burbank, CA 91505
    \*\*Animation
    Type: Television Production
    Andy Heyward . . . . . . . . . . . . . . . . . . . . . . . . . . . . . . . . . . . . . . . . President
    Bill Cooper . . . . . . . . . . . . . . . . . . . . . . . . . . . . . . . . . . . . Vice President-CFO
    Jeff Wernick . . . . . . . . . . . . . . . . . . . . . . . . . . . . . . . . . . . Exec. VP - COO
    Greg Payne . . . . . . . . . . . . . . . . . . . . . . . . Sr. VP, Legal/Business Affairs, Corp. Sect.
    Tricia Piascik . . . . . . . . . . . . . . . . . . . . . . . . . . . . . . . . . . . VP, Administration

**DISC INSURANCE SERVICES** ..................................... 818-973-4525/212-953-4336
   Fax:. . . . . . . . . . . . . . . . . . . . . . . . . . . . . . . . . . . . . . . . . . . . . . . . . . 818-972-4220
   3500 W. Olive Ave., Ste. 1180
   Burbank, CA 91505
   **ALSO: 820 2nd Ave, 7th Fl., New York, NY 10017
   Type: General Insurance
   Donna Taylor . . . . . . . . . . . . . . . . . . . . . . . . . . . . . . . . . . . . . . . Vice President-Gen. Mgr.

**\*DAMON PRODS. WORLDWIDE, MARK** ...................................... 310-226-8300
   Fax:. . . . . . . . . . . . . . . . . . . . . . . . . . . . . . . . . . . . . . . . . . . . . . . . . . 310-226-8350
   1925 Century Park East, Ste. 1700
   Los Angeles, CA 90067
   Type: Motion Picture Production
   *Mark Damon . . . . . . . . . . . . . . . . . . . . . . . . . . . . . . . . . . . . . . . . . . President
   Nancy Halloran . . . . . . . . . . . . . . . . . . . . . . . . . . . . . . . . . . . Chief Financial Officer
   *Richard Kiratsoulis . . . . . . . . . . . . . . . . . . . . . . . . . . . . . . . . Chief Operating Officer

**DANCING ASPARAGUS PRODS.** ........................................... 310-285-7774
   505 S. Beverly Dr., Ste. 238
   Beverly Hills, CA 90212
   Type: Motion Picture Production
   David Goldstein . . . . . . . . . . . . . . . . . . . . . . . . . . . . . . . . . . . VP, Business Affairs
   Richard Stein, Esq.. . . . . . . . . . . . . . . . . . . . . . . . . . . . . . . . . . VP, Legal Affairs

**DANJAQ INC.** ................................................... 310-449-3185
   Fax:. . . . . . . . . . . . . . . . . . . . . . . . . . . . . . . . . . . . . . . . . . . . . . . . . . 310-449-3189
   c/o MGM Plaza
   2401 Colorado Ave., Ste. 330
   Santa Monica, CA 90404
   Type: Motion Picture Production + Television Production
   Albert R. Broccoli . . . . . . . . . . . . . . . . . . . . . . . . . . . . . . . . . . . Chairman
   Dana Broccoli . . . . . . . . . . . . . . . . . . . . . . . . . . . . . . . . . . . Co-chairman
   Michael Wilson . . . . . . . . . . . . . . . . . . . . . . . . . . . . . . . . . . . President-CEO

**DAVIS ENTERTAINMENT CO.** .............................................. 310-556-3550
   Fax:. . . . . . . . . . . . . . . . . . . . . . . . . . . . . . . . . . . . . . . . . . . . . . . . . . 310-556-3688
   2121 Ave. of the Stars, Ste. 2900
   Los Angeles, CA 90067
   Type: Motion Picture Production
   Brooke Brooks . . . . . . . . . . . . . . . . . . . . . . . . . . . . . . . . . . . VP, Admin. Affairs

**DE PASSE ENTERTAINMENT** .............................................. 213-965-2580
   Fax:. . . . . . . . . . . . . . . . . . . . . . . . . . . . . . . . . . . . . . . . . . . . . . . . . . 213-965-2598
   5750 Wilshire Blvd., Ste. 640
   Los Angeles, CA 90036
   Type: Motion Picture Production + Television Production
   Arnold Brustin . . . . . . . . . . . . . . . . . . . . . . . . . . . . . . . . . . . Business Affairs
   Toni Patillo. . . . . . . . . . . . . . . . . . . . . . . . . . . . . . . . . . . . VP, Admin. & Finance

**\*DEAN WITTER REYNOLDS** ............................................. 818-907-2442
   Fax:. . . . . . . . . . . . . . . . . . . . . . . . . . . . . . . . . . . . . . . . . . . . . . . . . . 818-981-0963
   15490 Ventura Blvd., 3rd Fl.
   Sherman Oaks, CA 91403
   **Stock brokerage firm.
   Type: Financial Consulting
   *David S. Cooper . . . . . . . . . . . . . . . . . . . . . . . . . . . . . . . . . . . Account Executive
   *Tom Susan. . . . . . . . . . . . . . . . . . . . . . . . . . . . . . . . . . . . Account Executive

**DEL, RUBEL, SHAW, MASON & DERIN** . . . . . . . . . . . . . . . . . . . . . . . . . . . . . . . . . . . .310-772-2000
    Fax:. . . . . . . . . . . . . . . . . . . . . . . . . . . . . . . . . . . . . . . . . . . . . . . . . . .310-772-2777
    2029 Century Park East, Ste. 3910
    Los Angeles, CA 90067
    Type:  Entertainment Law
      Jeffrey D. Blye . . . . . . . . . . . . . . . . . . . . . . . . . . . . . . . . . . . . . . . . . . . . . Partner
      Ernest Del . . . . . . . . . . . . . . . . . . . . . . . . . . . . . . . . . . . . . . . . . . . . . . . . . Partner
      Greg Derin . . . . . . . . . . . . . . . . . . . . . . . . . . . . . . . . . . . . . . . . . . . . . . . . Partner
      Jeffrey S. Finkelstein . . . . . . . . . . . . . . . . . . . . . . . . . . . . . . . . . . . . . . . . . Partner
      Jonathon D. Moonves . . . . . . . . . . . . . . . . . . . . . . . . . . . . . . . . . . . . . . . . . Partner
      Michael Rubel . . . . . . . . . . . . . . . . . . . . . . . . . . . . . . . . . . . . . . . . . . . . . . Partner
      Nina L. Shaw . . . . . . . . . . . . . . . . . . . . . . . . . . . . . . . . . . . . . . . . . . . . . . . Partner
      Jean E. Tanaka . . . . . . . . . . . . . . . . . . . . . . . . . . . . . . . . . . . . . . . . . . . . . . Partner

**DELOITTE & TOUCHE** . . . . . . . . . . . . . . . . . . . . . . . . . . . . . . . . . . .310-551-6700/213-688-0800
    Fax:. . . . . . . . . . . . . . . . . . . . . . . . . . . . . . . . . . . . . . .310-284-9029/213-688-0100
    2029 Century Park East, Ste. 300
    Los Angeles, CA 90067-2900
    **ALSO: 1000 Wilshire Bl., LA 90017-2472 Telex:9103214090
    Type:  Financial Consulting + Business Management
      Don Rudkin . . . . . . . . . . . . . . . . . . . . . . . . . . . . . . . . . . . . . . . . . . . . . . . Partner
      Gary Dickey . . . . . . . . . . . . . . . . . . . . . . . . . . . . . . . . . Co-National Dir., Entertainment

**DERN & VEIN** . . . . . . . . . . . . . . . . . . . . . . . . . . . . . . . . . . . . . . . . . . . . . . . . . . . . .310-557-2244
    Fax:. . . . . . . . . . . . . . . . . . . . . . . . . . . . . . . . . . . . . . . . . . . . . . . . . . . .310-557-2224
    1901 Ave. of the Stars, Ste. 400
    Los Angeles, CA 90067
    Type:  Entertainment Law
      Dixon Q. Dern . . . . . . . . . . . . . . . . . . . . . . . . . . . . . . . . . . . . . . . . . . . . . Partner
      *Warren D. Dern . . . . . . . . . . . . . . . . . . . . . . . . . . . . . . . . . . . . . . . . . . Attorney
      *Jon F. Vein . . . . . . . . . . . . . . . . . . . . . . . . . . . . . . . . . . . . . . . . . . . Of Counsel
      *Bryan Wolf . . . . . . . . . . . . . . . . . . . . . . . . . . . . . . . . . . . . . . . . . . . Of Counsel

**DI BONA PRODS., VIN** . . . . . . . . . . . . . . . . . . . . . . . . . . . . . . . . . . . . . . . . . . . . . .310-442-5600
    Fax:. . . . . . . . . . . . . . . . . . . . . . . . . . . . . . . . . . . . . . . . . . . . . . . . . . . .310-442-5605
    12233 W. Olympic Blvd., Ste. 170
    Los Angeles, CA 90067
    Type:  Television Production
      *Terry Moore . . . . . . . . . . . . . . . . . . . . . . . . . . . . . . . . . . . . . . . VP, Operations
      Siow Vigman . . . . . . . . . . . . . . . . . . . . . . . . . . . . . . . . . . . . . . . . . . Controller

**DIAMOND JIM PRODUCTIONS** . . . . . . . . . . . . . . . . . . . . . . . . . . . . . . . . . . . . . . .818-988-4969
    5929 Hillview Park Ave.
    Sherman Oaks, CA 91401
    **Commercials, Music Video, Documentaries
    Type:  Television Production + Video Production + Motion Picture Production
      Mel Hilton . . . . . . . . . . . . . . . . . . . . . . . . . . . . . . . . . . VP, Business Affairs/Finance

**DISNEY CHANNEL, THE.** . . . . . . . . . . . . . . . . . . . . . . . . . . . . . . . . . . . . . . . . . . .818-569-7500
    Fax:. . . . . . . . . . . . . . . . . . . . . . . . . . . . . . . . . . . . . . . . . . . . . . . . . . . .818-566-1518
    3800 W. Alameda Ave.
    Burbank, CA 91505-4398
    Type:  Television Production
      Frederick Kuperberg . . . . . . . . . . . . . . . . . . . . . . . . . . . Sr. VP, Business/Legal Affairs
      Patrick T. Lopker . . . . . . . . . . . . . . . . . . . . . . . . . . . . . . . . Sr. VP, Finance & Admin.
      *Winifred B. Wechsler . . . . . . . . . . . . . . . . . . . . . . . . . . Sr. VP, New Business Development
      Chuck Kent . . . . . . . . . . . . . . . . . . . . . . . . . . . . . . . . . . . . . . . VP, Business Affairs
      *Maureen Whalen . . . . . . . . . . . . . . . . . . . . . . . . . . . . . . . . . . . . VP, Legal Affairs
      *Matt Krimmer . . . . . . . . . . . . . . . . . . . . . . . . . . . . . . . Dir., Business & Legal Affairs

**\*DOBSON GLOBAL ENTERTAINMENT** . . . . . . . . . . . . . . . . . . . . . . . . . . . . . . . . . . **404-848-8886**
    Fax: . . . . . . . . . . . . . . . . . . . . . . . . . . . . . . . . . . . . . . . . . . . . . . . . . . 404-848-8887
    3490 Piedmont Rd., #1206
    Atlanta, GA 30305
    Type:  Motion Picture Production + Television Production
    \*Bridget Dobson . . . . . . . . . . . . . . . . . . . . . . . . . . . . . . . . . . . . . . . . . President
    \*Andrew Dobson . . . . . . . . . . . . . . . . . . . . . . . . . . . . . Chief Financial Officer
    \*Thomas Collier . . . . . . . . . . . . . . . . . . . . . . . . . . . . . . . . . VP, Legal Affairs
    \*Mickie Hofmann . . . . . . . . . . . . . . . . . . . . . . . . . . . . . . . . . . . Accountant
    \*Paige White . . . . . . . . . . . . . . . . . . . . . . . . . . . . . Exec. Asst. to Dobsons

**DOCKRY PRODUCTIONS** . . . . . . . . . . . . . . . . . . . . . . . . . . . . . . . . . . . . **310-274-0761**
    Fax: . . . . . . . . . . . . . . . . . . . . . . . . . . . . . . . . . . . . . . . . . . . . . . . . . . 310-274-0762
    2528 Hutton Dr.
    Beverly Hills, CA 90210
    Type:  Motion Picture Production + Television Production + Video Production + Production Co-Financing +
Distribution
    Nancy Dockry . . . . . . . . . . . . . . . . . . . . . . . . . . . . . . . . . . . . . . . . . President
    Adolph Kaczynski . . . . . . . . . . . . . . . . . . . . . . . . . . . . . . . . . . . . . Treasurer

**\*DOG BEACH PRODUCTIONS** . . . . . . . . . . . . . . . . . . . . . . . . . . . . . . . . **310-479-5353**
    Fax: . . . . . . . . . . . . . . . . . . . . . . . . . . . . . . . . . . . . . . . . . . . . . . . . . . 310-479-4855
    11755 Wilshire Blvd., Ste. 1400
    Los Angeles, CA 90025
    Type:  Motion Picture Production
    \*David Fox . . . . . . . . . . . . . . . . . . . . . . . . . . . . . . . . . VP, Business Affairs

**\*DREAMWORKS/SKG** . . . . . . . . . . . . . . . . . . . . . . . . . . . . . . . . . . . . . . **818-733-6000**
    Fax: . . . . . . . . . . . . . . . . . . . . . . . . . . . . . . . . . . . . . . . . . . . . . . . . . . 818-733-5502
    100 Universal Plaza
    Universal City, CA 91608
    Type:  Motion Picture Production
    \*Steven Spielberg . . . . . . . . . . . . . . . . . . . . . . . . . . . . . . . . . . . . No Title
    \*Jeffrey Katzenberg . . . . . . . . . . . . . . . . . . . . . . . . . . . . . . . . . . . No Title
    \*David Geffen . . . . . . . . . . . . . . . . . . . . . . . . . . . . . . . . . . . . . . . No Title
    \*Helene Hahn . . . . . . . . . . . . . . . . . . . . . . . . . . . . . . . . . . . . . . . No Title
    \*Michael Montgomery . . . . . . . . . . . . . . . . . . . . . . . . . . . . . . . . . . No Title
    \*Ronald Nelson . . . . . . . . . . . . . . . . . . . . . . . . . . . . . . . . . . . . . . No Title

**DUITCH, POTESHMAN, FRANKLIN & CO.** . . . . . . . . . . . . . . . . . . . . . . . . **310-268-2000**
    Fax: . . . . . . . . . . . . . . . . . . . . . . . . . . . . . . . . . . . . . . . . . . . . . . . . . . 310-268-2001
    11601 Wilshire Blvd., 23rd Fl.
    Los Angeles, CA 90025-1759
    \*\*CPA
    Type:  Business Management
    Jeffrey Edell . . . . . . . . . . . . . . . . . . . . . . . . . . . . . . . . . . . . . . . . . Partner
    Lawrence Rudolph . . . . . . . . . . . . . . . . . . . . . . . . . . . . . . . . . . . Principal
    \*Mr. Hilly Gordon . . . . . . . . . . . . . . . . . . . . . . . . . . . . . . . . . . . . Partner

**E! ENTERTAINMENT TELEVISION** . . . . . . . . . . . . . . . . . . . . . . . . . . . . . **213-954-2400**
    Fax: . . . . . . . . . . . . . . . . . . . . . . . . . . . . . . . . . . . . . . . . . . . . . . . . . . 213-954-2620
    5670 Wilshire Blvd.
    Los Angeles, CA 90036
    \*\*24-hour cable entertainment news network
    Type:  Television Production
    Lee Masters . . . . . . . . . . . . . . . . . . . . . . . . . . . . . . . . . . . . . President-CEO
    Christopher Fager . . . . . . . . . . . . . . . . . . . . . . . . Sr. VP, Business/Legal Affairs
    \*William Keenan . . . . . . . . . . . . . . . . . . . . . . . . . . . . Sr. VP, Finance/CFO
    \*Mark Feldman . . . . . . . . . . . . . . . . . . . . . . . . . . VP, Business & Legal Affairs
    \*Michael Crabbe . . . . . . . . . . . . . . . . . . . . . . . . . . . . . . . . . . . Controller

**EGM FILM INTERNATIONAL INC.** ........................................... 310-260-9234
    Fax: ............................................................. 310-260-9244
    309 Santa Monica Blvd., Ste. 304
    Santa Monica, CA 90401
    Type:  Motion Picture Production
    John Eyres ............................................... President
    \*Paul Eyres ............................... VP, Distribution & Development

**ECHO ROCK ENTERTAINMENT** ............................................. 213-954-8323
    Fax: ............................................................. 213-954-0533
    8558 Holloway Dr., #201
    Los Angeles, CA 90069
    Type:  Motion Picture Production
    Michael Barnes ................................... Dir., Business Affairs

**EDELSTEIN, LAIRD & SOBEL** ................................. 310-274-6184/212-371-7111
    Fax: ................................................. 310-271-2664/212-644-5830
    9255 Sunset Blvd., Ste. 800
    Los Angeles, CA 90069
    \*\*ALSO: 32 E. 57th St., 15th Fl., New York, NY 10022
    Type:  Entertainment Law
    Gerald Edelstein ...................................... Sr. Partner (LA)
    Peter Laird ............................................. Sr. Partner
    \*William Sobel ......................................... Sr. Partner
    Paul Truss ............................................. Attorney (NY)

**ELKINS & ELKINS, AN ACCOUNTANCY CORP.** ............................... 818-789-3644
    Fax: ............................................................. 818-501-7733
    16830 Ventura Blvd., Ste 300
    Encino, CA 91436
    \*\*Writers - Actors - Directors
    Type:  Business Management
    Fred Elkins ............................................... President
    Gerald Elkins ................................... Secretary-Treasurer

**ELLIOTT ENT., LANG** ...................................................... 818-879-5300
    Fax: ............................................................. 818-879-5300
    P.O. Box 7419
    Thousand Oaks, CA 91359-7419
    Type:  Motion Picture Production + Television Production + Video Production + Distribution
    A. Edward Ezor ....................................... Corporate Counsel

**\*ELSBOY ENTERTAINMENT** ................................................ 213-656-3800
    Fax: ............................................................. 213-656-6311
    1581 N. Crescent Heights Blvd.
    Los Angeles, CA 90046-2405
    Type:  Motion Picture Production + Television Production
    \*Paul Aaron ............................................. Producer
    \*Jon Stokke ........................................... Dir., Finance

**ENTERTAINMENT BROKERS INTERNATIONAL** ............................. 310-824-0111
    Fax: ............................................................. 310-824-5733
    10940 Wilshire Blvd., 17th Floor
    Los Angeles, CA 90024
    \*\*Insuring Motion Pictures & Television Products
    Type:  General Insurance
    Don Cass ........................................... Managing Partner
    Jack Cave .......................................... Managing Partner

**\*ENTERTAINMENT FINANCIERS INC.** .................................... **310-276-1662**
    Fax:......................................................... 310-276-0166
    144 S. Beverly Dr., 6th Fl.
    Beverly Hills, CA 90212
    Type: Financial Consulting + Production Financing + Production Co-Financing
    \*Robert E. Solliday, Jr............................................... Chairman
    \*Rick E. Norris ........................................... Chief Executive Officer
    \*Richard M. Cavallero ............................................. President

**ENTERTAINMENT IND. FINANCIAL STRATEGIES ASSOC.** ..................... **818-587-4220**
    Fax:......................................................... 818-992-6134
    21700 Oxnard St., Ste. 1100
    Woodland Hills, CA 91367
    \*\*Retirement, Estate Plans, Financial Planning
    Type: Financial Consulting + General Insurance
    Rick Binder .......................................... Executive Director
    Leon Rousso, CFP ...................................... District Manager

**ERNST & YOUNG** ............................................ **310-551-5500/212-773-3000**
    1999 Ave. of the Stars, Ste. 2100
    Los Angeles, CA 90067
    \*\*ALSO: 787 7th Ave., New York, NY 10019
    Type: Business Management
    Harvey Gettleson ...................................... Business Mgmt., Partner
    Norman Marcus ....................................... Business Mgmt., Partner
    Mel Masuda .......................................... Audit Partner
    \*Kelly Rose .......................................... Office Managing, Partner

**ERVIN, COHEN & JESSUP** ....................................... **310-273-6333/310-281-6307**
    Fax:......................................................... 310-859-2325
    9401 Wilshire Blvd., 9th Fl.
    Beverly Hills, CA 90212-2974
    \*\*Telex: 9104905748, Answbk: JOLED LSA, Distribution
    Type: Entertainment Law + Financial Consulting + Production Financing
    Thomas F. R. Garvin ................................... Partner (310-281-6307)

**ESPARZA-KATZ PRODS.** ........................................... **310-281-3770**
    Fax:......................................................... 310-281-3777
    8899 Beverly Blvd., 8th Fl.
    Los Angeles, CA 90048
    Type: Motion Picture Production
    Steve Kalb .......................................... VP, Business Affairs
    Laura Caldera........................................ Accounting Admin.

**EVANS, DAVID J.** ............................................ **310-395-0965**
    1541 Ocean Ave. #300
    Santa Monica, CA 90401
    \*\*Motion Pictures, Television, Music
    Type: Entertainment Law
    David J. Evans, Esq.................................... Attorney

**EXCELSIOR PICTURES CORP.** ..................................... **310-289-8220**
    Fax:......................................................... 310-358-8768
    8544 Melrose Ave.
    West Hollywood, CA 90069
    \*\*Foreign sales
    Type: Motion Picture Production + Distribution + Production Co-Financing + Television Production
    Christopher Harbonville................................... President
    Adam Fast ........................................... VP, Business Affairs

**FX NETWORKS** . . . . . . . . . . . . . . . . . . . . . . . . . . . . . . . . . . . . . . . . . . . . . . . . . . . . . **310-369-3075**
    P.O. Box 900
    Beverly Hills, CA 90213-0900
    **ALSO: 10201 W. Pico Blvd. LA, CA 90025
    Type:  Television Production
    Anne Sweeney . . . . . . . . . . . . . . . . . . . . . . . . . . . . . . . . . . . . . . . Chairman-CEO, Fox Cable
    Bob Fleming. . . . . . . . . . . . . . . . . . . . . . . . . . . . . . . . . . . . . . . . . Sr. VP, Finance & Admin.

**FAMILY CHANNEL, THE** . . . . . . . . . . . . . . . . . . . . . . . . . . . . . . . . . . . . . . . . . **804-459-6000**
    Fax:. . . . . . . . . . . . . . . . . . . . . . . . . . . . . . . . . . . . . . . . . . . . . . . . . . . . . . . 804-459-6421
    2877 Guardian Lane
    Virginia Beach, VA 23452
    Type:  Television Production
    Larry Dantzler . . . . . . . . . . . . . . . . . . . . . . . . . . . . . . . . . . . . . . . . . . Vice President-CFO
    David Humphrey . . . . . . . . . . . . . . . . . . . . . . . . . . . . . . . . . . . . Sr. VP, Investor Relations
    Lou Isakoff. . . . . . . . . . . . . . . . . . . . . . . . . . . . . . . . . VP, Legal Affairs-Gen. Counsel
    Debra McKay . . . . . . . . . . . . . . . . . . . . . . . . . . . . . . . . . . . . . . . . . . . . . . . . Controller

**\*FEATURE FINANCE** . . . . . . . . . . . . . . . . . . . . . . . . . . . . . . . . . . . . . . . . . . . . . **310-470-8301**
    Fax:. . . . . . . . . . . . . . . . . . . . . . . . . . . . . . . . . . . . . . . . . . . . . . . . . . . . . . . 310-472-1481
    505 S. Beverly Drive #1020
    Beverly Hills, CA 90212
    **Dist. representation/consulting/sales
    Type:  Distribution
    *Cheryl Bartlam . . . . . . . . . . . . . . . . . . . . . . . . . . . . . . . . . . . . . . . . . . . . . . President

**FIELDS & HELLMAN CO., THE** . . . . . . . . . . . . . . . . . . . . . . . . . . . . . . . . . . . **310-276-6555**
    Fax:. . . . . . . . . . . . . . . . . . . . . . . . . . . . . . . . . . . . . . . . . . . . . . . . . . . . . . . 310-275-8198
    8899 Beverly Blvd., Ste. 918
    Los Angeles, CA 90048
    Type:  Motion Picture Production
    Freddie Fields. . . . . . . . . . . . . . . . . . . . . . . . . . . . . . . . . . . . . . . . . . Partner-Producer
    Jerome Hellman . . . . . . . . . . . . . . . . . . . . . . . . . . . . . . . . . . . . . . . . Partner-Producer

**FILM CAPITAL CORPORATION** . . . . . . . . . . . . . . . . . . . . . . . . . . . . . . . . . . **619-778-7617**
    Fax:. . . . . . . . . . . . . . . . . . . . . . . . . . . . . . . . . . . . . . . . . . . . . . . . . . . . . . . 619-778-7621
    2287 Hildy Lane
    Palm Springs, CA 92262-2410
    **Referrals to comple. bond, Ins. & Dist.
    Type:  Motion Picture Production + Television Production + Financial Consulting + PF
    *Marlene Mendoza . . . . . . . . . . . . . . . . . . . . . . . . . . . . . . . . . . . Exec. Producer/CEO
    *Chris Johnson . . . . . . . . . . . . . . . . . . . . . . . . . . . . . . . . . . . . . . . . Financial Officer

**FILM FINANCES, INC.** . . . . . . . . . . . . . . . . . . . . . . . . . . . . . . . . . . . . . . . . . . **310-275-7323**
    Fax:. . . . . . . . . . . . . . . . . . . . . . . . . . . . . . . . . . . . . . . . . . 310-275-1706/310-275-0723
    9000 Sunset Blvd., Ste. 1400
    Los Angeles, CA 90069
    Type:  Completion Bond + General Insurance + Production Financing
    Richard Soames . . . . . . . . . . . . . . . . . . . . . . . . . . . . . . . . . . . . . . . . . . . . . President
    Steve Ransohoff. . . . . . . . . . . . . . . . . . . . . . . . . . . . . . . . . . . . . . . . . Vice President
    *Marion Spiegelman. . . . . . . . . . . . . . . . . . . . . . . . . . . . . . . . VP, Business Affairs
    Kurt Woolner . . . . . . . . . . . . . . . . . . . . . . . . . . . . . . . . . . . . . . . . . . Vice President

**FILM FUNDING INC.** . . . . . . . . . . . . . . . . . . . . . . . . . . . . . . . . . . . . . . . . . . . **702-735-1922**
    Fax:. . . . . . . . . . . . . . . . . . . . . . . . . . . . . . . . . . . . . . . . . . . . . . . . . . . . . . . 702-735-0094
    1700 East Desert Inn Rd., Ste. 100
    Las Vegas, NV 89109
    Type:  Motion Picture Production + Television Production + Banking + Production Financing
    Raymond Girard. . . . . . . . . . . . . . . . . . . . . . . . . . . . . . . . . . . . . . . . . . . . . President
    Gary Vesperman . . . . . . . . . . . . . . . . . . . . . . . . . . . . . . . . . . . . . . . . Vice President
    John E. Neuenfeldt. . . . . . . . . . . . . . . . . . . . . . . . . . . . . . . . . . . . . . . . . . Treasurer

**FILM-VIDEO FINANCIAL PRESENTATIONS** . . . . . . . . . . . . . . . . . . . . . . . . . . . . . . **818-340-0175**
  Fax:. . . . . . . . . . . . . . . . . . . . . . . . . . . . . . . . . . . . . . . . . . . . . . . . . . . . . 818-340-6620
  7944 Capistrano Ave.
  West Hills, CA 91304
  **Create high quality financial presentations & bus. plan
Type:  Financial Consulting
  Alan Gadney . . . . . . . . . . . . . . . . . . . . . . . . . . . . . . . . . . . . . . . . . . . . . President

**FINDELLE LAW & MGMT., STANN**. . . . . . . . . . . . . . . . . . . . . . . . . . . . . . . . . . **310-552-1777**
  Fax:. . . . . . . . . . . . . . . . . . . . . . . . . . . . . . . . . . . . . . . . . . . . . . . . . . . 310-286-1990
  2049 Century Park East, Ste. 1100
  Los Angeles, CA 90067
Type:  Entertainment Law
  Stann Findelle . . . . . . . . . . . . . . . . . . . . . . . . . . . . . . . . . . . . . . . . . . Attorney

**FIRST CHARTER BANK** . . . . . . . . . . . . . . . . . . . . . . . . . . . . . . . . . . . . . . . . **310-278-7200**
  Fax:. . . . . . . . . . . . . . . . . . . . . . . . . . . . . . . . . . . . . . . . . . . . . . . . . . . 310-278-9543
  265 N. Beverly Dr.
  Beverly Hills, CA 90210
Type:  Banking
  Peter Bustetter . . . . . . . . . . . . . . . . . . . . . . . . . . . . . . . . . . . . . . . President-CEO
  Buddy Salzberg . . . . . . . . . . . . . . . . . . . . . . . . . . . . . . . . . . Sr. Vice President
  Jan Van Houdt . . . . . . . . . . . . . . . . . . . . . . . . . . . . . . . . . . VP-Mgr., Ent. Div.

**FIRST ENTERTAINMENT FEDERAL CREDIT UNION** . . . . . . . . . . . . . . . . . . . . . . . **213-851-3673**
  Fax:. . . . . . . . . . . . . . . . . . . . . . . . . . . . . . . . . . . . . . . . . . . . . . . . . . . 213-851-0383
  6735 Forest Lawn Dr.
  Hollywood, CA 90068
  **Branch: 10000 W. Washington Blvd. #1400, Culver City
Type:  Banking
  Charles Bruen. . . . . . . . . . . . . . . . . . . . . . . . . . . . . . . . . . . . . . . . President-CEO
  Michael Bare . . . . . . . . . . . . . . . . . . . . . . . . . . . . . . . VP, Finance/Data Processing
  Wm. Gary Moffatt . . . . . . . . . . . . . . . . . . . . . . . . . . . . . . . . . . VP, Operations
  Kathryn Harris . . . . . . . . . . . . . . . . . . . . . . . . . . . . Asst. VP, Operations (Culver City)
  James Marcellino . . . . . . . . . . . . . . . . . . . . . . . . . . . . Asst. VP, Central Services
  Lynn Muller . . . . . . . . . . . . . . . . . . . . . . . . . . . . Asst. VP, Operations (Hollywood)
  Roy MacKinnon. . . . . . . . . . . . . . . . . . . . . . . . . . . . . . . . . . Dir., Marketing

**FIRST INTERSTATE BANK OF CALIF - ENT. DIV.** . . . . . . . . . . . . . . . . . . . . . . . ***310-285-5768**
  Fax:. . . . . . . . . . . . . . . . . . . . . . . . . . . . . . . . . . . . . . . . . . . . . . . . . . ***310-285-5829**
  9601 Wilshire Blvd.
  Beverly Hills, CA 90210
  **All entertainment financing
Type:  Production Financing
  Lawrence Da Silva. . . . . . . . . . . . . . . . . . . . . . . . . . . . . . . . . VP-Mgr., Ent. Div.
  *Evelyn Sorrentino . . . . . . . . . . . . . . . . . . . . . . . . . . . . . Vice President (285-5872)

**FIRST LOOK PICTS./OVERSEAS FILMGROUP** . . . . . . . . . . . . . . . . . . . . . . . . . . **310-855-1199**
  Fax:. . . . . . . . . . . . . . . . . . . . . . . . . . . . . . . . . . . . . . . . . . . . . . . . . . . 310-855-0719
  8800 Sunset Blvd., Ste. 302
  Los Angeles, CA 90069
Type:  Motion Picture Production + Television Production + Distribution
  Robert Little . . . . . . . . . . . . . . . . . . . . . . . . . . . . . . . . . . . . . . . . Chairman
  Ellen Little . . . . . . . . . . . . . . . . . . . . . . . . . . . . . . . . . . . . . . . . . President
  *William Lischak . . . . . . . . . . . . . . . . . . . . . . . Chief Financial Officer/Chief Operations Officer
  *Susan Raines . . . . . . . . . . . . . . . . . . . . . . . . . . . . . . . . . . . . . . . Controller
  *Mansour Mostaedi . . . . . . . . . . . . . . . . . . . . . . . . . . . . . . VP, Finance & Accounting
  *David Steinberg. . . . . . . . . . . . . . . . . . . . . . . . . . . . . . . . VP, Legal/Business Affairs
  *Sharyn Yvloff . . . . . . . . . . . . . . . . . . . . . . . . . . . . . . . . . . Contract Administrator

**FIRST LOS ANGELES BANK, ENT. IND. DIV.** . . . . . . . . . . . . . . . . . . . . . . . . . . . . . . . . .310-557-1211
   Fax:. . . . . . . . . . . . . . . . . . . . . . . . . . . . . . . . . . . . . . . . . . . . . . . . . . . . . . .310-556-1205
   2049 Century Park East, 36th Fl.
   Los Angeles, CA 90067
   Type:  Production Financing
   \*Thomas H. Shaffer . . . . . . . . . . . . . . . . . . . . . . . . . . . . . . . . . . . . . . . President & CEO
   \*John Barritt . . . . . . . . . . . . . . . . . . . . . . . . . . . . . . . . . . . . . . . . . . . . . . . . . . . CFO
   \*Mario Garresi . . . . . . . . . . . . . . . . . . . . . . . . . . . . . . . . . . . . . . . Exec. Vice President

**FIRST NATIONAL BANK OF CHICAGO, THE.** . . . . . . . . . . . . . . . . . . . . . . . . . . . .312-732-4000
   Fax:. . . . . . . . . . . . . . . . . . . . . . . . . . . . . . . . . . . . . . . .312-732-8587/312-732-1117
   One First National Plaza, Ste. 0629
   Chicago, IL 60670
   \*\*Lending to the communications/entertainment industry.
   Type:  Motion Picture Production + Television Production
   Richard I. Elmendorf . . . . . . . . . . . . . . . . . . . . . . . . . . . . . . Vice President, Div. Head
   Steve Capouch . . . . . . . . . . . . . . . . . . . . . . . . . . . . . . . . . . . . . . . . . Vice President
   \*Michael Phelan . . . . . . . . . . . . . . . . . . . . . . . . . . . . . . . . . . . . . . . . Vice President
   John M. Speer . . . . . . . . . . . . . . . . . . . . . . . . . . . . . . . . . . . . . . . . . . Vice President

**FITZROY, ANNE STEWART.** . . . . . . . . . . . . . . . . . . . . . . . . . . . . . . . . . . . . . .212-370-4299
   Fax:. . . . . . . . . . . . . . . . . . . . . . . . . . . . . . . . . . . . . . . . . . . . . . . . .212-986-3498
   60 E. 42nd St.
   New York, NY 10165
   \*\*Accountant - Personal taxes - Theatrical Prods.
   Type:  Financial Consulting
   Anne Stewart FitzRoy . . . . . . . . . . . . . . . . . . . . . . . . . Certified Public Accountant

**FORTIS ENTERTAINMENT** . . . . . . . . . . . . . . . . . . . . . . . . . . . . . . . . . . . . . .310-226-7114
   9000 Sunset Blvd., Ste. 405
   Los Angeles, CA 90069
   Type:  Motion Picture Production + Television Production + Production Co-Financing
   Alex Rossu . . . . . . . . . . . . . . . . . . . . . . . . . . . . . . . . . . . . Chief Executive Officer
   Richard Huang . . . . . . . . . . . . . . . . . . . . . . . . . . . . . . . . . . VP, Business Affairs

**FOUR POINT ENTERTAINMENT** . . . . . . . . . . . . . . . . . . . . . . . . . . . . . . . . . . .213-850-1600
   Fax:. . . . . . . . . . . . . . . . . . . . . . . . . . . . . . . . . . . . . . . . . . . . . . . . .213-850-6709
   3575 Cahuenga Blvd. West, Ste. 600
   Los Angeles, CA 90068
   Type:  Television Production
   Shukri Ghalayini . . . . . . . . . . . . . . . . . . . . . . . . . . . . . . . . Co-owner-Chairman
   Ron Ziskin . . . . . . . . . . . . . . . . . . . . . . . . . . . . . . . . . . . . Co-owner-President
   Ariane Fleiderman . . . . . . . . . . . . . . . . . . . . . . . . . . . . . . . . . . . . . . Controller

**FOX BROADCASTING CO.** . . . . . . . . . . . . . . . . . . . . . . . . . . . . . . . . . . . . . .310-369-1000
   Fax:. . . . . . . . . . . . . . . . . . . . . . . . . . . . . . . . . . . . . . . . . . . . . . . . .310-369-2954
   10201 W. Pico Blvd.
   Los Angeles, CA 90035
   \*\*Business Affairs Fax: 310-369-3465
   Type:  Television Production
   David Grant . . . . . . . . . . . . . . . . . . . . . . . . . . . . . Exec. VP, Network Business Operations
   Ira Kurgan . . . . . . . . . . . . . . . . . . . . . . . . . . . . . . . . Executive VP, Business Affairs
   \*Larry Jacobson . . . . . . . . . . . . . . . . . . . . . . . . . . Chief Financial Officer/Exec. VP
   \*Richard Vokulich . . . . . . . . . . . . . . . . . . . . . . . . . . . . . . . Sr. VP, Business Affairs
   Eric Yeldell . . . . . . . . . . . . . . . . . . . . . . . . . . . . . . . . . . . . . Sr. VP, Legal Affairs
   \*Karen Fox . . . . . . . . . . . . . . . . . . . . . . . . . . . . . . . . . . . . . . . VP, Business Affairs
   Del Mayberry. . . . . . . . . . . . . . . . . . . . . . . . . . . . . VP-Controller, Fox Broadcasting
   David Talley. . . . . . . . . . . . . . . . . . . . . . . . . . . . . . . . . . . . . VP, Business Affairs
   Minna Taylor . . . . . . . . . . . . . . . . . . . . . . . . . . . . . . . . . . . . . VP, Legal Affairs

**\*FOX FILMED ENTERTAINMENT** . . . . . . . . . . . . . . . . . . . . . . . . . . . . . . . . . . . . . . . **310-369-1000**
  10201 W. Pico Blvd.
  Los Angeles, CA 90035
  Type: Motion Picture Production
  \*Peter Chernin . . . . . . . . . . . . . . . . . . . . . . . . . . . . . . . . . . . . . . . . . . . . . . . . . . CEO
  \*Bill Mechanic . . . . . . . . . . . . . . . . . . . . . . . . . . . . . . . . . . . . . . . . President/COO
  \*Simon Bax . . . . . . . . . . . . . . . . . . . . . . . . . . . . . . . . . . . . . . . . . . . . . . Sr. VP/CFO

**FOX TV STATIONS PRODS.** . . . . . . . . . . . . . . . . . . . . . . . . . . . . . . . . . . . . . . **213-856-1000**
  Fax: . . . . . . . . . . . . . . . . . . . . . . . . . . . . . . . . . . . . . . . . . . . . . . . . . . . 213-856-1594
  c/o Fox TV Center
  5746 Sunset Blvd.
  Los Angeles, CA 90028-8588
  Type: Television Production
  Gerry Freidman . . . . . . . . . . . . . . . . . . . . . . . . . . . . Sr. VP, Business/Legal Affairs
  Daphne Gronich . . . . . . . . . . . . . . . . . . . . . . . . . . . . . . VP, Business/Legal Affairs
  \*Denise Van Patten . . . . . . . . . . . . . . . . . . . . . . . . . . . VP, Business/Legal Affairs

**FRANKFURT, GARBUS, KLEIN & SELZ** . . . . . . . . . . . . . . . . . . . . . . . . . . **212-980-0120**
  488 Madison Ave.
  New York, NY 10022
  Type: Entertainment Law
  Ira Schreck . . . . . . . . . . . . . . . . . . . . . . . . . . . . . . . . . . . . . . . . . . . . . . Attorney

**FRANKLIN/WATERMAN ENT.** . . . . . . . . . . . . . . . . . . . . . . . . . . . . . . . . . . **310-452-9100**
  Fax: . . . . . . . . . . . . . . . . . . . . . . . . . . . . . . . . . . . . . . . . . . . . . . . . . . . 310-452-1771
  2644 30th St., 1st Fl.
  Santa Monica, CA 90405
  Type: Television Production + Distribution + Production Financing
  Jeff Franklin . . . . . . . . . . . . . . . . . . . . . . . . . . . . . . . . . . . . . . . . . Co-chairman
  Steve Waterman . . . . . . . . . . . . . . . . . . . . . . . . . . . . . . . . . . . . . . . Co-chairman
  B.L. Epstein . . . . . . . . . . . . . . . . . . . . . . . . . . . . . Exec. VP, Business Affairs

**FREEDMAN, BRODER & CO.** . . . . . . . . . . . . . . . . . . . . . . . . . . . . . . . . . . **310-449-6700**
  Fax: . . . . . . . . . . . . . . . . . . . . . . . . . . . . . . . . . . . . . . . . . . . . . . . . . . . 310-449-6789
  2501 Colorado Ave., Ste. 350
  Santa Monica, CA 90404
  Type: Business Management
  William Broder . . . . . . . . . . . . . . . . . . . . . . . . . . . . . . . . . . . . . . . . . Partner
  Stephen Michalski . . . . . . . . . . . . . . . . . . . . . . . . . . . . . . . . . . . . . . . Partner
  Debra Bonseigneur . . . . . . . . . . . . . . . . . . . . . . . . . . Certified Public Accountant
  Steve Wagner . . . . . . . . . . . . . . . . . . . . . . . . . . . . . Certified Public Accountant

**FRIES ENTERTAINMENT** . . . . . . . . . . . . . . . . . . . . . . . . . . . . . . . . . . . . . **213-466-2266**
  Fax: . . . . . . . . . . . . . . . . . . . . . . . . . . . . . . . . . . . . . . . . . . . . . . . . . . . 213-462-0881
  6922 Hollywood Blvd.
  Los Angeles, CA 90028-6133
  Type: Motion Picture Production + Production Co-Financing
  Charles W. Fries . . . . . . . . . . . . . . . . . . . . . . . . . . . . . . Chairman-President-CEO
  Neal Smaler . . . . . . . . . . . . . . . . . . . . . . . . . . . . . . . . . Chief Financial Officer
  \*Antony T. Ginnane . . . . . . . . . . . . . . . . . . . . . . . . . . . . Prod., Co-Financing
  Paul Landau, Esq. . . . . . . . . . . . . . . . . . . . . . . . . . . . Dir., Business/Legal Affairs

**FURMAN SELZ INC.** . . . . . . . . . . . . . . . . . . . . . . . . . . . . . . . . . . . . . . . . **212-309-8200**
  230 Park Ave., 13th Fl.
  New York, NY 10169
  Type: Banking
  Roy L. Furman . . . . . . . . . . . . . . . . . . . . . . . . . . . . . . . . . . . . . . . . . President
  Brian P. Friedman . . . . . . . . . . . . . . . . . . . . . . . . . . . . . Exec. Vice President
  Michael N. Garin . . . . . . . . . . . . . . . . . . . . . . Sr. Managing Dir., Media & Comm. Group
  Raymond J. Timothy . . . . . . . . . . . . . . . . . . . . . Sr. Managing Dir., Media & Comm. Group
  \*Bonnie Bown Zades . . . . . . . . . . . . . . . . . . . . . . . . . . . Dir., Investment Banking
  \*Gerald H. Cromack . . . . . . . . . . . . . . . . . . . . . . . . . . . . . . Managing Director
  \*Stephen Prough . . . . . . . . . . . . . . . . . . . . . . . . . . . . . . . . . . . . . . . Associate

**GEL PRODUCTION/DISTRIBUTION** . . . . . . . . . . . . . . . . . . . . . . . . . . . . . . . . . . **310-479-5619**
    Fax: . . . . . . . . . . . . . . . . . . . . . . . . . . . . . . . . . . . . . . . . . . . . . . . . . . . . 310-477-4447
    11075 Santa Monica Blvd., Ste. 250
    Los Angeles, CA 90025
    Type:  Motion Picture Production + Television Production + Distribution
    William A. Shields . . . . . . . . . . . . . . . . . . . . . . . . . . . . . . . . . . . . . . President-CEO
    Judi Becker . . . . . . . . . . . . . . . . . . . . . . . . . . . . . . . . . . . . . . . . . . . . . VP, Finance

**\*GAUMONT TELEVISION** . . . . . . . . . . . . . . . . . . . . . . . . . . . . . . . **818-505-6647/46-432306**
    Fax: . . . . . . . . . . . . . . . . . . . . . . . . . . . . . . . . . . . . . . . . . 818-505-6648/46-432320
    4125-1/2 Radford Ave.
    Studio City, CA 91604
    \*\*ALSO: 24 rue Jacques Dulud, 92200 Neuilly, France
    Type:  Television Production
    \*Christian Charret . . . . . . . . . . . . . . . . . . . . . . . . . . . . . . . . . . . President (Paris)
    \*Christine Camdessus . . . . . . . . . . . . . . . . . . . . . . . . . . . Business Affairs (Paris)

**GEFFEN PICTURES** . . . . . . . . . . . . . . . . . . . . . . . . . . . . . . . . . . . . . . . **310-278-9010**
    Fax: . . . . . . . . . . . . . . . . . . . . . . . . . . . . . . . . . . . . . . . . . . . . . . 310-273-1692
    9130 Sunset Blvd.
    Los Angeles, CA 90069
    Type:  Motion Picture Production
    David Geffen . . . . . . . . . . . . . . . . . . . . . . . . . . . . . . . . . . . . . . . . . . . Chairman
    Bonnie Lee . . . . . . . . . . . . . . . . . . . . . . . . . . . . . . . . . . . . . . . . . . . . President

**GELFAND, NEWMAN & WASSERMAN** . . . . . . . . . . . . . . . . . . . . . . . . . . . . **310-473-2522**
    Fax: . . . . . . . . . . . . . . . . . . . . . . . . . . . . . . . . . . . . . . . . . . . . . . 310-478-8392
    11500 W. Olympic Blvd., Ste. 404
    Los Angeles, CA 90064
    Type:  Business Management + General Insurance
    Charles Gelfand . . . . . . . . . . . . . . . . . . . . . . . . . . . . . . . . . . . . . . . . . Partner
    Michael Newman . . . . . . . . . . . . . . . . . . . . . . . . . . . . . . . . . . . . . . . . Partner
    Harmon Wasserman . . . . . . . . . . . . . . . . . . . . . . . . . . . . . . . . . . . . . . Partner

**GELFAND, RENNERT & FELDMAN** . . . . . . . . . . . . . . . . . . . . . . . . . . . . . . . **310-553-1707**
    Fax: . . . . . . . . . . . . . . . . . . . . . . . . . . . . . . . . . . . . . . . . . . . . . . 310-557-8412
    1880 Century Park East, 9th Fl.
    Los Angeles, CA 90067
    \*\*All areas of entertainment
    Type:  Business Management
    Nicholas Brown . . . . . . . . . . . . . . . . . . . . . . . . . . . . . . . . . . . . . Partner (LA)
    Steven L. Cantrock . . . . . . . . . . . . . . . . . . . . . . . . . . . . . . . . . Partner (LA/SF)
    Martin Feldman . . . . . . . . . . . . . . . . . . . . . . . . . . . . . . . . . . . . Partner (NY)
    Marshall M. Gelfand . . . . . . . . . . . . . . . . . . . . . . . . . . . . . . . . . Partner (LA)
    Todd E. Gelfand . . . . . . . . . . . . . . . . . . . . . . . . . . . . . . Partner, CPA (LA/SF)
    William L. Harper . . . . . . . . . . . . . . . . . . . . . . . . . . . . . . . Partner, CPA (LA)
    David Jackel . . . . . . . . . . . . . . . . . . . . . . . . . . . . . . . . . . Partner, CPA (LA)
    Jeffrey Kaye . . . . . . . . . . . . . . . . . . . . . . . . . . . . . . . . . . . Partner (London)
    Peter M. Levine . . . . . . . . . . . . . . . . . . . . . . . . . . . . . . . . Partner, CPA (NY)
    Edwin N. London . . . . . . . . . . . . . . . . . . . . . . . . . . . . . . . . . . . Partner (NY)
    Stephen Marks . . . . . . . . . . . . . . . . . . . . . . . . . . . . . . . . . . Partner (London)
    Ronald E. Nash . . . . . . . . . . . . . . . . . . . . . . . . . . . . . . . . . Partner, CPA (NY)
    John R. Phillips . . . . . . . . . . . . . . . . . . . . . . . . . . . . . . . . Partner, CPA (LA)
    Irwin L. Rennert . . . . . . . . . . . . . . . . . . . . . . . . . . . . . . . . . . . Partner (LA)
    Mario Testani . . . . . . . . . . . . . . . . . . . . . . . . . . . . . . . . . . Partner, CPA (NY)

**GENESIS ENTERTAINMENT** . . . . . . . . . . . . . . . . . . . . . . . . . . . **212-527-6400/818-706-6341**
    Fax: . . . . . . . . . . . . . . . . . . . . . . . . . . . . . . . . . . . . 212-527-6401/818-707-0785
    625 Madison Ave., 11th Fl.
    New York, NY 10022
    \*\*ALSO: 30501 Agoura Rd. #200, Agoura Hills, CA 91301
    Type:  Television Production
    \*Ronald Perelman . . . . . . . . . . . . . . . . . . . . . . . . . . . . . Chairman of the Board
    \*Bill Bevins . . . . . . . . . . . . . . . . . . . . . . . . . . . . . . . . . . . . . . . . . . . . . CEO
    Wayne Lepoff . . . . . . . . . . . . . . . . . . . . . . . . . . . . . . . . . . . President-COO
    Bob Berry . . . . . . . . . . . . . . . . . . . . . . . . . . . . . . . . . . . . Sr. VP, Finance
    Jeffrey S. Weiss . . . . . . . . . . . . . . . . . . . . . . . . . . . Sr. VP, Business/Legal Affairs

**GERBER ITC ENT. GROUP, THE** .............................................. 310-858-2600
  Fax:................................................................... 310-858-2606
  9200 Sunset Blvd., Ste. 1024
  Los Angeles, CA 90069
  Type:  Motion Picture Production + Television Production
  David Gerber ............................................................ President
  James Waldron.................................................. Sr. Vice President
  Honi Almond .......................................... VP, Business Affairs
  Kathi Weissberger ................................... Asst. to Pressident

**GIBSON, DUNN & CRUTCHER** ............................................. 310-552-8500
  Fax:................................................................... 310-277-5827
  2029 Century Park East, Ste. 4000
  Los Angeles, CA 90067
  **Telex: 674 930, Answbk: GIBTRASK LSA
  Type:  Entertainment Law
  Paul G. Bower ............................................................ Attorney
  Jeffrey C. Briggs ........................................................ Attorney
  James P. Clark ........................................................... Attorney
  Shari Leinwand ......................................................... Attorney
  Don Parris .............................................................. Attorney
  Leo G. Ziffren .......................................................... Attorney
  Lester Ziffren ........................................................... Attorney

**GIPSON HOFFMAN & PANCIONE** ......................................... 310-556-4660
  Fax:................................................................... 310-556-8945
  1901 Ave. of the Stars, Ste. 1100
  Los Angeles, CA 90067
  **ALSO: Zeppelinsterasse 28 CH-0857, Zurich, Switzerland
  Type:  Entertainment Law
  Markus W. Barmettler ........................................ Attorney (Zurich)
  *Lawrence Barnett ...................................................... Attorney
  Lindsey Bayman ........................................................ Attorney
  Vincent H. Chieffo....................................................... Attorney
  Ray Gross............................................................... Attorney
  *Janine Smith .......................................................... Attorney
  Robert H. Steinberg ..................................................... Attorney

**GOLDEN HARVEST FILMS** ............................................... 310-203-0722
  Fax:................................................................... 310-556-3214
  9884 Santa Monica Bl.
  Beverly Hills, CA 90212
  Type:  Motion Picture Production
  John W. Stuart ........................................................ Comptroller

**GOLDEN, RENEE WAYNE** ................................................ 310-550-8232
  Fax:................................................................... 310-276-7736
  8983 Norma Pl.
  West Hollywood, CA 90069
  Type:  Entertainment Law
  Renee Wayne Golden .................................................... Attorney

**GOLDMAN, SACHS & CO.** ............................................... 213-617-5820
  Fax:................................................................... 213-617-5812
  333 S. Grand Ave.
  Los Angeles, CA 90071
  **Full svc. investment bank to media/ent. professionals.
  Type:  Banking + Financial Consulting
  Jeff Colin ...................................................... Media & Ent. Group
  Todd Morgan ................................................... Media & Ent. Group

**GOLDWYN CO., SAMUEL**. . . . . . . . . . . . . . . . . . . . . . . . . . . . . . . . . . **310-552-2255/212-315-3030**
    Fax:. . . . . . . . . . . . . . . . . . . . . . . . . . . . . . . . . . . . . . . . . . 310-284-8493/212-307-6051
    10203 Santa Monica Blvd.
    Los Angeles, CA 90067
    **ALSO: 888 7th Ave. #2901, New York, NY 10106
    Type:  Motion Picture Production + Television Production + Distribution
    Samuel Goldwyn, Jr.. . . . . . . . . . . . . . . . . . . . . . . . . . . . . . Chairman of the Board-CEO
    Meyer Gottlieb. . . . . . . . . . . . . . . . . . . . . . . . . . . . . . . . . . . . . . . . . President-COO
    Hans Turner . . . . . . . . . . . . . . . . . . . . . . . . . . . . . . . . . . Chief Financial Officer-Sr. VP
    Norman Flicker . . . . . . . . . . . . . . . . . . . . . . . . . . . . . . . . . . . Sr. VP, Business Affairs
    *Lawrence Kirk, Jr.. . . . . . . . . . . . . . . . . . . . . . . . . . . . . . . . . . Sr. VP, Operations
    David Berson . . . . . . . . . . . . . . . . . . . . . . . . . . . . . . . . . . . . . VP, Business Affairs
    *Tom Fuelling. . . . . . . . . . . . . . . . . . . . . . . . . . . . . . . . . Vice President-Controller
    Jeffrey Glover . . . . . . . . . . . . . . . . . . . . . . . . . . . . . . . . . . . VP, Business Affairs

**GOODSON PRODS., MARK**. . . . . . . . . . . . . . . . . . . . . . . . . . . . . . . . . . . **213-965-6500**
    Fax:. . . . . . . . . . . . . . . . . . . . . . . . . . . . . . . . . . . . . . . . . . . . . 213-965-6527
    5750 Wilshire Blvd., Ste. 475W
    Los Angeles, CA 90036
    Type:  Television Production
    *Jonathan Goodson. . . . . . . . . . . . . . . . . . . . . . . . . President/Chief Executive Officer
    Harris Katleman. . . . . . . . . . . . . . . . . . . . . . . . . . . . . . . . Chief Operating Officer
    *Alan Sandler . . . . . . . . . . . . . . . . . . . . . . . . . . . . . . . . . Chief Financial Officer
    *Michael Brockman . . . . . . . . . . . . . . . . . . . . . . . . . . . . . . . . Sr. Vice President

**GORDON, THE LAW OFFICE OF PETER D.** . . . . . . . . . . . . . . . . . . . . . . . . . . **213-651-5111**
    Fax:. . . . . . . . . . . . . . . . . . . . . . . . . . . . . . . . . . . . . . . . . . . . . 213-651-3726
    8052 Melrose Ave., 2nd fl.
    Los Angeles, CA 90046
    **Motion Pictures, Television, Music
    Type:  Entertainment Law

**GRACIE FILMS** . . . . . . . . . . . . . . . . . . . . . . . . . . . . . . . . . . . . . . . . **310-280-4222**
    Fax:. . . . . . . . . . . . . . . . . . . . . . . . . . . . . . . . . . . . . . . . . . . . . 310-280-1530
    c/o Sony Film Corp.
    10202 W. Washington Blvd.
    Culver City, CA 90232
    **ALSO: 10201 W. Pico Blvd, LA, CA 90035
    Type:  Motion Picture Production + Television Production
    *Denise Sirkot. . . . . . . . . . . . . . . . . . . . . . . . . . . . . . . . . . Exec. Vice President

**\*GRAINY PICTURES, INC.** . . . . . . . . . . . . . . . . . . . . . . . . . . . . . . . . . . **914-265-2241**
    Fax:. . . . . . . . . . . . . . . . . . . . . . . . . . . . . . . . . . . . . . . . . . . . . 914-265-2543
    44 Market St.
    Cold Spring, NY 10516
    **Completion Financing
    Type:  Motion Picture Production
    John Pierson. . . . . . . . . . . . . . . . . . . . . . . . . . . . . . . . . . . . . . . . . . President
    Janet Pierson . . . . . . . . . . . . . . . . . . . . . . . . . . . . . . . . . . Dir., Special Projects

**GREENBERG GLUSKER FIELDS CLAMAN & MACHTINGER** .................. 310-553-3610
　Fax:.................................................................................. 310-553-0687
　1900 Ave. of the Stars, Ste. 2200
　Los Angeles, CA 90067
Type: Entertainment Law
　*Michael V. Bales......................................................................... Partner
　Nancy Bertrando ......................................................................... Partner
　Robert Chapman .......................................................................... Partner
　Bonnie E. Eskenazi ...................................................................... Partner
　Bertram Fields ............................................................................ Partner
　Mark Gochman ............................................................................ Partner
　E. Barry Haldeman........................................................................ Partner
　James Hornstein........................................................................... Partner
　Lawrence Iser............................................................................. Partner
　*Robert F. Marshall ...................................................................... Partner
　*Richard E. Posell......................................................................... Partner
　Charles Shephard ......................................................................... Partner
　Jill Smith .................................................................................. Partner
　Mark A. Stankevich....................................................................... Partner
　Eve Wagner ............................................................................... Partner

**GRUNDY PRODS. INC., REG** ..................................... 310-557-3555/212-752-0022
　Fax:....................................................................... 310-277-1687/212-752-0790
　9911 W. Pico Blvd., Ste. 1200
　Los Angeles, CA 90035
　**ALSO: 445 Park Ave. 20th Fl., New York, NY 10022
Type: Television Production
　Reg Grundy ............................................................................. Chairman
　Richard Barovick.......................................................... Chief Executive Officer
　Robert Crystal ............................................................. Sr. VP, Administration

**GUDVI, CHAPNICK & OPPENHEIM, INC.** ..................................... 818-990-0550
　Fax:.................................................................................. 818-990-5707
　15250 Ventura Blvd., Ste. 900
　Sherman Oaks, CA 91403
Type: Business Management
　Gerald Chapnick .......................................................................... Partner
　Bernard Gudvi ............................................................................ Partner
　Michael Oppenheim........................................................................ Partner

**GUILD MANAGEMENT CORPORATION** ................................... *310-277-9711
　Fax:.................................................................................. 310-785-9280
　9911 W. Pico Blvd., Penthouse A
　Los Angeles, CA 90035-2733
Type: Business Management
　*Robert Schiller ............................................................ Chairman of the Board
　Robert Colbert ......................................................................... President
　*Harry F. Schaffer ................................................................. Vice President

**HBO (L.A.)** .................................................. **310-201-9200**
  Fax: .......................................................... 310-201-9426
  2049 Century Park East, Ste. 4100
  Los Angeles, CA 90067-3215
  Type: Television Production
  *Chris Albrecht ............................ President, HBO Ind. Prods./Sr. VP, Original Prog.
  Robert Cooper .......................... Pres., HBO Worldwide Picts.-Sr.VP, HBO Picts.
  Rich Battaglia ................................... VP-Asst. Controller, West Coast
  Robert Roth ................................... Vice President-Controller
  Shelley Fischel ................................ Sr. VP, Human Resources
  Viviane Eisenberg .......................... VP-Chief Counsel, Original Programming
  Eric Levin ................................... VP, Finance & Analysis
  Michael Lombardo ........................ VP, Business Affairs, West Coast
  Scott McElhone ......................... VP-Asst. Controller, Cash and Rev. Ops.
  Jim Noonan ............................... VP, Corp. Affairs
  Mary Oldak .............................. VP-Asst. Controller Accounting Systems
  Keith Owitz .............................. VP, Finance & Analysis
  Joe Tarulli ............................ VP-Asst. Controller Financial Ops.& Reporting
  Glenn Whitehead ........................ VP, Business Affairs & Prod., West Coast
  Molly Wilson-Deloje ................... VP-Sr. Counsel, West Coast Programming
  Tom Woodbury ......................... VP-Chief Counsel Sales/Marketing

**HBO (NYC)** ............................................... **212-512-1000**
  Fax: .......................................................... 212-512-5572
  1100 Avenue of the Americas
  New York, NY 10036
  Type: Motion Picture Production + Television Production
  Michael Fuchs ............................... Chairman
  Eric Kessler .............................. President, HBO Video, Inc.
  Jeff Bewkes ................................. President
  *Bill Nelson ............................... Exec. VP, CFO
  *John Redpath ......................... Exec. VP, General Counsel
  Harold Akselrad ........................ Sr. VP, Business Affairs
  Richard Plepler ......................... Sr. VP, Corporate Affairs
  Angelo D'Amelio ....................... Sr. VP-CFO, HBO Video Inc.
  George Cooke .......................... VP-Sr. Counsel, Film Programming
  Bruce Grivetti .......................... VP, East Coast Business Affairs & Admin.
  Karen Levinson ....................... VP, Business Affairs, East Coast

**HBO INDEPENDENT PRODS.** ...................... **310-201-9300**
  Fax: .......................................................... 310-201-9529
  2049 Century Park East, Ste. 4200
  Los Angeles, CA 90067-3215
  Type: Television Production
  *Chris Albrecht ................................ President
  *Russell Schwartz ....................... Sr. VP, Business Affairs
  Pamela Baron .......................... Dir., Business Affairs

**HKM FILMS** ............................................. **213-465-9191**
  Fax: .......................................................... 213-465-4203
  1641 N. Ivar Ave.
  Hollywood, CA 90028
  Type: Motion Picture Production
  Larry Morris ............................. Chief Financial Officer
  *Dena Rendazzo ........................ Controller

**HALL COMMUNICATIONS, ARSENIO** ................. **310-280-6833**
  c/o Sony Entertainment
  10202 W. Washington Blvd. Capra 100
  Culver City, CA 90232
  Type: Motion Picture Production + Television Production + Video Production
  Arsenio Hall ........................... Exec. Producer
  *Kim Swann, ........................... Sr. Vice President

**HALL DICKLER KENT FRIEDMAN & WOOD** .................................**310-203-8410**
    Fax: .............................................................310-203-8559
    2029 Century Park East, Ste. 3590
    Los Angeles, CA 90067
    \*\*Motion Pictures & Music
    Type: Entertainment Law
    Fredric W. Ansis ......................................... Attorney
    Alan Feldstein ............................................ Attorney
    Jeffrey Lowy ............................................. Attorney

**HALPERN & MANTOVANI** ...........................................**310-277-2050**
    Fax: .............................................................310-553-2944
    1888 Century Park East, Ste. 910
    Los Angeles, CA 90067
    \*\*Actors- Writers- Producers- Partnerships- Corporations
    Type: Business Management
    Ted Halpern ............................................. Partner
    Frank Mantovani ........................................ Partner

**\*HAMILTON ENTERTAINMENT, INC., DEAN** ...........................**310-456-0072**
    Fax: .............................................................310-456-7080
    24568 Piuma Rd.
    Malibu, CA 90265
    Type: Motion Picture Production + Television Production + Distribution
    \*Dean Hamilton .......................................... President
    \*Don Borza ............................................... Controller

**HAMMER INTERNATIONAL** ..........................................**818-972-1749**
    Fax: .............................................................818-972-9021
    3900 W. Alameda, #1700
    Burbank, CA 91522
    Type: Motion Picture Production
    Roy Skeggs ............................................... Chairman-CEO
    \*Richelle Wilder ......................................... Exec. Vice President

**HANKIN & CO.** ....................................................**310-828-2222**
    Fax: .............................................................310-828-4422
    1620 26th St., Ste. 2000N
    Santa Monica, CA 90404-4039
    Type: Business Management + Financial Consulting
    Rock N. Hankin .......................................... Sr. Partner
    \*John D. Cheyne .......................................... Parnter
    Wallace B. Jones ......................................... Partner
    John R. Loevenguth ...................................... Partner
    \*David J. Nichols ......................................... Partner
    \*Jon W. Rasmussen ....................................... Partner
    Corey P. Schlossmann .................................... Partner
    \*Karl J. Schulze ......................................... Partner
    Elden L. Westhusing ..................................... Partner
    \*David E. Wilbur ........................................ Partner
    \*Dana L. Haynes .......................................... Principal
    Carol L. Odenberg ....................................... Dir., Administration

**HANNA-BARBERA, INC.** ......................................................213-851-5000
    Fax:.................................................................213-969-1201
    3400 Cahuenga Blvd.
    Hollywood, CA 90068-1376
    Type: Motion Picture Production + Television Production
    Joseph Barbera........................................Co-chairman-Founder
    William D. Hanna......................................Co-chairman-Founder
    Fred Seibert..................................................President
    *Jed Simmons......................................Exec. Vice President
    *Tom Barreca.............................VP, Hanna-Barbera Enterprises
    Joe Mazzuca...............................VP, Production Management
    Amanda Seward.............................VP, Business/Legal Affairs
    Alan Keith..................................Controller, Accounting
    *Buzz Potamkin.................................Executive Producer
    Julie Kane-Ritsch.......................Asst. VP, Business/Legal Affairs
    *Fonda Brewer..............................Dir., Human Resources
    *Christopher Jones....................Dir., Hanna-Barbera Enterprises
    *William Quarles..................Dir., Budgeting, Forcasting & Planning

**HARMONY GOLD** ..............................................................213-851-4900
    Fax:.................................................................213-851-5599
    7655 Sunset Blvd.
    Los Angeles, CA 90046
    Type: Television Production
    Kathy Ferrari..................................................Controller
    Robert Cohen..........................................VP, Business Affairs

**HART BROTHERS ENT. CORP.** .............................................818-504-4864
    Fax:.................................................................818-504-4868
    14755 Ventura Blvd., Ste. 716
    Sherman Oaks, CA 91403
    Type: Motion Picture Production + Television Production
    *Geno Hart....................................................President
    Ron Pope..............................................VP, Business Affairs

**HART III INSURANCE AGENCY, JOHN WILLIAM** ......................310-657-4278
    Fax:.................................................................310-273-2826
    8907 Wilshire Blvd. #204
    Beverly Hills, CA 90211
    Type: General Insurance
    Loriann Hart...................................................Partner
    Alison Hart.....................................................Partner
    Russell Hart....................................................Partner
    John Wm. Hart III..............................................Partner

**\*HARVEY ENTERTAINMENT COMPANY, THE.** ........................310-451-3377
    Fax:.................................................................310-458-6995
    100 Wilshire Blvd., Ste. 1400
    Santa Monica, CA 90401-1115
    Type: Motion Picture Production + Television Production
    *Jeffrey A. Montgomery....................................Chairman/CEO
    *Gregory M. Yulish.............................CFO/Exec. Vice President
    *Wendolyn Webb Schwarz...................Dir., Corporate Communications

**HAVOC** ...........................................212-924-1629/310-777-1970
    Fax:.......................................212-924-3105/310-777-4698
    16 W. 19th St., 12th Fl.
    New York, NY 10011
    **ALSO: 9247 Alden Dr., Beverly Hills, CA 90210
    Type: Motion Picture Production
    Tim Robbins........................Producer-Director-Writer-Actor
    Mark Seldis..............................Chief Financial Officer (LA)

**HAYES, HUME, PETAS, RICHARDS & COHANNE**.............................**310-284-7800**
    Fax:...............................................................310-284-7926
    10000 Santa Monica Blvd., Ste. 450
    Los Angeles, CA 90067
    Type: Entertainment Law
    Polin Cohanne ........................................... Partner
    Richard Scott Hume ...................................... Partner
    Mark Petas ............................................. Partner
    Peter C. Richards ....................................... Partner
    *Mary Muir ............................................ Associate

**HEARST ENTERTAINMENT** ...............................................**310-478-1700**
    Fax:...............................................................310-478-2202
    1640 S. Sepulveda Blvd., 4th Fl.
    Los Angeles, CA 90025-7510
    Type: Television Production
    Gerald Isenberg ..................................... Co-chairman-CEO
    Gerald W. Abrams ...................................... Co-chairman
    Marvin S. Katz ..................... Exec. VP, Business Affairs/Admin.
    Ronald Ulloa .................................... VP, Business Affairs

**HEENAN BLAIKIE** .....................................................**310-275-3600**
    Fax:...............................................................310-724-8340
    9401 Wilshire Blvd., Ste. 1100
    Beverly Hills, CA 90212
    Type: Entertainment Law
    Jeffrey Berkowitz....................................... Attorney
    Daniel H. Black ........................................ Attorney
    *Fred Fenster.......................................... Attorney
    Joel Goldman .......................................... Attorney
    *Daniel Leon........................................... Attorney
    *Scott Zolke .......................................... Attorney

**HEMDALE COMMUNICATIONS INC.**.......................................**213-966-3700**
    Fax:...............................................................213-653-5452
    7966 Beverly Blvd.
    Los Angeles, CA 90048
    **New York/Nashville/Dallas/Minneapolis/Calgary/London
    Type: Motion Picture Production + Television Production + Video Production + Distribution
    *Lawrence Abramson.................................... COO/Co-Chairman
    *Eric Parkinson....................................... CEO/Co-Chairman
    *Dorian Langdon .................... President, Hemdale Home Video Inc.
    Art Newberger ....................... President, Hemdale Int. TV
    *Tim Waters .................................... VP, General Mgr.

**HENSON PRODS., JIM** ..................................**213-960-4096/212-794-2400**
    Fax:....................................................213-960-4935/212-570-1147
    c/o Raleigh Studios
    5358 Melrose Ave., 300 W
    Hollywood, CA 90038
    **ALSO: 117 E. 69th St., New York, NY 10021
    Type: Motion Picture Production + Television Production + Video Production
    Brian Henson ........................... President-Chief Executive Officer
    *Charles Rivkin......................... President - Chief Operating Officer
    *Peter Schube ............... Sr. VP, Business/Legal Affairs-Gen. Counsel
    Linda Govreau ........................ VP, Finance/Accounting/Admin.
    Oscar Aguilar ................................ Corporate Controller

**HEYES COMPANY, THE** ..................................**818-222-1649/310-271-7133**
    Fax:...............................................................818-222-1649
    1227 Coldwater Canyon Dr.
    Beverly Hills, CA 90210
    Type: Motion Picture Production
    Peter Bierstedt .............................. Business/Legal Affairs

**HICKOX-BOWMAN PRODS., INC.** ........................................ **818-781-3885**
    Fax: ........................................................... 818-787-7264
    13634 Erwin St.
    Van Nuys, CA 91401
    Type: Motion Picture Production + Television Production
    Chuck Bowman ...................................... Chairman-Producer-Director
    S. Bryan Hickox ......................................... President-CEO-Producer
    Joanne Kraemer ......................................... Chief Financial Officer
    \*Lola Caldwell .......................................... Asst. to Mr. Bowman

**HILL WYNNE TROOP & MEISINGER** ............................... **310-824-7000**
    Fax: ........................................................... 310-443-7599
    10940 Wilshire Blvd., Ste. 800
    Los Angeles, CA 90024-3902
    Type: Entertainment Law
    \*Scott W. Alderton ............................................... Partner
    Mary K. Barnes ................................................... Partner
    \*Mary Craig Calkins .............................................. Partner
    \*Robert E. Duffy ................................................. Partner
    \*John M. Genga .................................................. Partner
    Marc J. Graboff .................................................. Partner
    \*Blaine E. Greenberg ............................................. Partner
    \*David Halberstadter ............................................. Partner
    \*Clyde M. Hettrick ............................................... Partner
    Dennis Hill ...................................................... Partner
    \*Robert M. Jason ................................................. Partner
    \*Martin D. Katz .................................................. Partner
    \*Thomas Glen Leo ................................................ Partner
    Louis M. Meisinger ............................................... Partner
    \*Robert S. Metzger ............................................... Partner
    \*Leigh B. Morris ................................................. Partner
    \*Neil R. O'Hanlon ................................................ Partner
    \*Anthony J. Oncidi ............................................... Partner
    Kirk A. Pasich ................................................... Partner
    \*Robert J. Plotkowski ............................................ Partner
    \*Curtis D. Porterfield ........................................... Partner
    \*C.N. Reddick III ................................................ Partner
    \*Ronald D. Reynolds .............................................. Partner
    \*David H. Samms ................................................. Partner
    \*Alan B. Spatz ................................................... Partner
    \*Scott W. Steuber ................................................ Partner
    Bruce D. Tobey ................................................... Partner
    \*Jeff A. Toder ................................................... Partner
    Richard Troop .................................................... Partner
    \*Rita L. Tuzon ................................................... Partner
    Robert J. Wynne .................................................. Partner
    Phil S. Levy ................................................ Exec. Director

**\*HILL/FIELDS ENT.** ............................................... **213-954-4500**
    Fax: ........................................................... 213-954-4550
    4500 Wilshire Blvd.
    Los Angeles, CA 90010
    Type: Motion Picture Production
    \*Tim Winteringham ............................................... Auditor

**HIRSCH, NOAH S.** ............................... **310-286-6724/310-550-4569**
    Fax: ........................................................... 310-550-4534
    1875 Century Park East, Ste. 2820
    Los Angeles, CA 90067
    \*\*Writers - Producers - Sports
    Type: Entertainment Law
    Noah S. Hirsch ................................................. Attorney

**HOFFMAN, NATHALIE R.** . . . . . . . . . . . . . . . . . . . . . . . . . . . . . . . . . **310-551-9195**
   Fax:. . . . . . . . . . . . . . . . . . . . . . . . . . . . . . . . . . . . . . . . . . . . . . . 310-552-6077
   1880 Century Park East, Ste. 1200
   Los Angeles, CA 90067
   **Music - Motion Pictures - Television
   Type: Entertainment Law
   Nathalie R. Hoffman . . . . . . . . . . . . . . . . . . . . . . . . . . . . . . . . . . Attorney

**HOPP, THOMAS.** . . . . . . . . . . . . . . . . . . . . . . . . . . . . **310-478-8818/805-985-1467**
   Fax:. . . . . . . . . . . . . . . . . . . . . . . . . . . . . . . . . . . . . . . . . . . . . . . 310-474-5878
   10880 Wilshire Blvd., Ste. 1111
   Los Angeles, CA 90024
   **CPA
   Type: Business Management
   *Thomas Hopp . . . . . . . . . . . . . . . . . . . . . . . . . . Certified Public Accountant

**HORWITZ ORGANIZATION, THE LEWIS** . . . . . . . . . . . . . . . . . . . . . . **310-275-7171**
   Fax:. . . . . . . . . . . . . . . . . . . . . . . . . . . . . . . . . . . . . . . . . . . . . . . 310-275-8055
   1840 Century Park East
   Los Angeles, CA 90067
   Type: Production Financing
   Lewis Horwitz . . . . . . . . . . . . . . . . . . . . . . . . . . . . . . . . . . . . . President
   Arthur Stribley . . . . . . . . . . . . . . . . . . . . . . . . . . . . . . . Sr. Vice President
   Brenda Doby . . . . . . . . . . . . . . . . . . . . . . . . . . . . . . . . Vice President
   Peter Lambert . . . . . . . . . . . . . . . . . . . . . . . . . . . . . . . . Vice President

**HOULIHAN LOKEY HOWARD & ZUKIN** . . . . . . . . . . . . . . . . . . . . . . **310-553-8871**
   Fax:. . . . . . . . . . . . . . . . . . . . . . . . . . . . . . . . . . . . . . . . . . . . . . . 310-553-2173
   1930 Century Park West, Ste. 200
   Los Angeles, CA 90067
   **Motion Pictures, Television, Music
   Type: Financial Consulting
   Robert F. Howard. . . . . . . . . . . . . . . . . . . . . . . . . . . . Managing Director
   *Roy A. Salter. . . . . . . . . . . . . . . . . . . . . . . . . . . . . . . Sr. Vice President
   *Darleen H. Armour . . . . . . . . . . . . . . . . . . . . . . . . . . . . Vice President

**I.N.I. ENTERTAINMENT GROUP INC.** . . . . . . . . . . . . . . . . . . . . . . . **310-479-6755**
   Fax:. . . . . . . . . . . . . . . . . . . . . . . . . . . . . . . . . . . . . . . . . . . . . . . 310-479-3475
   11845 Olympic Blvd. #1145
   Los Angeles, CA 90064
   Type: Motion Picture Production + Television Production + Video Production + Distribution
   Irv Holender. . . . . . . . . . . . . . . . . . . . . . . . . . . . . . . . . . Chairman-CEO
   *Michael Ricci . . . . . . . . . . . . . . . . . . . . . . . . . . . . . . . . President-COO
   Stephanie Zill . . . . . . . . . . . . . . . . . . . . . . . . . Exec. VP, Administration
   *Tara Spencer . . . . . . . . . . . . . . . . . . . . Contract Mgr., Int'l. Sales & Contracts
   Ralph Forman. . . . . . . . . . . . . . . . . . . . . . . . . . . . Operations Manager

**ING CAPITAL CORPORATION** . . . . . . . . . . . . . . . . . . . . . . . . . . . . . **213-617-9100**
   Fax:. . . . . . . . . . . . . . . . . . . . . . . . . . . . . . . . . . . . . . . . . . . . . . . 213-687-7324
   333 S. Grand Ave., Ste. 3000
   Los Angeles, CA 90071
   Type: Production Financing
   Loring Guessous . . . . . . . . . . . . . . . . . . . . . . . . . . . . . . . Vice President

**IRS MEDIA** . . . . . . . . . . . . . . . . . . . . . . . . . . . . . . . . . . . . . . . . . . . **310-838-7800**
   Fax:. . . . . . . . . . . . . . . . . . . . . . . . . . . . . . . . . . . . . . . . . . . . . . . 310-838-7814
   3520 Hayden Ave.
   Culver City, CA 90232
   Type: Motion Picture Production + Distribution
   Paul Colichman . . . . . . . . . . . . . . . . . . . . . . . . . . . . . . . President-CEO
   *Michael H. Lauer . . . . . . . . . . . . . . . . . . . . . . . . . . VP, Business Affairs
   *Bob Newport. . . . . . . . . . . . . . . . . . . . . . . . . . . . . . . . . . VP, Finance

**ITB CINEGROUP** . . . . . . . . . . . . . . . . . . . . . . . . . . . . . . . . . . . . . . . . . . . . . . . **213-469-7244 ext 18**
    Fax: . . . . . . . . . . . . . . . . . . . . . . . . . . . . . . . . . . . . . . . . . . . . . . . . . . . . . . . 213-463-7538
    c/o VPS Studios
    800 N. Seward
    Hollywood, CA 90038
    Type:  Motion Picture Production + Television Production
    Stephen S. Paik . . . . . . . . . . . . . . . . . . . . . . . . . . . . . . . . . . . . . . . VP, Business Affairs

**ITC ENT. GROUP** . . . . . . . . . . . . . . . . . . . . . . . . . . . . . . . . . . . . . . . . . . . . **818-760-2110**
    Fax: . . . . . . . . . . . . . . . . . . . . . . . . . . . . . . . . . . . . . . . . . . . . . . . . . . . . . . . 818-506-8189
    12711 Ventura Blvd., 3rd Fl.
    Studio City, CA 91604
    Type:  Motion Picture Production + Television Production
    Jules Haimovitz . . . . . . . . . . . . . . . . . . . . . . . . . . . . . . . . . . . . . . . . President-CEO
    Michael Birnbaum . . . . . . . . . . . . . . . . . . . . . . . . . . . . . . . . Exec. Vice President
    John Brady . . . . . . . . . . . . . . . . . . . . . . . . . . . . . . . . . . . . . . . . Exec. VP-CFO
    John Huncke . . . . . . . . . . . . . . . . . . . . . . . . . . . . Exec. VP-General Counsel
    David Hope . . . . . . . . . . . . . . . . . . . . . . . . . . . . . . . . . . . . Sr. Vice President

**ICON PRODUCTIONS INC.** . . . . . . . . . . . . . . . . . . . . . . . . . . . . . . . . . . . . . **818-954-2960**
    Fax: . . . . . . . . . . . . . . . . . . . . . . . . . . . . . . . . . . . . . . . . . . . . . . . . . . . . . . . 818-954-4212
    4000 Warner Blvd.
    Burbank, CA 91522-0001
    Type:  Motion Picture Production
    Bruce Davey . . . . . . . . . . . . . . . . . . . . . . . . . . . . . . . . . . . . . . . President-CEO
    Vicki Christianson . . . . . . . . . . . . . . . . . . . . . . . VP, Finance & Business Affairs
    Dana Ginsburg . . . . . . . . . . . . . . . . . . . . . . . . . . . VP, Legal/Business Affairs
    Chris Finigan . . . . . . . . . . . . . . . . . . . . . . . . . . . . . . Dir., Prod. Accounting
    *Heather Grossman . . . . . . . . . . . . . . . . . . . . . . . . . . . . . Financial Accountant

**IMAGE ORGANIZATION** . . . . . . . . . . . . . . . . . . . . . . . . . . . . . . . . . . . . . **310-278-8751**
    Fax: . . . . . . . . . . . . . . . . . . . . . . . . . . . . . . . . . . . . . . . . . . . . . . . . . . . . . . . 310-278-3967
    9000 Sunset Blvd., Ste. 915
    Los Angeles, CA 90069
    Type: Motion Picture Production
    Pierre David . . . . . . . . . . . . . . . . . . . . . . . . . . . . . . . Producer-Chairman-CEO
    Rene Malo . . . . . . . . . . . . . . . . . . . . . . . . . . . . . . . . . Producer-Co-chairman
    Larry Goebel . . . . . . . . . . . . . . . . . . . . . . . . . . . . . . . . . . . . . . . . President
    Carol Diesel Allison . . . . . . . . . . . . . . . . . . . . . . . . . . . . . . . . . . . Controller

**IMAGINE ENTERTAINMENT** . . . . . . . . . . . . . . . . . . . . . . . . . . . . . . . **310-277-1665**
    Fax: . . . . . . . . . . . . . . . . . . . . . . . . . . . . . . . . . . . . . . . . . . . . . . . . . . . . . . . 310-785-0107
    1925 Century Park East, 23rd Fl.
    Los Angeles, CA 90067-2734
    Type: Motion Picture Production
    Robin Barris . . . . . . . . . . . . . . . . . . . . . . . . . . . VP, Administration/Operations

**IMPERIAL BANK, ENT. IND. GROUP** . . . . . . . . . . . . . . . . . . . . . . . . . . **310-338-3100**
    Fax: . . . . . . . . . . . . . . . . . . . . . . . . . . . . . . . . . . . . . . . . . . . . . . . . . . . . . . . 310-338-3171
    9777 Wilshire Blvd., 4th Fl.
    Beverly Hills, CA 90212
    **Motion Pictures, Television, Interactive/Multimedia
    Type: Banking
    Morgan Rector . . . . . . . . . . . . . . . . . . . . . . . . . . . . . . . . . . . Sr. VP-Manager
    *Jeff Colvin . . . . . . . . . . . . . . . . . . . . . . . . . . . . . . . . . . . . . Vice President
    *Janice Zeitinger . . . . . . . . . . . . . . . . . . . . . . . . . . . . . . . . . . Vice President
    *Patrick Jack Lee . . . . . . . . . . . . . . . . . . . . . . . . . . . . . Asst. Vice President
    *Jared Underwood . . . . . . . . . . . . . . . . . . . . . . . . . . . . . Asst. Vice President

**IMPERIAL ENT.** . . . . . . . . . . . . . . . . . . . . . . . . . . . . . . . . . . . . . . . . . . . . **818-762-0005**
    Fax: . . . . . . . . . . . . . . . . . . . . . . . . . . . . . . . . . . . . . . . . . . . . . 818-762-0006
    4640 Lankershim Blvd., #201
    North Hollywood, CA 91602
    Type: Motion Picture Production
    Sunil R. Shah . . . . . . . . . . . . . . . . . . . . . . . . . . . . . . . . . . . . . . . . President
    Sundip Shah . . . . . . . . . . . . . . . . . . . . . . . . . . . . . . . . . Exec. Vice President
    Juan C. Collas . . . . . . . . . . . . . . . . . . . . . . VP, Finance & Operations-CFO
    Dolly M. Vergara . . . . . . . . . . . . . . . . . . . . . . . . . . . Contract Administrator

**IN PICTURES, LTD.** . . . . . . . . . . . . . . . . . . . . . . . . . . . . . . . . . . . . **212-925-0404**
    Fax: . . . . . . . . . . . . . . . . . . . . . . . . . . . . . . . . . . . . . . . . . . . . . 212-925-5656
    13-17 Laight St., Ste. 6-1
    New York, NY 10013
    **Domestic and international sales of finished films.
    Type: Production Financing + Motion Picture Production + Television Production
    Jamie Ader-Brown . . . . . . . . . . . . . . . . . . . . . . . . . . . . . . . Producer's Rep.
    Suzanne Fedak . . . . . . . . . . . . . . . . . . . . . . . . . . . . . . . . Producer's Rep.

**INGBER, JEFFREY C.** . . . . . . . . . . . . . . . . . . . . . . . . . . . . . . . . . . . **310-552-1047**
    Fax: . . . . . . . . . . . . . . . . . . . . . . . . . . . . . . . . . . . . . . . . . . . . . 310-286-1015
    1801 Century Park East, Ste. 2400
    Los Angeles, CA 90067
    **Motion Pictures, Television, Music
    Type: Entertainment Law
    Jeffrey C. Ingber . . . . . . . . . . . . . . . . . . . . . . . . . . . . . . . . . . . Attorney

**INTERMEDIA/FILM EQUITIES INC.** . . . . . . . . . . . . . . . . . . . . . . **310-777-7750**
    Fax: . . . . . . . . . . . . . . . . . . . . . . . . . . . . . . . . . . . . . . . . . . . . . 310-777-7751
    c/o The Ice House
    9348 Civic Center Dr., Ste. 250
    Beverly Hills, CA 90210
    Type: Financial Consulting + Banking
    Joseph N. Cohen . . . . . . . . . . . . . . . . . . . . . . . . . . . . . . . . Co-chairman
    Walter W. J. Olesiuk . . . . . . . . . . . . . . . . . . . . . . . . . . . . . Co-chairman
    Nigel Sinclair . . . . . . . . . . . . . . . . . . . . . . . . . . . . . . . . . . Co-chairman
    *Patrick Murray . . . . . . . . . . . . . . . . . . . . . . . . . Chief Operating Officer
    *Edith E. Myers . . . . . . . . . . . . . . . . . . . . . . . . . . . . . . . . . . Principal
    Adam Devejian . . . . . . . . . . . . . . . . . . . . . . . . . . . . . . . . . . Sr. Analyst

**INTERNATIONAL FILM GUARANTORS INC.** . . . . . . . . . . . . . . . . . **310-208-4500**
    Fax: . . . . . . . . . . . . . . . . . . . . . . . . . . . . . . . . . . . . . . . . . . . . . 310-443-8998
    10940 Wilshire Blvd., Ste. 2010
    Los Angeles, CA 90024
    Type: Completion Bond + Business Affairs + Legal Affairs
    *Kathleen Duke. . . . . . . . . . . . . . . . . . . . . . . . Sr. VP, Business/Legal Affairs
    Joan Stigliano . . . . . . . . . . . . . . . . . . . . . . . . Sr. VP, Business/Client Relations

**INTERNATIONAL FILM RESOURCE GROUP INC.** . . . . . . . . . . . . . . **207-864-5847**
    Fax: . . . . . . . . . . . . . . . . . . . . . . . . . . . . . . . . . . . . . . . . . . . . . 207-864-5863
    P.O. Box 1142
    Rangeley, ME 04970
    **Area of speciality: Motion Picture & Video Financing
    Type: Distribution + Production Financing
    Peter Lodise . . . . . . . . . . . . . . . . . . . . . . . . . . . . . . . . . . . . . President

**INTERSCOPE COMMUNICATIONS INC.** . . . . . . . . . . . . . . . . . . . . **310-208-8525**
    Fax: . . . . . . . . . . . . . . . . . . . . . . . . . . . . . . . . . . . . . . . . . . . . . 310-208-5425
    10900 Wilshire Blvd., Ste. 1400
    Los Angeles, CA 90024
    Type: Motion Picture Production
    Ted Field . . . . . . . . . . . . . . . . . . . . . . . . . . . . . . . . . . . . . Chairman-CEO
    Robert Cort. . . . . . . . . . . . . . . . . . . . . . . . . . . . . . . . . . . President-COO
    *Kathryn Nielsen . . . . . . . . . . . . . . . . . . . . . . . . . Chief Financial Officer
    Michael Helfant . . . . . . . . . . . . . . . . . . . . . . . . . . . . . Sr. Vice President
    Barbara Zipperman . . . . . . . . . . . . . . . . . . . . . VP, Business/Legal Affairs

**\*INTRAZONE INC./INTRAZONE INTERACTIVE LTD.** ...................... 310-659-1801
    Fax:................................................................. 310-659-1739
    8733 Sunset Blvd., Ste. 202
    Los Angeles, CA 90069
    \*\*Also video games
Type:  Motion Picture Production + Television Production
    Luigi Cingolani ............................................... President-CEO
    \*Lenore Van Camp.......................................... Chief Financial Officer
    Chris Walker ............................................ Chief Operating Officer
    \*Harmon Kaslow ..................................... Sr. VP, Legal/Business Affairs

**IRELL & MANELLA** ............................................ 310-277-1010/714-760-0721
    Fax:................................................................. 310-203-7199
    1800 Ave. of the Stars, Ste. 900
    Los Angeles, CA 90067-4276
    \*\*840 Newport Center Dr. #500, Newport Bch, CA 92660-6324
Type:  Entertainment Law
    Michael Gendler............................................ Entertainment Dept. Head
    Kevin M. Kelly ............................................ Entertainment Dept. Head
    David A. Dull................................................... Attorney
    John Fossum...................................... Attorney (714-760-0991)
    Joan Lesser....................................................... Attorney
    David Nimmer ................................................... Attorney
    Lois J. Scali ..................................................... Attorney
    Werner F. Wolfen .............................................. Attorney
    Juliette Youngblood............................................ Attorney
    Edward D. Zeldow............................................. Attorney
    \*Arthur Manella ............................................. Of Counsel

**\*ISLAND PICTURES CORP.** ................................................ 310-276-4500
    Fax:................................................................. 310-271-7840
    8920 Sunset Blvd., 2nd Fl.
    Los Angeles, CA 90069
Type:  Motion Picture Production
    \*Mark Burg....................................................... President
    \*Howie Lindenbaum............................................... CFO
    Jennifer Curran........................... VP, Legal Affairs/Business Affairs

**ISRAEL & BRAY** ......................................................... 212-319-3400
    Fax:................................................................. 212-755-9685
    919 Third Ave., 6th Fl.
    New York, NY 10022
Type:  Entertainment Law + Legal Affairs
    Larry E. Bray .................................................... Attorney

**IXTLAN** ................................................................. 310-395-0525
    Fax:................................................................. 310-395-1536
    201 Santa Monica Blvd., Ste. 610
    Santa Monica, CA 90401
Type:  Motion Picture Production
    \*Alan Chu .................................................. Business Affairs

**\*J & M ENT. LTD.** ...................................... 310-652-7733/171-723-6544
    Fax:.......................................... 310-652-0816/171-724-7541
    1289 Sunset Plaza Dr.
    Los Angeles, CA 90069
    \*\*2 Dorset Sq., London UK, NW1 6PU
Type:  Television Production + Video Production + Distribution
    \*Julie Palau ................................................... Co-Chairman
    \*Michael Ryan .................................................. Co-Chairman
    \*Anthony Miller ........................... Exec. VP - Head, Business Affairs

**JI BUSINESS SERVICES.** . . . . . . . . . . . . . . . . . . . . . . . . . . . . . . . . . . . . . . . . . . . . . **310-799-0536**
    Fax:. . . . . . . . . . . . . . . . . . . . . . . . . . . . . . . . . . . . . . . . . . . . . . . . . . . . . . . 310-799-0536
    12200 Montecito, Ste. F203
    Seal Beach, CA 90740
    **Unable to confirm by press time.
    Type: Business Management + Financial Consulting
    Diane L. Jankowski . . . . . . . . . . . . . . . . . . . . . . . . . . . . . . . . . . . . . . . . . . . President
    Ben Kalb. . . . . . . . . . . . . . . . . . . . . . . . . . . . . . . . . . . . . . . . . . . . . . . . . . Associate
    Sean McCormick . . . . . . . . . . . . . . . . . . . . . . . . . . . . . . . . . . . . . . . . . . . . Associate

**JVC ENTERTAINMENT, INC.** . . . . . . . . . . . . . . . . . . . . . . . . . . . . . . . . . . . . . **310-286-7212**
    Fax:. . . . . . . . . . . . . . . . . . . . . . . . . . . . . . . . . . . . . . . . . . . . . . . . . . . . . . . 310-286-7216
    2029 Century Park East, Ste. 970
    Los Angeles, CA 90067-2910
    Type: Distribution
    Isamu Tomitsuka . . . . . . . . . . . . . . . . . . . . . . . . . . . . . . . . . . . . . . . CEO-Chairman
    Barr B. Potter . . . . . . . . . . . . . . . . . . . . . . . . . . . . . . . . . . . . . . . President-COO
    *Osamu Namihisa. . . . . . . . . . . . . . . . . . . . . . . . . . . . Sr. VP, Secretary & Treasurer

**JACOBSON & COLFIN, P.C.** . . . . . . . . . . . . . . . . . . . . . . . . . . . . . . . . . . . . . . **212-691-5630**
    Fax:. . . . . . . . . . . . . . . . . . . . . . . . . . . . . . . . . . . . . . . . . . . . . . . . . . . . . . . 212-645-5038
    156 5th Ave., Ste. 434
    New York, NY 10010
    **Copyrights, Trademarks & Creative Arts
    Type: Entertainment Law
    Bruce E. Colfin . . . . . . . . . . . . . . . . . . . . . . . . . . . . . . . . . . . . . . . . . . . . Attorney
    Jeffrey E. Jacobson . . . . . . . . . . . . . . . . . . . . . . . . . . . . . . . . . . . . . . . . . . Attorney

**JAFFE BRAUNSTEIN FILMS** . . . . . . . . . . . . . . . . . . . . . . . . . . . . . . . . . . . . . **213-464-4100**
    Fax:. . . . . . . . . . . . . . . . . . . . . . . . . . . . . . . . . . . . . . . . . . . . . . . . . . . . . . . 213-878-0871
    7920 Sunset Blvd., 4th Fl.
    Los Angeles, CA 90046
    Type: Motion Picture Production + Television Production
    Barbara Carswell . . . . . . . . . . . . . . . . . . . . . . . . . . . . . . . . . . . . . . . . . . . . Finance

**\*JERSEY FILMS.** . . . . . . . . . . . . . . . . . . . . . . . . . . . . . . . . . . . . . . . . . . . . . . **310-280-4400**
    Fax:. . . . . . . . . . . . . . . . . . . . . . . . . . . . . . . . . . . . . . . . . . . . . . . . . . . . . . . 310-280-4411
    10202 W. Washington Blvd., Capra #112
    Culver City, CA 90232
    Type: Motion Picture Production
    *Danny DeVito. . . . . . . . . . . . . . . . . . . . . . . . . . . . . . . . . . . . . . . . . Co-chairman
    *Michael Shamberg . . . . . . . . . . . . . . . . . . . . . . . . . . . . . . . . . . . . . . Co-chairman
    *Stacey Sher . . . . . . . . . . . . . . . . . . . . . . . . . . . . . . . . . . . . . . . . . . . . President
    *Carla Macy . . . . . . . . . . . . . . . . . . . . . . . . . . . . . . . . . . . . . . . VP, Operations

**JOHNSON & ASSOC., NEVILLE L.** . . . . . . . . . . . . . . . . . . . . . . . . . . . . . . . . **310-826-2410**
    Fax:. . . . . . . . . . . . . . . . . . . . . . . . . . . . . . . . . . . . . . . . . . . . . . . . . . . . . . . 310-826-5450
    12121 Wilshire Blvd., Ste. 120
    Los Angeles, CA 90025
    Type: Entertainment Law
    Sally Koenig. . . . . . . . . . . . . . . . . . . . . . . . . . . . . . . . . . . . . . . . . . . . . . Attorney
    Neville L. Johnson . . . . . . . . . . . . . . . . . . . . . . . . . . . . . . . . . . . . . . . . . . . Attorney

**\*JOHNSON PRODUCTIONS, DON.** . . . . . . . . . . . . . . . . . . . . . . . . . . . . . . . . . **213-956-5000**
    c/o Paramount TV
    5555 Melrose Ave.
    Los Angeles, CA 90038
    Type: Motion Picture Production + Television Production
    *Martin Schuermann. . . . . . . . . . . . . . . . . . . . . . . . . . . . . . . . . . VP, Financial Officer

**JOHNSON, KATHLEEN K.** ............................................................. 213-957-2701
  6922 Hollywood Blvd., Ste. 500
  Hollywood, CA 90028
  **Contracts - Writers - Producers - Creators
  Type:  Entertainment Law
    Kathleen Johnson ................................................................... Attorney

**JONES-DAVID SALZMAN ENT., QUINCY** ....................................... 213-874-2009
  Fax: ............................................................................. 213-874-3364
  3800 Barham Blvd., Ste. 503
  Los Angeles, CA 90068
  Type:  Motion Picture Production + Television Production
    Quincy Jones .......................................... Co-chief Executive Officer
    David Salzman ......................................... Co-chief Executive Officer
    Jerry Gottlieb ............................................... Exec. Vice President

**JULIEN & ASSOCIATES INC.** ...................................................... 212-221-7575
  Fax: ............................................................................. 212-221-7386
  1501 Broadway, Ste. 2600
  New York, NY 10036
  Type:  Entertainment Law + Business Management + Motion Picture Production
    Jay Julien .............................................................. Owner
    Constantine Baris ...................................................... Principal

**KCET, COMMUNITY TV OF SO. CALIFORNIA** ............................... 213-666-6500
  Fax: .................................................... 213-953-5450/818-637-5290
  4401 Sunset Blvd.
  Los Angeles, CA 90027
  **ALSO: 425 E. Colorado, Glendale, CA 91205
  Type:  Television Production
    *Timothy Conroy .............................. Sr. VP, KCET Comm. (818-637-5253)
    *Gary Ferrell ............................................ CFO (213-953-5204)

**KPMG PEAT MARWICK** ............................................................ 310-499-4000
  Fax: ............................................................................. 310-436-4746
  1 World Trade Center, Ste. 1700
  Long Beach, CA 90831-1700
  **CPA & Consulting firm
  Type:  Business Management
    Bob Gagliano ..................................................... Managing Partner

**KATTEN MUCHIN ZAVIS & WEITZMAN** ....................................... 310-788-4400
  Fax: ............................................................................. 310-788-4471
  1999 Ave. of the Stars, Ste. 1400
  Los Angeles, CA 90067-6042
  Type:  Entertainment Law
    Katherine Goodman ...................................................... Partner
    Richard S. Harris ........................................................ Partner
    Larry Ulman ............................................................. Partner
    *Sara Frith ............................................................ Associate
    Immanuel Spira ......................................................... Associate
    *Mary Taten ............................................................ Associate
    Karen Randall ................................................... Co-managing Partner

**KAUFMAN ESQ., PETER L.** ....................................................... 310-788-2695
  Fax: ............................................................................. 310-788-0234
  1875 Century Park East, Ste. 700
  Los Angeles, CA 90067-2508
  **Motion Pictures, Television, Music, Video
  Type:  Entertainment Law + Motion Picture Production + Television Production + Distribution + Production
  Co-Financing + Business Affairs
    Peter L. Kaufman ....................................................... Attorney
    *Jerome Sussman ...................................................... Of Counsel

**KEHR CROOK TOVMASSIAN & FOX** ..................................... **310-479-5353**
    Fax: ................................................................ 310-479-4855
    11755 Wilshire Blvd., Ste. 1400
    Los Angeles, CA 90025-1520
    Type: Entertainment Law
    *George D. Crook ......................................................... Partner
    David M. Fox ............................................................. Partner
    Robert L. Kehr ........................................................... Partner
    Henry T. Tovmassian ..................................................... Partner

**KELTON, LAW OFFICE OF BRUCE J.** ..................................... **310-284-3257**
    Fax: ................................................................ 310-284-3259
    1888 Century Park East, Ste. 1900
    Los Angeles, CA 90067
    **Spec: Negotiation of tv/feature film rights; contracts.
    Type: Entertainment Law
    Bruce J. Kelton ................................................... Attorney at Law

**KENOFF & MACHTINGER** ................................................ **310-552-0808**
    Fax: ................................................................ 310-277-0653
    1999 Ave. of the Stars, Ste. 1250
    Los Angeles, CA 90067
    **Motion Pictures & Music
    Type: Entertainment Law
    Jay S. Kenoff ........................................................... Partner
    Leonard S. Machtinger ................................................... Partner
    William J. Immerman .................................................. Of Counsel
    Robert O. Kaplan .................................................... Of Counsel
    Lawrence E. May ..................................................... Of Counsel
    Susan Wolf ........................................................ Administrator

**\*KERMAN, LAW OFFICES OF THEA J.** ................................... **310-657-7007**
    Fax: ................................................................ 310-657-7233
    720 Huntley Drive, Ste. 213
    Los Angeles, CA 90069
    Type: Entertainment Law + Business Affairs + Legal Affairs
    *Thea J. Kerman ......................................................... Owner

**KERN, HAROLD B.** ..................................................... **310-205-2333**
    Fax: ................................................................ 310-278-2031
    9401 Wilshire Blvd., Ste. 700
    Beverly Hills, CA 90212-2961
    **CPA - Entertainers
    Type: Business Management
    Harold B. Kern ............................................ Certified Public Accountant

**KING WORLD PRODS.** ................................................... **310-826-1108**
    Fax: ................................................................ 310-207-2179
    12400 Wilshire Blvd., Ste. 1200
    Los Angeles, CA 90025-1019
    Type: Television Production
    Roger King ............................................................. Chairman
    Michael King ...................................................... President-CEO
    *Tony Hull ................................................. Chief Financial Officer
    Stephen W. Palley ................................................... Exec. VP-COO
    Jon Birkhahn ................................................ VP, Business Affairs
    *Ralph Goldberg ..................... VP, Legal Affairs Reality-Based Programming

**KINGS ROAD ENTERTAINMENT INC.** ..................................... **310-552-0057**
    Fax: ................................................................ 310-277-4468
    1901 Ave. of the Stars, Ste. 605
    Los Angeles, CA 90067
    Type: Motion Picture Production + Television Production
    *Stephen Friedman ................................................ President/CEO
    *Christopher Trunkey .......................................... Vice-President/CFO

**KIRSCHNER PRODS., DAVID** ............................................... 213-969-1258
    Fax: ....................................................................... 213-969-4169
    3330 Cahuenga Blvd., 2nd Fl.
    Hollywood, CA 90068
    Type:  Motion Picture Production
    David Kirschner .................................................................. Producer
    Paul Gertz ....................................................................... President
    Susan Roberts .............................................................. Office Manager

**KISMET ENTERTAINMENT INC.** ............................... 213-653-2600/071-495-4189
    Fax: ....................................................... 310-260-0033/071-495-4178
    8489 W. 3rd St.
    Los Angeles, CA 90048
    \*\*Unable to confirm by press time
    Type:  Motion Picture Production + Television Production
    Kelly Nine ................................................................ Principal-Writer
    Patricia Planck ......................................................... Principal-Producer
    Brian Norris ........................................................... Intl. Co. Producer
    Anita Mcgarr ........................................................ Dir., Business Affairs

**KOPELSON PRODS., ARNOLD** ............................................... 213-932-0500
    Fax: ....................................................................... 213-932-0238
    6100 Wilshire Blvd., Ste. 1500
    Los Angeles, CA 90048
    Type:  Motion Picture Production
    Arnold Kopelson ............................................................. Chairman-CEO
    Anne Kopelson ............................................................. Co-chairperson
    Stephen Brown ......................................................... Exec. Vice President
    Maria Norman ........................................................ VP, Administration

**KUSHNER-LOCKE CO.** ....................................................... 310-445-1111
    Fax: ....................................................................... 310-445-1191
    11601 Wilshire Blvd., 21st Fl.
    Los Angeles, CA 90025
    Type:  Motion Picture Production + Television Production + Distribution
    \*Peter Locke ................................................................. Co-chairman
    \*Donald Kushner ............................................................. Co-chairman
    \*Gregory Cascante ..................................................... President, K.L. Intl. Film
    \*Lawrence Mortoff ..................................................... President, K.L. Features
    \*Larry Friedricks ........................................................ President, K.L. Intl.
    \*Lenore Nelson ..................................................................... CFO
    Richard Marks ......................................................... VP, Legal Affairs
    Jerry Rubin ........................................................... VP, Business Affairs
    Douglas Lowell ....................................................... Dir., Financial Relations

**L.M.N. ENTERPRISES INC.** .................................................. 310-824-4269
    440 Veteran Ave., Ste. 306
    Los Angeles, CA 90024
    \*\*Funding for major feature films only.
    Type:  Motion Picture Production + Financial Consulting + Production Financing + Production Co-Financing
    Lynn Napoli ...................................................................... President

**LIVE ENTERTAINMENT COMPANIES** ......................................... 818-908-0303
    Fax: ....................................................................... 818-908-0320
    15400 Sherman Way, Ste. 500
    Van Nuys, CA 91406
    Type:  Distribution + Motion Picture Production + Production Financing + Production Co-Financing + Business Affairs
    Stewart Kleiner ..................................................... VP, Legal/Business Affairs

**LADENBURG, THALMANN & CO. INC.** . . . . . . . . . . . . . . . . . . . . . . . . . . . . . . . . . **212-872-1410**
   Fax:. . . . . . . . . . . . . . . . . . . . . . . . . . . . . . . . . . . . . . . . . . . . . . . . . . . . . 212-838-8072
   540 Madison Ave.
   New York, NY 10022
   Type: Financial Consulting + Banking
   Porter Bibb . . . . . . . . . . . . . . . . . . . . . . . . . . . . . . . . . Managing Director-Head, Mergers/Acquis.
   Peter Graham . . . . . . . . . . . . . . . . . . . . . . . . . . . . . . . . . . . . . . . . . . Managing Director

**LAIDLAW HOLDINGS INC.** . . . . . . . . . . . . . . . . . . . . . . . . . . . . . . . . . . . . . . . . . . **310-917-5656**
   Fax:. . . . . . . . . . . . . . . . . . . . . . . . . . . . . . . . . . . . . . . . . . . . . . . . . . . . . 310-917-5668
   100 Wilshire Blvd., Ste. 1620
   Santa Monica, CA 90401-1113
   **Investment bankers.
   Type: Financial Consulting
   Dimitri Villard . . . . . . . . . . . . . . . . . . . . . . . . . . . . . . . . . . . . . . . . . Managing Director
   *Sean Doyle . . . . . . . . . . . . . . . . . . . . . . . . . . . . . . . . . . . . . . . . . . . . . . Associate

**\*LAMBERT FINANCIAL SERVICES** . . . . . . . . . . . . . . . . . . . . . . . . . . . . . . . . . . **310-247-1931**
   Fax:. . . . . . . . . . . . . . . . . . . . . . . . . . . . . . . . . . . . . . . . . . . . . . . . . . . . . 818-243-1841
   11601 Wilshire Blvd., 5th Floor
   Los Angeles, CA 90025
   **Ivestment, Estate & Charitable Planning Firm
   Type: Business Management + Financial Consulting
   *Paul E. Lambert, ChFC . . . . . . . . . . . . . . . . . . . . . . . . . . . . . . . . . . . . . . . Principal
   *Denise R. Scher . . . . . . . . . . . . . . . . . . . . . . . . . . . . . . . . . . . . . . . . . . . Assistant

**LANCIT MEDIA PRODS.** . . . . . . . . . . . . . . . . . . . . . . . . . . . . . . . . . . . . . . . . . . **212-977-9100**
   Fax:. . . . . . . . . . . . . . . . . . . . . . . . . . . . . . . . . . . . . . . . . . . . . . . . . . . . . 212-977-9164
   601 W. 50th St., 6th Fl.
   New York, NY 10019
   Type: Television Production
   Gary Stein. . . . . . . . . . . . . . . . . . . . . . . . . . . . . . . . . . . . Exec. VP, Investors Relations
   Christie Rothenberg . . . . . . . . . . . . . . . . . . . . . . . . . . . . . Sr. VP, Business Affairs/Admin.

**LANDSBURG CO., THE** . . . . . . . . . . . . . . . . . . . . . . . . . . . . . . . . . . . . . . . . . . . **310-478-7878**
   Fax:. . . . . . . . . . . . . . . . . . . . . . . . . . . . . . . . . . . . . . . . . . . . . . . . . . . . . 310-477-7166
   11811 W. Olympic Blvd.
   Los Angeles, CA 90064-1113
   Type: Television Production
   Alan Landsburg . . . . . . . . . . . . . . . . . . . . . . . . . . . . . . . . . . . . . . . . . Chairman-CEO
   Howard Lipstone . . . . . . . . . . . . . . . . . . . . . . . . . . . . . . . . . . . . . . . President-COO
   *Rick Endelson . . . . . . . . . . . . . . . . . . . . . . . . . . . . . . . . . . . Chief Financial Officer
   Victor Paddock . . . . . . . . . . . . . . . . . . . . . . . . . . . . . . . . . . . . . VP, Business Affairs

**LANGBERG, LESLIE & GABRIEL** . . . . . . . . . . . . . . . . . . . . . . . . . . . . . . . . . . . **310-286-7700**
   Fax:. . . . . . . . . . . . . . . . . . . . . . . . . . . . . . . . . . . . . . . . . . . . . . . . . . . . . 310-284-8355
   2049 Century Park East, Ste. 3030
   Los Angeles, CA 90067
   **Entertainers - Production Co.
   Type: Entertainment Law
   Barry Langberg . . . . . . . . . . . . . . . . . . . . . . . . . . . . . . . . . . . . . . . Managing Partner

**LARGO ENTERTAINMENT** . . . . . . . . . . . . . . . . . . . . . . . . . . . . . . . . . . . . . . . . **310-203-0055**
   Fax:. . . . . . . . . . . . . . . . . . . . . . . . . . . . . . . . . . . . . . . . . . . . . . . . . . . . . 310-203-0254
   2029 Century Park East, Ste. 920
   Los Angeles, CA 90067
   Type: Distribution + Production Co-Financing
   *Barr B. Potter . . . . . . . . . . . . . . . . . . . . . . . . . . . . . . . . . . . . . . . . CEO/Chairman
   *Peter Elson . . . . . . . . . . . . . . . . . . . . . . . . . . . . . . . . . . . . . . Exec. Vice President
   *Bruce Vann, Esq. . . . . . . . . . . . . . . . . . . . . . . . . . . . . . . . . . . . . . . Legal Counsel
   *Robert Corzo . . . . . . . . . . . . . . . . . . . . . . . . . . . . . . . . . . . . . . . . . . VP, Finance

**\*LAUREN INTERNATIONAL** ................................................... **213-954-3791**
    Fax: ................................................................ 213-954-0902
    263 S. Van Ness Ave.
    Los Angeles, CA 90004
    Type: Motion Picture Production + Distribution
    \*Mishka Harnden ........................................... Vice President
    \*Eric M. Bernstein ................................................ Manager

**LE STUDIO CANAL + (U.S.)** ........................................ **310-247-0994**
    Fax: ................................................................ 310-247-0998
    301 N. Canon Dr., Ste. 228
    Beverly Hills, CA 90210
    Type: Motion Picture Production + Production Financing
    Richard Garzilli ................................ Exec. VP-General Counsel
    Michael Meltzer ....................................... Exec. VP-CFO
    Robert Chamberlain ................................... Controller

**LEDGER DOMAIN.** ................................................... **310-203-0262**
    Fax: ................................................................ 310-286-1141
    1180 S. Beverly Dr., Ste. 618
    Los Angeles, CA 90035-1153
    Type: Business Management
    Barbara Bryson ..................................................... Owner

**LEE, PATRICIA E.** .................................................... **310-271-1087**
    P.O. Box 16194
    Beverly Hills, CA 90209
    \*\*Contract neg. & drafting. Screenwriter/songwriter rep.
    Type: Entertainment Law
    Patricia E. Lee ............................................. Attorney at Law

**LEONARD, DICKER & SCHREIBER** ............................... **310-551-1987**
    Fax: ................................................................ 310-277-8050
    9430 Olympic Blvd., Ste. 400
    Beverly Hills, CA 90212
    Type: Entertainment Law
    \*Richard C. Leonard ................................................ Partner
    James P. Schreiber ................................................ Partner

**LERNER, LAWRENCE D., A BUS. MGMT. CORP.** ................. **818-719-6541/310-286-2552**
    Fax: ................................................................ 818-719-0242
    20501 Ventura Blvd., Ste. 392
    Woodland Hills, CA 91364
    Type: Business Management
    Lawrence Lerner ..................................................... Owner

**LEUCADIA FILM CORP.** .......................................... **801-521-1094/310-289-1668**
    Fax: ................................................. 801-524-1760/310-289-1578
    529 East S. Temple
    Salt Lake City, UT 84102
    \*\*ALSO: 8533 Rosewood Ave., Los Angeles, CA 90048
    Type: Motion Picture Production + Television Production + Video Production
    \*David Anderson ................................................ President
    \*Michael Beck ....................................... VP, Business Affairs

**LEVINE, PAUL S.** .................................................... **310-450-6711**
    Fax: ................................................................ 310-450-0181
    2828 Donald Douglas Loop N. Ste. 207
    Santa Monica, CA 90405-2959
    \*\*Book Publishing
    Type: Entertainment Law
    Paul S. Levine ....................................................... Attorney

**LICHTER ESQ., ROSALIND** ............................................... **212-941-4075**
    Fax: ............................................................... 212-941-4076
    375 Greenwich St., Ste. 714
    New York, NY 10013
    Type:  Entertainment Law
    Rosalind Lichter ........................................................... Attorney

**LIFETIME TELEVISION (NY)** .............................................. **212-424-7000**
    309 W. 49th St.
    New York, NY 10019
    Type:  Television Production
    *Douglas McCormick ...................................................... President
    Patrick Guy ................................................ Sr. VP, Business/Legal Affairs
    Jane Tollinger ............................................... Exec. VP, Administration
    *James Wesley ............................................................ Sr. VP, Financial
    Jeffrey Smith ............................................... VP, Business/Legal Affairs
    *Jean Rigg ................................................... VP, Business/Legal Affairs
    Alex Wagner .............................................. Dir., Editorial Services

**LIGHTSTORM ENTERTAINMENT INC.** ...................................... **310-587-2500**
    Fax: ............................................................... 310-393-3702
    919 Santa Monica Blvd.
    Santa Monica, CA 90401
    Type:  Motion Picture Production
    James Cameron ........................................................ Chairman-CEO
    Rae Sanchini ............................................................ President
    Carol Henry .................................................. Chief Financial Officer

**LILLISTON, LAW OFFICES OF BRUCE ST. J.** ............................... **310-319-3231**
    Fax: ............................................................... 310-451-4479
    1299 Ocean Ave., 5th Fl.
    Santa Monica, CA 90401
    **Motion Pictures, Television, Production Finance
    Type:  Entertainment Law
    Bruce St. J. Lilliston ....................................................... Attorney

**LITWAK, LAW OFFICES OF MARK** ........................................ **310-859-9595**
    Fax: ............................................................... 310-859-0806
    9595 Wilshire Blvd., Ste. 711
    Santa Monica, CA 90405
    **Represents independent filmakers, negotiate financing
    Type:  Entertainment Law

**LOEB & LOEB** ............................................. **310-282-2000/615-749-8300**
    Fax: ....................................................... 310-282-2191/615-749-8308
    10100 Santa Monica Blvd., Ste. 2200
    Los Angeles, CA 90067
    **ALSO: 45 Music Sq. West, Nashville, TN 37203
    Type:  Entertainment Law
    John Frankenheimer ....................................................... Co-chair
    Michael Mayerson ........................................................ Co-chair
    Philip J. Grosz ..................................................... Managing Partner
    Marc Chamlin .................................. President, Entertainment Div. (NY)
    Malcolm L. Mimms, Jr. ....................................... Partner (Nashville)
    Leroy Bobbitt ............................................................ Attorney
    Martin Fern ................................................ Attorney (213-688-3400)
    Joyce S. Jun ............................................................. Attorney
    Clark Siegel ............................................................. Attorney
    Myron L. Slobodien ...................................................... Attorney
    Rebel Steiner ............................................................ Attorney

**LONDINE PRODUCTIONS** . . . . . . . . . . . . . . . . . . . . . . . . . . . . . . . . . . . . . . . . . . . . . **310-281-7540**
    Fax: . . . . . . . . . . . . . . . . . . . . . . . . . . . . . . . . . . . . . . . . . . . . . . . . . . . . . . 310-822-9025
    1626 N. Wilcox Ave., Ste. 480
    Hollywood, CA 90028
    \*\*Also: Goods and Services
    Type:  Motion Picture Production + Television Production + Video Production + Production Co-Financing
    Cassius Vernon Weathersby . . . . . . . . . . . . . . . . . . . . . . . . . . . . . . . . . President-Producer
    Nadine Weathersby . . . . . . . . . . . . . . . . . . . . . . . . . . . . . . . . . Vice President-Producer

**LONDON & LICHTENBERG** . . . . . . . . . . . . . . . . . . . . . . . . . . . . . . . . . . . . . . . . **310-478-5151**
    Fax: . . . . . . . . . . . . . . . . . . . . . . . . . . . . . . . . . . . . . . . . . . . . . . . . . . . . 310-478-3696
    11601 Wilshire Blvd., Ste. 400
    Los Angeles, CA 90025
    Type:  Business Management
    Steven Barlevi . . . . . . . . . . . . . . . . . . . . . . . . . . . . . . . . . . . . . . . . . . . . . Partner
    Mathew Lichtenberg . . . . . . . . . . . . . . . . . . . . . . . . . . . . . . . . . . . . . . . . . Partner
    Robert Bernstein . . . . . . . . . . . . . . . . . . . . . . . . . . . . . . . . . . . . . . . . . Accountant

**LONE STAR PICTS. INTL. INC.** . . . . . . . . . . . . . . . . . . . . . . . . . . . . . . . . . . . . **214-696-8830**
    Fax: . . . . . . . . . . . . . . . . . . . . . . . . . . . . . . . . . . . . . . . . . . . . . . . . . . . . 214-521-6942
    4826 Greenville Ave.
    Dallas, TX 75206
    Type:  Motion Picture Production + Video Production
    Lee Thornburg . . . . . . . . . . . . . . . . . . . . . . . . . . . . . . . . . . . . . . . . . . . President
    John Boundy . . . . . . . . . . . . . . . . . . . . . . . . . . . . . . . . . . . . . . . Business Affairs

**LONGBOW PRODS.** . . . . . . . . . . . . . . . . . . . . . . . . . . . . . . . . . . . . . . . . . . . . **818-762-6600**
    Fax: . . . . . . . . . . . . . . . . . . . . . . . . . . . . . . . . . . . . . . . . . . . . . . . . . . . . 818-766-3657
    4181 Sunswept Dr., Ste. 100
    Studio City, CA 91604-2335
    Type:  Motion Picture Production + Television Production
    Richard Kughn . . . . . . . . . . . . . . . . . . . . . . . . . . . . . . . . . . . . . . . . . . . Chairman
    Ronnie D. Clemmer . . . . . . . . . . . . . . . . . . . . . . . . . . . . . . . . . . . . . . . . . President
    Bill Pace . . . . . . . . . . . . . . . . . . . . . . . . . . . . . . . . . . . . . . . . . . . . . . President
    \*Barbara J. McCarthy . . . . . . . . . . . . . . . . . . . . . . . . . . . . . . . . . Mgr., Business Affairs

**LONGFELLOW PRODS..** . . . . . . . . . . . . . . . . . . . . . . . . . . . . . . . . . . . . . . . . . **212-343-0452**
    145 Hudson Street, 12th Floor
    New York, NY 10013
    Type:  Motion Picture Production
    William R. Hearst III . . . . . . . . . . . . . . . . . . . . . . . . . . . . . . . . . Chief Executive Officer
    Andrew Karsch . . . . . . . . . . . . . . . . . . . . . . . . . . . . . . . . . . . . President-Producer
    Rachael Horovitz . . . . . . . . . . . . . . . . . . . . . . . . . . . . . . . . . . . . . . Vice President

**\*LOTUS PICTURES INC.** . . . . . . . . . . . . . . . . . . . . . . . . . . . . . . . . . . . . . . . . **213-651-4411**
    Fax: . . . . . . . . . . . . . . . . . . . . . . . . . . . . . . . . . . . . . . . . . . . . . . . . . . . . 213-651-1401
    8489 W. Third St., Ste. 1041-B
    Los Angeles, CA 90048
    Type:  Motion Picture Production + Television Production
    \*Sidney Kiwitt . . . . . . . . . . . . . . . . . . . . . . . . . . . . . . . . . . . . . . . Business Affairs

**LUMIERE FILMS INC.** . . . . . . . . . . . . . . . . . . . . . . . . . . . . . . . . . . . . . . . . . **213-653-7878**
    Fax: . . . . . . . . . . . . . . . . . . . . . . . . . . . . . . . . . . . . . . . . . . . . . . . . . . . . 213-653-8877
    8442 Melrose Pl.
    Los Angeles, CA 90069
    Type:  Motion Picture Production
    Claudia Buchanan, Esq. . . . . . . . . . . . . . . . . . . . . . . . . . . . . . . . . . Business Affairs
    Dana Padgett . . . . . . . . . . . . . . . . . . . . . . . . . . . . . . . . . . . . . . . Administration

**LYNCH ENTERTAINMENT** . . . . . . . . . . . . . . . . . . . . . . . . . . . . . . . . . **213-469-7166/310-473-5217**
   Fax: . . . . . . . . . . . . . . . . . . . . . . . . . . . . . . . . . . . . . . . . . . . . . . . . . . . . . 310-473-9847
   2001 S. Barrington Ave. #200
   Los Angeles, CA 90025
   Type: Television Production
     Thomas Lynch . . . . . . . . . . . . . . . . . . . . . . . . . . . . . . . . . . . . . . . . . President
     *John D. Lynch . . . . . . . . . . . . . . . . . . . . . . . . . . . . . . . . . . . . . . . Vice President

**MCA INC.** . . . . . . . . . . . . . . . . . . . . . . . . . . . . . . . . . . . . . . . . . . . . . . . . **818-777-1000**
   100 Universal City Plaza
   Universal City, CA 91608-1085
   Type: Motion Picture Production + Television Production
     Lew R. Wasserman . . . . . . . . . . . . . . . . . . . . . . . . . . . Chairman of the Board-CEO
     Sidney Sheinberg . . . . . . . . . . . . . . . . . . . . . . . . . . . . . . . . . . . . President-COO
     Thomas Wertheimer . . . . . . . . . . . . . . . . . . . . . . . . . . . . . . . Exec. Vice President
     Tom Pollock . . . . . . . . . . . . . . . . . . . . . . . . . . . . Chairman, Motion Picture Group
     *Joseph A Fischer . . . . . . . . . . . . . . . . . . . . . . . . Exec. VP, Motion Picture Group
     *Ann Busby . . . . . . . . . . . . . . . . . . . . . . . . . . . . . Sr. VP, Motion Picture Group
     Pamela Cherney . . . . . . . . . . . . . . . . . . . . . . . . . . . . . . . . . . . . . . . . Treasurer

**MCA TV ENTERTAINMENT** . . . . . . . . . . . . . . . . . . . . . . . . . . . . . . . . . **818-777-1000**
   Fax: . . . . . . . . . . . . . . . . . . . . . . . . . . . . . . . . . . . . . . . . . . . . . . . . . . . . . 818-733-1457
   100 Universal City Plaza, 507 PH-2
   Universal City, CA 91608-1085
   Type: Television Production
     Barbara Fisher . . . . . . . . . . . . . . . . . . . . . . . . . . . . . . . . . . . . . . . . . President
     Bob Kelley . . . . . . . . . . . . . . . . . . . . . . . . . . . . . . . . . . . . Exec. Vice President
     *Jerome F. Clark . . . . . . . . . . . . . . . . . . . . . . . . . . . . . . . . . . Sr. VP, Finance
     Ed Rothman, Esq. . . . . . . . . . . . . . . . . . . . . . . . . . . . . . . . . . . . . Legal Affairs
     Jerry Clark . . . . . . . . . . . . . . . . . . . . . . . . . . . . . . . VP, Finance, MCA TV Group
     Sally Holland . . . . . . . . . . . . . . . . . . . . . . . . . . . . . . . . . Dir., Business Affairs

**MCEG STERLING ENT.** . . . . . . . . . . . . . . . . . . . . . . . . . . . . . . . . . . . . . **310-282-0871**
   Fax: . . . . . . . . . . . . . . . . . . . . . . . . . . . . . . . . . . . . . . . . . . . . . . . . . . . . . 310-282-8303
   1888 Century Park East, Ste. 1777
   Los Angeles, CA 90067-1721
   Type: Motion Picture Production + Television Production + Distribution + Financial Consulting
     John Hyde . . . . . . . . . . . . . . . . . . . . . . . . . . . . . . . . . . . Chief Executive Officer
     Kathryn Cass . . . . . . . . . . . . . . . . . . . . . . . . . . . . . . . . . . . . . . Exec. VP-COO
     Ann K. Jacobus . . . . . . . . . . . . . . . . . . . . . . . . . . . . Exec. VP-General Counsel
     *Ray Barber . . . . . . . . . . . . . . . . . . . . . . . . . . . . . . . VP, Corporate Controller
     Kate Morris . . . . . . . . . . . . . . . . . . . . . . . . . . . . . VP, Admin.-Corp. Secretary

**MGM WORLDWIDE TV GROUP** . . . . . . . . . . . . . . . . . . . . . . . . . . . . . . . **310-449-3000**
   2500 Broadway St.
   Santa Monica, CA 90404-3061
   Type: Television Production
     John Symes . . . . . . . . . . . . . . . . . . . . . . . . . . . . . . . . . . . . . . . . . . President
     *Cecelia Andrews . . . . . . . . . . . . . . . . . . . . . . . . . . . Sr. VP, TV Business Affairs
     Thomas Malanga . . . . . . . . . . . . . . . . . . . . . . . . . . Sr. VP, Finance/Administration
     *Shelley Brown . . . . . . . . . . . . . . . . . . . . . . . . . . . . . . Exec. Dir., TV Finance

**MTM** . . . . . . . . . . . . . . . . . . . . . . . . . . . . . . . . . . . . . . . . . . . . . . . . . . . . . **818-755-2400**
   Fax: . . . . . . . . . . . . . . . . . . . . . . . . . . . . . . . . . . . . . . . . . . . . . . . . . . . . . 818-755-2448
   12700 Ventura Blvd.
   Studio City, CA 91604
   Type: Television Production + Distribution
     Bill Allen . . . . . . . . . . . . . . . . . . . . . . . . . . . . . . . . . . . . . . Pres., Television
     Charles Larsen . . . . . . . . . . . . . . . . . . . . . . . . . . . . . . . Pres., Worldwide Dist.
     Scott Higgins . . . . . . . . . . . . . . . . . . . . . . . . . . . . Sr. VP, Finance & Administration
     Neil Strum . . . . . . . . . . . . . . . . . . . . . . . . . . . . . . Sr. VP, Business/Legal Affairs

**MTV NETWORKS** . . . . . . . . . . . . . . . . . . . . . . . . . . . . . . . . . . . . . . . . . . **212-258-8000**
    Fax:. . . . . . . . . . . . . . . . . . . . . . . . . . . . . . . . . . . . . . . . . . . . . . 212-258-8303
    1515 Broadway
    New York, NY 10036
    \*\*VH-1 - Nick At Nite
    Type:  Television Production
    Thomas E. Freston . . . . . . . . . . . . . . . . . . . . . . . . . . . . . Chairman-CEO, MTV Networks
    Geraldine Laybourne . . . . . . . . . . . . . . . . . . . . . . . . . . . . Vice Chairman, MTV Networks
    Judy McGrath. . . . . . . . . . . . . . . . . . . . . . . . . . . . . . . . . . . President-Creative Dir.
    Lois Eisenstein. . . . . . . . . . . . . . . . . . . . . Sr. VP, Business Affairs-Gen. Counsel, MTV Net.
    \*Kevin Lavan . . . . . . . . . . . . . . . . . . . . . Chief Financial Officer-Sr. VP, MTV Networks

**MAGNUS FILM GROUP**. . . . . . . . . . . . . . . . . . . . . . . . . . . . . . . . . . . . . . **310-914-7699**
    Fax:. . . . . . . . . . . . . . . . . . . . . . . . . . . . . . . . . . . . . . . . . . . . . . 310-914-7695
    3241 Military Ave.
    Los Angeles, CA 90034
    Type:  Motion Picture Production
    Julie Kemper . . . . . . . . . . . . . . . . . . . . . . . . . . . . . . . . . . . . . President-CEO
    \*Larry Markowski . . . . . . . . . . . . . . . . . . . . . . . . . . . . . . . Dir., Business Affairs

**MAIN LINE PICTURES** . . . . . . . . . . . . . . . . . . . . . . . . . . . . . . . . . . . . . . **213-851-5555**
    Fax:. . . . . . . . . . . . . . . . . . . . . . . . . . . . . . . . . . . . . . . . . . . . . . 213-851-2191
    7920 Sunset Blvd., Ste. 250
    Los Angeles, CA 90046
    Type:  Motion Picture Production
    James Schaeffer . . . . . . . . . . . . . . . . . . . . . . . . . . . . . . . . . . . . Chairman
    Carl Mazzocone . . . . . . . . . . . . . . . . . . . . . . . . . . . . . . . . . . . . . President
    \*Nancy Carlucci . . . . . . . . . . . . . . . . . . . . . . . . . . . . . . . . . . . . Controller

**MANATT, PHELPS & PHILLIPS** . . . . . . . . . . . . . . . . . . . . . . . . . . . . . . . **310-312-4000**
    Fax:. . . . . . . . . . . . . . . . . . . . . . . . . . . . . . . . . . . . . . . . . . . . . . 310-312-4224
    11355 W. Olympic Blvd.
    Los Angeles, CA 90064
    \*\*All areas of entertainment
    Type:  Entertainment Law
    Lawrence J. Blake . . . . . . . . . . . . . . . . . . . . . . . . . . . . . . . . . . . . Attorney
    Mark O. Fleischer . . . . . . . . . . . . . . . . . . . . . . . . . . . . . . . . . . . . Attorney
    Joseph Horacek . . . . . . . . . . . . . . . . . . . . . . . . . . . . . . . . . . . . . Attorney
    Laurence M. Marks . . . . . . . . . . . . . . . . . . . . . . . . . . . . . . . . . . . Attorney
    L.Lee Phillips . . . . . . . . . . . . . . . . . . . . . . . . . . . . . . . . . . . . . . . Attorney

**MAREE JR. & ASSOCS. INC., A. MORGAN**. . . . . . . . . . . . . . . . . . . . . . . **213-939-8700**
    Fax:. . . . . . . . . . . . . . . . . . . . . . . . . . . . . . . . . . . . . . . . . . . . . . 213-939-5544
    4727 Wilshire Blvd., Ste. 600
    Los Angeles, CA 90010-3875
    Type:  Business Management
    Hugh Duff Robertson. . . . . . . . . . . . . . . . . . . . . . . . . . . . . . . . President-CEO

**MAROEVICH, O'SHEA AND COGHLAN INS. BROKERS** . . . . . . . . . . . . . . . . . **800-951-0600**
    Fax:. . . . . . . . . . . . . . . . . . . . . . . . . . . . . . . . . . . . . . . . . . . . . . 415-957-0577
    425 Market St., 10th Fl.
    San Francisco, CA 94105
    \*\*Entertainment insurance brokers
    Type:  General Insurance
    Van Maroevich. . . . . . . . . . . . . . . . . . . . . . . . . . . . . . . . . . . . . . President
    \*Gerald Clifford . . . . . . . . . . . . . . . . . . . . . . . . . . . . . . . . Chief Financial Officer
    \*Stephen R. Elkins . . . . . . . . . . . . . . . . . . . . . . . . . . . . Acct. Mgr./Entertainment Division
    \*Donald R. Reid . . . . . . . . . . . . . . . . . . . . . . . . . . . . . . Acct. Mgr./Entertainment Division

**MARSH & MCLENNAN INC.** ............................................... **212-345-6260**
    Fax:................................................................ 212-345-5811
    1166 Ave. of the Americas
    New York, NY 10036
    **All entertainment insurance is here.
    Type:  General Insurance
    A. Le Conte Moore ............................................ Sr. VP-Dept. Mgr.
    Robert A. Boyar............................................. Sr. Vice President
    Alice Fay Prine.................................................. Vice President
    Tracey Quinn ................................................... Vice President

**\*MARTINDALE, C.P.A., LARRY** ........................................... **310-474-0810**
    Fax:................................................................ 310-475-2041
    10780 Santa Monica Blvd., Ste. 280
    Los Angeles, CA 90025
    **All areas but music
    Type:  Business Management
    Larry Martindale ...................................................... Partner

**MARVEL FILMS** ....................................................... **310-444-8632**
    Fax:................................................................ 310-444-8518
    1440 S. Sepulveda Blvd., Ste. 114 & 126
    Los Angeles, CA 90025-3400
    **Animation
    Type:  Motion Picture Production + Television Production
    Stan Lee ........................................................... Chairman
    Avi Arad.......................................................... President-CEO
    Bill Kerstetter .................................................... Exec. VP-COO

**MATLEN & ASSOCIATES, C.P.A., H. ROY** .................................... **818-981-7911**
    Fax:................................................................ 818-981-2678
    16027 Ventura Blvd., Ste. 420
    Encino, CA 91436
    Type:  Business Management
    H. Roy Matlen ....................................................... Owner
    Lee Edwards........................................................ Accountant
    Kandy de Prosse.................................................... Accountant

**MATTHAU COMPANY, THE** ............................................... **310-557-2727**
    1999 Ave. of the Stars, Ste. 2100
    Los Angeles, CA 90067
    Type:  Motion Picture Production + Television Production
    Walter Matthau ..................................................... Chairman
    Charles Matthau................................................ CEO-President

**MAVERICK** ........................................................... **213-852-1177**
    8000 Beverly Blvd.
    Los Angeles, CA 90048
    Type:  Motion Picture Production + Television Production
    Madonna Ciccone ........................................ Co-chief Executive Officer
    Freddy DeMann........................................... Co-chief Executive Officer
    Ronnie Dashev........................................... Exec. Vice President

**MAXWELL GROUP, THE** ................................................. **818-753-2747**
    Fax:................................................................ 818-753-2810
    4821 Lankershim #F
    N. Hollywood, CA 91602
    Type:  Business Management
    *Adrienne Maxwell ............................................. Business Manager

**MEDIA SERVICES GROUP INC.** . . . . . . . . . . . . . . . . . . . . . . . . . . . . . . . . . . . . . . . . . **401-454-3130**
   Fax:. . . . . . . . . . . . . . . . . . . . . . . . . . . . . . . . . . . . . . . . . . . . . . . . . . . . . . . . . . . . . 401-454-3131
   170 Westminster St., Ste. 701
   Providence, RI 02903
   \*\*radio stations & cable television stations
   Type: Financial Consulting
   Robert J. Maccini. . . . . . . . . . . . . . . . . . . . . . . . . . . . . . . . . . . . . . . . . . . . . . . . . . . Partner

**MELENDEZ PRODS., BILL** . . . . . . . . . . . . . . . . . . . . . . . . . . . . . . . . . . . . . . . . . . . . . **213-463-4101**
   Fax:. . . . . . . . . . . . . . . . . . . . . . . . . . . . . . . . . . . . . . . . . . . . . . . . . . . . . . . . . . . . . 213-469-0195
   439 N. Larchmont Blvd.
   Los Angeles, CA 90004
   Type: Motion Picture Production
   Bill Melendez. . . . . . . . . . . . . . . . . . . . . . . . . . . . . . . . . . . . . . . . . . . . . . . . . . . . President
   Carol Neal . . . . . . . . . . . . . . . . . . . . . . . . . . . . . . . . . . . . . . . . . . . . Financial Supervisor

**MENES LAW CORP.** . . . . . . . . . . . . . . . . . . . . . . . . . . . . . . . . . . . **310-277-4895/310-286-1313**
   Fax:. . . . . . . . . . . . . . . . . . . . . . . . . . . . . . . . . . . . . . . . . . . . . . . . . . . . . . . . . . . . . 310-556-5695
   1901 Ave. of the Stars, 20th Fl.
   Los Angeles, CA 90067
   \*\*Also: 310-286-1310; Telex: 317 948, Answbk: MLCLSA
   Type: Entertainment Law
   Barry A. Menes . . . . . . . . . . . . . . . . . . . . . . . . . . . . . . . . . . . . . . . Attorney (286-1310)
   Paul I. Menes . . . . . . . . . . . . . . . . . . . . . . . . . . . . . . . . . . . . . . . . Attorney (286-1313)
   \*Marc Messineo . . . . . . . . . . . . . . . . . . . . . . . . . . . . . . . . . . . . . . . . . . . . . . Associate

**MERCANTILE NATIONAL BANK - ENT. IND. DIV.** . . . . . . . . . . . . . . . . . . . . . . . . . . . **310-277-2265**
   Fax:. . . . . . . . . . . . . . . . . . . . . . . . . . . . . . . . . . . . . . . . . . . . . . . . . . . . . . . . . . . . . 310-203-0894
   1840 Century Park East, 2nd fl.
   Los Angeles, CA 90067
   Type: Production Financing + Banking
   \*Gwen T. Miller . . . . . . . . . . . . . . . . . . . . . . . . . . . . . . . . . . Sr. VP, Entertainment Division
   \*Cindy W. Kirven. . . . . . . . . . . . . . . . . . . . . . . . . . . . . . . . . . . . VP, Entertainment Division

**MESIROW PRIVATE EQUITY** . . . . . . . . . . . . . . . . . . . . . . . . . . . . . . . . . . . . . . . . . . . **312-595-6099**
   Fax:. . . . . . . . . . . . . . . . . . . . . . . . . . . . . . . . . . . . . . . . . . . . . . . . . . . . . . . . . . . . . 312-595-6211
   350 N. Clark
   Chicago, IL 60610
   Type: Financial Consulting
   \*Thomas E. Caluhn. . . . . . . . . . . . . . . . . . . . . . . . . . . . . . . . . . . . . . Managing Director
   \*William P. Futter. . . . . . . . . . . . . . . . . . . . . . . . . . . . . . . . . . . . . . . Managing Director
   Daniel P. Howell . . . . . . . . . . . . . . . . . . . . . . . . . . . . . . . . . . . . . . . Managing Director
   \*Michael J. Barrett . . . . . . . . . . . . . . . . . . . . . . . . . . . . . . . . . . . . . . . . Vice President
   Michael Smith . . . . . . . . . . . . . . . . . . . . . . . . . . . . . . . . . . . . . . . . . . . . . . . Associate

**METRO-GOLDWYN-MAYER INC.** . . . . . . . . . . . . . . . . . . . . . . . . . . . . . . . . . . . . . . . **310-449-3000**
   2500 Broadway St.
   Santa Monica, CA 90404
   Type: Motion Picture Production
   \*Alan Cole-Ford. . . . . . . . . . . . . . . . . . . . . . . . . . . . . . . . . . Exec. VP, Strategy & Development
   Frank Davis . . . . . . . . . . . . . . . . . . . . . . . . . . . . . . . . . . Sr. Exec. VP, Business Affairs Div.
   Trevor Fetter . . . . . . . . . . . . . . . . . . . . . . . . . . . . . . . . . . . . Exec. Vice President-CFO
   Michael S. Hope. . . . . . . . . . . . . . . . . . . . . . . . . . . . . . . . . . . . . Exec. Vice President
   \*David Johnson. . . . . . . . . . . . . . . . . . . . . . . . . . . . . . . . . . . Exec. VP-General Counsel
   A. Robert Pisano . . . . . . . . . . . . . . . . . . . . . . . . . . . . . . . . . . . . . Exec. Vice President
   \*William Jones . . . . . . . . . . . . . . . . . . . . . . . . . . . . . . . . . . . Exec. VP, Corporate Affairs
   Darci Denkert. . . . . . . . . . . . . . . . . . . . . . . . . . . . . . . . . . . Executive VP, Business Affairs
   Deborah Arvesen . . . . . . . . . . . . . . . . . . . . . . . . . . . . . . . . . . . . . . VP, Corporate Tax
   Charlie Cohen . . . . . . . . . . . . . . . . . . . . . . . . . . . . . . . . . . Sr. VP, Financial Analysis
   Maria Angeletti . . . . . . . . . . . . . . . . . . . . . . . . . . . . . . . . . . . . . . . . . VP-Asst. Sec.
   Terry Buckland . . . . . . . . . . . . . . . . . . . . . . . . . . . . . . . . . . . . . . . VP, Corporate Audit
   Margaret Collins . . . . . . . . . . . . . . . . . . . . . . . . . . . . . . . . . . . . . . . . . VP, Litigation
   Luba Keske . . . . . . . . . . . . . . . . . . . . . . . . . . . . . . . . . . . VP, Admin. Business Affairs
   Libby Pachares. . . . . . . . . . . . . . . . . . . . . . . . . . . . . . . . . . . . . VP, Business Affairs
   Daniel Rosset . . . . . . . . . . . . . . . . . . . . . . . . . . . . . . . . . Vice President-Corp. Controller
   Mike Smarinsky . . . . . . . . . . . . . . . . . . . . . . . . . . . . . . . . . . . . . . VP, Corporate Legal

**MIRAGE ENTERPRISES** . . . . . . . . . . . . . . . . . . . . . . . . . . . . . . . . . . . . . . . . **213-956-5600**
    Fax: . . . . . . . . . . . . . . . . . . . . . . . . . . . . . . . . . . . . . . . . . . . . . . . 213-956-1166
c/o Paramount
5555 Melrose Ave., Demille Bldg. 1st Fl.
Los Angeles, CA 90038-3197
Type: Motion Picture Production
    *Lindsay Doran . . . . . . . . . . . . . . . . . . . . . . . . . . . . . . . . . . . . . . . . . . President
    *Jenny McLaren . . . . . . . . . . . . . . . . . . . . . . . . . . . . . . . . . . VP, Business Affairs

**MIRAMAX FILMS** . . . . . . . . . . . . . . . . . . . . . . . . . . . . . . . **212-941-3800/213-969-2000**
    Fax: . . . . . . . . . . . . . . . . . . . . . . . . . . . . . . . . . . 212-941-3949/213-969-9840
c/o Tribeca Film Center
375 Greenwich St.
New York, NY 10013
    **ALSO: 7920 Sunset Blvd. #230, Los Angeles, CA 90046
Type: Motion Picture Production + Distribution
    Harvey Weinstein . . . . . . . . . . . . . . . . . . . . . . . . . . . . . . . . . . . . . . . . Co-chair
    Bob Weinstein . . . . . . . . . . . . . . . . . . . . . . . . . . . . . . . . . . . . . . . . . . Co-chair
    John Logigian . . . . . . . . . . . . . . . . . . . . . . . . . . . Exec. VP, Business/Legal Affairs
    Irwin Reiter . . . . . . . . . . . . . . . . . . . . . . . . . . . . . . Chief Financial Officer (NY)
    Scott Greenstein . . . . . . . . . . . . . . . VP, In Charge of Motion Picts./Music/New Media
    Agnes Mentre . . . . . . . . . . . . . . . . . . . . . . . . . . VP, Business Affairs & Production
    Deborah Branch . . . . . . . . . . . . . . . . . . . . . . . . . . . . Dir., Business/Legal (NY)
    *Neil Sacker . . . . . . . . . . . . . . . . . . . . . . . . . . . . VP, Legal/Business Affairs (LA)

**MISS UNIVERSE INC.** . . . . . . . . . . . . . . . . . . . . . . . . . . . . . . . . . . **310-553-2555**
    Fax: . . . . . . . . . . . . . . . . . . . . . . . . . . . . . . . . . . . . . . . . . . . . 310-553-0234
1801 Century Park East, Ste. 2100
Los Angeles, CA 90067
Type: Television Production
    *Martin Brooks . . . . . . . . . . . . . . . . . . . . . . . . . . . . . . . . . . . . . . . . . President
    Gail Rosenblum . . . . . . . . . . . . . . . . . . . . . . . . . . . . VP, Legal/Business Affairs
    Scott Wherity . . . . . . . . . . . . . . . . . . . . . . . . . . . . . Mgr., Financial Analysis
    Carl Allison . . . . . . . . . . . . . . . . . . . . . . . . . . . . . . . . . . . Sr. Accountant

**MISTER/SISTER PRODS.** . . . . . . . . . . . . . . . . . . . . . . . . . . . . . . . **213-653-8822**
    Fax: . . . . . . . . . . . . . . . . . . . . . . . . . . . . . . . . . . . . . . . . . . . . 213-653-5767
6535 Wilshire Blvd., Ste. 250
Los Angeles, CA 90048
Type: Motion Picture Production + Television Production + Video Production + Production Co-Financing + Business Affairs + Legal Affairs
    David K. Brownstein . . . . . . . . . . . . . . . . . . . . . . . . . . . . . Principal/Attorney
    Majken M. Gilmartin . . . . . . . . . . . . . . . . . . . . . . . . . . . . . . . . . . Principal

**MITCHELL, SILBERBERG & KNUPP** . . . . . . . . . . . . . . . . . . . . . . . . . . . . . . . . . . . . . . . . . **310-312-2000**
 Fax: . . . . . . . . . . . . . . . . . . . . . . . . . . . . . . . . . . . . . . . . . . . . . . . . . . . . . . . . 310-312-3785
 11377 W. Olympic Blvd.
 Los Angeles, CA 90064
 \*\*Motion Pictures, Television, Music
Type:  Entertainment Law
 Michael Adler . . . . . . . . . . . . . . . . . . . . . . . . . . . . . . . . . . . . . . . . . . . . . . Partner
 Seymour Bricker . . . . . . . . . . . . . . . . . . . . . . . . . . . . . . . . . . . . . . . . . . . Partner
 Gary Concoff . . . . . . . . . . . . . . . . . . . . . . . . . . . . . . . . . . . . . . . . . . . . . . Partner
 Philip Davis . . . . . . . . . . . . . . . . . . . . . . . . . . . . . . . . . . . . . . . . . . . . . . . Partner
 Bernard Donnenfeld. . . . . . . . . . . . . . . . . . . . . . . . . . . . . . . . . . . . . . . . . Partner
 Harold Friedman . . . . . . . . . . . . . . . . . . . . . . . . . . . . . . . . . . . . . . . . . . . Partner
 William Kaplan . . . . . . . . . . . . . . . . . . . . . . . . . . . . . . . . . . . . . . . . . . . . Partner
 Roger Sherman. . . . . . . . . . . . . . . . . . . . . . . . . . . . . . . . . . . . . . . . . . . . . Partner
 \*Gene Solomon. . . . . . . . . . . . . . . . . . . . . . . . . . . . . . . . . . . . . . . . . . . . Partner
 Donald Steele. . . . . . . . . . . . . . . . . . . . . . . . . . . . . . . . . . . . . . . . . . . . . Partner
 Douglas Stone . . . . . . . . . . . . . . . . . . . . . . . . . . . . . . . . . . . . . . . . . . . . Partner
 \*Mary Sullivan . . . . . . . . . . . . . . . . . . . . . . . . . . . . . . . . . . . . . . . . . . . . Partner
 \*Jennifer Justman . . . . . . . . . . . . . . . . . . . . . . . . . . . . . . . . . . . . . . . . . Associate
 \*David Miercort . . . . . . . . . . . . . . . . . . . . . . . . . . . . . . . . . . . . . . . . . . Associate
 \*Lauren Stogel . . . . . . . . . . . . . . . . . . . . . . . . . . . . . . . . . . . . . . . . . . . Associate
 Christine Cuddy . . . . . . . . . . . . . . . . . . . . . . . . . . . . . . . . . . . . . . . . Of Counsel
 \*Diane Golden . . . . . . . . . . . . . . . . . . . . . . . . . . . . . . . . . . . . . . . . . Of Counsel
 \*Steven Katz . . . . . . . . . . . . . . . . . . . . . . . . . . . . . . . . . . . . . . . . . . Of Counsel
 \*Charles Silverberg. . . . . . . . . . . . . . . . . . . . . . . . . . . . . . . . . . . . . . Of Counsel

**MORGAN CREEK PRODS.** . . . . . . . . . . . . . . . . . . . . . . . . . . . . . . . . . . . . . . . **818-954-4800**
 Fax: . . . . . . . . . . . . . . . . . . . . . . . . . . . . . . . . . . . . . . . . . . . . . . . . . . . . . . . . 818-954-4811
 4000 Warner Blvd., Bldg. 76
 Burbank, CA 91522
Type:  Motion Picture Production
 James G. Robinson. . . . . . . . . . . . . . . . . . . . . . . . . . . . . . . . . . . . . . Chairman-CEO
 \*Gary Barber. . . . . . . . . . . . . . . . . . . . . . . . . . . . . . . . . . . . . . . . Vice Chairman
 Andrew Larner . . . . . . . . . . . . . . . . . . . . . . . . . . . . . . . . . . . Director, Legal Affairs

**MORGAN, C.P.A., ROBERT F.** . . . . . . . . . . . . . . . . . . . . . . . . . . . . . . . . . . . . **310-475-1647**
 Fax: . . . . . . . . . . . . . . . . . . . . . . . . . . . . . . . . . . . . . . . . . . . . . . . . . . . . . . . . 310-475-2041
 10780 Santa Monica Blvd., Ste. 280
 Los Angeles, CA 90025
 \*\*All areas but music
Type:  Business Management
 Robert Morgan. . . . . . . . . . . . . . . . . . . . . . . . . . . . . . . . . . . . . . . . . . . . Partner

**MORRISON & FOERSTER** . . . . . . . . . . . . . . . . . . . . . . . . . . . . . **213-892-5200/212-468-8000**
 Fax: . . . . . . . . . . . . . . . . . . . . . . . . . . . . . . . . . . . . . . . . . 213-892-5454/212-468-7900
 555 W. 5th St.
 Los Angeles, CA 90013-1024
 \*\*ALSO: 1290 Ave. of Americas, New York, NY 10104
Type:  Entertainment Law
 Pauline Stevens . . . . . . . . . . . . . . . . . . . . . . . . . . . . . . . . . . . . . . . . Partner (LA)
 David Hollander. . . . . . . . . . . . . . . . . . . . . . . . . . . . . . . . . . . . . . Of Counsel (NY)

**MOTION PICTURE CORP. OF AMERICA.** . . . . . . . . . . . . . . . . . . . . . . . . . . . . **310-319-9500**
 Fax: . . . . . . . . . . . . . . . . . . . . . . . . . . . . . . . . . . . . . . . . . . . . . . . . . . . . . . . . 310-319-9501
 1401 Ocean Ave., #301
 Santa Monica, CA 90401
Type:  Motion Picture Production
 Brad Krevoy. . . . . . . . . . . . . . . . . . . . . . . . . . . . . . . . . . . . . . . . . . . Co-chairman
 Steven Stabler . . . . . . . . . . . . . . . . . . . . . . . . . . . . . . . . . . . . . . . . Co-chairman
 \*Jeff Ivers . . . . . . . . . . . . . . . . . . . . . . . . . . . . . . . . . . . . . . . . . . . . . . . CFO
 \*RJ Murillo . . . . . . . . . . . . . . . . . . . . . . . . . . . . . . . . . . . . . . Dir., Business Affairs

**MOVICORP HOLDINGS, INC.** . . . . . . . . . . . . . . . . . . . . . . . . . . . . . . . . . . . . . . **310-553-4300**
   Fax:. . . . . . . . . . . . . . . . . . . . . . . . . . . . . . . . . . . . . . . . . . . . . . . . . . . . 310-553-1159
   9887 Santa Monica Blvd.
   Beverly Hills, CA 90212-1604
Type:  Motion Picture Production + Television Production + Production Financing + Production
Co-Financing
   Robert Schnitzer. . . . . . . . . . . . . . . . . . . . . . . . . . . . . . . . . . . . . . . . President
   Paul Kijzer . . . . . . . . . . . . . . . . . . . . . . . . . . . . . . . . . . . . Advisor to the Board

**MOVIE GROUP, THE** . . . . . . . . . . . . . . . . . . . . . . . . . . . . . . . . . . . . . . . . . . . **310-556-2830**
   Fax:. . . . . . . . . . . . . . . . . . . . . . . . . . . . . . . . . . . . . . . . . . . . . . . . . . . . 310-277-1490
   1900 Ave. of the Stars, Ste. 1425
   Los Angeles, CA 90067
   **Finances and Distributes Independently Produced Films
Type:  Motion Picture Production
   Peter E. Strauss . . . . . . . . . . . . . . . . . . . . . . . . . . . . . . . . . . . President-CEO
   Ann Oliver . . . . . . . . . . . . . . . . . . . . . . . . . . . . . . . . . Chief Financial Officer
   Jed Daly . . . . . . . . . . . . . . . . . . . . . . . . . . . . . . Sr. VP, Legal/Business Affairs
   Randy Klinenberg . . . . . . . . . . . . . . . . . . . . . . . . . . . . . . . . . VP, Operations

**MRUVKA ENTERTAINMENT, ALAN.** . . . . . . . . . . . . . . . . . . . . . . . . . . . . . . . . **310-271-5400**
   Fax:. . . . . . . . . . . . . . . . . . . . . . . . . . . . . . . . . . . . . . . . . . . . . . . . . . . . 310-271-3479
   9220 Sunset Blvd., Ste. 224
   Los Angeles, CA 90069
Type:  Motion Picture Production + Television Production
   *Alan Mruvka. . . . . . . . . . . . . . . . . . . . . . . . . . . . . . . . . . . . . . Co-Chairman
   *Marilyn Vance. . . . . . . . . . . . . . . . . . . . . . . . . . . . . . . . . . . . . Co-Chairman
   Edward Hazan . . . . . . . . . . . . . . . . . . . . . . . . . . . . . . Chief Financial Officer

**MULTIMEDIA INC.** . . . . . . . . . . . . . . . . . . . . . . . . . . . . . . . . . . . . . . . . . . . . . **803-298-4373**
   Fax:. . . . . . . . . . . . . . . . . . . . . . . . . . . . . . . . . . . . . . . . . . . . . . . . . . . . 803-298-4271
   P.O. Box 1688
   Greenville, SC 29602
Type:  Television Production
   Robert E. Hamby Jr.. . . . . . . . . . . . . . . . . . . . . . . . . Sr. VP, Finance/Admin.-CFO
   *Frederick G. Lohman . . . . . . . . . . . . . . . . . . . . . . . . . . . . . VP, Controller
   Alan D. Austin . . . . . . . . . . . . . . . . . . . . . . . . . . . . . . . . . . . . . . . . Treasurer

**MURPHY PRODS., EDDIE** . . . . . . . . . . . . . . . . . . . . . . . . . . . . **212-399-9900/213-956-4545**
   Fax:. . . . . . . . . . . . . . . . . . . . . . . . . . . . . . . . . . . . . . 212-399-0555/213-956-3767
   152 W. 57th St., 47th Fl.
   New York, NY 10019
   **ALSO: c/o Paramount, 5555 Melrose Ave., LA, CA 90038
Type:  Motion Picture Production + Television Production
   Eddie Murphy . . . . . . . . . . . . . . . . . . . . . . . . . . . . . . . . . . . . . . . . . . . CEO
   Mark E. Landesman. . . . . . . . . . . . . . . . . . . . . . . . . . . Chief Financial Officer
   *Mark D. Lipsky. . . . . . . . . . . . . . . . . . . . . . . . . . . . . . . . . . Vice President

**\*MYMAN, ABELL, FINEMAN, GREENSPAN & ROWAN** . . . . . . . . . . . . . . . . . . . . . . **310-820-7717**
   Fax:. . . . . . . . . . . . . . . . . . . . . . . . . . . . . . . . . . . . . . . . . . . . . . . . . . . . 310-207-2680
   11777 San Vicente Blvd., Ste. 880
   Los Angeles, CA 90049
Type:  Entertainment Law + Business Management + Financial Consulting + Production Financing + Legal
Affairs
   *Leslie B. Abell . . . . . . . . . . . . . . . . . . . . . . . . . . . . . . . . . . . . . . . . Partner
   *Thomas J. Fineman. . . . . . . . . . . . . . . . . . . . . . . . . . . . . . . . . . . . . Partner
   *Eric R. Greenspan. . . . . . . . . . . . . . . . . . . . . . . . . . . . . . . . . . . . . . Partner
   *Jeffrey Taylor Light . . . . . . . . . . . . . . . . . . . . . . . . . . . . . . . . . . . . Partner
   *Robert M. Myman. . . . . . . . . . . . . . . . . . . . . . . . . . . . . . . . . . . . . Partner
   *Thomas P. Rowan. . . . . . . . . . . . . . . . . . . . . . . . . . . . . . . . . . . . . . Partner
   *Robert M. Angel . . . . . . . . . . . . . . . . . . . . . . . . . . . . . . . . . . . . Associate
   *Michael K. Goldsmith. . . . . . . . . . . . . . . . . . . . . . . . . . . . . . . . . Associate

**NBC ENTERTAINMENT** . . . . . . . . . . . . . . . . . . . . . . . . . . . . . . . . . . . . . **818-840-4444/212-664-4444**
3000 W. Alameda Blvd.
Burbank, CA 91523-0001
\*\*ALSO: 30 Rockefeller Plaza, New York, NY 10112
Type:  Television Production
John Agoglia . . . . . . . . . . . . . . . . . . . . . . . . . . . . . . . . . . . . . . . . . . . . Pres., NBC Enterprises
Harold Brook . . . . . . . . . . . . . . . . . . . . . . . . . . . . . . . . Sr. VP, Business Affairs & Admin.
Joseph Bures . . . . . . . . . . . . . . . . . . . . . . . . . . . . . . . . . Sr. VP, Business Affairs & Admin.
Warren Jenson . . . . . . . . . . . . . . . . . . . . . . . . . . . . . . . . . . . . . Sr. VP, Finance (NY)
Gerard Petry . . . . . . . . . . . . . . . . . . . . . . . . . . . . . . Sr. VP, Finance & Bus. Ops. West Coast
\*Rosalyn Weinman . . . . . . . . . . . . . . . . . . . . . . . . . . . . . . . . . . Sr. VP, Broadcast Standards
Ted Cordes . . . . . . . . . . . . . . . . . . . . . . . . . . . . . . . . VP, Broadcast Standards West Coast
Anne Egerton . . . . . . . . . . . . . . . . . . . . . . . . . . . . . VP, Sr. Litigation Counsel West Coast
Craig Hunegs . . . . . . . . . . . . . . . . . . . . . . . . . . . . . . . . . . . . . . VP, Business Affairs
James A. Henry . . . . . . . . . . . . . . . . . . . . . . . Dir., Prog. & Talent Neg./Business Affairs
Anne Kurrasch . . . . . . . . . . . . . . . . . . . . . . . . . . . . . . . . . . . . . Dir., Business Affairs
\*Marjorie Neufeld . . . . . . . . . . . . . . . . . . . . . . . . . . . . . . . . . . . Dir., Business Affairs
Kesa Tsuda . . . . . . . . . . . . . . . . . . . . . . . . . . . . . . . . . . . . . . . . Dir., Finance Admin.
Nicole Ungerman . . . . . . . . . . . . . . . . . . . . . . . . . . . . . . . . . . . Dir., Business Affairs

**NBC INC.** . . . . . . . . . . . . . . . . . . . . . . . . . . . . . . . . . . . . . . . . . . **818-840-4444/212-664-4444**
Fax: . . . . . . . . . . . . . . . . . . . . . . . . . . . . . . . . . . . . . . . . . . . . . . 818-840-3952
3000 W. Alameda Blvd.
Burbank, CA 91523-0001
\*\*ALSO: 30 Rockefeller Plaza, New York, NY 10112
Type:  Television Production
Rick Cotton . . . . . . . . . . . . . . . . . . . . . . . . . . . . . . . . Exec. VP-General Counsel (NY)
\*Warren Jenson . . . . . . . . . . . . . . . . . . . . . . . . . . . . . . . . . . . . . Sr. VP, CFO (NY)
Stephen Stander . . . . . . . . . . . . . . . . . . . . . . . . . . . . . . . . . . . . . Sr. VP, Law (NY)
\*Susan Costley . . . . . . . . . . . . . . . . . . . . . . . . . . . . . . VP, International Finance (NY)
\*Larry Rutkowski . . . . . . . . . . . . . . . . . . . . . . . . . . . . . VP, Corporate Finance (NY)

**NBC PRODUCTIONS** . . . . . . . . . . . . . . . . . . . . . . . . . . . . . . . . . . . . . . **818-840-7500**
Fax: . . . . . . . . . . . . . . . . . . . . . . . . . . . . . . . . . . . . . . . . . . . . . . 818-840-7673
330 Bob Hope Dr.
Burbank, CA 91523-0001
Type:  Television Production + Business Affairs
\*John Agoglia . . . . . . . . . . . . . . . . . . . . . . . . . . . . . . President, NBC Prods. (818-840-3833)
Lorna Bitensky . . . . . . . . . . . . . . . . . . . . . . . . . . Sr. VP, Prod. Business Affairs (818-840-7615)
\*Gerard DiCanio . . . . . . . . . . . . . . . . . . . . . . . . . . . . . . . . VP, Finance (818-840-7547)
Albert Spevak . . . . . . . . . . . . . . . . . . . . . . . . . . VP, Prod. Business Affairs (818-840-7610)

**NATIONAL LAMPOON** . . . . . . . . . . . . . . . . . . . . . . . . . . . . . . . . . . . . . **310-474-5252**
Fax: . . . . . . . . . . . . . . . . . . . . . . . . . . . . . . . . . . . . . . . . . . . . . . 310-474-1219
10850 Wilshire Blvd., Ste. 1000
Los Angeles, CA 90024
Type:  Motion Picture Production + Television Production + Video Production + Distribution
\*James P. Jimirro . . . . . . . . . . . . . . . . . . . . . . . . . . . . . . . . . . . . . President/CEO
Gary Cowan . . . . . . . . . . . . . . . . . . . . . . . . . . . . . . . . . . . Chief Financial Officer

**NEAR NORTH INSURANCE BROKERAGE, INC.** . . . . . . . . . . . . . . . . . . **310-556-1900/212-935-7373**
Fax: . . . . . . . . . . . . . . . . . . . . . . . . . . . . . . . . . . 310-556-4702/212-629-4854
2121 Avenue of the Stars #2060
Los Angeles, CA 90067
\*\*ALSO: 55 E. 52nd St. #3100, New York NY 10055
Type:  General Insurance
Diane Brinson . . . . . . . . . . . . . . . . . . . . . . . . . . . . . . . . . . . Sr. Vice President (LA)
Ron Cohen . . . . . . . . . . . . . . . . . . . . . . . . . . . . . . . . . . . . . Sr. Vice President (NY)
Marc Federman . . . . . . . . . . . . . . . . . . . . . . . . . . . . . . . . . . Sr. Vice President (LA)
Greg Jones . . . . . . . . . . . . . . . . . . . . . . . . . . . . . . . . . . . . . Sr. Vice President (LA)
\*Christine Sadofsky . . . . . . . . . . . . . . . . . . . . . . . . . . . . . . . . Sr. Vice President (NY)
Eve Stilts . . . . . . . . . . . . . . . . . . . . . . . . . . . . . . . . . . . Account Executive (Chicago)

**NEILA INC.** . . . . . . . . . . . . . . . . . . . . . . . . . . . . . . . . . . . . . . . . . . . . . **310-559-7826**
    Fax:. . . . . . . . . . . . . . . . . . . . . . . . . . . . . . . . . . . . . . . . . . . . . . 310-559-3969
    P.O. Box 3605
    Beverly Hills, CA 90212
    Type:  Motion Picture Production + Television Production
    Stanley Ralph Ross . . . . . . . . . . . . . . . . . . . . . . . . . . . . . . . . . Exec. Vice President
    Daniel Harrison . . . . . . . . . . . . . . . . . . . . . . . . . . . . . . . . . . . VP, Business Affairs

**NELSON, GUGGENHEIM, FELKER & LEVINE**. . . . . . . . . . . . . . . . . . . . . . . . **310-207-8337**
    Fax:. . . . . . . . . . . . . . . . . . . . . . . . . . . . . . . . . . . . . . . . . . . . . 310-207-0855
    12424 Wilshire Blvd., Ste. 1120
    Los Angeles, CA 90025
    Type:  Entertainment Law
    Peter Martin Nelson . . . . . . . . . . . . . . . . . . . . . . . . . . . . . . . . . Partner
    Alfred Kim Guggenheim . . . . . . . . . . . . . . . . . . . . . . . . . . . . . . Partner
    Patti C. Felker. . . . . . . . . . . . . . . . . . . . . . . . . . . . . . . . . . . . . Partner
    Jared E. Levine. . . . . . . . . . . . . . . . . . . . . . . . . . . . . . . . . . . . Partner
    Danny Hayes . . . . . . . . . . . . . . . . . . . . . . . . . . . . . . . . . . . . . Attorney
    Jody Simon. . . . . . . . . . . . . . . . . . . . . . . . . . . . . . . . . . . . . . . Attorney

**NEMSCHOFF, LOUISE**. . . . . . . . . . . . . . . . . . . . . . . . . . . . . . . . . . . . . . . . **310-274-4627**
    Fax:. . . . . . . . . . . . . . . . . . . . . . . . . . . . . . . . . . . . . . . . . . . . . 310-274-5039
    433 N. Camden Dr., Ste. 1200
    Beverly Hills, CA 90210-4416
    **Motion Pictures, Television, Video, Interactive
    Type:  Entertainment Law
    Louise Nemschoff . . . . . . . . . . . . . . . . . . . . . . . . . . . . . . . . . . Attorney

**\*NEO MOTION PICTURES, INC.**. . . . . . . . . . . . . . . . . . . . . . . . . . . . . . . . . **213-653-6007**
    Fax:. . . . . . . . . . . . . . . . . . . . . . . . . . . . . . . . . . . . . . . . . . . . . 213-653-0409
    8315 Beverly Blvd.
    Los Angeles, CA 90048
    Type:  Motion Picture Production
    \*Robin Hewitt. . . . . . . . . . . . . . . . . . . . . . . . . . . . . . . . . . . . . . Controller

**NEUMAN & ASSOCIATES, C.P.A.S** . . . . . . . . . . . . . . . . . . . . . . . . . . . . . . . **818-995-4404**
    Fax:. . . . . . . . . . . . . . . . . . . . . . . . . . . . . . . . . . . . . . . . . . . . . 818-995-1132
    16255 Ventura Blvd., Ste. 920
    Encino, CA 91436
    **Corporate accounting, tax and business management.
    Type:  Business Management + Financial Consulting
    Harley J. Neuman, CPA. . . . . . . . . . . . . . . . . . . . . . . . . . . . . . Managing Partner

**NEW DAWN ENTERTAINMENT** . . . . . . . . . . . . . . . . . . . . . . . . . . . . . . . . . **310-559-1622**
    Fax:. . . . . . . . . . . . . . . . . . . . . . . . . . . . . . . . . . . . . . . . . . . . . 310-559-1623
    9027 Larke Ellen Circle
    Los Angeles, CA 90035-4222
    **Unable to confirm by press time
    Type:  Motion Picture Production + Television Production
    Richard Rosen . . . . . . . . . . . . . . . . . . . . . . . . . . . . . . . . . . . . VP, Business Affairs

**NEW DEAL PRODS., INC.** . . . . . . . . . . . . . . . . . . . . . . . . . . . . . . . . . . . . . **310-280-4504**
    Fax:. . . . . . . . . . . . . . . . . . . . . . . . . . . . . . . . . . . . . . . . . . . . . 310-280-1518
    c/o Columbia Pictures
    10202 W. Washington Blvd., Capra 203
    Culver City, CA 90232-3195
    Type:  Motion Picture Production + Television Production
    \*John Singleton. . . . . . . . . . . . . . . . . . . . . . . . . . . . . . . . . . . . President

**NEW LINE CINEMA** . . . . . . . . . . . . . . . . . . . . . . . . . . . . . . . . . . . . . . . . . . **310-854-5811/212-649-4900**
    Fax:. . . . . . . . . . . . . . . . . . . . . . . . . . . . . . . . . . . . . . . . . . . . . . . . . . . . . 310-854-1824
    116 N. Robertson Blvd., Ste. 200
    Los Angeles, CA 90048
    **ALSO: 888 Seventh Ave., New York, NY 10106
    Type:  Motion Picture Production
    Sara Risher . . . . . . . . . . . . . . . . . . . . . . . . . . . . . . . . . . . . . . Chairman, New Line Prods.
    Robert Shaye . . . . . . . . . . . . . . . . . . . . . . . . . . . . . . . . . . . . . . . . . . . Chairman-CEO
    Michael De Luca . . . . . . . . . . . . . . . . . . . . . . . . . . . . . . Pres.-COO, New Line Prods.
    Michael Lynne . . . . . . . . . . . . . . . . . . . . . . . . . . . . . . . . . . . Chief Financial Officer
    Benjamin Zinkin . . . . . . . . . . . . . . . . . . . . . . . . . Exec. VP, Business/Legal Affairs (NY)
    Steve Abramson. . . . . . . . . . . . . . . . . . . . . . . . . . . . . . Sr. VP-Treasurer-CFO (NY)
    *Judd Funk . . . . . . . . . . . . . . . . . . . . . . . . . . . . . . . . . . Sr. VP, Business Affairs
    Phillip Rosen . . . . . . . . . . . . . . . . . . . . . . . . . . . . . . . . . Sr. VP, Business Affairs
    Michele Gotlib . . . . . . . . . . . . . . . . . . . . . . . . . . . . . . . . VP, New Business Mgmt.
    *Paul Prokop. . . . . . . . . . . . . . . . . . . . . . . . . . . . . . . . . VP, Production Finance
    Jim Rosenthal. . . . . . . . . . . . . . . . . . . . . . . . . . . . . . . . . . VP, Business Affairs
    Michael Spatt . . . . . . . . . . . . . . . . . . . . . . . . . . . . . . . . . . . . . VP, Finance (NY)
    *Susan Schalbe . . . . . . . . . . . . . . . . . . . . . . . . . . . . . Dir., Human Resources & Admin.

**NEW REGENCY PRODS. INC.** . . . . . . . . . . . . . . . . . . . . . . . . . . . . . . . . . . . . **818-954-3044**
    Fax:. . . . . . . . . . . . . . . . . . . . . . . . . . . . . . . . . . . . . . . . . . . . . . . . . 818-954-3295
    4000 Warner Blvd.
    Burbank, CA 91522-0001
    Type:  Motion Picture Production
    *Arnon Milchan . . . . . . . . . . . . . . . . . . . . . . . . . . . . . . . . . . . . . . . . . . Producer
    *Michael Nathanson . . . . . . . . . . . . . . . . . . . . . . . . . . . . . . . . . . . . Chairman/CEO
    *David Matalon. . . . . . . . . . . . . . . . . . . . . . . . . . . . . . . . . . . . . . President/COO
    *Kathleen Amundson . . . . . . . . . . . . . . . . . . . . . . . . . . . . . . . . . . . . Sr. VP/CFO
    William S. Weiner . . . . . . . . . . . . . . . . . . . . . . . . . . . . . . . . . VP, Legal Affairs

**NEW WORLD ENTERTAINMENT** . . . . . . . . . . . . . . . . . . . . . . . **212-527-4800/310-444-8100**
    Fax:. . . . . . . . . . . . . . . . . . . . . . . . . . . . . . . . . . . . . . . 212-527-4801/310-444-8540
    625 Madison Ave.
    New York, NY 10022
    **ALSO: 1440 S. Sepulveda Blvd., Los Angeles CA 90025
    Type:  Television Production + Distribution
    *Brandon Tartikoff . . . . . . . . . . . . . . . . . . . . . . . . . . . . . . . . . . . . . . . . Chairman
    *James McNamara . . . . . . . . . . . . . . . . . . . . . . . . . . . . . . . . . . . . President-CEO
    *Harvey Finkel . . . . . . . . . . . . . . . . . . . . . . . . . . . . . . . Sr. Vice President-CFO
    *Lorna Shepard. . . . . . . . . . . . . . . . . . . . . . . . . . . . . . . Sr. VP, Business Affairs
    *Paul A. Birmingham . . . . . . . . . . . . . . . . . . . . . . . . . . . . . VP, Administration
    *Carolyn Siffermann. . . . . . . . . . . . . . . . . . . . . . . . . . . . . . . . . . . VP, Finance

**NICKELODEON** . . . . . . . . . . . . . . . . . . . . . . . . . . . . . . . . . . . . . . . . . . . **212-258-7500**
    Fax:. . . . . . . . . . . . . . . . . . . . . . . . . . . . . . . . . . . . . . . . . . . . . . . . . 212-258-7705
    1515 Broadway, 38th Fl.
    New York, NY 10036
    Type:  Television Production
    Jeffrey Dunn. . . . . . . . . . . . . . . . . . . . . . . . . . Exec. VP, Strategy & Business Operations
    *Rich Cronin . . . . . . . . . . . . . . . . . . . . . . . . . . . . General Mgr., Sr. VP, Nick-at-Nite
    *Andra Shapiro . . . . . . . . . . . . . . . . . . . . . . . . . . . . . . . Sr. VP, Business Affairs

**NORTHSTAR ENT. GROUP, INC.** . . . . . . . . . . . . . . . . . . . . . . . . . . . . . . . . **804-579-2250**
    Fax:. . . . . . . . . . . . . . . . . . . . . . . . . . . . . . . . . . . . . . . . . . . . . . . . . 804-579-2253
    977 Centerville Turnpike
    Virginia Beach, VA 23463-0001
    Type:  Motion Picture Production + Television Production
    Susan Rohrer . . . . . . . . . . . . . . . . . . . . . . . . . . . . . . . Prod. Director (804-579-2284)
    *Allison Wilson . . . . . . . . . . . . . . . . . . . . . . . . . . . . . . . . VP, Finance (804-579-2658)

**NORWITZ ATTORNEY AT LAW, ERIC.** . . . . . . . . . . . . . . . . . . . . . . . . . . . . **213-389-3477**
    3333 W. 2nd St., Ste. 52-214
    Los Angeles, CA 90004
    Type:  Entertainment Law
    Eric Norwitz. . . . . . . . . . . . . . . . . . . . . . . . . . . . . . . . . . . . . . . . . . . . Attorney

© 1995 Hollywood Financial Directory No. 3
310-315-4815 or 800-815-0503 outside California

**NOSTALGIA TELEVISION** . . . . . . . . . . . . . . . . . . . . . . . . . . . . . . . . . . . . . . . . . . . . . . . . . **202-289-6633**
   Fax:. . . . . . . . . . . . . . . . . . . . . . . . . . . . . . . . . . . . . . . . . . . . . . . . . . . . . . . . . 202-289-6632
   650 Mass Ave., N.W.
   Washington, DC 20001
   Type: Television Production
     *John Heim . . . . . . . . . . . . . . . . . . . . . . . . . . . . . . . . . . . . . . . . . . . President/CEO
     *Daniel Holdgreiwe . . . . . . . . . . . . . . . . . . . . . . . . . . . . . . . . . . . . General Counsel
     *Martin Gallogy . . . . . . . . . . . . . . . . . . . . . . . . . . . . . . . . . . . . . . . . . . . . . . CFO

**NU IMAGE** . . . . . . . . . . . . . . . . . . . . . . . . . . . . . . . . . . . . . . . . . . . . . . . . . . . . . . . . . **310-246-0240**
   Fax:. . . . . . . . . . . . . . . . . . . . . . . . . . . . . . . . . . . . . . . . . . . . . . . . . . . . . . . . . 310-246-1655
   110 N. Doheny
   Beverly Hills, CA 90211
   Type: Motion Picture Production
     Avi Lerner . . . . . . . . . . . . . . . . . . . . . . . . . . . . . . . . . . . . . . . . . . . Chairman
     Danny Dimbort . . . . . . . . . . . . . . . . . . . . . . . . . . . . . . . . . . . . . . . . . President
     Kurtis Kent. . . . . . . . . . . . . . . . . . . . . . . . . . . . . . . . . . . . . . . Office Manager

**O'HARA-HOROWITZ PRODUCTIONS** . . . . . . . . . . . . . . . . . . . . . . . . . . . . . . **818-986-7150**
   Fax:. . . . . . . . . . . . . . . . . . . . . . . . . . . . . . . . . . . . . . . . . . . . . . . . . . . . . . . . . 818-986-8226
   16633 Ventura Blvd., Ste. 1330
   Encino, CA 91436
   Type: Television Production
     Michael O'Hara . . . . . . . . . . . . . . . . . . . . . . . . . . . . . . . . . . . . . . . President
     Jennifer H. Barnes . . . . . . . . . . . . . . . . . . . . . . . . . . . . Chief Financial Officer
     Dr. Lawrence Horowitz . . . . . . . . . . . . . . . . . . . . . . . . . . Chief Executive Officer

**O'HARA/GREGG FILMS** . . . . . . . . . . . . . . . . . . . . . . . . . . . . . . . . . . . . . . . . . **818-846-4874**
   4204 National Ave.
   Toluca Lake, CA 91505
   **MAIL TO: P.O. Box 2187, Beverly Hills, CA 90213
   Type: Motion Picture Production + Television Production
     Albert Dorsey, III. . . . . . . . . . . . . . . . . . . . . . . . . . . . . . . . . . . . . VP, Finance

**O'MELVENY & MYERS**. . . . . . . . . . . . . . . . . . . . . . . . . . . . . . . . . . . . . . . . . . . **310-553-6700**
   1999 Ave. of the Stars, Ste. 700
   Los Angeles, CA 90067-6035
   **Institutional, Studio & Indep. Prod. Cos.
   Type: Entertainment Law
     Donald Petroni . . . . . . . . . . . . . . . . . . . . . . . . . . . . . . . . . . . . . . Sr. Partner
     Kendall Bishop. . . . . . . . . . . . . . . . . . . . . . . . . . . . . . . . . . Managing Partner

**OBERMAN, TIVOLI & MILLER LTD.** . . . . . . . . . . . . . . . . . . . . . . . . . . . . . . **310-471-9300**
   Fax:. . . . . . . . . . . . . . . . . . . . . . . . . . . . . . . . . . . . . . . . . . . . . . . . . . . . . . . . . 310-471-4702
   500 S. Sepulveda Blvd., Ste. 500
   Los Angeles, CA 90049
   **All areas
   Type: Business Management
     Julie Miller. . . . . . . . . . . . . . . . . . . . . . . . . . . . . . . . . . . . . . . . . . . Partner
     Robert Oberman. . . . . . . . . . . . . . . . . . . . . . . . . . . . . . . . . . . . . . . . Partner
     Alan Tivoli . . . . . . . . . . . . . . . . . . . . . . . . . . . . . . . . . . . . . . . . . . . Partner

**OLYMPIC ENTERTAINMENT GROUP** . . . . . . . . . . . . . . . . . . . . . . . . . . . . . . **818-556-6300**
   Fax:. . . . . . . . . . . . . . . . . . . . . . . . . . . . . . . . . . . . . . . . . . . . . . . . . . . . . . . . . 818-556-6363
   801 Main St.
   Burbank, CA 91506
   Type: Motion Picture Production + Television Production
     Dominic Orsatti . . . . . . . . . . . . . . . . . . . . . . . . . . . . . . . . . . . Chairman-CEO
     *Paul Cameron . . . . . . . . . . . . . . . . . . . . . . . . . . . . . . . . . . . . . . . President
     Janet Wood. . . . . . . . . . . . . . . . . . . . . . . . . . . . . . . . . . Chief Financial Officer

**ONCE UPON A TIME FILMS, LTD.** . . . . . . . . . . . . . . . . . . . . . . . . . . . . . . . . . . . . . . **310-392-3500**
    Fax:. . . . . . . . . . . . . . . . . . . . . . . . . . . . . . . . . . . . . . . . . . . . . . . . 310-392-9484
    3110 Main St., Ste. 210
    Santa Monica, CA 90405
    Type:  Motion Picture Production + Television Production
    *Richard Olshansky . . . . . . . . . . . . . . . . . . . . . . . . . . . . . . . . . Exec. VP, Business Affairs

**OPPENHEIM ESQ., ROBERT L.** . . . . . . . . . . . . . . . . . . . . . . . . . . . . . . . . . **310-556-4423**
    Fax:. . . . . . . . . . . . . . . . . . . . . . . . . . . . . . . . . . . . . . . . . . . . . . . . 310-556-4425
    1875 Century Park East, Ste. 1500
    Los Angeles, CA 90067
    **Motion Pictures, Music, Television, Video
    Type:  Entertainment Law
    Robert L. Oppenheim, Esq. . . . . . . . . . . . . . . . . . . . . . . . . . . . . . . . . . . . Attorney

**OPPENHEIMER & CO. INC.** . . . . . . . . . . . . . . . . . . . . . . . . . . . . . . . . . . . . **212-667-5028**
    c/o Oppenheimer Tower
    World Financial Center
    New York, NY 10281
    Type:  Banking
    Mark A. Leavitt . . . . . . . . . . . . . . . . . . . . . . . . . . . . . . . . . Managing Director
    *Fritz T. Beesemyer . . . . . . . . . . . . . . . . . . . . . . . . . . . . . . . Sr. Vice President
    *John G. Lapham III . . . . . . . . . . . . . . . . . . . . . . . . . . . . . . . Sr. Vice President

**ORION PICTURES CORPORATION** . . . . . . . . . . . . . . . . . . . . . . . . . . . . . . **310-282-0550**
    Fax:. . . . . . . . . . . . . . . . . . . . . . . . . . . . . . . . . . . . . . . . . . . . . . . . 310-201-0798
    1888 Century Park East
    Los Angeles, CA 90067-1728
    Type:  Motion Picture Production + Video Production + Distribution + Production Co-Financing
    John W. Kluge . . . . . . . . . . . . . . . . . . . . . . . . . . . . . . . . . Chairman of the Board
    Stuart Subotnick . . . . . . . . . . . . . . . . . . . . . . . . . . . . . . . . . . Vice Chairman
    Leonard White . . . . . . . . . . . . . . . . . . . . . . . . . . . . . . . . . President-CEO
    John Hester. . . . . . . . . . . . . . . . . . . . . . . . . . . . . . Exec. VP-General Counsel
    *Silvia Kessel . . . . . . . . . . . . . . . . . . . . . . . . . . . . . . . . Exec. Vice President
    Cynthia Friedman. . . . . . . . . . . . . . . . . . . . . . . . . . . . . . . . . . Sr. VP-CFO
    Gregory Arvesen . . . . . . . . . . . . . . . . . . . . . . . . . . . . . . . . . VP-Treasurer
    Timothy Campbell . . . . . . . . . . . . . . . . . . . . . . . . . . VP, Contract Accounting
    Joseph Colleran . . . . . . . . . . . . . . . . . . . VP, Corporate Audit/Special Projects
    Barbara Custer . . . . . . . . . . . . . . . . . . . . . . . . . . . VP, Business/Legal Affairs
    *Vincent Famulari. . . . . . . . . . . . . . . . . . . VP, Intl. Finance for Orion Picts. Intl.
    Rhonda Gale. . . . . . . . . . . . . . . . . . . . . . . . . . . . . VP, Business Affairs
    *Sandra Gong . . . . . . . . . . . . . . . . . . . . . . . . . . . . . . . VP-Controller
    *Catherine Houser . . . . . . . . . . . . . . . . . . . . . . . . . . . . VP, Administration
    Julie Landau . . . . . . . . . . . . . . . . . . . . . . . . . . . . VP, Production Finance
    *Christine Mackinnon. . . . . . . . . . . . . . . . . . . . . . . . . . . . . . . VP, MIS
    *Robert M. Mott . . . . . . . . . . . . . . VP, Fin/Admin for Orion Picts. Dist. Group
    Debra Roth . . . . . . . . . . . . . . . . . . . . . . . . . . . . . . VP, Business Affairs

**OVERSEAS FINANCIAL SERVICES** . . . . . . . . . . . . . . . . . . . . . . . . . . . . . . **800-220-4260**
    Fax:. . . . . . . . . . . . . . . . . . . . . . . . . . . . . . . . . . . . . . . . . . . . . . . . 818-343-5708
    19528 Ventura Blvd., Ste 339
    Tarzana, CA 91356
    **Intl. Consulting / Offshore Banking / Intl. Royalties
    Type:  Financial Consulting
    Ron Milco . . . . . . . . . . . . . . . . . . . . . . . . . . . . . . . . . . . . . . . . Sr. Director
    James Sutherland . . . . . . . . . . . . . . . . . . . . . . . . . . . . . . . . . Hong Kong Rep

**PBS** . . . . . . . . . . . . . . . . . . . . . . . . . . . . . . . . . . . . . . . . . . . . . . . . . . . . . . . . . . **703-739-5000**
   Fax: . . . . . . . . . . . . . . . . . . . . . . . . . . . . . . . . . . . . . . . . . . . . . . . . . . . . . . 703-739-0775
   1320 Braddock Place
   Alexandria, VA 22314-1698
   Type: Television Production
   Ervin Duggan . . . . . . . . . . . . . . . . . . . . . . . . . . . . . . . . . . . . . . . . . President-CEO
   *John C. Hollar . . . . . . . . . . . . . . . . . . . . . . . . . . . . . . Exec. VP, Learning Ventures
   Robert Ottenhoff . . . . . . . . . . . . . . . . . . . . . . . . . . . . . . . . . . . . . . Exec. VP-COO
   Elizabeth Wolfe . . . . . . . . . . . . . . . . . . . . . . . . . . . . . . . . Chief Financial Officer
   M. Peter Downey . . . . . . . . . . . . . . . . . . . . . . . . . Sr. VP, Program Business Affairs
   Paula Jameson . . . . . . . . . . . . . . . . . . . . . . . . . Sr. VP-General Counsel-Secretary
   James Scalem . . . . . . . . . . . . . . . . . . . . . . . . . . . . . . VP, Fundraising Programming

**\*PACHYDERM ENTERTAINMENT** . . . . . . . . . . . . . . . . . . . . . . . . . . . **310-264-4144/212-840-8414**
   Fax: . . . . . . . . . . . . . . . . . . . . . . . . . . . . . . . . . . . . . . . . . . . . . . . . . . 310-264-4145
   3000 W. Olympic Blvd., Ste. 1372
   Santa Monica, CA 90404
   **ALSO: 1560 Broadway Ste.600, NY, NY 10036
   Type: Motion Picture Production + Television Production
   *Dori Berinstein . . . . . . . . . . . . . . . . . . . . . . . . . . . . . . . . . . . . . . . . . . . Partner
   *Kenneth Feld . . . . . . . . . . . . . . . . . . . . . . . . . . . . . . . . . . . . . . . . . . . . Partner
   *James Freydberg . . . . . . . . . . . . . . . . . . . . . . . . . . . . . . . . . . . . . . . . . Partner
   *Michelle Leslie . . . . . . . . . . . . . . . . . . . . . . . . . . . . . . . . . . . . Administration
   *Ralph Sevush . . . . . . . . . . . . . . . . . . . . . . . . . . . . . . . . . . . . Business Affairs

**PACIFIC ARTS** . . . . . . . . . . . . . . . . . . . . . . . . . . . . . . . . . . . . . . . . . . . . . . . **310-820-0991**
   Fax: . . . . . . . . . . . . . . . . . . . . . . . . . . . . . . . . . . . . . . . . . . . . . . . . . . 310-826-4779
   11858 La Grange Ave.
   Los Angeles, CA 90025
   Type: Motion Picture Production + Video Production + Distribution
   Michael Nesmith . . . . . . . . . . . . . . . . . . . . . . . . . . . . . . Chairman of the Board
   *Bob Bunshaft . . . . . . . . . . . . . . . . . . . . . . President, Pacific Arts Publishing, Inc.
   *George Steele . . . . . . . . . . . . . . . . . . . . . . . . . . . . . . President, Rio Records
   *Ward Sylvester . . . . . . . . . . . . . . . . . . . . . . . . . . . . . President, Media Group
   *Michael Hamill . . . . . . . . . . . . . . . . . . . . . . . . . . CFO, Nesmith Media Group
   *Jim Cowan . . . . . . . . . . . . . . . . . . . . . . . . . VP/General Manager of Rio Records

**PACIFIC WESTERN PRODS.** . . . . . . . . . . . . . . . . . . . . . . . . . . . . . . . . . . **213-956-8601**
   Fax: . . . . . . . . . . . . . . . . . . . . . . . . . . . . . . . . . . . . . . . . . . . . . . . . . . 213-956-1101
   5555 Melrose Ave., Lubitich Annex #119
   Hollywood, CA 90038
   Type: Motion Picture Production + Television Production
   Julie Thomson . . . . . . . . . . . . . . . . . . . . . . . . . . . . . . . . . . . . . . . . VP, Finance

**PADELL, NADELL, FINE, WEINBERGER & CO.** . . . . . . . . . . . . . . . . . . **212-957-0900**
   Fax: . . . . . . . . . . . . . . . . . . . . . . . . . . . . . . . . . . . . . . . . . . . . . . . . . . 212-262-2769
   156 West 56th St.
   New York, NY 10019
   Type: Business Management
   Bert Padell . . . . . . . . . . . . . . . . . . . . . . . . . . . . . . . . . . . . . . . . . . . . Chairman
   Bruce Nadell . . . . . . . . . . . . . . . . . . . . . . . . . . . . . . . . . . . . . . . . Sr. Partner
   *Jake Fine . . . . . . . . . . . . . . . . . . . . . . . . . . . . . . . . . . Administrative Partner
   Aaron Weinberger . . . . . . . . . . . . . . . . . . . . . . . . . . . . . . . . . . . . . . . Partner
   Frank Franco . . . . . . . . . . . . . . . . . . . . . . . . . . . . . . . . . . . . . . . . . . Partner
   *Karl Graham . . . . . . . . . . . . . . . . . . . . . . . . . . . . . . . . . . . . . . . . . Partner
   *Ira Herzog . . . . . . . . . . . . . . . . . . . . . . . . . . . . . . . . . . . . . . . . . . . Partner
   David Levin . . . . . . . . . . . . . . . . . . . . . . . . . . . . . . . . . . . . . . . . . . . Partner
   *Jeff Schwartz . . . . . . . . . . . . . . . . . . . . . . . . . . . . . . . . . . . . . . . . . Partner
   *Seymour Straus . . . . . . . . . . . . . . . . . . . . . . . . . . . . . . . . . . . . . . . Partner

**PANITCH & CO., INC., HERSH** . . . . . . . . . . . . . . . . . . . . . . . . . . . . . . . . . **818-999-2530**
   Fax: . . . . . . . . . . . . . . . . . . . . . . . . . . . . . . . . . . . . . . . . . . . . . . . . . . 818-999-6935
   21243 Ventura Blvd., Ste. 101
   Woodland Hills, CA 91364
   Type: Business Management
   Hersh Panitch . . . . . . . . . . . . . . . . . . . . . . . . . . . . . . . . . . . . . . . . . . . . Owner

**PAPAZIAN-HIRSCH ENTERTAINMENT** . . . . . . . . . . . . . . . . . . . . . . . . . . . . . . . . . . . . **310-471-2332**
    Fax: . . . . . . . . . . . . . . . . . . . . . . . . . . . . . . . . . . . . . . . . . . . . . . . . . . . . . . 310-471-3352
    500 S. Sepulveda Blvd., Ste. 600
    Los Angeles, CA 90049
    Type:  Television Production
    Robert A. Papazian . . . . . . . . . . . . . . . . . . . . . . . . . . . . . . . . . . . . . . . . . President
    James G. Hirsch . . . . . . . . . . . . . . . . . . . . . . . . . . . . . . . . . . . . . Secretary-Treasurer
    Pattee Roedig . . . . . . . . . . . . . . . . . . . . . . . . . . . . . . . . . . . . . Exec. Vice President

**PARAGON ENTERTAINMENT CORP.** . . . . . . . . . . . . . . . . . . . . . . . . . **310-478-7272/416-977-2929**
    Fax: . . . . . . . . . . . . . . . . . . . . . . . . . . . . . . . . . . . . . . . . 310-479-2314/416-977-0489
    11400 W. Olympic Blvd., 16th Floor
    Los Angeles, CA 90064
    Type:  Motion Picture Production + Television Production
    Jon Slan . . . . . . . . . . . . . . . . . . . . . . . . . . . . . . . . . . . . . . CEO-Chairman of the Board
    *Richard Borchiver . . . . . . . . . . . . . . . . . . . . . . . . . . President - Paragon Ent. Corp. (Toronto)
    Gary Randall . . . . . . . . . . . . . . . . . . . . . . . . . . . . . . . . President - Paragon Productions
    Harry Tremain . . . . . . . . . . . . . . . . . . . . . . . . . . . . . . . . . . . . . . . . . VP, Finance
    Laura Polley . . . . . . . . . . . . . . . . . . . . . . . . . Mgr., Business Affairs (Toronto) (416-977-2929)

**\*PARAMOUNT DOMESTIC DISTRIBUTION** . . . . . . . . . . . . . . . . . . . . . . . . . . . . . . . **213-956-5000**
    5555 Melrose Ave.
    Los Angeles, CA 90038-3197
    Type:  Motion Picture Production
    *Wayne Lewellen . . . . . . . . . . . . . . . . . . . . . . . . . . . . . . . . . . . . . . . . . President
    *Paul Springer . . . . . . . . . . . . . . . . . . . . . . . . . . . . . . . Sr. VP, Asst. General Counsel
    *John Hersker . . . . . . . . . . . . . . . . . . . . . . . . . . . . . . . . . . . VP, Sales Adminstration

**PARAMOUNT DOMESTIC TV** . . . . . . . . . . . . . . . . . . . . . . . . . . . . . . . . . . . . . **213-956-5000**
    5555 Melrose Ave.
    Los Angeles, CA 90038-3197
    Type:  Television Production
    Steven Goldman . . . . . . . . . . . . . . . . . . . . . . . . . . . . . . . . . . . . Pres., Domestic TV
    Frank Kelly . . . . . . . . . . . . . . . . . . . . . . . . . . . . . . . . . . President, Creative Affairs
    Joel Berman . . . . . . . . . . . . . . . . . . . . . . . . . . . . . . . . . . . President, Distribution
    *Meryl Cohen . . . . . . . . . . . . . . . . . . . . . . . . . . . . . . . . . . . President, Marketing
    Robert Sheehan . . . . . . . . . . . . . . . . . . . . . . . . . . . Exec. VP, Business Affairs/Finance
    Bruce Pottash . . . . . . . . . . . . . . . . . . . . . . . . . . . . . . Sr. VP, Legal/Business Affairs
    *Christine Cunningham . . . . . . . . . . . . . . . . . . . . . . . . . . . . . . . . VP, Business Affairs
    Carole Harmon . . . . . . . . . . . . . . . . . . . . . . . . . . . . VP, Sales/Contracts Administration
    Peter Kane . . . . . . . . . . . . . . . . . . . . . . . . . . . . . . . . . VP, Business Affairs & Legal
    *Karen Kanemoto . . . . . . . . . . . . . . . . . . . . . . . . . . . . . . . . VP, Domestic TV Finance
    Robert G. Mendez . . . . . . . . . . . . . . . . . . . . . . . . . . . . . . . . . . VP, Business Affairs
    *Phillip Murphy . . . . . . . . . . . . . . . . . . . . . . . . . . . . . . . . . . VP, Group Operations
    *Cynthia Teele . . . . . . . . . . . . . . . . . . . . . . . . . . . . . . . . . . . . . . . . . VP, Legal

**PARAMOUNT HOME VIDEO DISTRIBUTION** . . . . . . . . . . . . . . . . . . . . . . . . . . . . **213-956-5000**
    5555 Melrose Ave.
    Los Angeles, CA 90038-3197
    Type: Video Production
    *Eric Doctorow . . . . . . . . . . . . . . . . . . . . . . . . . . . . . . . . . . Pres., Worldwide Video
    Jack Waterman . . . . . . . . . . . . . . . . . . . . . . . . . . . . . Pres., Worldwide Pay Television
    *Steven Madoff . . . . . . . . . . . . . . . . . . . . . . . . . . . . . Sr. VP, Business Affairs & Legal
    Jonathan Bader . . . . . . . . . . . . . . . . . . . . . . . . . . . . VP, Business Affairs (Acquisitions)
    Gari Ann Douglass . . . . . . . . . . . . . . . . . . . . . . . . . . . . . . . . . . . . . . . VP, Finance
    Harold Fraser . . . . . . . . . . . . . . . . . . . . . . . . . . . . . . . . . . . . . . . . VP, Operations

**PARAMOUNT NETWORK TV** . . . . . . . . . . . . . . . . . . . . . . . . . . . . . . . . . . . . . . . . . **213-956-5000**
5555 Melrose Ave.
Los Angeles, CA 90038-3197
Type:  Television Production
Kerry Mc Cluggage . . . . . . . . . . . . . . . . . . . . . . . . . . . . . . . . . . Chairman, Television Group
Garrett S. Hart . . . . . . . . . . . . . . . . . . . . . . . . . . . . . . . . . . . President, Network TV
*Richard Lindheim . . . . . . . . . . . . . . . . . . . . . . . . . . . . . . . Exec. VP, Television Group
*Gerald Goldman . . . . . . . . . . . . . . . . . . . . . . . Sr. VP, Finance & Longform Production
*Jake Jacobson . . . . . . . . . . . . . . . . . . . . . . . . . . . . . . Sr. VP, Business Affairs
Milinda McNeely . . . . . . . . . . . . . . . . . . . . . . . . . . . . . . . . . . Sr. VP, Legal
*Cheryl Birch . . . . . . . . . . . . . . . . . . . . . . . . . . . . . . . . . . VP, Business Affairs
Eileen Ige-Wong . . . . . . . . . . . . . . . . . . . . . . . . . . . . . . . . VP, Network Finance
*Michael Masters . . . . . . . . . . . . . . . . . . . . . . . . . . . . . . . . . . . VP, Finance
*J.R. McGinnis . . . . . . . . . . . . . . . . . . . . . . . . . . . . . . . . . . VP, Business Affairs

**PARAMOUNT PICTURES** . . . . . . . . . . . . . . . . . . . . . . . . . . . . . . . . . . . . . **213-956-5000**
5555 Melrose Ave.
Los Angeles, CA 90038-3197
**ALSO: 15 Columbus Circle, New York, NY 10023-7780
Type:  Motion Picture Production + Television Production
William Bernstein . . . . . . . . . . . . . . . . . . . . . . . . . . . Exec. VP, Paramount Picts.
Patrick B. Purcell . . . . . . . . . . . . . . . . . . . . . Exec. VP-CFO & Admin. Officer
Mark Badagliacca . . . . . . . . . . . . . . . . . . . . . . . . . . . . . Sr. VP, Planning
Alan J. Bailey . . . . . . . . . . . . . . . . . . . . . . . . . . . . . . . Sr. VP-Treasurer
William Hawkins . . . . . . . . . . . . . . . . . . . . . . . . . . . Sr. VP, Human Resources
*Stephen Koppekin . . . . . . . . . . . . . . . . . . . . . . . . Sr. VP, Industrial Relations
J. Jay Rakow . . . . . . . . . . . . . . . . . . . . . . . . . . . . Sr. VP-General Counsel
Stephen P. Taylor . . . . . . . . . . . . . . . . . . . . . . . . . . . . . Sr. VP, Finance
*Ed Trainor . . . . . . . . . . . . . . . . . . . . . . . . . . . . . . . . . . . . Sr. VP, IS
*Stan Balcomb . . . . . . . . . . . . . . . . . . . . . . . . . . VP, Information Processing/IS
Carmen Desiderio . . . . . . . . . . . . . . . . . . . . . . . . . VP, Contract Accounting
Rosemary Di Pietra . . . . . . . . . . . . . . . . . . . . . . . . . . . VP, Administration
JoAnne Griffith . . . . . . . . . . . . . . . . . . . . . . . . . . . . VP, Human Resources
Louis Gutierrez . . . . . . . . . . . . . . . . . . . . . . . . . . . . . . . . . VP, Legal
*Kathleen Hoops . . . . . . . . . . . . . . . . . . . . . . . . . . . . . . VP, Residuals
*Lola Langner . . . . . . . . . . . . . . . . . . . . . . . . . . . . . . VP, Legal (NY)
*Rina Roselli . . . . . . . . . . . . . . . . . . . VP, Employee Relations Legal Services
Thomas A. Zimmerman . . . . . . . . . . . . . . . . . . . . . . . . . VP-Controller

**PARAMOUNT PICTURES MOTION PICTURE GROUP** . . . . . . . . . . . . . . . . . . **213-956-5000**
5555 Melrose Ave.
Los Angeles, CA 90038-3197
Type:  Motion Picture Production
*Sherry Lansing . . . . . . . . . . . . . . . . . . . . . . . . . . . . . . Chairman & CEO
*Barry London . . . . . . . . . . . . . . . . . . . . . . . . . . . . . . . Vice Chairman
*John Goldwyn . . . . . . . . . . . . . . . . . . . . . . . . . . . . . . . . . President
*Rochel Blachman . . . . . . . . . . . . . . . . . . . . . . . . . Sr. VP, Business Affairs
Richard Fowkes . . . . . . . . . . . . . . . . . . . . . . . . . . Sr. VP, Business Affairs
*Karen Magid . . . . . . . . . . . . . . . . . . . . . . . . . . . . . Sr. VP, Legal Affairs
*Linda Wohl . . . . . . . . . . . . . . . . . . . . . . . . . . Sr. VP, Music Legal Affairs
*Alan Heppel . . . . . . . . . . . . . . . . . . . . . . . . . . . . . . . . . VP, Legal
Kevin Koloff . . . . . . . . . . . . . . . . . . . . . . . . . . VP, Music Business Affairs
*Claudia Martin . . . . . . . . . . . . . . . . . . . . . . . . . . . . VP, Credits/Titles
*Scott Martin . . . . . . . . . . . . . . . . . . . . . . . . . . VP, Intellectual Properties
*Michael O'Sullivan . . . . . . . . . . . . . . . . . . . . . . . VP, International (London)
*Steven Plum . . . . . . . . . . . . . . . . . . . . . . . . . . . . . VP, Business Affairs

**PASAROW, AVERILL C.** . . . . . . . . . . . . . . . . . . . . . . . . . . . . . . . . **818-779-1601**
Fax: . . . . . . . . . . . . . . . . . . . . . . . . . . . . . . . . . . . . . . . . . . . . 818-779-1505
14407 Hamlin St., Ste. H
Van Nuys, CA 91401
**Music & records
Type:  Entertainment Law
Averill C. Pasarow . . . . . . . . . . . . . . . . . . . . . . . . . . . . . . . . . Attorney

**PASCOTTO & GALLAVOTTI**..................................................310-203-7515
   Fax:.................................................................310-284-3021
   1800 Avenue of the Stars, Ste. 600
   Los Angeles, CA 90067
   Type:  Entertainment Law
   Alvaro Pascotto .......................................................... Attorney

**PATCHETT KAUFMAN ENTERTAINMENT** ...................................310-838-7000
   Fax:.................................................................310-838-8430
   8621 Hayden Place
   Culver City, CA 90232
   Type:  Television Production
   Tom Patchett ........................................ Chief Executive Officer
   Kenneth Kaufman ........................................................ President
   *Ann Kindberg ....................................... VP, Production (Bus. Affairs)
   *Debbie Smith........................................ Mgr., Production Services (Acctng.)

**PAUL, HASTINGS, JANOSKY & WALKER**........................ 310-319-3300/213-683-6000
   Fax:.................................................................310-393-3652
   1299 Ocean Ave., 5th Fl.
   Santa Monica, CA 90401
   **ALSO: 555 S. Flower, 23rd fl., Los Angeles, CA 90071
   Type:  Entertainment Law
   *Nancy Abell ............................................................. Partner
   *Toliver Besson .......................................................... Partner
   *Jamie Broder ........................................................... Partner
   Robert M. Dudnik ................................................ Partner, S.M.
   *Leonard Janofsy ........................................................ Partner
   *Eris Joss................................................................ Partner
   *Keith Meyer ............................................................ Partner
   *Patrick Ramsey ......................................................... Partner
   *Carl Shapiro ............................................................ Partner
   *Robert Span............................................................. Partner
   *Dennis Vaughn .......................................................... Partner
   *Robert Walker........................................................... Partner
   *Charles Walker .......................................................... Partner
   *Harry Zinn.............................................................. Partner

**\*PEACOCK FILMS INC.** ......................................................213-874-6000
   Fax:.................................................................213-874-4252
   3439 Cahuenga Blvd. West
   Hollywood, CA 90068
   Type:  Motion Picture Production
   *Moshe Bibiyan ...................................... Chief Executive Officer
   *Simon Bibiyan........................................................ President
   *Scott Paterra ............................................................. CFO
   *Jeffrey Miles ........................................ Legal & Business Affairs

**PERCENTERPRISES COMPLETION BONDS, INC.** .............................310-551-0371
   Fax:.................................................................310-551-0518
   1901 Ave. of the Stars, Ste. 2000
   Los Angeles, CA 90067
   **Assoc. w/Motion Pict. Guarantors Ltd, Toronto Canada
   Type:  Completion Bond
   Lionel A. Ephraim ..................................................... President
   Walter Mandell ............................................... Financial Consultant

**PERLBERGER, LAW OFFICES OF MARTIN** ...................... 213-850-8100/212-233-3676
   Fax:.......................................................213-851-0909/212-233-3678
   Email:........................................................... ag45g @ lafn.org
   3251 Bennett Dr.
   Los Angeles, CA 90068
   **ALSO: 15 Park Row #500, NY, NY 10038
   Type:  Business Affairs + Entertainment Law
   Martin Perlberger .................................... Owner-Chief Executive

**PERLMUTTER, SAM, LAW OFFICES OF** ........................................ **213-931-1017**
   Fax: ............................................................. 213-857-1351
   5757 Wilshire Blvd., Ste. 636
   Los Angeles, CA 90036
   **Litigation, Actor Contracts, all areas of entertainment
  Type: Entertainment Law
   Karen S. Newman ....................................................... Attorney
   Sam Perlmutter ........................................................ Attorney

**PERRY & NEIDORF** ............................................. **310-550-1254**
   9720 Wilshire Blvd., 3rd Fl.
   Beverly Hills, CA 90212-2013
  Type: Business Management
   Michael Neidorf ........................................................ Partner
   Murray Neidorf ........................................................ Partner

**PERSKY PRODS., LESTER** ...................................... **310-476-9697**
   Fax: ............................................................. 310-476-6665
   935 Bel Air Road
   Los Angeles, CA 90077
  Type: Motion Picture Production + Television Production
   Lester Persky ......................................................... President
   Camille Pollock ....................................................... Controller
   Tomlinson Dean ................................................... Vice President
   *Jonas Neilson .............................................. Asst. to the Producer

**\*PETERS ENTERTAINMENT** ..................................... **818-954-ext.**
   Fax: ............................................................. 818-954-4976
   4000 Warner Blvd., Bldg. 15
   Burbank, CA 91522
  Type: Motion Picture Production
   *Jon Peters ..................................... Chairman (818-954-4960)
   *Tracy Barone .................................. President (818-954-2441)

**PHILIPS MEDIA ELECTRONIC PUBLISHING** ........................ **310-444-6600/6500**
   Fax: ............................................................. 310-445-5777
   10960 Wilshire Blvd., Stc. 700
   Los Angeles, CA 90024
   **Interactive Publisher & Distributer
  Type: Distribution
   Scott Marden ..................................................... CEO-President
   *Dave McElhatten ....................................... President, Philips Media Games
   *Sarina Simon ................................. President, Home & Family Entertainment
   Craig Cox ....................................................... Sr. VP, Finance
   Emiel Petrone ............................................... Sr. VP, Acquisitions
   Brad Auerbach ............................................... VP, Business Affairs

**\*PHOENICIAN FILMS** .......................................... **213-848-3444**
   Fax: ............................................................. 213-848-9612
   8228 Sunset Blvd., #311
   Los Angeles, CA 90046
  Type: Motion Picture Production
   *Elie Samaha ......................................................... President
   *Mark McGarry ........................................................... CFO
   *Kevin Bernhardt ..................................................... Secretary

**PICTUREMAKER PRODS.** ........................................ **310-581-6608**
   Fax: ............................................................. 310-581-6609
   2821 Main St.
   Santa Monica, CA 90405
  Type: Motion Picture Production + Television Production
   Mark H. Ovitz .................................................... COO-Producer

**PIRROMOUNT PICTURES** ............................................... **818-994-3262**
    Fax:............................................................ 818-994-3262 (notify)
    7321 Lennox Ave., F-10
    Van Nuys, CA 91405
    Type:  Motion Picture Production + Television Production
    *Mark Pirro............................................................. President
    Steve Neimand ...................................................... Business Affairs

**PLAYBOY ENTERTAINMENT GROUP INC.** ....................... **310-246-4000**
    Fax:........................................................................ 310-246-4050
    9242 Beverly Blvd.
    Beverly Hills, CA 90210
    Type:  Television Production
    Myron DuBow ..................................... Sr. VP, Bus./Legal Affairs
    Rebecca Maskey ................... Sr. VP, Finance & Treasurer (312-751-8000)
    Stuart Kricun ................................... Dir., Business/Legal Affairs

**\*POLLACK & ASSOCIATES, ROBERT** .......................... **212-459-8926**
    Fax:........................................................................ 212-977-5012
    433 W. 43rd St. #3A
    New York, NY 10036
    Type:  Motion Picture Production + Production Financing + Production Co-Financing
    *Robert Pollack........................................................... President
    *Sheri Rose ................................................ VP, Bus. & Legal Affairs

**POLYGRAM VIDEO** ...................................................... **212-333-8000**
    Fax:........................................................................ 212-603-7960
    825 8th Ave.
    New York, NY 10019
    Type:  Distribution
    *Gene Silverman....................................................... President & CEO
    *Rand Hoffman ........................................................ VP, Business Affairs
    *Brian Berger............................................ Dir.,  Finance & Administration

**POLYGRAM FILMED ENT.** ............................................. **310-777-7700**
    Fax:........................................................................ 310-777-7709
    9348 Civic Center Dr., Ste. 300
    Beverly Hills, CA 90210
    Type:  Motion Picture Production
    Michael Kuhn............................................................. President
    Rick Finkelstein ...................................................... Exec. Vice President
    Malcolm Ritchie........................................................ Chief Operating Officer
    David Daugherty .................................................. VP, Business/Legal Affairs

**\*PREFERRED INVESTMENT GROUP LTD.** ......................... **310-471-5344**
    Fax:........................................................................ 310-471-9744
    15430 Brownwood Place
    Bel Air, CA 90077
    Type:  Financial Consulting + Banking + Business Affairs
    *Ron Goldstein ........................................................ President

**PRELUDE PICTURES** .................................................... **213-956-8646**
    Fax:........................................................................ 213-956-0060
    c/o Paramount Pictures
    5555 Melrose Ave., Dressing Rm Bl. #205
    Los Angeles, CA 90038
    Type:  Motion Picture Production
    Mike Ilitch, Jr. ...................................................... Co-chairman
    *Mark Koch ............................................................. Chairman
    *Stuart Pollok .......................................... VP, Business Affairs/Special Projects

**PRICE WATERHOUSE**. . . . . . . . . . . . . . . . . . . . . . . . . . . . . . . . . . . . . . . **310-553-6030/213-236-3000**
    Fax:. . . . . . . . . . . . . . . . . . . . . . . . . . . . . . . . . . . . . . . . . . . . . 310-788-9298/213-622-9062
    1880 Century Park East, Ste. 1600
    Los Angeles, CA 90067
    **ALSO: 400 S. Hope St., Los Angeles CA 90071-2889
    Type: Business Management
    Franklin R. Johnson . . . . . . . . . . . . . . . . . . . . . . . . . Managing Partner, Ent. Prac. Grp (310-201-1803)
    Steven M. Abraham . . . . . . . . . . . . . . . . . . . . . . . . . Partner, Mgmt. Consulting Svcs. (213-236-3131)
    Saul J. Berman . . . . . . . . . . . . . . . . . . . . . . . . . . . Partner, Strategic Consulting Grp (310-201-1909)
    James H. Dezart . . . . . . . . . . . . . . . . . . . . . . . . . . . . . . Partner, Valuation Services (213-236-3573)
    Burton N. Forester . . . . . . . . . . . . . . . . . . . . . . . . . . . . . . . Partner, Tax Services (310-201-1938)
    W. Reed Graves . . . . . . . . . . . . . . . . . . . . . . . . . . . . . Partner, Intl. Tax Services (213-236-3490)
    Robert R. Keenan. . . . . . . . . . . . . . . . . . . . . . . . . . . . . . . Partner, Audit Services (310-201-1968)
    John R. Stubbs . . . . . . . . . . . . . . . . . . . . . . . . . . . Partner, Mgmt. Consulting Svcs. (213-236-3324)
    Robert M. Wagman . . . . . . . . . . . . . . . . . . . . . . . . . . . . Partner, Business Mgmt. (310-201-1868)
    Richard J. Withey. . . . . . . . . . . . . . . . . . . . . . . . . . . . . . Partner, Audit Services (310-201-1806)

**PRIME SPORTS** . . . . . . . . . . . . . . . . . . . . . . . . . . . . . . . . . . . . . . . . . . . . . . . . . **310-286-3800**
    Fax:. . . . . . . . . . . . . . . . . . . . . . . . . . . . . . . . . . . . . . . . . . 310-286-3876/310-286-3875
    10000 Santa Monica Blvd., Ste. 200
    Los Angeles, CA 90067-7007
    Type: Television Production
    *Kathryn Cohen . . . . . . . . . . . . . . . . . . . . . . . . . . . . . . . . . . . . . . . . . . . . . General Mgr.
    Tony Acone . . . . . . . . . . . . . . . . . . . . . . . . . . . . . . . . . . . . . . . . . Asst. to Chairman
    Julian Quattlebaum . . . . . . . . . . . . . . . . . . . . . . . . . . . . . . . . . . . . . General Counsel

**PRISM ENTERTAINMENT CORP.** . . . . . . . . . . . . . . . . . . . . . . . . . . . . . . . . . . **310-277-3270**
    Fax:. . . . . . . . . . . . . . . . . . . . . . . . . . . . . . . . . . . . . . . . . . . . . . . . . . 310-203-8036
    1888 Century Park East, Ste. 350
    Los Angeles, CA 90067
    Type: Motion Picture Production + Video Production + Distribution
    Earl Rosenstein . . . . . . . . . . . . . . . . . . . . . . . . . . . . . . . . . . . . . . . . Sr. VP-CFO
    Cynthia Berry Meyer . . . . . . . . . . . . . . . . . . . . . . . . . . . . . . . VP, Business Affairs

**PRODUCER & MANAGEMENT ENT. GROUP** . . . . . . . . . . . . . . . . . . . . . . . . . . **213-466-5319**
    Fax:. . . . . . . . . . . . . . . . . . . . . . . . . . . . . . . . . . . . . . . . . . . . . . . . . . 213-466-1892
    6255 Sunset Blvd., Ste. 2000
    Los Angeles, CA 90028
    Type: Motion Picture Production + Television Production
    Richard Robbins. . . . . . . . . . . . . . . . . . . . . . . . . . . . . . . . . VP, Business Affairs

**PRODUCERS ENT. GROUP LTD., THE** . . . . . . . . . . . . . . . . . . . . . . . . . . . . . . . **310-285-0400**
    Fax:. . . . . . . . . . . . . . . . . . . . . . . . . . . . . . . . . . . . . . . . . . . . . . . . . . 310-281-2585
    9150 Wilshire Blvd., Ste. 205
    Beverly Hills, CA 90212
    Type: Motion Picture Production + Television Production
    *Irwin Meyer. . . . . . . . . . . . . . . . . . . . . . . . . . . . . . . . . . . . . . . . President/CEO
    Arthur H. Bernstein . . . . . . . . . . . . . . . . . . . . . . . . . . . . . . . . . Sr. Vice President
    Terri MacInnis . . . . . . . . . . . . . . . . . . . . . . . . . . . . . . . . . . . . Investor Relations

**PROGRAM POWER ENT. INC.**. . . . . . . . . . . . . . . . . . . . . . . . . . **310-981-2033/310-426-2001**
    Fax:. . . . . . . . . . . . . . . . . . . . . . . . . . . . . . . . . . . . . . . . . . . . . . . . . . 310-426-5323
    3300 Cherry Ave.
    Long Beach, CA 90807
    **Producer's representatives
    Type: Motion Picture Production + Television Production + Distribution + Production Co-Financing
    James T. Flocker . . . . . . . . . . . . . . . . . . . . . . . . . . . . . . . . . . . . . . . . . President
    Eric S. Jacobson. . . . . . . . . . . . . . . . . . . . . . . . . . . . . . . . . . . . . . Legal Affairs

**PROGRESSIVE ASSET MGMT.** . . . . . . . . . . . . . . . . . . . . . . . . . . . **510-834-3722/800-786-2998**
    Fax:. . . . . . . . . . . . . . . . . . . . . . . . . . . . . . . . . . . . . . . . . . . . . . . . . . 510-836-1621
    1814 Franklin St., Ste. 710
    Oakland, CA 94612
    **Specializing in socially responsible investments
    Type: Business Management + Financial Consulting
    Daniel Ratner-Guanche . . . . . . . . . . . . . . . . . . . . . . . . . . . . . Investment Consultant

**PROMARK ENTERTAINMENT GROUP** . . . . . . . . . . . . . . . . . . . . . . . . . . . . . . . . . . . . . **213-878-0404**
    Fax:. . . . . . . . . . . . . . . . . . . . . . . . . . . . . . . . . . . . . . . . . . . . . . . . . . . . . . . . . 213-878-0486
    3599 Cahuenga Blvd. West, 3rd Fl.
    Los Angeles, CA 90068
    Type: Motion Picture Production + Television Production
    *Jonathan M. Kramer . . . . . . . . . . . . . . . . . . . . . . . . . . . . . . . . . . . . . . . President

**PROPAGANDA FILMS** . . . . . . . . . . . . . . . . . . . . . . . . . . . . . . . . . . . . . . . . . . **213-462-6400**
    Fax:. . . . . . . . . . . . . . . . . . . . . . . . . . . . . . . . . . . . . . . . . . . . . . . . . . . . . . . . . 213-463-7874
    940 N. Mansfield Ave.
    Los Angeles, CA 90038-3197
    **PolyGram Filmed Entertainment
    Type: Motion Picture Production + Television Production
    *Steve Golin . . . . . . . . . . . . . . . . . . . . . . . . . . . . . . . . . . . . . . . . . . . . . Chairman
    James Tauber . . . . . . . . . . . . . . . . . . . . . . . . . . . . . . . . . . . . . . . President-COO
    Ted MacKinney . . . . . . . . . . . . . . . . . . . . . . . . . . . . . . . Chief Financial Officer
    *Paul Green. . . . . . . . . . . . . . . . . . . . . . . . . . . . . . . . . . . Legal/Business Affairs

**PROSKAUER, ROSE, GOETZ & MENDELSOHN.** . . . . . . . . . . . . . . . . . . . . . . . . . . . **310-557-2900**
    Fax:. . . . . . . . . . . . . . . . . . . . . . . . . . . . . . . . . . . . . . . . . . . . . . . . . . . . . . . . . 310-557-2193
    2121 Ave. of the Stars, Ste. 2700
    Los Angeles, CA 90067-5010
    Type: Entertainment Law
    Howard Behar . . . . . . . . . . . . . . . . . . . . . . . . . . . . . . . . . . . . . . . . . . Attorney
    Steven G. Drapkin . . . . . . . . . . . . . . . . . . . . . . . . . . . . . . . . . . . . . . . Attorney
    Howard D. Fabrick. . . . . . . . . . . . . . . . . . . . . . . . . . . . . . . . . . . . . . . . Attorney
    Bernard D. Gold . . . . . . . . . . . . . . . . . . . . . . . . . . . . . . . . . . . . . . . . . Attorney

**QUINCE PRODS., INC.** . . . . . . . . . . . . . . . . . . . . . . . . . . . . . . . . . . . . . . . . . **818-761-6991**
    Fax:. . . . . . . . . . . . . . . . . . . . . . . . . . . . . . . . . . . . . . . . . . . . . . . . . . . . . . . . . 818-761-6996
    12725 Ventura Blvd., Ste. H
    Studio City, CA 91604
    Type: Motion Picture Production + Television Production
    Edward Asner. . . . . . . . . . . . . . . . . . . . . . . . . . . . . . . . . . . . . . . . . . President
    Matthew Asner. . . . . . . . . . . . . . . . . . . . . . . . VP, Development & Business Affairs
    *Paige Lipman . . . . . . . . . . . . . . . . . . . . . . . . . . . . . . . . . Asst. to Mr. Asner

**RCS/PMP FILMS** . . . . . . . . . . . . . . . . . . . . . . . . . . . . . . . . . . . . . . . . . . . **310-888-4100**
    Fax:. . . . . . . . . . . . . . . . . . . . . . . . . . . . . . . . . . . . . . . . . . . . . . . . . . . . . . . . . 310-888-4111
    9348 Civic Center Dr., Mezz
    Beverly Hills, CA 90210
    **aka Percy Main Productions
    Type: Motion Picture Production
    Ridley Scott . . . . . . . . . . . . . . . . . . . . . . . . . . . . . . . . . . . . . . . . . . Chairman
    Tony Scott . . . . . . . . . . . . . . . . . . . . . . . . . . . . . . . . . . . . . . . . Co-chairman
    Mimi Polk. . . . . . . . . . . . . . . . . . . . . . . . . . . . . . . . . . . . . . . . . . . President
    Philip Elway. . . . . . . . . . . . . . . . . . . . . . . . . . . . . . Exec. VP, Business Affairs
    Robert Norton . . . . . . . . . . . . . . . . . . . . CFO-Exec. VP, Finance & Administration
    Steve Richards . . . . . . . . . . . . . . . . . . . . . . . . . . . . . . . . . . . . . . . Controller
    Jerry Heiss . . . . . . . . . . . . . . . . . . . . . . . . . . . . . . . . . . Asst. to Tony Scott
    *Anne Lai . . . . . . . . . . . . . . . . . . . . . . . . . Asst. to Ridley Scott & Mimi Polk
    Brandi Miles. . . . . . . . . . . . . . . . . . . . . . . . . . . . . . . . Asst. to Robert Norton
    *Mark Nelson . . . . . . . . . . . . . . . . . . . . . . . . . . . . . . . . Asst. to Philip Elway
    Cindy Pierson. . . . . . . . . . . . . . . . . . . . . . . Asst. to Ridley Scott & Mimi Polk
    *Pete Toumasis . . . . . . . . . . . . . . . . . . . . . . . . . . . . . . . Asst. to Tony Scott

**RHH/ALBERT G. RUBEN INS. SERVICES INC.** ..................................310-551-1101
  Fax: ..................................................................310-201-0847
  2121 Ave. of the Stars, Ste. 700
  Los Angeles, CA 90067
  Type: General Insurance
   C. Scott Milne ....................................................... Chairman
   Tom McCaffrey ................................................. President-CEO
   Robert Gellen ............................................... Exec. Vice President
   Michael McAllister ............................................ Sr. Vice President
   Dick Friese ....................................................... Vice President
   Shirley Griffith ................................................... Vice President
   Buckley Norris .................................................... Vice President
   Marcia Rutledge ................................................... Vice President
   Brian Kingman .................................................... Vice President

**RHI ENTERTAINMENT** .......................................310-358-8500/212-977-9001
  Fax: .............................................310-854-1822/212-977-9049
  116 N. Robertson Blvd., Ste. 506
  Los Angeles, CA 90048
  **ALSO: 156 W. 56th St., #1901, New York 10019
  Type: Motion Picture Production + Television Production
   Robert Halmi, Sr. .......................................... Chairman-Producer
   Robert Halmi Jr. .............................................. President-CEO
   *Mike Durney ......................................... Sr. VP, Finance, CFO
   Anthony Guido ................................... Sr. VP, Legal/Business Affairs
   Timothy Clyne ......................................... Vice President-Controller

**RKO PICTURES, INC.** .........................................310-277-0707/212-644-0600
  Fax: .............................................310-284-8574/212-319-2610
  1875 Century Park East, #2410
  Los Angeles, CA 90067
  **ALSO: 551 Madison Ave, 14th Fl. New York 10022
  Type: Motion Picture Production
   Ted Hartley .................................................... Chairman-CEO
   Dina Merrill ................................................... Vice Chairman
   *Carol Hamilton ........................................... Dir., Business Affairs

**RABBIT EARS PRODS.** ..............................................203-857-3760
  Fax: ..................................................................203-857-3777
  131 Rowayton Ave.
  Rowayton, CT 06853
  **Multimedia product development
  Type: Video Production + Television Production
   Mark Sottnick .................................................. CEO-Chairman
   Mark Grayson .................................................... President
   *Kathleen Konopka ........................................... Vice President/CFO

**\*RANKIN/BASS** .....................................................212-582-4017
  Fax: ..................................................................212-582-0937
  24 W. 55th St.
  New York, NY 10019
  Type: Motion Picture Production
   *Arthur Rankin ................................................. President-CEO
   *Norman Topper ......................................... Vice President-Treasurer

**RASTAR PRODS.** ...................................................310-280-7871
  Fax: ..................................................................310-280-2331
  10202 W. Washington, Hepburn West Bldg.
  Culver City, CA 90232
  Type: Motion Picture Production + Television Production
   *Ray Stark .............................................. Chairman of the Board
   *Marykay Powell .................................................... President
   *John Morrissey ........................................... Exec. Vice President
   *Susanne A. Guercioni ................................ Sr. VP, Business Affairs

**REES ASSOCS., MARIAN.** . . . . . . . . . . . . . . . . . . . . . . . . . . . . . . . . . . . . . . . . . . . **818-508-5599**
    Fax:. . . . . . . . . . . . . . . . . . . . . . . . . . . . . . . . . . . . . . . . . . . . . . . . . . . . 818-508-8012
    4125 Radford Ave.
    Studio City, CA 91604
    **Prod. Office: 818-769-5120
    Type: Motion Picture Production
    Marian Rees . . . . . . . . . . . . . . . . . . . . . . . . . . . . . . . . . . . . . . . . . . . . President
    Anne Hopkins . . . . . . . . . . . . . . . . . . . . . . . . . . . . . . . . . . . . . . Vice President
    Jane Thompson . . . . . . . . . . . . . . . . . . . . . . . . . . . . . . . . . . . . Business Affairs

**REIFF & ASSOCIATES, D.R.** . . . . . . . . . . . . . . . . . . . . . . . . . . . . . . . . . . . . . . . . **212-603-0231**
    Fax:. . . . . . . . . . . . . . . . . . . . . . . . . . . . . . . . . . . . . . . . . . . . . . . . . . . . 212-247-0739
    320 W. 57th St.
    New York, NY 10019
    **Entertainment Insurance Brokers
    Type: General Insurance
    Dennis R. Reiff . . . . . . . . . . . . . . . . . . . . . . . . . . . . . . . . . . . . . . . . . . Principal

**REITER MANAGEMENT.** . . . . . . . . . . . . . . . . . . . . . . . . . . . . . **310-287-0176-310-287-0177**
    Fax:. . . . . . . . . . . . . . . . . . . . . . . . . . . . . . . . . . . . . . . . . . . . . . . . . . . . 310-287-0776
    2732 McConnell Dr.
    Los Angeles, CA 90064-3405
    Type: Business Management
    Harriet Namiot Reiter. . . . . . . . . . . . . . . . . . . . . . . . Certified Public Accountant

**REPUBLIC PICTURES CORP.** . . . . . . . . . . . . . . . . . . . . . . . . . . . . . . . . . . . . . **213-965-6900**
    Fax:. . . . . . . . . . . . . . . . . . . . . . . . . . . . . . . . . . . . . . . . . . . . . . . . . . . . 213-965-6963
    5700 Wilshire Blvd., Ste. 525, N. Tower
    Los Angeles, CA 90036-3659
    Type: Television Production + Video Production
    *Robert Sigman. . . . . . . . . . . . . . . . . . . . . . . . . . . . . . . . . . . . . President/CEO
    Jeffrey Brauer. . . . . . . . . . . . . . . . . . . . . . . . . . . . Sr. VP, Business/Legal Affairs
    Kim Swartz. . . . . . . . . . . . . . . . . . . . . . . . . . . . . . . . VP, Business Legal Affairs

**RESOURCE ONE INC.** . . . . . . . . . . . . . . . . . . . . . . . . . . . . . . . . . . . . . . . . . . **310-275-6188**
    Fax:. . . . . . . . . . . . . . . . . . . . . . . . . . . . . . . . . . . . . . . . . . . . . . . . . . . . 310-246-4490
    438 N. Bedford Dr.
    Beverly Hills, CA 90210
    Type: Business Management + Financial Consulting
    Ric Mandelbaum . . . . . . . . . . . . . . . . . . . . . . . . . . . . . . . Chief Executive Officer

**REYNOLDS & REYNOLDS INC.** . . . . . . . . . . . . . . . . . . . . . . . **515-243-1724/800-767-1724**
    Fax:. . . . . . . . . . . . . . . . . . . . . . . . . . . . . . . . . . . . . . . . . . . . . . . . . . . . 515-243-6664
    c/o The Plaza
    300 Walnut St., Ste. 200
    Des Moines, IA 50309-2239
    Type: General Insurance
    Stanley J. Reynolds . . . . . . . . . . . . . . . . . . . . . . . . . . . . . . . . . . . . . President
    Ron Fry . . . . . . . . . . . . . . . . . . . . . . . . . . . . . . . . . . . . Exec. Vice President
    Steve Gooding . . . . . . . . . . . . . . . . . . . . . . . . . . . . . Dir., Employee Benefits
    Sandy Bell . . . . . . . . . . . . . . . . . . . . . . . . . . . . . . . Mgr., Theatre Insurance
    Kent McLaughlin. . . . . . . . . . . . . . . . . . . . . . . . . . . . . . . Account Executive

**ROBERTS, ANDREW S.** . . . . . . . . . . . . . . . . . . . . . . . . . . **805-496-7777/818-597-0633**
    Fax:. . . . . . . . . . . . . . . . . . . . . . . . . . . . . . . . . . . . . . . 805-497-2700/805-379-2055
    960 S. Westlake Blvd., Ste. 208
    Westlake Village, CA 91361
    **A professional law corporation.
    Type: Entertainment Law
    Andrew S. Roberts. . . . . . . . . . . . . . . . . . . . . . . . . . . . . . . . . . . . . . President

**ROBINSON/JEFFREY ASSOC. INC.** . . . . . . . . . . . . . . . . . . . . . . . . . . . . . . . . . . . . . . **810-644-0006**
    Fax:. . . . . . . . . . . . . . . . . . . . . . . . . . . . . . . . . . . . . . . . . . . . . . . . . . . . . 810-645-1853
    400 W. Maple, Ste. 300
    Birmingham, MI 48009
    Type: Business Management + Financial Consulting
    Peter Robinson . . . . . . . . . . . . . . . . . . . . . . . . . . . . . . . . . . . . . . . . . . . . . No title

**ROCKET PICTURES**. . . . . . . . . . . . . . . . . . . . . . . . . . . . . . . . . . . . . . . . . . . . . **310-550-3300**
    Fax:. . . . . . . . . . . . . . . . . . . . . . . . . . . . . . . . . . . . . . . . . . . . . . . . . . . . . 310-550-1126
    9536 Wilshire Blvd., #410
    Beverly Hills, CA 90212
    Type: Motion Picture Production
    Thomas J. Coleman . . . . . . . . . . . . . . . . . . . . . . . . . . . . . . . . . . Chairman-President
    Jon Turtle . . . . . . . . . . . . . . . . . . . . . . . . . . . . . . . . . . . . . . . . . . . . . President
    Laura Mills . . . . . . . . . . . . . . . . . . . . . . . . . . . . . . . . . . . . . . . Dir., Operations

**RODEO DRIVE FINANCIAL MGMT.** . . . . . . . . . . . . . . . . . . . . . . . . . . . . . . . . . . **310-556-9741**
    Fax:. . . . . . . . . . . . . . . . . . . . . . . . . . . . . . . . . . . . . . . . . . . . . . . . . . . . . 310-284-8968
    1875 Century Park East, Ste. 150
    Los Angeles, CA 90067-2502
    **Unable to confirm by press time
    Type: Business Management
    Larry Oglesby . . . . . . . . . . . . . . . . . . . . . . . . . . . . . . . . . . . . . . . . . . President

**ROSENFELD, MEYER & SUSMAN** . . . . . . . . . . . . . . . . . . . . . . . . . . . . . . . . . . . . . . . . . .**310-858-7700**
    Fax:. . . . . . . . . . . . . . . . . . . . . . . . . . . . . . . . . . . . . . . . . . . . . . . . . . . . . . . . . .310-271-6430
    9601 Wilshire Blvd., 4th Floor
    Beverly Hills, CA 90210-5288
    **Telex: 194 195
    Type: Entertainment Law
    *Greg S. Bernstein . . . . . . . . . . . . . . . . . . . . . . . . . . . . . . Partner, Entertainment/Media Finance
    *Todd W. Bonder . . . . . . . . . . . . . . . . . . . . . . . . . . . . . . . . . . . . . . . . . . Partner, Litigation
    *Stacey M. Byrnes . . . . . . . . . . . . . . . . . . . . . . . . . . . . . . . . . . . . . . . . Partner, Litigation
    *Maren Christensen . . . . . . . . . . . . . . . . . . . . . . . . . . . . . . . . . . . . . . Partner, Litigation
    Steven Fayne . . . . . . . . . . . . . . . . . . . . . . . . . . . . . . Partner, Entertainment/Media Finance
    *David F. Graber. . . . . . . . . . . . . . . . . . . . . . . . . . . . . . . . . . . . . . . . . . Partner, Litigation
    *Kirk M. Hallam . . . . . . . . . . . . . . . . . . . . . . . . . . . . . . . . . . . . . . . . . . Partner, Litigation
    *Harris J. Kane . . . . . . . . . . . . . . . . . . . . . . . . . . . . . . . . . . . . . . . . . . Partner, Litigation
    *Donald Karl. . . . . . . . . . . . . . . . . . . . . . . . . . . . . . . . . . . . . . Partner, Corporate/Interactive
    Lawrence S. Kartiganer . . . . . . . . . . . . . . . . . . . . . . . . . . . . . . . . . Partner, Entertainment
    *Burt Levitch . . . . . . . . . . . . . . . . . . . . . . . . . . . . . . . . . . . . . Partner, Trusts & Estates
    Marvin B. Meyer . . . . . . . . . . . . . . . . . . . . . . . . . . . . . . . . . . . . . Partner, Entertainment
    *Ovvie Miller . . . . . . . . . . . . . . . . . . . . . . . . . . . . . . . . . . . Partner, Litigation/Family Law
    *Jeffrey L. Nagin . . . . . . . . . . . . . . . . . . . . . . . . . . . . . . . Partner, Entertainment/Corporate
    *Michael A. Robbins . . . . . . . . . . . . . . . . . . . . . . . . . . . . . . . . Partner, Litigation/Labor
    *William M. Ross . . . . . . . . . . . . . . . . . . . . . . . . . . . . . . . . . . . . . . . Partner, Corporate
    *James L. Seal . . . . . . . . . . . . . . . . . . . . . . . . . . . . . . . . . . . . . . . . . Partner, Litigation
    Jeffrey L. Shumway. . . . . . . . . . . . . . . . . . . . . . . . . . . . . . . . . . . Partner, Entertainment
    William J. Skrzyniarz. . . . . . . . . . . . . . . . . . . . . . . . . . Partner, Entertainment/Interactive
    Allen E. Susman. . . . . . . . . . . . . . . . . . . . . . . . . . . . . . . . . . . . . . Partner, Entertainment
    *Robert H. Thau . . . . . . . . . . . . . . . . . . . . . . . . . . . . . . . . . . . . . . . . Partner, Litigation
    *Gail Migdal Title. . . . . . . . . . . . . . . . . . . . . . . . . . . . . . . . . . . . . . Partner, Litigation
    *David D. Wexler . . . . . . . . . . . . . . . . . . . . . . . . . . . . . . . . . . . . . . . Partner, Corporate
    *Kathryn A. Young. . . . . . . . . . . . . . . . . . . . . . . . . . . . . . Partner, Litigation/Insurance
    *Mel Ziontz . . . . . . . . . . . . . . . . . . . . . . . . . . . . . . . . . . . . . . . . . . . Partner, Corporate
    *John P. Burke . . . . . . . . . . . . . . . . . . . . . . . . . . . . . Of Counsel, Corporate/Media Finance
    *Bernard Greenberg . . . . . . . . . . . . . . . . . . . . . . . . . . . . . Of Counsel, Trusts & Estates
    *James M.A. Murphy . . . . . . . . . . . . . . . . . . . . . . . Of Counsel, Corporate/Trusts & Estates
    Michael Rosenfeld . . . . . . . . . . . . . . . . . . . . . . . . . . . . . . . . . Of Counsel, Entertainment
    *Jeffrey Abrams . . . . . . . . . . . . . . . . . . . . . . . . . . . . . . . . . . . Associate, Litigation
    *Stacy Barancik . . . . . . . . . . . . . . . . . . . . . . . . . . . . . . . . . Associate, Entertainment
    *Scott Barker. . . . . . . . . . . . . . . . . . . . . . . . . . . . . . . . . . Associate, Litigation/Labor
    *Norman H. Becker . . . . . . . . . . . . . . . . . . . . . . . . . . . . . . . . . Associate, Litigation
    Renee A. Galka . . . . . . . . . . . . . . . . . . . . . . . . . . . . . . . . . Associate, Entertainment
    David L. Hirshland. . . . . . . . . . . . . . . . . . . . . . . . . . . . . . . Associate, Entertainment
    *Susan E. Holley. . . . . . . . . . . . . . . . . . . . . . . . . . . . . . . . Associate, Litigation/Labor
    *Lisa Jacobsen . . . . . . . . . . . . . . . . . . . . . . . . . . . . . . . . . Associate, Litigation/Labor
    *Cameron Jones . . . . . . . . . . . . . . . . . . . . . . . . . . . . . . . . . Associate, Entertainment
    *David A. Karnes . . . . . . . . . . . . . . . . . . . . . . . . . . . . . . . . . . . Associate, Litigation
    *Suzanne H. Kessler . . . . . . . . . . . . . . . . . . . . . . . . . . . . . . . . . Associate, Litigation
    *Brian McPherson . . . . . . . . . . . . . . . . . . . . . . . . . . . . . . . Associate, Entertainment
    *Peter Spelman . . . . . . . . . . . . . . . . . . . . . . . . . . . . . Associate, Litigation/Family Law
    *Darren M. Trattner . . . . . . . . . . . . . . . . . . . . . . . . . . . . . . . . . Associate, Litigation
    *Thomas D. Triggs . . . . . . . . . . . . . . . . . . . . . . . . . . . . . . . . . Associate, Litigation
    *Lior Z. Zohar. . . . . . . . . . . . . . . . . . . . . . . . . . . . . . . . . . . . Associate, Litigation

**ROYAL & ASSOCIATES, INC.** . . . . . . . . . . . . . . . . . . . . . . . . . . . . . . . . . . . . . . . . .**213-852-0412**
    Fax:. . . . . . . . . . . . . . . . . . . . . . . . . . . . . . . . . . . . . . . . . . . . . . . . . . . . . .213-653-7553
    8421 Wilshire Blvd., Penthouse
    Beverly Hills, CA 90211
    Type: Business Management
    *David Royal . . . . . . . . . . . . . . . . . . . . . . . . . . . . . . . . . . . . . . . . Managing Director
    Steven Frey . . . . . . . . . . . . . . . . . . . . . . . . . . . . . . . . . . . . . . . CPA-Dir., Finance
    Michael Bolger. . . . . . . . . . . . . . . . . . . . . . . . . . . . . . . . . . Mgr., Client Affairs

© 1995 Hollywood Financial Directory No. 3
310-315-4815 or 800-815-0503 outside California

**RUBENSTIEN & FINCH** . . . . . . . . . . . . . . . . . . . . . . . . . . . . . . . . . . . . . . . . . . . . . . . . **310-277-1646**
    Fax: . . . . . . . . . . . . . . . . . . . . . . . . . . . . . . . . . . . . . . . . . . . . . . . . . . . . . . . . . 310-277-4259
    1901 Ave. of the Stars, Ste. 1774
    Los Angeles, CA 90067-6018
    Type: Entertainment Law + Business Management
    *Roxanne T. Finch . . . . . . . . . . . . . . . . . . . . . . . . . . . . . . . . . . . . . . . . . . . . . . . . . Partner
    *Steven M. Rubenstein . . . . . . . . . . . . . . . . . . . . . . . . . . . . . . . . . . . . . . . . . . . . Partner
    *Loren A. Detres . . . . . . . . . . . . . . . . . . . . . . . . . . . . . . . . . . . . . . . . . . . . . . Associate
    *Tami A. Holsten . . . . . . . . . . . . . . . . . . . . . . . . . . . . . . . . . . . . . . . . . . . . . . Associate

**\*RUBIN, RICHARDS & CO.** . . . . . . . . . . . . . . . . . . . . . . . . . . . . . . . . . . . . . . . . . . . **818-772-0430**
    Fax: . . . . . . . . . . . . . . . . . . . . . . . . . . . . . . . . . . . . . . . . . . . . . . . . . . . . . . . . . 818-772-1053
    8817 Lindley Ave.
    Northridge, CA 91325
    Type: Business Management
    *Lawrence M. Rubin . . . . . . . . . . . . . . . . . . . . . . . . . . . . . . . . . . . . . . . . . Sr. Partner
    *Eva Munoz-Richards . . . . . . . . . . . . . . . . . . . . . . . . . . . . . . . . . . . . . . . . . . Partner

**RUST PRODS., PATRICIA** . . . . . . . . . . . . . . . . . . . . . . . . . . . . . . . . . . . . . . . . . . . . **310-477-4417**
    Fax: . . . . . . . . . . . . . . . . . . . . . . . . . . . . . . . . . . . . . . . . . . . . . . . . . . . . . . . . . 310-477-3342
    12021 Wilshire Blvd., Ste. 924
    Los Angeles, CA 90025
    Type: Motion Picture Production + Television Production + Distribution
    Patricia Rust . . . . . . . . . . . . . . . . . . . . . . . . . . . . . . . . . . . . . . . . . . . . . . . . . President
    Lillian Balteanu . . . . . . . . . . . . . . . . . . . . . . . . . . . . . . . . . . . . . VP, Business Affairs

**RYSHER ENTERTAINMENT** . . . . . . . . . . . . . . . . . . . . . . . . . . . . . . . . . . . . . . . . . . **818-846-0030**
    Fax: . . . . . . . . . . . . . . . . . . . . . . . . . . . . . . . . . . . . . . . . . . . . . . . . . . . . . . . . . 818-557-3766
    3400 Riverside Dr., Ste 600
    Burbank, CA 91505
    Type: Television Production + Motion Picture Production + Distribution
    *Keith Samples . . . . . . . . . . . . . . . . . . . . . . . . . . . . . . . . . . . . . . . . . . . . . Chairman
    *Tim Helfet . . . . . . . . . . . . . . . . . . . . . . . . . . . . . . . . . . . . . . . . . . . . . . . . President
    *Adina Savin . . . . . . . . . . . . . . . . . . . . . . . . . . . . . . . Sr. VP, Business/Legal Affairs
    Randy Stargel . . . . . . . . . . . . . . . . . . . . . . . . . . . . . . . . . . . . . . . . . Sr. VP, Finance
    Jean Hein . . . . . . . . . . . . . . . . . . . . . . . . . . . . . . . . . . . . . . . . . . . . . . . Controller
    Jeff Thomas . . . . . . . . . . . . . . . . . . . . . . . . . . . . . Dir., Financial Reporting & Planning

**SABAN ENTERTAINMENT** . . . . . . . . . . . . . . . . . . . . . . . . . . . . . . . . . . . **818-972-4879/212-779-7750**
    Fax: . . . . . . . . . . . . . . . . . . . . . . . . . . . . . . . . . . . . . . . . . . . . . . 818-972-4895/212-779-7751
    4000 W. Alameda Ave., 5th Fl.
    Burbank, CA 91505
    **ALSO: 477 Madison Ave., 10th Fl., New York, NY 10022
    Type: Motion Picture Production + Television Production
    Haim Saban . . . . . . . . . . . . . . . . . . . . . . . . . . . . . . . . . . . . . . . . . . . Chairman-CEO
    Mel Woods . . . . . . . . . . . . . . . . . . . . . . . . . . . . . . . . . . . . . . . . . . . . President-COO
    *Peter Dang . . . . . . . . . . . . . . . . . . . . . . . . . . President, Childrens Entertainment Group
    *Stan Golden . . . . . . . . . . . . . . . . . . . . . . . . President, Saban International Services
    Bill Josey . . . . . . . . . . . . . . . . . . . . . . . . . . . . . . . . . . Sr. VP, Business/Legal Affairs
    Mark Ittner . . . . . . . . . . . . . . . . . . . . . . . . . . . . . . . . . . . . . . . . . . . . . VP, Finance

**SACKS, SAMUEL** . . . . . . . . . . . . . . . . . . . . . . . . . . . . . . . . . . . . . . . . . **310-277-6228/277-0553**
    Fax: . . . . . . . . . . . . . . . . . . . . . . . . . . . . . . . . . . . . . . . . . . . . . . . . . . . . . . . . . 310-286-1289
    211 S. Spalding Dr., Ste. 606N
    Beverly Hills, CA 90212-3622
    **Motion Pictures, Television
    Type: Entertainment Law + Business Affairs
    Samuel Sacks . . . . . . . . . . . . . . . . . . . . . . . . . . . . . . . . . . . . . . . . . . . . . . Attorney

**SANCTUARY WOODS MULTIMEDIA CORP.** ................................. **415-286-6000**
Fax:. . . . . . . . . . . . . . . . . . . . . . . . . . . . . . . . . . . . . . . . . . . . . . 415-286-6010
1875 S. Grant St.
San Mateo, CA 94402
Type:  Television Production
Brian Beninger. . . . . . . . . . . . . . . . . . . . . . . . . . . . . . . . . . . . . . . Chairman
Scott Walchek . . . . . . . . . . . . . . . . . . . . . . . . . . . . . . . . . . . . . President
*Allen Barr . . . . . . . . . . . . . . . . . . . . . . . . . . . . . . . . . . VP, Finance, CFO

**SATIN & COMPANY** . . . . . . . . . . . . . . . . . . . . . . . . . . . . . . . . . . . . . **310-553-1040**
1901 Ave. of the Stars, Ste. 1450
Los Angeles, CA 90067
**Royalty Audits, Music catalog valuation
Type:  Business Management
Robert Satin . . . . . . . . . . . . . . . . . . . . . . . . . . . . . . . . . . . . President
*Linda Becker. . . . . . . . . . . . . . . . . . . . . . . . . . . . . . . . . Dir., Royalties

**SATRIANO & HILTON, INC.**. . . . . . . . . . . . . . . . . . . . . . . . . . . . . . . . **310-826-8356**
Fax:. . . . . . . . . . . . . . . . . . . . . . . . . . . . . . . . . . . . . . . . . . . . 310-820-8373
11661 San Vicente Blvd., Ste. 615
Los Angeles, CA 90049
Type:  Business Management
Thomas V. Satriano, CPA . . . . . . . . . . . . . . . . . . . . . . . . Head, Business Mgmt. Div.

**\*SAVITSKY SATIN & GEIBELSON.** . . . . . . . . . . . . . . . . . . . . . . . . . **310-553-1040**
Fax:. . . . . . . . . . . . . . . . . . . . . . . . . . . . . . . . . . . . . . . . . . . . 310-201-3732
1901 Avenue of the Stars #1450
Los Angeles, CA 90067
**All segments of the entertainment industry
Type:  Business Management
*George Savitsky . . . . . . . . . . . . . . . . . . . . . . . . . . . . . . . . . . President
*Jeffrey Geibelson . . . . . . . . . . . . . . . . . . . . . . . . . . . . . . Vice President

**SAVOY PICTURES** . . . . . . . . . . . . . . . . . . . . . . . . . . . **310-247-7930/212-247-5810**
Fax:. . . . . . . . . . . . . . . . . . . . . . . . . . . . . . . . . . . . . . . . . . . . 310-247-7929
c/o The Water Gardens
2425 Olympic Blvd.
Santa Monica, CA 90404
Type: Motion Picture Production + Television Production + Distribution
*Howard K. Bass . . . . . . . . . . . . . . . . . . . . . . . . . . . . . . . . Sr. VP, CFO
Harris Maslansky . . . . . . . . . . . . . . . . . . . . . . . . . . Sr. VP, Business Affairs
Jessica Roddy. . . . . . . . . . . . . . . . . . . . . . . . . . . . . . . . Sr. VP, Legal
*James Miller . . . . . . . . . . . . . . . . . . . . . . . . . . . . . . . . VP-Controller

**SCALA PRODS.** . . . . . . . . . . . . . . . . . . . . . . . . . . . . . . . . . . . **310-659-5573**
Fax:. . . . . . . . . . . . . . . . . . . . . . . . . . . . . . . . . . . . . . . . . . . . 310-659-5716
949 Larrabee St., Ste. 208
Los Angeles, CA 90069
**Unable to confirm by press time
Type: Motion Picture Production
Nik Powell . . . . . . . . . . . . . . . . . . . . . . . . . . . . . . . . . . Co-chairman
Stephen Woolley . . . . . . . . . . . . . . . . . . . . . . . . . . . . . . . Co-chairman

**SCHAEFER, LAW OFFICES OF SUSAN G.** . . . . . . . . . . . . . . . . **310-277-7025/310-442-6610**
Fax:. . . . . . . . . . . . . . . . . . . . . . . . . . . . . . . . . . 310-277-1183/310-442-6606
1990 S. Bundy Dr., Ste. 630
Los Angeles, CA 90025
Type:  Entertainment Law
Susan G. Schaefer . . . . . . . . . . . . . . . . . . . . . . . . . . . . . . . Principal
Robert A. Niers . . . . . . . . . . . . . . . . . . . . . . . . . . . . . . Legal Assistant

**SCHIFF A PROFESSIONAL CORP., GUNTHER H.** . . . . . . . . . . . . . . . . . . . . . . . . . . . . . **310-557-9081**
  Fax:. . . . . . . . . . . . . . . . . . . . . . . . . . . . . . . . . . . . . . . . . . . . . . . . . . . . . . . . . . . . . . . . . 310-277-8050
  9230 Olympic Blvd., Ste. 400
  Beverly Hills, CA 90212-4552
  Type: Entertainment Law
  Gunther H. Schiff, Esq. . . . . . . . . . . . . . . . . . . . . . . . . . . . . . . . . . . . . . . . . . . . . . . . . Attorney

**SCHLATTER PRODS., GEORGE** . . . . . . . . . . . . . . . . . . . . . . . . . . . . . . . . . . . . . . . **213-655-1400**
  Fax:. . . . . . . . . . . . . . . . . . . . . . . . . . . . . . . . . . . . . . . . . . . . . . . . . . . . . . . . . . . . . . . . . 213-852-1640
  8321 Beverly Blvd.
  Los Angeles, CA 90048
  Type: Television Production
  Gary Necessary . . . . . . . . . . . . . . . . . . . . . . . . . . . . . . . . . . . . . . . Exec. in Charge of Prod.
  Nathan Golden . . . . . . . . . . . . . . . . . . . . . . . . . . . . . . . . . . . . . . . . . . . . . . . . . . Accountant

**SCHOLASTIC PRODS.** . . . . . . . . . . . . . . . . . . . . . . . . . . . . . . . . . . . . . . . . . . . . . . **212-529-6300**
  Fax:. . . . . . . . . . . . . . . . . . . . . . . . . . . . . . . . . . . . . . . . . . . . . . . . . . . . . . . . . . . . . . . . . 212-228-7546
  740 Broadway
  New York, NY 10003
  Type: Television Production
  Deborah Forte . . . . . . . . . . . . . . . . . . . . . . . . . . . . . . . . . . . . . . . . Exec. Vice President
  Jane Startz . . . . . . . . . . . . . . . . . . . . . . . . . . . . . . . . . . . . . . . . . . . Exec. Vice President
  *Robin Grey . . . . . . . . . . . . . . . . . . . . . . . . . . . . . . . . . . . . . . VP, Business/Legal Affairs

**SCHUSTER & ASSOCIATES** . . . . . . . . . . . . . . . . . . . . . . . . . . . . . . . . . . . . . . . . **310-596-5900**
  Fax:. . . . . . . . . . . . . . . . . . . . . . . . . . . . . . . . . . . . . . . . . . . . . . . . . . . . . . . . . . . . . . . . . 310-431-4540
  8327 N. Marina Pacifica
  Long Beach, CA 90803
  **Motion Pictures, Television, Music
  Type: Entertainment Law + Business Management
  Jeremy G. Schuster . . . . . . . . . . . . . . . . . . . . . . . . . . . . . . . . . . . . . . . . . . . . Sr. Counsel

**\*SCRIPPS HOWARD PRODUCTIONS** . . . . . . . . . . . . . . . . . . . . . . . . . . . . . . . . . **310-264-3000**
  Fax:. . . . . . . . . . . . . . . . . . . . . . . . . . . . . . . . . . . . . . . . . . . . . . . . . . . . . . . . . . . . . . . . . 310-264-3111
  2425 Olympic Blvd., Ste. 5005
  Santa Monica, CA 90404
  Type: Television Production
  *David Percelay . . . . . . . . . . . . . . . . . . . . . . . . . . . . . . . . . . . . . . . . . . . . President-CEO
  *Allan Chalfin. . . . . . . . . . . . . . . . . . . . . . . . . . . . . . . . . . VP, Finance/Admin./Prod.
  *Debbie Stasson . . . . . . . . . . . . . . . . . . . . . . . . . . . . . . . . . . . . . . . . . Business Affairs

**\*SECOND CITY ENTERTAINMENT, INC., THE** . . . . . . . . . . . . . . . . . . . . . . . . . . **312-664-4032**
  Fax:. . . . . . . . . . . . . . . . . . . . . . . . . . . . . . . . . . . . . . . . . . . . . . . . . . . . . . . . . . . . . . . . . 312-664-9837
  1616 N. Wells St.
  Chicago, IL 60614
  Type: Television Production
  *Andrew Alexander . . . . . . . . . . . . . . . . . . . . . . . . . . . . . . . . . . . . . . . . . . . . President
  *Will Graber . . . . . . . . . . . . . . . . . . . . . . . . . . . . . . . . . . . . . . . . . . . . . . VP, Finance

**SENTINEL TELEVISION CORPORATION** . . . . . . . . . . . . . . . . . . . . . . . . . . . . . . **310-820-7767**
  Fax:. . . . . . . . . . . . . . . . . . . . . . . . . . . . . . . . . . . . . . . . . . . . . . . . . . . . . . . . . . . . . . . . . 310-442-9850
  12304 Santa Monica Blvd., Ste. 100
  Los Angeles, CA 90025
  Type: Motion Picture Production + Television Production + Video Production + Distribution
  *Michael W. Leighton . . . . . . . . . . . . . . . . . . . . . . . . . . . . . . . . . . . . . President-CEO
  *James R. Zatolokin . . . . . . . . . . . . . . . . . . . . . . . . . . . . . . . . . Exec. Vice President
  *Dr. Kyo R. Jhin. . . . . . . . . . . . . . . . . . . . . . . . . . . . . . . . . . VP, Asian-American Affairs
  *Maj. Gen. John K. Singlaub, USA (Ret.) . . . . . . . . . . . . . . . . . . . . . VP, Wash. Affairs
  *William J. Kushner . . . . . . . . . . . . . . . . . . . . . . District Representative - Network Affairs

**SHANE CO., A** . . . . . . . . . . . . . . . . . . . . . . . . . . . . . . . . . . . . . . . . . . . . . . . . . . . **310-456-5655**
  21355 Pacific Coast Hwy., Ste. 201
  Malibu, CA 90265
  Type: Television Production
  Joan Conrad Erwin. . . . . . . . . . . . . . . . . . . . . . . . . . . . . . . . . Chief Executive Officer

**SHAPIRO ENT. INC., RICHARD & ESTHER**.............................310-271-2202
   Fax:.............................................................310-271-8990
   335 N. Maple Dr., Ste. 245
   Beverly Hills, CA 90210-3867
   Type:  Motion Picture Production
   Richard Shapiro ..........................................Chairman
   Esther Shapiro ......................................President-CEO
   M. Jack Mayesh .............................Chief Operating Officer

**SHOWTIME NETWORKS INC.**.......................................818-505-7700
   Fax:.............................................................818-505-7773
   10 Universal City Plaza, 31st Fl.
   Universal City, CA 91608-1097
   Type:  Television Production
   *Jerry Cooper .............Sr. VP,Chief Financial Officer (NY) (212-708-1326)
   Nora Ryan ..........................Exec. VP, Business Development
   Jeff Silberman ...............Sr. VP, New Business Dev. (818-505-7736)
   *Cathryn Green........................... VP, Brand Development
   Roy Langbord ..........VP, Business Affairs/Brand Devl. (212-708-1454)

**SIDLEY & AUSTIN**...............................................213-896-6000
   Fax:.............................................................213-896-6600
   555 W. 5th St.
   Los Angeles, CA 90013
   Type:  Production Financing + Production Co-Financing
   Gary Cohen ...................................................Partner
   Moshe J. Kupietzky ...........................................Partner

**SINCLAIR, TENENBAUM, OLESIUK & CO., INC.**......................310-285-6222
   9348 Civic Center Dr., Ste. 200
   Beverly Hills, CA 90210
   Type:  Entertainment Law
   Nigel Sinclair .................................................Partner
   Irwin Tenenbaum...............................................Partner
   *Walter Olesiuk .................................................Partner
   *Craig Emanuel..................................................Partner
   *David Freedman ...............................................Partner
   *Nigel Pearson ................................................Partner

**SINGER LEWAK GREENBAUM & GOLDSTEIN CPAS & MGMT CONSULT**........310-477-3924
   Fax:.............................................................310-478-6070
   10960 Wilshire Blvd., Ste. 1100
   Los Angeles, CA 90024-3783
   **Production Accounting
   Type:  Business Management
   Norman L. Greenbaum ....................... Certified Public Accountant
   Janice D. McKenna ........................ Certified Public Accountant

**SINGER PRODS. INC., JOSEPH M.**.................................310-551-2277
   Fax:.............................................................310-556-3760
   2121 Ave. of the Stars, Ste. 2900
   Los Angeles, CA 90067
   Type:  Motion Picture Production
   Joseph M. Singer .................................Chairman-Producer
   Jeffrey Levy .......................Exec. VP, Business Affairs (NY)

**\*SINGLE SPARK PICTURES**......................................310-315-4779
   Fax:.............................................................310-315-4773
   3000 W. Olympic Blvd. Ste. 2337
   Santa Monica, CA 90404
   Type: Motion Picture Production + Television Production + Video Production + Distribution + Production Financing + Production Co-Financing
   *Mark Mori.......................................................President
   *Thorpe Mori .............................................VP, Finance
   *Thea Boyanowsky...........................................Exec. Asst.

**SIPOS, THOMAS M.** .................................................... **310-458-6048**
    Fax: ................................................................ 310-458-6048
    P.O. Box 1903
    Santa Monica, CA 90406-1903
    **Motion Pictures, Television, Music
    Type:  Entertainment Law
    Thomas M. Sipos ............................................... Attorney

**SKADDEN, ARPS, SLATE, MEAGHER & FLOM** ............................... **213-687-5000**
    Fax: ................................................................ 213-687-5600
    300 S. Grand Ave.
    Los Angeles, CA 90071
    Type:  Entertainment Law
    Frank Rothman. .................................................. Partner
    Jeff Valley ....................................................... Partner

**SKOURAS PICTS. INC.** .................................................. **310-285-5455**
    Fax: ................................................................ 310-285-5466
    335 N. Maple Dr., Ste. 248
    Beverly Hills, CA 90210
    Type:  Motion Picture Production + Video Production + Distribution
    Tom Skouras .................................................. President-CEO
    Jeff Holmes ................................................... Exec. VP-COO
    JoAnn Lawrence .............................................. VP, Finance & Admin.

**SLAFF, MOSK, & RUDMAN** ............................................... **310-275-5351**
    Fax: ................................................................ 310-273-8706
    9200 Sunset Blvd., Ste. 825
    Los Angeles, CA 90069
    Type:  Entertainment Law
    Valerie Flugge ................................................... Partner
    Norman Rudman ................................................. Partner
    Marc Stein ....................................................... Partner

**SLOANE, OWEN** ...................................................... **310-393-5345**
    Fax: ................................................................ 310-395-8782
    100 Wilshire Blvd., Ste. 2040
    Santa Monica, CA 90401-1116
    Type:  Entertainment Law
    Wofford Denius .................................................. Attorney
    Lindsey Feldman ................................................ Attorney
    Owen Sloane .................................................... Attorney

**SLOSS, LAW OFFICE P.C.** .............................................. **212-627-9898**
    Fax: ................................................................ 212-627-9498
    170 Fifth Ave., Ste. 800
    New York, NY 10010-5911
    Type:  Entertainment Law + Production Financing + Production Co-Financing
    John Sloss. ...................................................... Principal
    Jodi Peikoff ..................................................... Associate

**SMITH AFFILIATED CAPITAL CORP.** ..................................... **212-644-9440**
    Fax: ................................................................ 212-644-1979
    880 Third Ave.
    New York, NY 10022
    Type:  Financial Consulting
    Robert G. Smith, Ph.D. .......................................... President
    Robert G. Smith, III ............................................. Exec. Vice President
    *Martin B. Tolep. ............................................... Sr. Vice President
    John A. Jenney ................................................... Vice President
    John F. Pandolfino ............................................... Vice President

**SMITH BARNEY INC.** . . . . . . . . . . . . . . . . . . . . . . . . . . . . . . . . . . . . **516-791-4300/310-551-9400**
   1465 Broadway
   Hewlett, NY 11567
   **ALSO: 1875 Century Pk. E., #1950, LA 90067
   Type:  Financial Consulting
   Anthony Calabrese . . . . . . . . . . . . . . . . . . . . . . . . . . . . Financial Consultant (LA) (310-551-9457)
   Barry Ringelheim . . . . . . . . . . . . . . . . . . . . . . . . . . . . . . . . . . . . . . . . . Financial Consultant

**SMITH, BARAB, SIMPSON** . . . . . . . . . . . . . . . . . . . . . . . . . . . . . . . . . . . . **310-859-6644**
   Fax: . . . . . . . . . . . . . . . . . . . . . . . . . . . . . . . . . . . . . . . . . . . . . . . . . . . . 310-859-6650
   9606 Santa Monica Blvd., 3rd Fl.
   Beverly Hills, CA 90210
   Type:  Entertainment Law
   Martin J. Barab . . . . . . . . . . . . . . . . . . . . . . . . . . . . . . . . . . . . . . . . . . . . . Partner
   Robert A. Klein . . . . . . . . . . . . . . . . . . . . . . . . . . . . . . . . . . . . . . . . . . . . . Attorney

**SOJOURN ENTERTAINMENT** . . . . . . . . . . . . . . . . . . . . . . . . . . . . . . . . . . **310-446-4414**
   Fax: . . . . . . . . . . . . . . . . . . . . . . . . . . . . . . . . . . . . . . . . . . . . . . . . . . . . 310-446-4412
   1916 Pelham Ave. #100
   Los Angeles, CA 90025
   Type:  Motion Picture Production + Video Production
   *Jack Teetor . . . . . . . . . . . . . . . . . . . . . . . . . . . . . . . . . . . . . . . . . . . . . . . President
   Cary Fitchey . . . . . . . . . . . . . . . . . . . . . . . . . . . . . . . . . . . . Chief Operating Officer
   Craig Keshishian . . . . . . . . . . . . . . . . . . . . . . . . . . . . . . . . VP, Business Affairs
   *Guy Morris . . . . . . . . . . . . . . . . . . . . . . . . . . . . . . . . . . . VP, Finance & Operations

**SOMMER & BEAR** . . . . . . . . . . . . . . . . . . . . . . . . . . . . . . . . . . . . . . . . . . **310-858-4989**
   Fax: . . . . . . . . . . . . . . . . . . . . . . . . . . . . . . . . . . . . . . . . . . . . . . . . . . . . 310-858-0775
   9777 Wilshire Blvd., Ste. 512
   Beverly Hills, CA 90212
   **Writers - Directors - Producers - Packaging
   Type:  Entertainment Law
   *Jeffrey Bear . . . . . . . . . . . . . . . . . . . . . . . . . . . . . . . . . . . . . . . . . . . . . . Partner
   *Paul Sommer . . . . . . . . . . . . . . . . . . . . . . . . . . . . . . . . . . . . . . . . . . . . . . Partner

**SONY PICTURES ENTERTAINMENT** . . . . . . . . . . . . . . . . . . . . . . . . . . . . **310-280-8000**
   10202 W. Washington Blvd.
   Culver City, CA 90232-3195
   Type:  Motion Picture Production + Television Production
   Alan J. Levine . . . . . . . . . . . . . . . . . . . . . . . . . . . . . . . . . . . . . . . . President-COO
   Kenneth Lemberger . . . . . . . . . . . . . . . . . . . . . . . . . . . . . . . Exec. Vice President
   *Dennis Miller . . . . . . . . . . . . . . . . . . . . . . . . . . . . . . . . . . . Exec. Vice President
   *Ted Howells, Jr. . . . . . . . . . . . . . . . . . . . . . . . . . . . . . . . . . . . . . . Sr. VP/CFO
   Ronald Jacobi . . . . . . . . . . . . . . . . . . . . . . . . . . . . . . . Sr. VP & General Counsel
   *Lucy Wander-Perna . . . . . . . . . . . . . . . . . . . . . . . . . . . . . . . . Sr. Vice President
   Kenneth Willaims . . . . . . . . . . . . . . . . . . . . . . . . . . . . . . . . . . Sr. Vice President
   *Susan Jameson . . . . . . . . . . . . . . . . . . . . . . . . . . . . . . . . . . . . . Vice President
   *Joe Kraft . . . . . . . . . . . . . . . . . . . . . . . . . . . . . . . . . . . . . . . . . VP/Treasurer
   *Robert M. Moses . . . . . . . . . . . . . . . . . . . . . . . . . . . . . . . . . . . . . Vice President
   *Beth Berke . . . . . . . . . . . . . . . . . . . . . . . . . . . . . . . . . . . . . . . . Asst. Secretary
   *Robert Eichorn . . . . . . . . . . . . . . . . . . . . . . . . . . . . . . . . . . . . . Asst. Secretary
   *Jared Jussim . . . . . . . . . . . . . . . . . . . . . . . . . . . . . . . . . . . . . . . Asst. Secretary

**SONY TELEVISION ENTERTAINMENT** . . . . . . . . . . . . . . . . . . . . . . . . . . . **310-280-8000**
   Fax: . . . . . . . . . . . . . . . . . . . . . . . . . . . . . . . . . . 310-280-1352/310-280-1244
   10202 W. Washington Blvd.
   Culver City, CA 90232
   Type:  Television Production
   *Mel Harris . . . . . . . . . . . . . . . . . . . . . . . . . . . . . . . . . . . . . . . . . . . President
   *Greg Boone . . . . . . . . . . . . . . . . . . . . . . . . . . . . . . . . . . Sr. VP, Legal Affairs
   *Mary O'Hare . . . . . . . . . . . . . . . . . . . . . . . . . . . . . . . . . . . Sr. Vice President
   *Joe Stevens . . . . . . . . . . . . . . . . . . . . . . . . . . . . . . . . . . . . . Sr. VP, Finance
   Mark Lebowitz . . . . . . . . . . . . . . . . . . . . . . . . . . . . . . . Vice President-Controller
   *Mitch McDiffett . . . . . . . . . . . . . . . . . . . . . . . . . . VP, Financial Planning and Analysis
   *Mike Viebrock . . . . . . . . . . . . . . . . . . . . . . . . . . . . VP, Legal & Business Affairs

**SPECTACOR FILMS** . . . . . . . . . . . . . . . . . . . . . . . . . . . . . . . . . . . . . . . . . . . . . . . . . **310-271-9990**
    Fax:. . . . . . . . . . . . . . . . . . . . . . . . . . . . . . . . . . . . . . . . . . . . . . . . . . . . . 310-247-0412
    9000 Sunset Blvd., Ste. 1550
    West Hollywood, CA 90069
    Type: Motion Picture Production
    David Newlon . . . . . . . . . . . . . . . . . . . . . . . . . . . . . . . . . . . . . . . . Exec. Vice President
    Dino Gioia . . . . . . . . . . . . . . . . . . . . . . . . . . . . . . . . . . . . . . . . . . . . . . . . Controller

**SPELLING ENTERTAINMENT GROUP INC.** . . . . . . . . . . . . . . . . . . . . . . . . . . . . . . **213-965-5729**
    Fax:. . . . . . . . . . . . . . . . . . . . . . . . . . . . . . . . . . . . . . . . . . . . . . . . . . . . . 213-965-5829
    5700 Wilshire Blvd., 5th Fl.
    Los Angeles, CA 90036-3696
    Type: Television Production + Motion Picture Production + Video Production + Distribution
    Steven R. Berrard. . . . . . . . . . . . . . . . . . . . . . . . . . . . . . . . . . . . . . President-CEO
    *Peter Bachmann . . . . . . . . . . . . . . . . . . . . . . . . . . . . . Exec. VP, Business Affairs
    *Thomas P. Carson . . . . . . . . . . . . . . . . . . . . . . . . . . . . . . . . Exec. VP, CFO
    *Kathy Coughlan . . . . . . . . . . . . . . . . . . . . . . . . . . . . Sr. VP-Corporate Controller

**SPELLING TELEVISION INC.** . . . . . . . . . . . . . . . . . . . . . . . . . . . . . . . . . . . . . . . . **213-965-5700**
    Fax:. . . . . . . . . . . . . . . . . . . . . . . . . . . . . . . . . . . . . . . . . . . . . . . . . . . . . 213-965-5895
    5700 Wilshire Blvd., 5th Fl.
    Los Angeles, CA 90036-3696
    Type: Motion Picture Production + Television Production
    Aaron Spelling . . . . . . . . . . . . . . . . . . . . . . . . . . . . . . Chairman of the Board-CEO
    E. Duke Vincent. . . . . . . . . . . . . . . . . . . . . . . . . . . . . . . . . . . . Vice Chairman
    Lawrence Lyttle . . . . . . . . . . . . . . . . . . . . . . . . . . . . . . . . . . . . . . President
    Ed Melocoton. . . . . . . . . . . . . . . . . . . . . . . . . . . . . . . . . . . . . . VP-Controller
    Barbara Rubin . . . . . . . . . . . . . . . . . . . . . . . . . . . . . . . . VP, Business Affairs
    Lougenia Patrick . . . . . . . . . . . . . . . . . . . . . . . . . . . Exec. Dir., Business Affairs

**SQUEAK PICTURES INC.** . . . . . . . . . . . . . . . . . . . . . . . . . . . . . . . . . . . . . . . . **818-980-0800**
    Fax:. . . . . . . . . . . . . . . . . . . . . . . . . . . . . . . . . . . . . . . . . . . . . . . . . . . . . 818-980-1640
    3753 Cahuenga Blvd. West
    Studio City, CA 91604
    Type: Video Production
    Pamela Tarr . . . . . . . . . . . . . . . . . . . . . . . . . . . . . . . . . . President-Exec. Prod.
    Timothy Fryman . . . . . . . . . . . . . . . . . . . . . . . . . . . Head, Finance/Business Affairs

**ST. CLARE ENTERTAINMENT** . . . . . . . . . . . . . . . . . . . . . . . . . . . . . . . . . . . . **818-777-7633**
    Fax:. . . . . . . . . . . . . . . . . . . . . . . . . . . . . . . . . . . . . . . . . . . . . . . . . . . . . 818-733-1437
    c/o Universal Studios
    100 Universal City Plaza
    Universal City, CA 91608
    Type: Television Production
    John Landis . . . . . . . . . . . . . . . . . . . . . . . . . . . . . . . . . . . . . . . . Chairman
    Robert K. Weiss. . . . . . . . . . . . . . . . . . . . . . . . . . . . . . . . . . . . . President
    Leslie Belzberg . . . . . . . . . . . . . . . . . . . . . . . . . . . . . . Chief Operating Officer

**STAENBERG, THE LAW OFFICES OF MARC R.** . . . . . . . . . . . . . . . . . . . . . . **310-829-1700**
    Fax:. . . . . . . . . . . . . . . . . . . . . . . . . . . . . . . . . . . . . . . . . . . . . . . . . . . . . 310-829-2148
    2530 Wilshire Blvd., 2nd Fl.
    Santa Monica, CA 90403
    **Motion Pictures, Television, Music
    Type: Entertainment Law
    Marc R. Staenberg . . . . . . . . . . . . . . . . . . . . . . . . . . . . . . . . . . . . . . Attorney

**STANBURY, FISHELMAN & LEVY.** . . . . . . . . . . . . . . . . . . . . . . . . . . . . . . . . . **310-278-1800**
    Fax:. . . . . . . . . . . . . . . . . . . . . . . . . . . . . . . . . . . . . . . . . . . . . . . . . . . . . 310-278-1802
    9200 Sunset Blvd., Penthouse 30
    Los Angeles, CA 90069-3607
    Type: Entertainment Law
    *Bruce C. Fishelman. . . . . . . . . . . . . . . . . . . . . . . . . . . . President & Partner
    Harold Levy . . . . . . . . . . . . . . . . . . . . . . . . . . . . . . . . . . . . . . . . . Partner
    *George Stanbury . . . . . . . . . . . . . . . . . . . . . . . . . . . . . . . . . . . . . . Partner
    *Tom Kerr. . . . . . . . . . . . . . . . . . . . . . . . . . . . . . . . . . . . . . . . . . . Associate

**STEINHART, TERRAN T.** . . . . . . . . . . . . . . . . . . . . . . . . . . . . . . . . . . . . **213-933-8263**
    Fax: . . . . . . . . . . . . . . . . . . . . . . . . . . . . . . . . . . . . . . . . . . . . . . 213-933-2391
    431 S. Fairfax Ave., 4th Fl.
    Los Angeles, CA 90036-3123
    Type: Entertainment Law
    Terran T. Steinhart . . . . . . . . . . . . . . . . . . . . . . . . . . . . . . . . . . . . . Attorney

**STEINHAUER, PHYLLIS A.** . . . . . . . . . . . . . . . . . . . . . . . . . . . . . . . **310-318-8461**
    Fax: . . . . . . . . . . . . . . . . . . . . . . . . . . . . . . . . . . . . . . . . . . . . . . 310-318-3249
    128 Eighth St.
    Manhattan Beach, CA 90266
    \*\*Copyright, trademark and tax law.
    Type: Entertainment Law
    Phyllis Steinhauer . . . . . . . . . . . . . . . . . . . . . . . . . . . . . . . . . . . . . Attorney

**STEPHENS & ASSOCIATES** . . . . . . . . . . . . . . . . . . . . . . . . . . . **310-395-6621/310-841-0340**
    Fax: . . . . . . . . . . . . . . . . . . . . . . . . . . . . . . . . . . . . 310-395-6621/310-841-0342
    1341 Ocean Ave., Ste. 293
    Santa Monica, CA 90401
    \*\*ALSO: 433 N. Camden Dr., PH Bev. Hills, CA 90210
    Type: Financial Consulting + Production Financing + Production Co-Financing
    \*Theresa Stephens . . . . . . . . . . . . . . . . . . . . . . . . . . . . . . . . . . . . . Partner
    David Dizenfeld . . . . . . . . . . . . . . . . . . . . . . . . . . Business Affairs-Prod. Exec.

**STEPHENS INC.** . . . . . . . . . . . . . . . . . . . . . . . . . . . . . . . . . . . . . . . . **501-374-4361**
    Fax: . . . . . . . . . . . . . . . . . . . . . . . . . . . . . . . . . . . . . . . . . . . . . . 501-377-2666
    111 Center St.
    Little Rock, AK 72201
    Type: Banking
    \*Warren A. Stephens . . . . . . . . . . . . . . . . . . . . . . . . . . . . . . . . . President
    \*David Knight . . . . . . . . . . . . . . . . . . . . . . . . . . . . . . . . Sr. Vice President
    \*Mark Doramus . . . . . . . . . . . . . . . . . . . . . . . . . . . . . . . . . Vice President

**STEWART & HARRIS.** . . . . . . . . . . . . . . . . . . . . . . . . . . . . . . . . . . . **818-577-4100**
    Fax: . . . . . . . . . . . . . . . . . . . . . . . . . . . . . . . . . . . . . . . . . . . . . . 818-577-5105
    150 E. Colorado Blvd., Ste. 216
    Pasadena, CA 91105
    \*\*Motion Pictures, Television
    Type: Entertainment Law
    Garry D. Stewart . . . . . . . . . . . . . . . . . . . . . . . . . . . . . . . . . . . Sr. Partner

**STILETTO ENTERTAINMENT** . . . . . . . . . . . . . . . . . . . . . . . . . . . **310-306-4490**
    Fax: . . . . . . . . . . . . . . . . . . . . . . . . . . . . . . . . . . . . . . . . . . . . . . 310-306-5350
    5443 Beethoven St.
    Los Angeles, CA 90066
    \*\*Music
    Type: Business Management
    Garry Kief . . . . . . . . . . . . . . . . . . . . . . . . . . . . . . . . . . . . . . . . . . . Owner
    Edna Collison . . . . . . . . . . . . . . . . . . . . . . . . . . . . . . . . . . . . . . . Partner
    Steve Wax . . . . . . . . . . . . . . . . . . . . . . . . . . . . . . . . . . . . . . . . . . Partner

**STONE & ASOOCIATES** . . . . . . . . . . . . . . . . . . . . . . . . . . . . . . . . . **310-273-2905**
    Fax: . . . . . . . . . . . . . . . . . . . . . . . . . . . . . . . . . . . . . . . . . . . . . . 310-273-9059
    280 S. Beverly Dr., Ste. 513
    Beverly Hills, CA 90212
    Type: Business Management
    \*Behnam Heshejin . . . . . . . . . . . . . . . . . . . . . . . . . . . . . . . . . . . . Partner
    Ronald Stone . . . . . . . . . . . . . . . . . . . . . . . . . . . . . . . . . . . . . . . . Partner

© 1995 Hollywood Financial Directory No. 3
310-315-4815 or 800-815-0503 outside California

**STRAIGHTLEY FILMS** . . . . . . . . . . . . . . . . . . . . . . . . . . . . . . . . . . **714-636-4300**
   Fax:. . . . . . . . . . . . . . . . . . . . . . . . . . . . . . . . . . . . . . . . . . . 714-636-0309
   P.O. Box 1951
   Beverly Hills, CA 90213
   **Also: Music
   Type: Motion Picture Production + Television Production + Distribution + Production Financing
   John Levingston. . . . . . . . . . . . . . . . . . . . . . . . . . . . . . . . . . . . Chairman-CEO
   Joseph Benti . . . . . . . . . . . . . . . . . . . . . . . . . . . . . . . . . . VP, Creative Business

**SULLIVAN ENT.**. . . . . . . . . . . . . . . . . . . . . . . . . . **310-247-0166/416-921-7177**
   Fax:. . . . . . . . . . . . . . . . . . . . . . . . . . . . . . . . . . . . . . . . . . . 310-247-1945
   9465 Wilshire Blvd., Ste. 605
   Beverly Hills, CA 90212
   Type: Motion Picture Production
   Aldo De Felice . . . . . . . . . . . . . . . . . . . . . . . . . . . Legal/Business Affairs (Toronto)

***SUNBOW PRODS.** . . . . . . . . . . . . . . . . . . . . . . . . . . . . . . . . . . **212-886-4900**
   Fax:. . . . . . . . . . . . . . . . . . . . . . . . . . . . . . . . . . . . . . . . . . . 212-366-4242
   100 Fifth Ave., 3rd Floor
   New York, NY 10011-4340
   Type: Television Production
   *C.J. Kettler . . . . . . . . . . . . . . . . . . . . . . . . . . . . . . . . . . . . . . . President
   *N. Linsey Tully . . . . . . . . . . . . . . . . . . . . . . . . . . . . . . . . . . . . . . . CFO

**SUPNIK, PAUL D.**. . . . . . . . . . . . . . . . . . . . . . . . . . . . . . . . . . . **310-205-2050**
   Fax:. . . . . . . . . . . . . . . . . . . . . . . . . . . . . . . . . . . . . . . . . . . 310-205-2011
   433 N. Camden Dr., Ste. 1200
   Beverly Hills, CA 90210
   Type: Entertainment Law
   Paul D. Supnik . . . . . . . . . . . . . . . . . . . . . . . . . . . . . . . . . . . . . Attorney

**SUSSMAN, JEROME J.** . . . . . . . . . . . . . . . . . . . . . . . . . . . . . . . . . **310-788-2744**
   Fax:. . . . . . . . . . . . . . . . . . . . . . . . . . . . . . . . . . . . . . . . . . . 310-788-0103
   1875 Century Park East, Ste. 700
   Los Angeles, CA 90067
   Type: Entertainment Law
   Jerome J. Sussman . . . . . . . . . . . . . . . . . . . . . . . . . . . . . . . . . . . Attorney
   *James E. Blancarte . . . . . . . . . . . . . . . . . . . . . . . . . Attorney, Of Counsel
   *Jack R. Luellen . . . . . . . . . . . . . . . . . . . . . . . . . . . . Attorney, Of Counsel

**TNT/TURNER PICTURES INC.**. . . . . . . . . . . . . . . . . . . **310-551-6300/404-827-1500**
   Fax:. . . . . . . . . . . . . . . . . . . . . . . . . . . . . . . . . . . . . . . . . . . 310-551-6344
   1888 Century Park East, 14th Fl.
   Los Angeles, CA 90067
   **ALSO: 1050 Techwood Dr., Atlanta, GA 30318-5604
   Type: Television Production
   Roger Mayer . . . . . . . . . . . . . . . . . . . . . . . President-COO, Turner Entertainment Co.
   *Robert M. Osher . . . . . . . . . . . . . . . . . . . . . . Exec. VP, Turner Pictures Group
   Neal Baseman . . . . . . . . . . . . . . . . . . . Sr. VP, Business Affairs, Turner Pictures Inc.
   Susan O. Gross. . . . . . . . . . . . . . . . . . . . Sr. VP, Business Affairs, Turner Pictures Inc.
   *Ronni Coulter . . . . . . . . . . . . . . . . . . . . . . VP, Business Affairs, Turner Pictures Inc.
   Andre Carey. . . . . . . . . . . . . . . . . . . . Exec. Dir., Business Affairs, Turner Pictures Inc.
   *Jonathan Harris . . . . . . . . . . . . . . . . . . Exec. Dir., Business Affairs, Turner Pictures Inc

**TAFFNER ENTERTAINMENT LTD.** . . . . . . . . . . . . . . . . **213-937-1144/212-245-4680**
   Fax:. . . . . . . . . . . . . . . . . . . . . . . . . . . . . . . . 310-284-3176/212-315-1132
   1888 Century Park East, 19th Floor
   Los Angeles, CA 90067
   **ALSO: 31 W. 56th St., NY, NY 10019
   Type: Television Production + Distribution + Business Affairs + Legal Affairs
   *Don Taffner, Jr.. . . . . . . . . . . . . . . . . . . . . . . . . . . Exec. VP, CEO (NY & LA)
   *Jeff Cotugno . . . . . . . . . . . . . . . . . . . . . . . . . . . . . . . . . . CFO (NY)
   Emmet G. Lavery, Jr.. . . . . . . . . . . . . . . . . . . . . . . VP, Business Affairs (LA)
   *Meg Lewis. . . . . . . . . . . . . . . . . . . . . . . . . . . . . . VP, Legal Affairs (NY)

**TANNEN, KATHY L.**......................................................**818-501-7517**
   Fax:....................................................................818-501-2053
   P.O. Box 55004
   Sherman Oaks, CA 91413
   \*\*Develop. & prod. contracts - international distribution
   Type: Entertainment Law + Distribution + Business Affairs + Legal Affairs + Television Production
   Kathy L. Tannen ........................................................ Attorney

**TASHJIAN AND TASHJIAN** ............................................**310-207-2026**
   Fax:....................................................................310-207-1416
   11726 San Vicente Blvd., Ste. 650
   Los Angeles, CA 90049
   \*\*Immigration law for entertainers
   Type: Entertainment Law
   H. Richard Tashjian ..................................................... Attorney

**TELEPICTURES PRODS.**..................................................**818-972-0777**
   Fax:....................................................................818-972-0864
   3500 Riverside Dr., Ste. 1000
   Burbank, CA 91505
   Type: Television Production
   \*James Paratore........................................................President
   \*Joseph Reilly ................................................ VP, Business Affairs
   \*Alan Solomon ........................................................ Comptroller

**TELESCENE COMMUNICATIONS INC.** .........................**310-821-5353/514-737-5512**
   Fax:........................................................310-577-6727/514-737-7945
   13323 Washington Blvd., Ste. 205
   Los Angeles, CA 90066
   \*\*London: ph 71-384-1022 fax: 71-384-1246
   Type: Motion Picture Production + Television Production
   Robin Spry ................................................. President (Montreal)
   Paul Painter ......................................... Exec. VP-Sec.-Treas. (Montreal)
   \*Bruce Moccia ..................................... Sr. VP, USA Division (LA)

**TEMPLE, MARK S.**......................................................**310-444-8337**
   Fax:....................................................................310-444-8407
   1440 S. Sepulveda Blvd.
   Los Angeles, CA 90025
   \*\*Motion Pictures, Television
   Type: Entertainment Law + Business Affairs + Legal Affairs
   Mark S. Temple ........................................................ Attorney

**THIRD EYE TELEPICTURES**...............................................**818-222-4376**
   c/o Third Eye Plaza
   4354 Park Vicente
   Calabasas, CA 91302
   Type: Motion Picture Production + Television Production + Business Affairs + Legal Affairs
   \*Michael J. Herman .................................................. President/CEO
   Jeffrey S. Berger ........................................ Sr. Exec. VP- Production Counsel

**THOMPSON ORGANIZATION, LARRY** .....................................**310-288-0700**
   Fax:....................................................................310-288-0711
   335 N. Maple Dr., Ste. 361
   Beverly Hills, CA 90210
   Type: Motion Picture Production
   Larry Thompson........................................................Chairman-CEO

**TIFFANY & ASSOCIATES, CATHERINE** ....................................**310-397-0043**
   Fax:....................................................................310-397-6404
   253-A 26th St., Ste. 308
   Santa Monica, CA 90402
   \*\*Financial mgr. for directors, actors, producers.
   Type: Business Management
   Catherine Tiffany ................................................. Business Manager

**TISCH CO., THE STEVE** . . . . . . . . . . . . . . . . . . . . . . . . . . . . . . . . . . . . . . . . . . **310-838-2500**
    Fax:. . . . . . . . . . . . . . . . . . . . . . . . . . . . . . . . . . . . . . . . . . . . . . . . . . . 310-204-2713
    3815 Hughes Ave.
    Culver City, CA 90232-2715
    Type: Motion Picture Production + Television Production
    Steve Tisch. . . . . . . . . . . . . . . . . . . . . . . . . . . . . . . . . . . . . . . . . . . . . . . . . President
    Wendy Kopeikin . . . . . . . . . . . . . . . . . . . . . . . . . . . . . . . . . . . . . . . . . . . . Controller
    *Andrea Schlupp. . . . . . . . . . . . . . . . . . . . . . . . . . . . . . . . . . . . . . Asst. to Steve Tisch

**\*TORONTO/ONTARIO FILM DEVELOPMENT CORP.** . . . . . . . . . . . . . . . . . . . . . . **213-960-4787**
    Fax:. . . . . . . . . . . . . . . . . . . . . . . . . . . . . . . . . . . . . . . . . . . . . . . . . . . 213-960-4786
    650 N. Bronson Ave., B-130
    Los Angeles, CA 90004
    Type: Motion Picture Production + Television Production + Guild/Union + Production Co-Financing
    *Alison Emilio . . . . . . . . . . . . . . . . . . . . . . . . . . . . . . . . . . . . . . . . . Marketing Agent

**\*TRANS PACIFIC FILMS.** . . . . . . . . . . . . . . . . . . . . . . . . . . . . . . . . . . . . . . . . . **310-777-3521**
    Fax:. . . . . . . . . . . . . . . . . . . . . . . . . . . . . . . . . . . . . . . . . . . . . . . . . . . 310-858-0410
    9348 Civic Center Drive, Ste. 200
    Beverly Hills, CA 90210
    Type: Motion Picture Production
    *Patrick Murray . . . . . . . . . . . . . . . . . . . . . . . . . . . . . . . . . . . . . . . . . Exec. VP-COO

**TRANSATLANTIC ENTERPRISES (TAE) PRODUCTIONS.** . . . . . . . . . . . . . . . . . . . . . **310-451-0011**
    Fax:. . . . . . . . . . . . . . . . . . . . . . . . . . . . . . . . . . . . . . . . . . . . . . . . . . . 310-451-6011
    201 Wilshire Blvd., Atrium 17
    Santa Monica, CA 90401
    Type: Motion Picture Production + Television Production + Distribution
    Robert D. Kline . . . . . . . . . . . . . . . . . . . . . . . . . . . . . . . . . . . . . . . . President-CEO
    *Michael Schneider. . . . . . . . . . . . . . . . . . . . . . . . . . . . . . . . . . . . . . . . . . . . CFO

**TRAVELERS INSURANCE CO.** . . . . . . . . . . . . . . . . . . . . . . . . . . . . . . . . . . . . . . . **203-277-5952**
    Fax:. . . . . . . . . . . . . . . . . . . . . . . . . . . . . . . . . . . . . . . . . . . . . . . . . . . 203-954-4755
    c/o Securities Dept. 9PB
    One Tower Square
    Hartford, CT 06183-2030
    Type: General Insurance
    Teresa M. Torrey . . . . . . . . . . . . . . . . . . . . . . . . . . . . . . . . . . . . Second Vice President
    Pamela D. Westmoreland. . . . . . . . . . . . . . . . . . . . . . . . . . . . . . . . Investment Officer

**\*TRAVELERS INSURANCE CO.- INVESTMENT GROUP (NY)** . . . . . . . . . . . . . . . . . . **212-816-3184**
    Fax:. . . . . . . . . . . . . . . . . . . . . . . . . . . . . . . . . . . . . . . . . . . . . . . . . . . 212-816-3320
    388 Greenwich St.
    New York, NY 10013
    Type: General Insurance

**TRISTAR PICTURES** . . . . . . . . . . . . . . . . . . . . . . . . . . . . . . . . . . . . . . . . . . . . **310-280-7700**
    Fax:. . . . . . . . . . . . . . . . . . . . . . . . . . . . . . . . . . . . . . . . . . . . . . . . . . . 310-280-1569
    c/o TriStar Building
    10202 W. Washington Blvd.
    Culver City, CA 90232-3195
    Type: Motion Picture Production
    Marc Platt. . . . . . . . . . . . . . . . . . . . . . . . . . . . . . . . . . . . . . . . . . . . . . President
    *Liz Aschenbrenner . . . . . . . . . . . . . . . . . . . . . . . . . . . . . . Exec. VP, Legal Affairs
    Robert Geary . . . . . . . . . . . . . . . . . . . . . . . . . . . . . . . . Exec. VP, Business Affairs
    Gary Hirsch . . . . . . . . . . . . . . . . . . . . . . . . . . . . . . . . . . Sr. VP, Business Affairs
    *John S. Levy . . . . . . . . . . . . . . . . . . . . . . . . . . . . . . . . . . Sr. VP, Business Affairs
    *Paul Smith. . . . . . . . . . . . . . . . . . . . . . . . . . Sr. VP, Operations & Business Affairs
    *Luis Allen . . . . . . . . . . . . . . . . . . . . . . . . . . . . . . . . . . . . . . . VP, Legal Affairs
    Cassandra Barbour. . . . . . . . . . . . . . . . . . . . . . . . . . . . . . VP, Legal Administration
    Jon Gibson . . . . . . . . . . . . . . . . . . . . . . . . . . . . . . . . . . . . . VP, Business Affairs
    Mark Horowitz. . . . . . . . . . . . . . . . . . . . . . . . . . . . . . . VP, Business Affairs Admin.
    *Andrea Levitt . . . . . . . . . . . . . . . . . . . . . . . . . . . . . . . . . . . . . VP, Legal Affairs

**TRISTAR TV** . . . . . . . . . . . . . . . . . . . . . . . . . . . . . . . . . . . . . . . . . . . . **310-202-1234**
   Fax:. . . . . . . . . . . . . . . . . . . . . . . . . . . . . . . . . . . . . . . . . . 310-202-4922
   9336 W. Washington Blvd.
   Culver City, CA 90232
   Type:  Television Production
   Sandra Stern . . . . . . . . . . . . . . . . . . . . . . . . . . . . . . . . . Exec. VP, Business Affairs
   Mary O'Hare . . . . . . . . . . . . . . . . . . . . . . . . . . . . Sr. VP, Legal Affairs (310-280-7024)
   Bob Chasin. . . . . . . . . . . . . . . . . . . . . . . . . . . . . . . . . . . . . VP, Business Affairs
   Clay Lorinsky. . . . . . . . . . . . . . . . . . . . . . . . . . . . . . . . . . VP, Business Affairs

**TRIMARK HOLDINGS INC.** . . . . . . . . . . . . . . . . . . . . . . . . . . . . . . . . . . **310-314-2000**
   Fax:. . . . . . . . . . . . . . . . . . . . . . . . . . . . . . . . . . . . . . . . . . 310-399-8022
   2644 30th St., 2nd Fl.
   Santa Monica, CA 90405
   Type:  Motion Picture Production + Distribution
   Mark Amin. . . . . . . . . . . . . . . . . . . . . . . . . . . . . . . . . . . . . . . . . . . Chairman
   James Keegan. . . . . . . . . . . . . . . . . . . . . . . . . . . . . . . . . . . . . . Sr. VP-CFO
   *Wescott Guarino . . . . . . . . . . . . . . . . . . . . . . . . . . . . . . . . . . . . . Controller
   Bruce Eisen . . . . . . . . . . . . . . . . . . . . . . . . . . . . . Dir., Legal/Business Affairs

**TRIPLE-7 ENTERTAINMENT** . . . . . . . . . . . . . . . . . . . . . . . . **619-244-7557/818-985-0207**
   Fax:. . . . . . . . . . . . . . . . . . . . . . . . . . . . . . . . . . . . . . . . . . 619-244-7666
   11812 Moorpark St., Unit F
   Studio City, CA 91604
   Type:  Motion Picture Production + Television Production
   *Dian Eaton. . . . . . . . . . . . . . . . . . . . . . . . . . . . . . . . . . . . . . . . President
   James Banks, Esq. . . . . . . . . . . . . . . . . . . . . . . . . . VP, Business/Legal Affairs

**\*TRIVISION PICTURES INC.** . . . . . . . . . . . . . . . . . . . . . . . . . **213-655-5055/310-264-6565**
   Fax:. . . . . . . . . . . . . . . . . . . . . . . . . . . . . . . . . . . . . . . . . . 213-655-5158
   222A S. Tower Dr.
   Beverly Hills, CA 90211
   Type:  Motion Picture Production + Television Production
   *Alexander Tabrizi . . . . . . . . . . . . . . . . . . . . . . . . . . . . . . . . . . . Chairman
   *Alan Roberts . . . . . . . . . . . . . . . . . . . . . . . . . . . . . . . . . . . . . President
   *George Hernandez . . . . . . . . . . . . . . . . . . . . . . . . . . . . . VP, Business Affairs

**\*TROMA INC.** . . . . . . . . . . . . . . . . . . . . . . . . . . . . . . . . . . **212-757-4555/213-960-4012**
   Fax:. . . . . . . . . . . . . . . . . . . . . . . . . . . . . . . . 212-399-9885/213-960-4013
   733 9th Ave.
   New York, NY 10019
   **ALSO: 650 N. Bronson, #103, LA, CA 90004
   Type:  Motion Picture Production
   *Lloyd Kaufman. . . . . . . . . . . . . . . . . . . . . . . . . . . . . . . . . . . . . President
   *Michael Herz. . . . . . . . . . . . . . . . . . . . . . . . . . . . . . . . . . Vice President
   *Kim Bieber . . . . . . . . . . . . . . . . . . . . . . . . . . . . Dir., Los Angeles Operations

**TROUBLESHOOTERS, INC.** . . . . . . . . . . . . . . . . . . . . . . . . . . . . . . . . **310-451-8747**
   Fax:. . . . . . . . . . . . . . . . . . . . . . . . . . . . . . . . . . . . . . . . . . 310-458-7317
   1640 5th St., Ste. 106
   Santa Monica, CA 90401
   **Actors - Producers
   Type:  Business Management
   Arlyne Medann . . . . . . . . . . . . . . . . . . . . . . . . . . . . . . . . . . . . . President
   Ruth Staub . . . . . . . . . . . . . . . . . . . . . . . . . . . . . . . . . . . . Vice President

**TRUMAN VAN DYKE CO.** . . . . . . . . . . . . . . . . . . . . . . . . . . . . . . . . . . **213-462-3300**
   6255 Sunset Blvd., Ste. 1401
   Hollywood, CA 90028
   Type:  General Insurance
   Truman Van Dyke . . . . . . . . . . . . . . . . . . . . . . . . . . . . . . . President-Owner
   Rose Van Dyke . . . . . . . . . . . . . . . . . . . . . . . . . . . . Chief Financial Officer

**\*TULCHIN & ASSOCIATES, HARRIS** .......................................... **310-914-7979**
    Fax:................................................................. 310-914-7927
    11377 W. Olympic Blvd., 2nd Floor
    Los Angeles, CA 90064
    Type:  Entertainment Law + Financial Consulting + Production Co-Financing + Business Affairs + Legal
Affairs
    \*Harris E. Tulchin, Esq. .......................................... Owner
    \*David Bargman, Esq. .......................................... Of Counsel
    \*Jean-Christophe Barjon. .......................................... Of Counsel
    \*Jean-Francois Joffre ............................................. Of Counsel
    \*Lawrence J. Langs. .............................................. Of Counsel
    \*Silvio Tonazzi, Esq. ............................................. Of Counsel

**TURNER ACCOUNTANCY CORP.** ............................................ **310-273-4260**
    Fax:................................................................. 310-273-1869
    9200 Sunset Blvd., Ste. 701
    Los Angeles, CA 90069
    \*\*All areas
    Type:  Business Management
    Ralph Turner ..................................................... President

**TURNER BROADCASTING SYSTEM** ......................................... **404-827-1717**
    1 CNN Center, P.O. Box 105366
    Atlanta, GA 30348
    Type:  Television Production
    Wayne H. Pace ............................................. VP, Finance-CFO
    Carla LaMorta ............................................. Dir., Financial Systems

**TURNER ORIGINAL PRODUCTIONS** ....................................... **404-827-1700**
    Fax:........................................................ 404-885-4433/404-885-4188
    1050 Techwood Dr. NW
    Atlanta, GA 30318
    Type:  Television Production + Distribution
    Marshall Orson......................................... VP, Business Affairs
    \*Lee Rivera ........................................... Legal (404-827-4945)

**TURNER, LAWRENCE J.** ..................................................... **310-273-4858**
    Fax:................................................................. 310-273-1869
    9200 Sunset Blvd., Ste. 701
    Los Angeles, CA 90069
    \*\*All areas
    Type:  Entertainment Law + Business Management
    \*Lawrence J. Turner ....................................... Attorney/CPA

**TWENTIETH CENTURY FOX FILM CORP.** ................................... **310-369-1000**
    10201 W. Pico Blvd.
    Los Angeles, CA 90035
    Type:  Motion Picture Production
    \*Steven Bersch ..................................... Exec. VP, Business Affairs
    \*Robert Cohen ..................................... Exec. VP, Legal Affairs
    Lyman Gronemeyer.............................. Exec. VP, Legal & General Counsel
    Michael Doodan.......................... Sr. VP, Legal Affairs-Asst. Gen. Counsel
    \*Jay Dougherty ............................... Sr. VP, Legal Affairs - Production
    Daniel Ferleger................................ Sr. VP, Business Affairs
    Mark H. Resnick ............................ Sr. VP, Business Affairs
    \*Peter Cyffka ..................................... VP & Controller
    Joseph M. De Marco ......................... VP, Business Affairs
    \*Joan Hansen ................................... VP, Legal Affairs
    \*Steven Pena..................................... VP, Legal Affairs
    \*Victoria Rossellini. ........................... VP, Legal Affairs
    \*Sandra K. Smokler ........................... VP, Legal Affairs
    \*Greg Sneed ................................ VP, Finance & Administration
    \*David Stern ..................................... VP, Legal Affairs

**TWENTIETH CENTURY FOX TELEVISION** .................................... **310-369-1000**
   Fax: ........................................................ 310-369-1872 (legal)
   10201 W. Pico Blvd.
   Los Angeles, CA 90035
   **fax: 310-369-4088 (business)
   Type: Television Production + Business Affairs + Legal Affairs
   Charlie Goldstein ........................................ Exec. VP, Prod. & Finance
   Gary Newman ........................................ Exec. VP, Business/Legal Affairs
   *Robert Barron ................................................. Sr. VP, Finance
   Kimberly Brightman ............................................... VP, Finance
   Kelly Cline ................................................ VP, Legal Affairs
   David M. Robinson ...................................... VP, Business Affairs
   Michelle Lautanen ................................ Exec. Dir., Business Affairs
   Gordon E. Wood ................................. Exec. Dir., Business Affairs

**TWENTIETH TV** .................................................... **310-369-3924**
   Fax: ................................................................ 310-369-3899
   2121 Ave. of the Stars
   Los Angeles, CA 90067
   Type: Television Production
   Vance S. Van Petten ........................... Executive VP, Business/Legal Affairs
   Benson H. Begun ........................... VP, Business Affairs, Intl. TV
   *Eric Jacobson .................................. VP, Business/Legal Affairs
   *Sandra Ortiz ................................... VP, Business/Legal Affairs
   *Hubert T. Smith, Jr. ................... Counsel, Business/Legal Affairs
   *Andrew Thau ......................... Counsel, Business/Legal Affairs
   Marisa Fermin .......................... Dir., Business/Legal Affairs

**U.S. FILM CORP.** ................................................. **310-475-4547**
   Fax: ................................................................ 310-475-3797
   2029 Century Park East, Ste. 1260
   Los Angeles, CA 90067-3088
   Type: Motion Picture Production + Distribution
   Robert M. Nau .................................................. President
   Kimberly Wick McClain ................................... Exec. VP-COO
   Beverly Graham ................................... Mgr., Customer Service

**USA NETWORK** ................................................... **212-408-9100**
   Fax: ................................................................ 212-408-8063
   1230 Avenue of the Americas
   New York, NY 10020
   Type: Television Production
   Kay Koplovitz .................................... Founder-President-CEO
   Stephen Brenner ............. Exec. Sr. VP, Bus. Affairs/Operations/Gen. Counsel
   Douglas Hamilton ................................... CFO-VP, Admin.
   Richard Lynn ....................................... VP, Business Affairs

**UNION BANK MEDIA GROUP** .................................... **213-236-5780**
   Fax: ................................................................ 213-236-5747
   445 S. Figueroa St., 15th Fl.
   Los Angeles, CA 90071-1602
   Type: Production Financing
   Craig Dougherty .............................. Sr. VP, Communications/Media

**\*UNISTAR ENTERTAINMENT** ................................... **213-462-7991**
   Fax: ................................................................ 213-462-3752
   6363 Sunset Blvd., Ste. 930C
   Los Angeles, CA 90028
   Type: Motion Picture Production + Television Production + Production Financing + Production Co-Financing
   *Gloria Bartholomew Morrison ....................................... CEO

**UNITED JERSEY BANK** . . . . . . . . . . . . . . . . . . . . . . . . . . . . . . . . . . . . . . . . . . **609-987-3497**
  Fax: . . . . . . . . . . . . . . . . . . . . . . . . . . . . . . . . . . . . . . . . . . . . . . . . . . . . 609-734-9125
  301 Carnegie Center
  Princeton, NJ 08540
  Type:  Banking
    Henry G. Kush Jr. . . . . . . . . . . . . . . . . . . . . . . . . . . . . . . . . . . . . . . Vice President
    Kenneth B. Stoddard . . . . . . . . . . . . . . . . . . . . . . . . . . . . . . . . . . . . Vice President

**\*UNITED PARAMOUNT NETWORK** . . . . . . . . . . . . . . . . . . . . . . . . . . . . . . . **213-956-5000**
  5555 Melrose Ave.
  Los Angeles, CA 90038-3197
  Type:  Motion Picture Production
    *Lucie Salhany . . . . . . . . . . . . . . . . . . . . . . . . . . . . . . . . . . . . . . President/CEO
    *Michael Sullivan . . . . . . . . . . . . . . . . . . . . . . . . . . . . . . President, Entertainment
    *Len Grossi . . . . . . . . . . . . . . . . . . . . . . . . . . . . . . . . . . . . . . Sr. Exec. VP
    *Valerie Cavanaugh . . . . . . . . . . . . . . . . . . . . . . . . . Sr. VP, Business/Legal Affairs
    *Barry Gordon . . . . . . . . . . . . . . . . . . . . . . . . . . . . . VP, Business/Legal Affairs

**\*UNITY COMMUNICATIONS, INC.** . . . . . . . . . . . . . . . . . . . . . . . . . . . . . . . . **213-463-7659**
  Fax: . . . . . . . . . . . . . . . . . . . . . . . . . . . . . . . . . . . . . . . . . . . . . . . . . . . . 213-878-6769
  2001 S. Barrington Ave., Ste. 210
  Los Angeles, CA 90025
  Type:  Motion Picture Production + Television Production + Production Co-Financing
    *Harry Bernsen . . . . . . . . . . . . . . . . . . . . . . . . . . . . . . . . . . . . . . . . President
    *Roger N. Golden . . . . . . . . . . . . . . . . . . . . . . . . . . . . . . . . VP, Business Affairs

**UNIVERSAL PICTURES** . . . . . . . . . . . . . . . . . . . . . . . . . . . . . . . . . . . . . . . . . . **818-777-1000**
  Fax: . . . . . . . . . . . . . . . . . . . . . . . . . . . . . . . . . . . . . . . . . . . . . . . . . . . . 818-777-0662
  100 Universal City Plaza
  Universal City, CA 91608-1085
  Type:  Motion Picture Production
    *Casey Silver . . . . . . . . . . . . . . . . . . . . . . . . . . . . . President, Universal Pictures
    *Hal Lieberman . . . . . . . . . . . . . . . . . . . . . . . . . . . . . . President, Production
    *Jon Gumpert . . . . . . . . . . . . . . . . . . . . . . . . . . . Exec. VP, Business/Legal Affairs
    *Jim Burk . . . . . . . . . . . . . . . . . . . . . . . . . . . Sr. VP, Finance, Mot. Pict. Group
    Jeffrey A. Korchek . . . . . . . . . . . . . . . . . . . . . . . . . . . . . Sr. VP, Business Affairs
    *Mary Ledding . . . . . . . . . . . . . . . . . . . . . . . . . . . . . . . Sr. VP, Legal Affairs
    *Gerald S. Barton . . . . . . . . . . . . . . . . . . . . . . . . . . Business Affairs Consultant
    Paul Farberman . . . . . . . . . . . . . . . . . . . . . . . . . . VP, Music Business Affairs
    *Carlos Penera . . . . . . . . . . . . . . . . . . . . . . . . . . . . . . . . . VP/Controllor
    *Joseph Randazzo . . . . . . . . . . . . . . . . . . . . . . . . . . . . . . VP, Participations
    Robert W. Rubin . . . . . . . . . . . . . . . . . . . . . . . . . . . . . . VP, Business Affairs
    *Greg Anderson . . . . . . . . . . . . . . . . . . . . . . . . . Dir., Business Affairs Admin.
    *George Davis . . . . . . . . . . . . . . . . . . . . . . . . . . . . . . . . Dir., Business Affairs
    *Tony Grana . . . . . . . . . . . . . . . . . . . . . . . . . . . . . Dir., Production Resources
    *Bill Greenberg . . . . . . . . . . . . . . . . . . . . . . . . . . . . Dir., Feature Estimating
    Larry Weier . . . . . . . . . . . . . . . . . . . . . . . Dir., Feature Prod. Information Services

**UNIVERSAL TELEVISION** . . . . . . . . . . . . . . . . . . . . . . . . . . . . . . . . . . . . . . . **818-777-1000**
  100 Universal City Plaza
  Universal City, CA 91608-1085
  Type:  Television Production
    Tom Thayer . . . . . . . . . . . . . . . . . . . . . . . . . . . . . . . . . . . . . . . . President
    Susan Workman . . . . . . . . . . . . . . . . . . . . . . . . . Exec. VP, Business Affairs/Admin.
    *Charles Engel . . . . . . . . . . . . . . . . . . . . . . . . . . . Sr. VP, Universal Television
    James Brock . . . . . . . . . . . . . . . . . . . . . . . . . . . . . . . . VP, Business Affairs
    Sheldon Mittleman . . . . . . . . . . . . . . . . . . . . . . . . . . . . . VP, Business Affairs
    *Ralph Sariego . . . . . . . . . . . . . . . . . . . . . . VP, Television Production Management

**VH1** . . . . . . . . . . . . . . . . . . . . . . . . . . . . . . . . . . . . . . . . . . . . . . . . . . . . . . . **212-258-7840**
  Fax: . . . . . . . . . . . . . . . . . . . . . . . . . . . . . . . . . . . . . . . . . . . . . . . . . . . . 212-258-7955
  1515 Broadway
  New York, NY 10036
  Type:  Television Production
    *Gil Aronow . . . . . . . . . . . . . . . . . . . . . . . . . VP, General Counsel, MTV Europe

**VANDERKLOOT FILM & TELEVISION INC.** .................................. 404-221-0236
    Fax:. ........................................................ 404-584-5247
750 Ralph McGill Blvd. NE
Atlanta, GA 30312
Type:  Motion Picture Production + Television Production
    William VanDerKloot ........................................... President
    Charlie Willis. ........................................ Vice President-Gen. Mgr.
    Paul A. Johns ............................................... Comptroller

**VANSA INSURANCE SERVICES** .............................................. 818-763-9365
    Fax:. ........................................................ 818-762-2242
11365 Ventura Blvd., Ste. 113
Studio City, CA 91604
**Formerly DeWitt Stern of California
Type:  General Insurance
    Bill Hudson ............................................. Mgr., Ent. Div.
    Sarah Legan ....................................... Asst. Manager, Ent. Div.
    Tom Putnam. ...................................... Entertainment Division

***VENTURA ENTERTAINMENT GROUP LTD.**. ................................. 310-820-0607
    Fax:. ........................................................ 310-820-0692
11466 San Vicente Blvd.
Los Angeles, CA 90049
**Specialty: marketing, corp. sponsorship, lic. merchand.
Type:  Television Production + Video Production + Distribution
    *Floyd Kephart ........................................... CEO/Chairman
    *Ray Volpe. .................................................. President
    *David Ward. ..................................................... CFO
    Marti Fischer ................... VP, Corp. Sponsorship & Destination Mktg.

**VIACOM PRODUCTIONS** .................................................. 818-505-7500
    Fax:. ........................................................ 818-505-7599
10 Universal City Plaza
Universal City, CA 91608-1002
Type:  Television Production
    Roger Kirman ................................. Sr. VP, Business Affairs
    *Adene Lacy .................................. VP, Finance/Operations

***VIACOM, INC.** .......................................... 212-258-6000/212-373-7000
    Fax:. ....................................... 212-258-6175/212-373-8228
1515 Broadway
New York, NY 10036
**ALSO: 15 Columbus Circle, NY NY 10023-7780
Type:  Motion Picture Production
    *Phillippe P. Dauman ................... Exec. VP, General Counsel & CAO
    *Sumner M. Redstone. ....................................... Chairman
    *Frank J. Biondi ......................................... President-CEO
    *Thomas E. Dooley .................................... Exec. VP, CFO
    *Vaughn A. Clarke. ................................... Sr. VP- Treasurer
    Steven S. Fadem. ............................... Sr. VP, Business Affairs
    *Carl D. Folta ............................... Sr. VP, Corporate Relations
    *Michael D. Fricklas. .................... Sr. VP, Deputy General Counsel
    *Rudolph L. Hertlein .......................... Sr. VP, Corp. Development
    Lawrence Levinson ....................... Sr. VP, Government Relations
    *William A. Roskin ................... Sr. VP, Human Resources & Admin.
    *George Smith Jr. ....................... Sr. VP-Chief Financial Officer
    *Mark M. Weinstein. ....................... Sr. VP, Government Affairs
    *Peter Butler ................................... VP, Risk Management
    *Stephanie Storms ................... VP-Deputy General Counsel, Cable
    Norman A. Tsacalis ............................... VP, Internal Audit

**VIDEFILM PRODUCERS INTL.** ........................................... 310-550-7588
    Fax:. ........................................................ 310-550-1009
8899 Beverly Blvd., Ste. 999
Los Angeles, CA 90048
Type:  Television Production + Video Production + Distribution
    *Kirk D'Amico. ............................................... President

**VIEWER'S CHOICE** .............................................. 310-785-9094/212-486-6600
    Fax:. ........................................................ 310-785-9195/212-688-9497
    1888 Century Park East, Ste. 830
    Los Angeles, CA 90067
    **ALSO: 909 Third Ave. 21st Fl., New York, NY 10022
    Type:  Television Production
    Kim Cunningham. ..................................................... VP, Business Affairs
    Sandra E. Landau. .................................................. VP-General Counsel (NY)


**VISION INTERNATIONAL** .................................................. **310-843-0900**
    Fax:. ............................................................. 310-843-9010
    1875 Century Park East, Ste. 200
    Los Angeles, CA 90067
    Type:  Motion Picture Production + Distribution
    Stephen Monas. .............................................................. President
    Stephen Greenwald ............................................. Chief Executive Officer
    *Deborah Chiramonte. ............................................. Dir., Legal Affairs


**VIVIANI ESQ., THE LAW OFFICE OF DOUGLAS D.** ........................... **516-427-1502**
    Fax:. ............................................................. 516-427-1516
    33 Walt Whitman Rd., Ste. 307
    Melville, NY 11746
    **Area of specialty: Motion Pictures/Television/Music
    Type:  Entertainment Law
    Douglas D. Viviani, Esq. ...................................................... Attorney


**WALT DISNEY COMPANY, THE.** ........................................ **818-560-1000**
    500 S. Buena Vista St.
    Burbank, CA 91521-0001
    Type:  Motion Picture Production + Television Production
    Michael D. Eisner ................................................ Chairman of the Board-CEO
    Roy E. Disney ..................................................... Vice Chairman of the Board
    *Sanford Litvack. .................................................... Sr. Exec. VP - CCO
    Lawrence P. Murphy ....................................... Exec. VP, Strategic Planning & Develop.
    *John Cooke ........................................ Exec. VP, Corp. Affairs/Govt. Relations
    *Richard D. Nanula ...................................................... Exec. VP-CFO
    Joseph M. Santaniello ......................................................... Sr. VP
    John Garand. ................................................... VP, Planning & Control
    Peter Murphy ...................................................... VP, Strategic Planniing
    Mark Rozells ................................................ Vice President-Asst. Treasurer
    Jeff Smith. ................................................................. VP-Counsel
    Valerie Cohen ........................................... VP-Asst. General Counsel
    Peter F. Nolan ............................................ VP-Asst. General Counsel
    Edward Nowak. .......................................... VP-Asst. General Counsel
    David Thompson ......................................... VP-Asst. General Counsel
    Marsha L. Reed ............................................... Corporate Secretary

## WALT DISNEY MOTION PICTURES GROUP .................................. 818-560-1000
500 S. Buena Vista St.
Burbank, CA 91521-0001
**Hollywood/Touchstone/Walt Disney Pictures
Type: Motion Picture Production
*Chris McGurk ........................................................ President
*Bernadine Brandis ................................................... Exec. VP
Robert DeBitetto ............................................. Sr. VP, Business Affairs
*Robert Moore ............................................. Sr. VP, Planning & Analysis
Kathleen O'Connell ........................................... Sr. VP, Business Affairs
Steven C. Bardwil ................................................ VP, Legal Affairs
Kevin Breen .................................... VP, Music Business & Legal Affairs
Merritt Farren ............................... VP, Business/Legal Affairs - Interactive
Laura Fox ....................................................... VP, Legal Affairs
Art Frazier .................................................. VP, Business Affairs
Steven Gerse ............................... VP, Theatrical Anim. Business Affairs
Robert W. Johnson .............................................. VP, Labor Relations
Phillip Muhl .................................................. VP, Business Affairs
Paul Steinke ............................................... VP, Production Finance
*Sylvia J. Krask ....................................... Dir., Music Business Affairs
*David B. Rone ............................................. Dir., Business Affairs
Karen Dane ........................................................... Attorney
Chris Floyd .......................................................... Attorney
Lisa A. Franklin ..................................................... Attorney
*Asa Hung ........................................................... Attorney
Gabrielle Klatsky .................................................... Attorney

## WALT DISNEY TV ANIMATION ............................................. 818-754-7100
500 S. Buena Vista St.
Burbank, CA 91521
**MESSENGER:5200 Lankershim Blvd., North Hollywood, 91601
Type: Television Production
Gary Krisel ......................................................... President
Rob Hummel .............................................. VP, New Technologies
Mark Kenchelian ........................................... VP, Business Affairs
*Fred Paccone ............................................... VP, Finance

## WALT DISNEY TELEVISION & TELECOMMUNICATIONS ..................... 818-560-1000
500 S. Buena Vista St.
Burbank, CA 91521-0001
Type: Motion Picture Production + Television Production
*Dennis Hightower ................................................... President
W. Randolph Reiss ............................................ Exec. Vice President
*Laurie Younger ......................... Sr. VP, Business Affairs & Corp. Admin..
Scottye Hedstrom ............................... VP, Network TV Business Affairs
*Michael Maloney ............................................... VP, Legal Affairs
Rosalind Marks ................................ VP, Network TV Business Affairs
Walter O'Neal ............................................ VP, TV Prod. Finance
Joanna Spak .............................................. VP, Network TV Finance

## WALTERS, THE LAW OFFICES OF GARY ................................... 213-656-5100
Fax: ..................................................... 213-656-5373
8205 Santa Monica Blvd., Ste. I-122
Los Angeles, CA 90046
**Unable to confirm by press time
Type: Entertainment Law
Gary Walters ......................................................... Attorney

## WARNER BROS. DOMESTIC TV DISTRIBUTION ........................... 818-954-6000
4000 Warner Blvd.
Burbank, CA 91522-0001
Type: Distribution
Lenny Bart ............................................. Sr. VP, Administration

**WARNER BROS. HOME VIDEO** .............................................. **818-954-6000**
4000 Warner Blvd.
Burbank, CA 91522
Type: Video Production
Marsha K. King ........................................ Sr. VP, Business Affairs (818-954-2346)

**WARNER BROS. INTL. TV DISTRIB.** ........................................ **818-954-4068**
Fax: ................................................................ 818-954-6539
4000 Warner Blvd., The Tower, 14th Fl.
Burbank, CA 91522
Type: Television Production
Jeffrey R. Schlesinger ................................................... President
John Chickering ............................................ VP, Financial Admin.
Tommie J. Redwine .......................................... VP, Intl. Sales Admin.
John Whitesell .............................................. VP, Intl. Sales Admin.
Gwen Whitson .......................................... Vice Pres.-Gen. Counsel

**\*WARNER BROS. NETWORK** ......................................... **818-954-6000 x4580**
Fax: ................................................................ 818-954-6808
4000 Warner Blvd.
Burbank, CA 91522-0001
Type: Television Production
\*Mitchell Nedick ........................................ Head, Finance/Administration
\*Jed Petrick ................................................ Head, Media Sales

**WARNER BROS. PAYTV** .................................................. **212-484-8000**
Fax: ................................................................ 212-397-0728
75 Rockefeller Plaza
New York, NY 10019
Type: Television Production
Jeffrey Calman ................................... VP, Sales/Planning/Business Affairs
J.T. Shadoan .............................................. VP, Financial Affairs
Tony Cochi ................................................ Dir., Financial Affairs

**WARNER BROS. PICTURES** ............................................... **818-954-6000**
Fax: .......................................................... 818-954-2487/bus.affairs
4000 Warner Blvd.
Burbank, CA 91522-0001
Type: Motion Picture Production
\*Michael Goodnight ........................................ Sr. VP, Assistant Controller
Steven Spira ..................................... Sr. VP, Theatrical Business Affairs
Jeremy Williams ........................... Sr. VP-General Counsel, Theatrical Legal
Patti J. Connolly ............................................ VP, Business Affairs
Dan Furie ................................................ VP, Business Affairs
Jack Sattinger ............................................. VP, Theatrical Legal
\*Marshall Silvermann ...................... VP, Assoc. General Counsel - Theatrical
\*Jodi Levinson ............................................ Dir., Business Affairs

**WARNER BROS. TELEVISION** ............................................. **818-954-6000**
Fax: ................................................................ 818-954-7367
4000 Warner Blvd.
Burbank, CA 91522-0001
Type: Television Production
Leslie Moonves ........................................................ President
Art Stolnitz ................................... Exec. VP, Business/Financial Affairs
Paul Stager ................................... Sr. VP, Studio General Counsel
\*Nancy Tellem ................................. Sr. VP, Business/Financial Affairs
\*Julie Waxman ....................... Sr. VP, Business Affairs/Intl. Co-prods.
Karen Cease .............................................. VP, Business Affairs
\*Don Feldgraber .......................................... VP, Business Affairs
\*Wilt Haff ................................................ VP, Business Affairs
Irwin Moss ................................................ VP, Business Affairs
Roni Mueller .............................................. VP, Business Affairs
Dorothy Relyea ...................................... VP, Production Control/Estimating

**WARNER BROS. WORLDWIDE** ............................................... **818-954-6000**
c/o Warner Bros. Studio
4000 Warner Blvd.
Burbank, CA 91522-0001
Type: Distribution
Edward A. Romano ............................................... Exec. VP-CFO (818-954-1441)
*Reginald G. Harpur ............................................ Sr. VP-Controller (818-954-5449)


**WARNER BROS.**.............................................................. **818-954-6000**
Fax: .................................................................... 818-954-3182
4000 Warner Blvd.
Burbank, CA 91522-0001
Type: Motion Picture Production + Television Production
*Robert A. Daly ............................................................. Chairman/Co-CEO
*Terry Semel ................................................................. Chairman/Co-CEO
*Ed Romano ............................................................ Exec. VP-Treasurer
Gary Meisel ...................................................... Sr. VP-Deputy General Counsel
Shelley Presser .................................................. Sr. VP-Deputy General Counsel


**WEINSTEIN & HART** .................................................... **310-274-7157**
Fax: .................................................................... 310-288-1884
433 N. Camden Dr., Ste. 600
Beverly Hills, CA 90210
Type: Entertainment Law
Joseph Hart.................................................................... Partner
Jerome Weinstein.............................................................. Partner


**WEISSMANN, WOLFF, BERGMAN, COLEMAN & SILVERMAN** .................. **310-858-7888**
Fax: .................................................................... 310-550-7191
9665 Wilshire Blvd., Ste. 900
Beverly Hills, CA 90212
Type: Entertainment Law
Stewart Brookman ............................................................. Partner
David Colden ................................................................. Partner
Stan Coleman .................................................................. Partner
Alan Grodin .................................................................. Partner
Henry Holmes ................................................................. Partner
Steven Katleman ............................................................... Partner
Eric Weissmann ............................................................... Partner
Ira Epstein ............................................................... Of Counsel
*Joel Mckvin............................................................... Associate
*Todd Stern................................................................ Associate


**WESTBERG ENTERTAINMENT** ............................................. **213-874-5544**
Fax: .................................................................... 213-874-7757
1604 N. Vista St.
Hollywood, CA 90046-2818
Type: Motion Picture Production + Television Production
David Westberg ............................................................. President-COO


**WILEY, DAN** ......................................................... **213-876-5824**
2341 Zorada Ct.
Los Angeles, CA 90046
**Entertainers
Type: Business Management
Dan Wiley .............................................................. Business Manager


**WILSHIRE COURT PRODS.** .............................................. **310-557-2444**
Fax: .................................................................... 310-557-0017
1840 Century Park East, Ste. 400
Los Angeles, CA 90067
Type: Television Production
Paul Marquez ......................................................... Sr. VP, Operations
Jack Angeles ........................................................ VP, Business Affairs

**WISEMAN & BURKE, INC.** . . . . . . . . . . . . . . . . . . . . . . . . . . . . . . . . . . . . . **818-247-1007**
   Fax:. . . . . . . . . . . . . . . . . . . . . . . . . . . . . . . . . . . . . . . . . . . . . . . . . . 818-247-1861
   206 S. Brand Blvd.
   Glendale, CA 91204
   \*\*Entertainment & fraud auditors
   Type: Business Management + Financial Consulting + Legal Affairs
     Bruce Wiseman . . . . . . . . . . . . . . . . . . . . . . . . . . . . . . . . . . . . . . . . . President
     Kevin Burke . . . . . . . . . . . . . . . . . . . . . . . . . . . . . . . . . . Exec. Vice President
     \*Robert LaRose. . . . . . . . . . . . . . . . . . . . . . . . . . . . . . . . . . . . . . . CPA, CFE

**WISHIK, LAW OFFICES OF GARY S.** . . . . . . . . . . . . . . . . . . . . . . . . . . . . **310-278-3092**
   Fax:. . . . . . . . . . . . . . . . . . . . . . . . . . . . . . . . . . . . . . . . . . . . . . . . . . 310-273-5602
   9107 Wilshire Blvd., Ste. 300
   Beverly Hills, CA 90210
   Type: Entertainment Law
     Gary Wishik . . . . . . . . . . . . . . . . . . . . . . . . . . . . . . . . . . . . . . . . . . Attorney

**WOLF, MARVIN LOUIS.** . . . . . . . . . . . . . . . . . . . . . . . . . . . . . . . . . . . . . . **310-553-5674**
   Fax:. . . . . . . . . . . . . . . . . . . . . . . . . . . . . . . . . . . . . . . . . . . . . . . . . . 310-282-0974
   2049 Century Park East, 18th Fl.
   Los Angeles, CA 90067
   Type: Entertainment Law
     Marvin Louis Wolf . . . . . . . . . . . . . . . . . . . . . . . . . . . . . . . . . . . . . Attorney

**WOLPER ORG. INC., THE.** . . . . . . . . . . . . . . . . . . . . . . . . . . . . . . . . . . . . **818-954-1707**
   Fax:. . . . . . . . . . . . . . . . . . . . . . . . . . . . . . . . . . . . . . . . . . . . . . . . . . 818-954-4380
   c/o Warner Bros.
   4000 Warner Blvd., West Admin. #12
   Burbank, CA 91522-0001
   Type: Motion Picture Production + Television Production + Distribution
     David L. Wolper . . . . . . . . . . . . . . . . . . . . . . . . . . . . . . . . . . . . . Chairman
     Mark M. Wolper . . . . . . . . . . . . . . . . . . . . . . . . . . . . . . . . . . . . . President
     Auriel Sanderson . . . . . . . . . . . . . . . . . . . . . . . . . . . . Sr. VP, Administration

**WOOD & FREEMAN BUSINESS MANAGEMENT.** . . . . . . . . . . . . . . . . . . . . . . . **213-469-5196**
   Fax:. . . . . . . . . . . . . . . . . . . . . . . . . . . . . . . . . . . . . . . . . . . . . . . . . . 213-962-6111
   2018 N. Vine St.
   Hollywood, CA 90068
   \*\*Entertainment industry tax experts
   Type: Business Management
     Stuart Freeman . . . . . . . . . . . . . . . . . . . . . . . . . . . . . . . . . . . . . . Co-owner
     Beverly Freeman . . . . . . . . . . . . . . . . . . . . . . . . . . . . . . . . . . . . . Co-owner
     \*Chris Frank . . . . . . . . . . . . . . . . . . . . . . . . . . . . . . . . . . . . . . . . . . . CPA

**WORLD TRADE BANK** . . . . . . . . . . . . . . . . . . . . . . . . . . . . . . . . . . . . . . . . **310-551-0100**
   Fax:. . . . . . . . . . . . . . . . . . . . . . . . . . . . . . . . . . . . . . . . . . . . . . . . . . 310-203-8310
   9944 Santa Monica Blvd.
   Beverly Hills, CA 90212
   Type: Banking
     W. Chris Broquist . . . . . . . . . . . . . . . . . . . . . . . . . . VP, Entertainment Industries

**YANKEE ENTERTAINMENT GROUP** . . . . . . . . . . . . . . . . . . . . . . . . . . . . . . **818-954-0780**
   Fax:. . . . . . . . . . . . . . . . . . . . . . . . . . . . . . . . . . . . . . . . . . . . . . . . . . 818-954-0964
   3815 W. Olive Ave., #201
   Burbank, CA 91505
   Type: Motion Picture Production
     Robert Magaudda. . . . . . . . . . . . . . . . . . . . . . . . . . . . Chief Financial Officer
     Donald C. McKeon . . . . . . . . . . . . . . . . . . . . . . . . . . Chief Executive Officer

**YOUNG & COMPANY, M.G., A BUS. MGMT. CORP.** ............................ 310-284-7000
    Fax: ............................................................... 310-552-7925
    2049 Century Park East, Ste. 2580
    Los Angeles, CA 90067
    \*\*Music & General Entertainment
    Type: Business Management
    Melody Young .......................................................... Principal

**\*ZENITH ENTERTAINMENT** .................................................. 213-960-4986
    Fax: ............................................................... 213-960-4987
    c/o Raleigh Studios
    5300 Melrose Ave., Bldg. East Ste. 204
    Hollywood, CA 90038
    Type: Motion Picture Production + Television Production + Production Co-Financing
    \*Pamela Alster ............................................... Dir., Business Affairs
    \*John Jahrmarkt ................................................. Dir., Legal Affairs

**ZIFFREN BRITTENHAM BRANCA & FISCHER** ............................... 310-552-3388
    Fax: ............................................................... 310-553-7068
    2121 Ave. of the Stars, Ste. 3200
    Los Angeles, CA 90067
    \*\*Motion Pictures, Television, Music
    Type: Entertainment Law
    Harry Brittenham ..................................................... Sr. Partner
    Kenneth Ziffren ...................................................... Sr. Partner
    Kenneth August ......................................................... Partner
    John G. Branca ......................................................... Partner
    Paul Brindze ........................................................... Partner
    \*Steve Burkon .......................................................... Partner
    Samuel Fischer ......................................................... Partner
    Clifford Gilbert-Lurie .................................................. Partner
    Kathleen Hallberg ...................................................... Partner
    Dennis Luderer ......................................................... Partner
    David Nochimson ........................................................ Partner
    Gary Stiffelman ........................................................ Partner
    Mitchell Tenzer ........................................................ Partner
    Jamie Young ............................................................ Partner
    \*Jamey Cohen ......................................................... Associate
    \*David Laude ......................................................... Associate

**ZIVETZ, SCHWARTZ & SALTSMAN, CPA'S** ................................... 310-826-1040
    Fax: ............................................................... 310-826-1065
    11900 W. Olympic Blvd., Ste. 650
    Los Angeles, CA 90064-1151
    Type: Business Management + Financial Consulting
    David L. Bass ............................................. Certified Public Accountant
    Michael D. Saltsman ...................................... Certified Public Accountant
    Lester J. Schwartz ....................................... Certified Public Accountant
    Susan B. Windle .......................................... Certified Public Accountant
    Michael A. Brown ............................................... Enrolled Agent

**ZOLLO PRODUCTIONS.** ...................................................... 212-957-1300
    Fax: ............................................................... 212-957-1315
    257 W. 52nd St.
    New York, NY 10019-5803
    Type: Motion Picture Production
    Nicholas Paleologos ..................................................... VP, Finance

# SECTION B.

## Companies Cross-Referenced by Type

## SECTION B.
## COMPANIES INDEXED BY TYPE

### Business Affairs

Berkover & Co., CPA, Rosalyn
Chrystie & Berle
Corber, Brian Lee
International Film Guarantors Inc.
Kerman, Law offices of Thea J.
NBC Productions
Perlberger, Law Offices of Martin
Preferred Investment Group Ltd.
Sacks, Samuel
Taffner Entertainment Ltd.
Tannen, Kathy L.
Temple, Mark S.
Third Eye Telepictures
Tulchin & Associates, Harris
Twentieth Century Fox Television

### Banking

AmSouth Bank, N.A.
Bank of America, Ent. & Media Ind. Group
Bank of America, NT&SA
Bank of Montreal
Banque Paribas
California United Bank
Carolina Barnes Capital Inc.
City National Bank - Ent. Div.
Crestar Bank
Film Funding Inc.
First Charter Bank
First Entertainment Federal Credit Union
Furman Selz Inc.
Goldman, Sachs & Co.
Imperial Bank, Ent. Ind. Group
InterMedia/Film Equities Inc.
Ladenburg, Thalmann & Co. Inc.
Mercantile National Bank - Ent. Ind. Div.
Oppenheimer & Co. Inc.
Preferred Investment Group Ltd.
Stephens Inc.
United Jersey Bank
World Trade Bank

### Business Management

Artists Financial Management, Ltd.
BDO Seidman
Bamberger Business Mgmt.
Bedker, London & Kossow
Beldock Levine & Hoffman
Berger, Kahn, Shafton, Moss, Figler, Simon & Gladstone
Berkover & Co., CPA, Rosalyn
Berlin, Ann Lurie, Fiddleheads, Ltd.
Bernstein, Fox, Goldberg & Licker
Braverman, Codron & Co.
Business Management Office, The
C.M. Management
Capell, Coyne & Co.
Carlton, Rosanne
Coudert Bros.
Countryman & McDaniel

Deloitte & Touche
Duitch, Poteshman, Franklin & Co.
Elkins & Elkins, An Accountancy Corp.
Ernst & Young
Freedman, Broder & Co.
Gelfand, Newman & Wasserman
Gelfand, Rennert & Feldman
Gudvi, Chapnick & Oppenheim, Inc.
Guild Management Corporation
Halpern & Mantovani
Hankin & Co.
Hopp, Thomas
JI Business Services
Julien & Associates Inc.
KPMG Peat Marwick
Kern, Harold B.
Lambert Financial Services
Ledger Domain
Lerner, Lawrence D., A Bus. Mgmt. Corp.
London & Lichtenberg
Maree Jr. & Assocs. Inc., A. Morgan
Martindale, C.P.A., Larry
Matlen & Associates, C.P.A., H. Roy
Maxwell Group, The
Morgan, C.P.A., Robert F.
Myman, Abell, Fineman, Greenspan & Rowan
Neuman & Associates, C.P.A.s
Oberman, Tivoli & Miller Ltd.
Padell, Nadell, Fine, Weinberger & Co.

Panitch & Co., Inc., Hersh
Perry & Neidorf
Price Waterhouse
Progressive Asset Mgmt.
Reiter Management
Resource One Inc.
Robinson/Jeffrey Assoc. Inc.
Rodeo Drive Financial Mgmt.
Royal & Associates, Inc.
Rubenstien & Finch
Rubin, Richards & Co.
Satin & Company
Satriano & Hilton, Inc.
Savitsky Satin & Geibelson
Schuster & Associates
Singer Lewak Greenbaum & Goldstein CPAs & Mgmt Consult.
Stiletto Entertainment
Stone & Asoociates
Tiffany & Associates, Catherine
Troubleshooters, Inc.
Turner Accountancy Corp.
Turner, Lawrence J.
Wiley, Dan
Wiseman & Burke, Inc.
Wood & Freeman Business Management
Young & Company, M.G., A Bus. Mgmt. Corp
Zivetz, Schwartz & Saltsman, CPA's

### Completion Bonds

Complete Film Corp.
Coulter & Sands, Inc.
Film Finances, Inc.
International Film Guarantors Inc.
Percenterprises Completion Bonds, Inc.

## Distribution

A-PIX Entertainment
ABC Cable & Intl. Broadcast Group
Active Entertainment
Banner Assocs., Bob
Betzer Films Inc., Just
Blockbuster Entertainment Group
Blue Rider Pictures
Bohbot Entertainment
British Connection
Buena Vista International
Buena Vista Picts. Distrib.
Buena Vista Television
Burrud Productions, Bill
Cabin Fever Entertainment
Carsey-Werner Co., The
Columbia TriStar Home Video
Columbia TriStar TV Distribution
Elliott Ent., Lang
Excelsior Pictures Corp.
Feature Finance
First Look Picts./Overseas Filmgroup
Franklin/Waterman Ent.
GEL Production/Distribution
Goldwyn Co., Samuel
Hamilton Entertainment, Inc., Dean
Hemdale Communications Inc.
I.N.I. Entertainment Group Inc.
IRS Media
International Film Resource Group Inc.
J & M Ent. Ltd.
JVC Entertainment, Inc.
Kaufman Esq., Peter L.
Kushner-Locke Co.
LIVE Entertainment Companies
Largo Entertainment
Lauren International
MCEG Sterling Ent.
MTM
Miramax Films
National Lampoon
New World Entertainment
Orion Pictures Corporation

Pacific Arts
Philips Media Electronic Publishing
PolyGram Video
Prism Entertainment Corp.
Program Power Ent. Inc.
Rust Prods., Patricia
Rysher Entertainment
Savoy Pictures
Sentinel Television Corporation
Single Spark Pictures
Skouras Picts. Inc.
Spelling Entertainment Group Inc.
Straightley Films
Taffner Entertainment Ltd.
Tannen, Kathy L.
TransAtlantic Enterprises (TAE) Productions
Trimark Holdings Inc.
Turner Original Productions
U.S. Film Corp.
Ventura Entertainment Group Ltd.
Videfilm Producers Intl.

Vision International
Warner Bros. Domestic TV Distribution
Warner Bros. Worldwide
Wolper Org. Inc., The

## Entertainment Law

Albright, Yee & Schimt
Alperin, Esq., Howard K.
Armstrong, Hirsch, Jackoway, Tyerman & Wertheimer
Artists Legal & Accounting Assistance
Asherson & Klein
Ashley & Frisby
Atkinson Esq., Heather R.
Barab, Vaughan & Kline
Baron Law Office, Stephen
Bedker, London & Kossow
Behr & Robinson
Beldock Levine & Hoffman
Berger, Kahn, Shafton, Moss, Figler, Simon & Gladstone
Berggren, Arthur T.
Berke, Jeff
Bienstock & Clark
Blackman, A. Lee
Blackwell, The Law Offices of William W.
Blanc, Williams, Johnston & Kronstadt
Blau, Edward
Bloom Dekom Hergott & Cook
Bortman, David Attorney At Law
Browning, Jacobson & Klein
Buchalter, Nemer, Fields & Younger
Cavella, Catherine A.
Chrystie & Berle
Codikow & Carroll
Cohen & Luckenbacher
Cohen, Allan S.
Coplan, Daniel J.
Corber, Brian Lee
Coudert Bros.
Countryman & McDaniel
Del, Rubel, Shaw, Mason & Derin
Dern & Vein
Edelstein, Laird & Sobel
Ervin, Cohen & Jessup
Evans, David J.
Findelle Law & Mgmt., Stann
Frankfurt, Garbus, Klein & Selz
Gibson, Dunn & Crutcher
Gipson Hoffman & Pancione
Golden, Renee Wayne

Gordon, The Law Office Of Peter D.
Greenberg Glusker Fields Claman & Machtinger
Hall Dickler Kent Friedman & Wood
Hayes, Hume, Petas, Richards & Cohanne
Heenan Blaikie
Hill Wynne Troop & Meisinger
Hirsch, Noah S.
Hoffman, Nathalie R.
Ingber, Jeffrey C.
Irell & Manella
Israel & Bray
Jacobson & Colfin, P.C.
Johnson & Assoc., Neville L.
Johnson, Kathleen K.
Julien & Associates Inc.
Katten Muchin Zavis & Weitzman
Kaufman Esq., Peter L.
Kehr Crook Tovmassian & Fox

Kelton, Law Office of Bruce J.
Kenoff & Machtinger
Kerman, Law offices of Thea J.
Langberg, Leslie & Gabriel
Lee, Patricia E.
Leonard, Dicker & Schreiber
Levine, Paul S.
Lichter Esq., Rosalind
Lilliston, Law Offices of Bruce St. J.
Litwak, Law Offices Of Mark
Loeb & Loeb
Manatt, Phelps & Phillips
Menes Law Corp.
Mitchell, Silberberg & Knupp
Morrison & Foerster
Myman, Abell, Fineman, Greenspan & Rowan
Nelson, Guggenheim, Felker & Levine
Nemschoff, Louise
Norwitz Attorney at Law, Eric
O'Melveny & Myers
Oppenheim Esq., Robert L.
Pasarow, Averill C.
Pascotto & Gallavotti
Paul, Hastings, Janosky & Walker
Perlberger, Law Offices of Martin
Perlmutter, Sam, Law offices of
Proskauer, Rose, Goetz & Mendelsohn
Roberts, Andrew S.
Rosenfeld, Meyer & Susman
Rubenstien & Finch

Sacks, Samuel
Schaefer, Law Offices of Susan G.
Schiff A Professional Corp., Gunther H.
Schuster & Associates
Sinclair, Tenenbaum, Olesiuk & Co., Inc.
Sipos, Thomas M.
Skadden, Arps, Slate, Meagher & Flom
Slaff, Mosk, & Rudman
Sloane, Owen
Sloss, Law Office P.C.
Smith, Barab, Simpson
Sommer & Bear
Staenberg, The Law Offices of Marc R.
Stanbury, Fishelman & Levy
Steinhart, Terran T.
Steinhauer, Phyllis A.
Stewart & Harris
Supnik, Paul D.
Sussman, Jerome J.
Tannen, Kathy L.
Tashjian and Tashjian
Temple, Mark S.
Tulchin & Associates, Harris
Turner, Lawrence J.
Viviani Esq., The Law Office of Douglas D.
Walters, The Law Offices of Gary
Weinstein & Hart
Weissmann, Wolff, Bergman, Coleman & Silverman
Wishik, Law Offices of Gary S.
Wolf, Marvin Louis
Ziffren Brittenham Branca & Fischer

### Financial Consulting

Abraham & Company, David
AdMedia Corporate Advisors Inc.
Banque Paribas

Berger, Kahn, Shafton, Moss, Figler, Simon & Gladstone
Berkover & Co., CPA, Rosalyn
Braverman, Codron & Co.
Budgets By Design
Carolina Barnes Capital Inc.
Cassandra Group Inc., The
Cineworld Pictures, Ltd.
Crestar Bank
Dean Witter Reynolds
Deloitte & Touche
Entertainment Financiers Inc.
Entertainment Ind. Financial Strategies Assoc.
Ervin, Cohen & Jessup
Film Capital Corporation
Film-Video Financial Presentations
FitzRoy, Anne Stewart
Goldman, Sachs & Co.
Hankin & Co.
Houlihan Lokey Howard & Zukin
InterMedia/Film Equities Inc.
JI Business Services
L.M.N. Enterprises Inc.
Ladenburg, Thalmann & Co. Inc.
Laidlaw Holdings Inc.
Lambert Financial Services
MCEG Sterling Ent.
Media Services Group Inc.
Mesirow Private Equity
Myman, Abell, Fineman, Greenspan & Rowan
Neuman & Associates, C.P.A.s
Overseas Financial Services
Preferred Investment Group Ltd.
Progressive Asset Mgmt.
Resource One Inc.
Robinson/Jeffrey Assoc. Inc.
Smith Affiliated Capital Corp.
Smith Barney Inc.
Stephens & Associates
Tulchin & Associates, Harris
Wiseman & Burke, Inc.
Zivetz, Schwartz & Saltsman, CPA's

### General Insurance

AON Entertainment Ltd. Ins. Services
American Business Ins. Brokers LA, Inc./Acordia
American Specialty Underwriters (ASU)
Berger, Kahn, Shafton, Moss, Figler, Simon & Gladstone
Chubb Insurance Co.
Coulter & Sands, Inc.
DISC Insurance Services
Entertainment Brokers International
Entertainment Ind. Financial Strategies Assoc.
Film Finances, Inc.
Gelfand, Newman & Wasserman
Hart III Insurance Agency, John William
Maroevich, O'Shea and Coghlan Ins. Brokers
Marsh & McLennan Inc.
Near North Insurance Brokerage, Inc.
RHH/Albert G. Ruben Ins. Services Inc.
Reiff & Associates, D.R.
Reynolds & Reynolds Inc.
Travelers Insurance Co.
Travelers Insurance Co.- Investment Group (NY)
Truman Van Dyke Co.
Vansa Insurance Services

## Guild/Union

Actor's Equity Association (A.E.A.)
Toronto/Ontario Film Development Corp.

## Legal Affairs

Bienstock & Clark
Chrystie & Berle
Corber, Brian Lee
International Film Guarantors Inc.
Israel & Bray
Kerman, Law offices of Thea J.
Taffner Entertainment Ltd.
Tannen, Kathy L.
Temple, Mark S.
Third Eye Telepictures
Twentieth Century Fox Television
Wiseman & Burke, Inc.

## Motion Picture Production

21st Century Film Corp.
40 Acres & A Mule Filmworks Inc.
AEI - Atchity Ent. Intl.
About Face Prods.
Active Entertainment
Alliance Communications
Amblin Entertainment
American First Run Studios
American Playhouse
Angelika Films
Arama Entertainment
August Entertainment
Austin Prods., Bruce
Avenue Pictures
Baltimore Pictures
Beacon Pictures
Bell Associates, Dave
Betzer Films Inc., Just
Big Sky Entertainment
Black & White Television, Inc.
Blue Rider Pictures
Boz Productions
Braun Productions, David
Brooksfilms, Ltd.
Buckeye Communications
Cannon Pictures
Capella Films Inc.
Carolco Pictures
Carsey-Werner Co., The
Carthay Circle Pictures & Mgmt.
Castle Rock Entertainment
Chancellor Entertainment
Check Entertainment
Cine Grande Corporation
Cinema Line Films Corp.
Cinema Seven Prods.
Cinequanon Pictures Intl. Inc.
Cinergi Pictures Entertainment Inc.
Cinetel Films
Cineville Inc.
Citadel Entertainment, L.P.
Clark Prods., Dick

Colossal Pictures

Columbia Pictures
Columbia TriStar Motion Picture Companies
Concorde/New Horizons Corp.
Creative Road Corp.
Crown Intl. Pictures
Culver Studios, The
Damon Prods. Worldwide, Mark
Dancing Asparagus Prods.
Danjaq Inc.
Davis Entertainment Co.
De Passe Entertainment
Diamond Jim Productions
Dobson Global Entertainment
Dockry Productions
Dog Beach Productions
Dreamworks/SKG
EGM Film International Inc.
Echo Rock Entertainment
Elliott Ent., Lang
Elsboy Entertainment
Esparza-Katz Prods.
Excelsior Pictures Corp.
Fields & Hellman Co., The
Film Capital Corporation
Film Funding Inc.
First Look Picts./Overseas Filmgroup
First National Bank of Chicago, The
Fortis Entertainment
Fox Filmed Entertainment
Fries Entertainment
GEL Production/Distribution
Geffen Pictures
Gerber ITC Ent. Group, The
Golden Harvest Films
Goldwyn Co., Samuel
Gracie Films
Grainy Pictures, Inc.
HBO (NYC)
HKM Films
Hall Communications, Arsenio
Hamilton Entertainment, Inc., Dean
Hammer International
Hanna-Barbera, Inc.
Hart Brothers Ent. Corp.

Harvey Entertainment Company, The
Havoc
Hemdale Communications Inc.
Henson Prods., Jim
Heyes Company, The
Hickox-Bowman Prods., Inc.
Hill/Fields Ent.
I.N.I. Entertainment Group Inc.
IRS Media
ITB CineGroup
ITC Ent. Group
Icon Productions Inc.
Image Organization
Imagine Entertainment
Imperial Ent.
In Pictures, Ltd.
Interscope Communications Inc.
Intrazone Inc./Intrazone Interactive Ltd.
Island Pictures Corp.
Ixtlan
Jaffe Braunstein Films
Jersey Films
Johnson Productions, Don
Jones-David Salzman Ent., Quincy

Julien & Associates Inc.
Kaufman Esq., Peter L.
Kings Road Entertainment Inc.
Kirschner Prods., David
Kismet Entertainment Inc.
Kopelson Prods., Arnold
Kushner-Locke Co.
L.M.N. Enterprises Inc.
LIVE Entertainment Companies
Lauren International
Le Studio Canal + (U.S.)
Leucadia Film Corp.
Lightstorm Entertainment Inc.
Londine Productions
Lone Star Picts. Intl. Inc.
Longbow Prods.
Longfellow Prods.
Lotus Pictures Inc.
Lumiere Films Inc.
MCA Inc.
MCEG Sterling Ent.

Magnus Film Group
Main Line Pictures
Marvel Films
Matthau Company, The
Maverick
Melendez Prods., Bill
Metro-Goldwyn-Mayer Inc.
Mirage Enterprises
Miramax Films
Mister/SISTER Prods.
Morgan Creek Prods.
Motion Picture Corp. of America
Movicorp Holdings, Inc.
Movie Group, The
Mruvka Entertainment, Alan
Murphy Prods., Eddie
National Lampoon
Neila Inc.
Neo Motion Pictures, Inc.
New Dawn Entertainment
New Deal Prods., Inc.
New Line Cinema
New Regency Prods. Inc.
NorthStar Ent. Group, Inc.
Nu Image
O'Hara/Gregg Films
Olympic Entertainment Group
Once Upon A Time Films, Ltd.
Orion Pictures Corporation
Pachyderm Entertainment
Pacific Arts
Pacific Western Prods.
Paragon Entertainment Corp.
Paramount Domestic Distribution
Paramount Pictures .
Paramount Pictures Motion Picture Group
Peacock Films Inc.
Persky Prods., Lester
Peters Entertainment
Phoenician Films
Picturemaker Prods.
Pirromount Pictures
Pollack & Associates, Robert
Polygram Filmed Ent.
Prelude Pictures

Prism Entertainment Corp.

Producer & Management Ent. Group
Producers Ent. Group Ltd., The
Program Power Ent. Inc.
Promark Entertainment Group
Propaganda Films
Quince Prods., Inc.
RCS/PMP Films
RHI Entertainment
RKO Pictures, Inc.
Rankin/Bass
Rastar Prods.
Rees Assocs., Marian
Rocket Pictures
Rust Prods., Patricia
Rysher Entertainment
Saban Entertainment
Savoy Pictures
Scala Prods.
Sentinel Television Corporation
Shapiro Ent. Inc., Richard & Esther
Singer Prods. Inc., Joseph M.
Single Spark Pictures
Skouras Picts. Inc.
Sojourn Entertainment
Sony Pictures Entertainment
Spectacor Films
Spelling Entertainment Group Inc.
Spelling Television Inc.
Straightley Films
Sullivan Ent.
Telescene Communications Inc.
Third Eye Telepictures
Thompson Organization, Larry
Tisch Co., The Steve
Toronto/Ontario Film Development Corp.
Trans Pacific Films
TransAtlantic Enterprises (TAE) Productions
TriStar Pictures
Trimark Holdings Inc.
Triple-7 Entertainment
Trivision Pictures Inc.
Troma Inc.
Twentieth Century Fox Film Corp.
U.S. Film Corp.

Unistar Entertainment
United Paramount Network
Unity Communications, Inc.
Universal Pictures
VanDerKloot Film & Television Inc.
Viacom, Inc.
Vision International
Walt Disney Company, The
Walt Disney Motion Pictures Group
Walt Disney Television & Telecommunications
Warner Bros. Pictures
Warner Bros..
Westberg Entertainment
Wolper Org. Inc., The
Yankee Entertainment Group
Zenith Entertainment
Zollo Productions

### Production Co-Financing

Bank of California, The
Baron Law Office, Stephen
Betzer Films Inc., Just

British Connection
Cineworld Pictures, Ltd.
Dockry Productions
Entertainment Financiers Inc.
Excelsior Pictures Corp.
Fortis Entertainment
Fries Entertainment
L.M.N. Enterprises Inc.
LIVE Entertainment Companies
Largo Entertainment
Londine Productions
Mister/SISTER Prods.
Movicorp Holdings, Inc.
Orion Pictures Corporation
Pollack & Associates, Robert
Program Power Ent. Inc.
Sidley & Austin
Sloss, Law Office P.C.
Stephens & Associates
Toronto/Ontario Film Development Corp.
Tulchin & Associates, Harris
Unistar Entertainment
Unity Communications, Inc.
Zenith Entertainment


## Production Financing

Bank of America, Ent. & Media Ind. Group
Bank of America, NT&SA
Bank of California, The
Banque Paribas
Betzer Films Inc., Just
British Connection
Buckeye Communications
Chemical Bank, Ent. Ind. Group
Chrystie & Berle
Cineworld Pictures, Ltd.
City National Bank - Ent. Div.
Communication for Transformation
Entertainment Financiers Inc.
Ervin, Cohen & Jessup
Film Capital Corporation
Film Finances, Inc.
Film Funding Inc.
First Interstate Bank of Calif - Ent. Div.
First Los Angeles Bank, Ent. Ind. Div.
Franklin/Waterman Ent.
Horwitz Organization, The Lewis
ING Capital Corporation
In Pictures, Ltd.
International Film Resource Group Inc.
L.M.N. Enterprises Inc.
LIVE Entertainment Companies
Le Studio Canal + (U.S.)
Mercantile National Bank - Ent. Ind. Div.
Movicorp Holdings, Inc.
Myman, Abell, Fineman, Greenspan & Rowan
Pollack & Associates, Robert


Sidley & Austin
Sloss, Law Office P.C.
Stephens & Associates
Straightley Films
Union Bank Media Group
Unistar Entertainment


## Television Production

A&E Television Networks
ABC Cable & Intl. Broadcast Group
ABC Entertainment
ABC Productions
AEI - Atchity Ent. Intl.
Alliance Communications
Amblin Entertainment
American First Run Studios
American Playhouse
August Entertainment
Austin Prods., Bruce
Avenue Pictures
Baltimore Pictures
Banner Assocs., Bob
Baywatch Production Co.
Beacon Pictures
Bell Associates, Dave
Big Sky Entertainment
Black & White Television, Inc.
Black Entertainment TV
Bochco Prods., Steven
Braun Productions, David
Buckeye Communications
Buena Vista Television
Burrud Productions, Bill
CBS Entertainment
Cannell Prods. Inc., Stephen J.
Carsey-Werner Co., The
Carthay Circle Pictures & Mgmt.
Castle Rock Entertainment
Chancellor Entertainment
Check Entertainment
Citadel Entertainment, L.P.
Clark Prods., Dick
Colossal Pictures
Columbia Picts. Television
Columbia TriStar Television
Comedy Central
Cramer Company, The
Creative Road Corp.
Culver Studios, The
DIC Entertainment
Danjaq Inc.
De Passe Entertainment
Di Bona Prods., Vin
Diamond Jim Productions
Disney Channel, The
Dobson Global Entertainment
Dockry Productions
E! Entertainment Television
Elliott Ent., Lang
Elsboy Entertainment
Excelsior Pictures Corp.
FX Networks
Family Channel, The
Film Capital Corporation
Film Funding Inc.
First Look Picts./Overseas Filmgroup
First National Bank of Chicago, The
Fortis Entertainment
Four Point Entertainment
Fox Broadcasting Co.
Fox TV Stations Prods.
Franklin/Waterman Ent.
GEL Production/Distribution
Gaumont Television

Genesis Entertainment
Gerber ITC Ent. Group, The
Goldwyn Co., Samuel
Goodson Prods., Mark
Gracie Films
Grundy Prods. Inc., Reg
HBO (L.A.)
HBO (NYC)
HBO Independent Prods.
Hall Communications, Arsenio
Hamilton Entertainment, Inc., Dean
Hanna-Barbera, Inc.
Harmony Gold
Hart Brothers Ent. Corp.
Harvey Entertainment Company, The
Hearst Entertainment
Hemdale Communications Inc.
Henson Prods., Jim
Hickox-Bowman Prods., Inc.
I.N.I. Entertainment Group Inc.
ITB CineGroup

ITC Ent. Group
In Pictures, Ltd.
Intrazone Inc./Intrazone Interactive Ltd.
J & M Ent. Ltd.
Jaffe Braunstein Films
Johnson Productions, Don
Jones-David Salzman Ent., Quincy
KCET, Community TV of So. California
Kaufman Esq., Peter L.
King World Prods.
Kings Road Entertainment Inc.
Kismet Entertainment Inc.
Kushner-Locke Co.
Lancit Media Prods.
Landsburg Co., The
Leucadia Film Corp.
Lifetime Television (NY)
Londine Productions
Longbow Prods.
Lotus Pictures Inc.
Lynch Entertainment
MCA Inc.
MCA TV Entertainment
MCEG Sterling Ent.
MGM Worldwide TV Group
MTM
MTV Networks
Marvel Films
Matthau Company, The
Maverick
Miss Universe Inc.
Mister/SISTER Prods.
Movicorp Holdings, Inc.
Mruvka Entertainment, Alan
Multimedia Inc.
Murphy Prods., Eddie
NBC Entertainment
NBC Inc.
NBC Productions
National Lampoon
Neila Inc.
New Dawn Entertainment
New Deal Prods., Inc.
New World Entertainment
Nickelodeon

NorthStar Ent. Group, Inc.

Nostalgia Television
O'Hara-Horowitz Productions
O'Hara/Gregg Films
Olympic Entertainment Group
Once Upon A Time Films, Ltd.
PBS
Pachyderm Entertainment
Pacific Western Prods.
Papazian-Hirsch Entertainment
Paragon Entertainment Corp.
Paramount Domestic TV
Paramount Network TV
Paramount Pictures .
Patchett Kaufman Entertainment
Persky Prods., Lester
Picturemaker Prods.
Pirromount Pictures
Playboy Entertainment Group Inc.
Prime Sports
Producer & Management Ent. Group
Producers Ent. Group Ltd., The
Program Power Ent. Inc.
Promark Entertainment Group
Propaganda Films
Quince Prods., Inc.
RHI Entertainment
Rabbit Ears Prods.
Rastar Prods.
Republic Pictures Corp.
Rust Prods., Patricia
Rysher Entertainment
Saban Entertainment
Sanctuary Woods Multimedia Corp.
Savoy Pictures
Schlatter Prods., George
Scholastic Prods.
Scripps Howard Productions
Second City Entertainment, Inc., The
Sentinel Television Corporation
Shane Co., A
Showtime Networks Inc.
Single Spark Pictures
Sony Pictures Entertainment
Sony Television Entertainment

Spelling Entertainment Group Inc.
Spelling Television Inc.
St. Clare Entertainment
Straightley Films
Sunbow Prods.
TNT/Turner Pictures Inc.
Taffner Entertainment Ltd.
Telepictures Prods.
Telescene Communications Inc.
Third Eye Telepictures
Tisch Co., The Steve
Toronto/Ontario Film Development Corp.
TransAtlantic Enterprises (TAE) Productions
TriStar TV
Triple-7 Entertainment
Trivision Pictures Inc.
Turner Broadcasting System
Turner Original Productions
Twentieth Century Fox Television
Twentieth TV
USA Network
Unistar Entertainment
Unity Communications, Inc.
Universal Television

VH1
VanDerKloot Film & Television Inc.
Ventura Entertainment Group Ltd.
Viacom Productions
Videfilm Producers Intl.
Viewer's Choice
Walt Disney Company, The
Walt Disney TV Animation
Walt Disney Television & Telecommunications
Warner Bros. Intl. TV Distrib.
Warner Bros. Network
Warner Bros. PayTV
Warner Bros. Television
Warner Bros..
Westberg Entertainment
Wilshire Court Prods.
Wolper Org. Inc., The
Zenith Entertainment

## Video Production

Barr Films
Big Sky Entertainment
Buckeye Communications
Buena Vista Home Video
Burrud Productions, Bill
Celebrity Home Ent.
Cineville Inc.
Diamond Jim Productions
Dockry Productions
Elliott Ent., Lang
Hall Communications, Arsenio
Hemdale Communications Inc.
Henson Prods., Jim
I.N.I. Entertainment Group Inc.
J & M Ent. Ltd.
Leucadia Film Corp.
Londine Productions
Lone Star Picts. Intl. Inc.
Mister/SISTER Prods.
National Lampoon
Orion Pictures Corporation
Pacific Arts
Paramount Home Video Distribution
Prism Entertainment Corp.
Rabbit Ears Prods.
Republic Pictures Corp.
Sentinel Television Corporation
Single Spark Pictures
Skouras Picts. Inc.
Sojourn Entertainment
Spelling Entertainment Group Inc.
Squeak Pictures Inc.
Ventura Entertainment Group Ltd.
Videfilm Producers Intl.
Warner Bros. Home Video

# SECTION C.

## Names

## Cross-Referenced

## by Company

## SECTION C.
## NAMES CROSS-REFERENCED BY COMPANY

| | |
|---|---|
| *AARON, PAUL | Elsboy Entertainment |
| *ABELL, LESLIE B. | Myman, Abell, Fineman, Greenspan & Rowan |
| *ABELL, NANCY | Paul, Hastings, Janosky & Walker |
| ABRAHAM, DAVID | Abraham & Company, David |
| ABRAHAM, STEVEN M. | Price Waterhouse |
| ABRAM, STEVE | American Business Ins. Brokers LA, Inc./Acordia |
| ABRAMS, GERALD W. | Hearst Entertainment |
| *ABRAMS, JEFFREY | Rosenfeld, Meyer & Susman |
| *ABRAMS, JOSEPH Y. | ABC Cable & Intl. Broadcast Group |
| ABRAMSON, CURTIS | Braverman, Codron & Co. |
| ABRAMSON, HOWARD | Behr & Robinson |
| *ABRAMSON, LAWRENCE | Hemdale Communications Inc. |
| ABRAMSON, STEVE | New Line Cinema |
| ACESTE, JOAN | Comedy Central |
| ACONE, TONY | Prime Sports |
| *ADAMSON, SUSAN C. | Armstrong, Hirsch, Jackoway, et al. |
| ADELSON, AMY | ABC Productions |
| ADER-BROWN, JAMIE | In Pictures, Ltd. |
| ADLER, MICHAEL | Mitchell, Silberberg & Knupp |
| AGOGLIA, JOHN | NBC Entertainment |
| *AGOGLIA, JOHN | NBC Productions |
| AGUILAR, OSCAR | Henson Prods., Jim |
| AKSELRAD, HAROLD | HBO (NYC) |
| *ALBRECHT, CHRIS | HBO (L.A.) |
| *ALBRECHT, CHRIS | HBO Independent Prods. |
| ALBRIGHT, CLIFTON | Albright, Yee & Schimt |
| *ALDERTON, SCOTT W. | Hill Wynne Troop & Meisinger |
| *ALEXANDER, ALLAN L. | Armstrong, Hirsch, Jackoway, et al. |
| *ALEXANDER, ANDREW | Second City Entertainment, Inc., The |
| ALLEN, BILL | MTM |
| *ALLEN, LUIS | TriStar Pictures |
| ALLISON, CARL | Miss Universe Inc. |
| ALLISON, CAROL DIESEL | Image Organization |
| ALMOND, HONI | Gerber ITC Ent. Group, The |
| *ALPERIN, HOWARD K. | Alperin, Esq., Howard K. |
| *ALPEROVICH, ADRIAN | Columbia TriStar Home Video |
| *ALSTER, PAMELA | Zenith Entertainment |
| ALTMANN, PHIL | Beacon Pictures |
| AMIN, MARK | Trimark Holdings Inc. |
| *AMUNDSON, KATHLEEN | New Regency Prods. Inc. |
| *ANDERSON, DAVID | Leucadia Film Corp. |
| *ANDERSON, GREG | Universal Pictures |
| *ANDRES, MICHAEL | Bank of Montreal |
| *ANDREWS, CECELIA | MGM Worldwide TV Group |
| *ANEY, SCOTT | Bank of America, NT&SA |
| *ANGEL, ROBERT M. | Myman, Abell, Fineman, Greenspan & Rowan |
| ANGELES, JACK | Wilshire Court Prods. |
| ANGELETTI, MARIA | Metro-Goldwyn-Mayer Inc. |
| ANSIS, FREDRIC W. | Hall Dickler Kent Friedman & Wood |
| ARAD, AVI | Marvel Films |
| *ARAMA, SHIMON | Arama Entertainment |
| *ARMOUR, DARLEEN H. | Houlihan Lokey Howard & Zukin |
| ARMSTRONG, ARTHUR | Armstrong, Hirsch, Jackoway, et al. |
| ARNTZEN, DAVID | Business Management Office, The |
| ARNTZEN, NANCY | Business Management Office, The |
| *ARONOW, GIL | VH1 |
| ARVESEN, DEBORAH | Metro-Goldwyn-Mayer Inc. |
| ARVESEN, GREGORY | Orion Pictures Corporation |
| *ASCHENBRENNER, LIZ | TriStar Pictures |
| ASHERSON, NEVILLE | Asherson & Klein |
| ASHLEY, STEPHEN | Ashley & Frisby |
| ASNER, EDWARD | Quince Prods., Inc. |
| ASNER, MATTHEW | Quince Prods., Inc. |
| *ATCHITY, KENNETH | AEI - Atchity Ent. Intl. |
| *ATKINSON, HEATHER R. | Atkinson Esq., Heather R. |
| AUERBACH, BRAD | Philips Media Electronic Publishing |
| AUGUST, KENNETH | Ziffren Brittenham Branca & Fischer |
| *AUSTEN, KARL R. | Armstrong, Hirsch, Jackoway, Tyerman & Wertheimer |
| AUSTIN, ALAN D. | Multimedia Inc. |
| *AUSTIN, BRUCE | Austin Prods., Bruce |
| *BACHMANN, PETER | Spelling Entertainment Group Inc. |
| BADAGLIACCA, MARK | Paramount Pictures . |
| BADER, JONATHAN | Paramount Home Video Distribution |
| *BADISH, KENNETH | Active Entertainment |
| BAER, WILLI | Capella Films Inc. |
| BAGDASARIAN, ANNA | Bank of California, The |
| BAILEY, ALAN J. | Paramount Pictures . |
| BAKSHI, CAROLE | California United Bank |
| *BALCOMB, STAN | Paramount Pictures . |
| *BALES, MICHAEL V. | Greenberg Glusker Fields Claman & Machtinger |
| BALTEANU, LILLIAN | Rust Prods., Patricia |
| BAMBERGER, HENRY J. | Bamberger Business Mgmt. |
| BANKS, ESQ., JAMES | Triple-7 Entertainment |
| BANNER, BOB | Banner Assocs., Bob |
| BANNER, CHUCK | Banner Assocs., Bob |
| BARAB, MARTIN J. | Smith, Barab, Simpson |
| BARAK-MILGROM, DEBORAH | CBS Entertainment |
| *BARANCIK, STACY | Rosenfeld, Meyer & Susman |
| *BARBER, GARY | Morgan Creek Prods. |
| *BARBER, RAY | MCEG Sterling Ent. |
| BARBERA, JOSEPH | Hanna-Barbera, Inc. |
| BARBOUR, CASSANDRA | TriStar Pictures |
| *BARCLAY, PARIS | Black & White Television, Inc. |
| BARDWIL, STEVEN C. | Walt Disney Motion Pictures Group |
| BARE, MICHAEL | First Entertainment Federal Credit Union |
| *BARGMAN, ESQ., DAVID | Tulchin & Associates, Harris |
| BARIS, CONSTANTINE | Julien & Associates Inc. |
| *BARJON, JEAN-CHRISTOPHE | Tulchin & Associates, Harris |
| *BARKER, SCOTT | Rosenfeld, Meyer & Susman |
| BARLEVI, STEVEN | London & Lichtenberg |
| BARMETTLER, MARKUS W. | Gipson Hoffman & Pancione |
| BARNES, JENNIFER H. | O'Hara-Horowitz Productions |
| BARNES, MARY K. | Hill Wynne Troop & Meisinger |
| BARNES, MICHAEL | Echo Rock Entertainment |
| BARNES, STEPHEN D. | Bloom Dekom Hergott & Cook |
| BARNES III, FRANK E. | Carolina Barnes Capital Inc. |
| *BARNETT, LAWRENCE | Gipson Hoffman & Pancione |
| BARNWELL, ANDRE | Black Entertainment TV |
| BARON, PAMELA | HBO Independent Prods. |
| BARON, STEPHEN | Baron Law Office, Stephen |
| *BARONE, TRACY | Peters Entertainment |
| BAROVICK, RICHARD | Grundy Prods. Inc., Reg |
| *BARR, ALLEN | Sanctuary Woods Multimedia Corp. |
| *BARRECA, TOM | Hanna-Barbera, Inc. |
| *BARRETT, MICHAEL J. | Mesirow Private Equity |
| BARRIS, ROBIN | Imagine Entertainment |
| *BARRITT, JOHN | First Los Angeles Bank, Ent. Ind. Div. |
| *BARRON, ROBERT | Twentieth Century Fox Television |
| *BARRY, JOHN | Castle Rock Entertainment |
| BART, LENNY | Warner Bros. Domestic TV Distribution |
| *BARTHOLOMEW MORRISON, GLORIA | Unistar Entertainment |
| *BARTLAM, CHERYL | Feature Finance |
| *BARTON, GERALD S. | Universal Pictures |
| BARUC, ROBERT | A-PIX Entertainment |
| BASEMAN, NEAL | TNT/Turner Pictures Inc. |
| BASS, DAVID L. | Zivetz, Schwartz & Saltsman, CPA's |
| *BASS, HOWARD K. | Savoy Pictures |
| *BASS, NINA | Carsey-Werner Co., The |
| *BASS, RONALD J. | Armstrong, Hirsch, Jackoway, Tyerman & Wertheimer |
| BATTAGLIA, RICH | HBO (L.A.) |
| *BAX, SIMON | Fox Filmed Entertainment |
| BAYMAN, LINDSEY | Gipson Hoffman & Pancione |
| *BEAR, JEFFREY | Sommer & Bear |
| *BECK, MICHAEL | Leucadia Film Corp. |
| BECKER, JUDI | GEL Production/Distribution |
| *BECKER, LINDA | Satin & Company |
| BECKER, MORTIMER | Bedker, London & Kossow |
| *BECKER, NORMAN H. | Rosenfeld, Meyer & Susman |
| *BEESEMYER, FRITZ T. | Oppenheimer & Co. Inc. |
| BEGUN, BENSON H. | Twentieth TV |
| BEHAR, HOWARD | Proskauer, Rose, Goetz & Mendelsohn |
| BEHR, JOEL | Behr & Robinson |
| BELL, ALEX | Barr Films |
| BELL, SANDY | Reynolds & Reynolds Inc. |
| BELZBERG, LESLIE | St. Clare Entertainment |
| BENINGER, BRIAN | Sanctuary Woods Multimedia Corp. |
| *BENNETT, GEORGE | About Face Prods. |
| *BENNETT, YUDI | Budgets By Design |
| BENTI, JOSEPH | Straightley Films |
| * BERGER, Brian | Polygram VIdeo |
| BERGER, JEFFREY S. | Third Eye Telepictures |
| BERGGREN, ARTHUR | Berggren, Arthur T. |
| BERGMAN, AVIVA | Clark Prods., Dick |
| *BERINSTEIN, DORI | Pachyderm Entertainment |
| BERK, MICHAEL | Baywatch Production Co. |
| *BERKE, BETH | Sony Pictures Entertainment |
| BERKE, JEFF | Berke, Jeff |
| *BERKOVER, ROSALYN | Berkover & Co., CPA, Rosalyn |
| BERKOWITZ, JEFFREY | Heenan Blaikie |

BERLE, ELIHU M. .........................................Chrystie & Berle
BERLIN, ANN LURIE .........................Berlin, Ann Lurie, Fiddleheads, Ltd.
BERMAN, JOEL .......................................Paramount Domestic TV
BERMAN, SAUL J. ..........................................Price Waterhouse
*BERNHARDT, KEVIN ...................................Phoenician Films
*BERNSEN, HARRY ...........................Unity Communications, Inc.
BERNSTEIN, ARMYAN.................................Beacon Pictures
*BERNSTEIN, ARNOLD..................Bernstein, Fox, Goldberg & Licker
BERNSTEIN, ARTHUR H. ..............Producers Ent. Group Ltd., The
*BERNSTEIN, ERIC M. .......................................Lauren International
*BERNSTEIN, FRED ...............Columbia TriStar Motion Picture Companies
*BERNSTEIN, GREG S. ..................Rosenfeld, Meyer & Susman
BERNSTEIN, ROBERT........................London & Lichtenberg
BERNSTEIN, WILLIAM .................................Paramount Pictures .
BERRARD, STEVEN R. ...............Spelling Entertainment Group Inc.
*BERRARD, STEVEN R. ...........Blockbuster Entertainment Group
BERRY, BOB .......................................Genesis Entertainment
*BERSCH, STEVEN .....................Twentieth Century Fox Film Corp.
BERSON, DAVID .......................................Goldwyn Co., Samuel

BERTRANDO, NANCY......Greenberg Glusker Fields Claman & Machtinger
*BESSON, TOLIVER....................Paul, Hastings, Janosky & Walker
BETZER, JUST ...........................................Betzer Films Inc., Just
*BEVINS, BILL ....................................Genesis Entertainment
BEWKES, JEFF..........................................................HBO (NYC)
BIBB, PORTER ........................Ladenburg, Thalmann & Co. Inc.
*BIBIYAN, MOSHE...................................Peacock Films Inc.
*BIBIYAN, SIMON....................................Peacock Films Inc.
*BIEBER, KIM ...........................................................Troma Inc.
BIENSTOCK, TERRY................................Bienstock & Clark
BIERSTEDT, PETER....................................Heyes Company, The
BINDER, RICK ..........Entertainment Ind. Financial Strategies Assoc.
BINGHAM, JULIA..........................Castle Rock Entertainment
*BIONDI, FRANK J. ..........................................Viacom, Inc.
*BIRCH, CHERYL ..............................Paramount Network TV
BIRKHAHN, JON ......................................King World Prods.
*BIRMINGHAM, PAUL A. ...............New World Entertainment
BIRNBAUM, MICHAEL.................................ITC Ent. Group
BISHOP, KENDALL ...............................O'Melveny & Myers
BITENSKY, LORNA ....................................NBC Productions
*BLACHMAN, ROCHEL.............Paramount Pictures Motion Picture Group
BLACK, DANIEL H. ......................................Heenan Blaikie
*BLACK, LAURA ...............................Carsey-Werner Co., The
BLACKMAN, A. LEE.......................................Blackman, A. Lee
BLACKMAN, LEA ................................Cinema Seven Prods.
BLACKWELL, WILLIAM..........Blackwell, The Law Offices of William W.
BLAKE, LAWRENCE J. .....................Manatt, Phelps & Phillips
*BLANC, RONALD L. ...........Blanc, Williams, Johnston & Kronstadt
*BLANCARTE, JAMES E. .....................Sussman, Jerome J.
*BLANK, MATHEW ...............Blockbuster Entertainment Group
BLAU, EDWARD ..................................................Blau, Edward
BLAYLOCK, WILLIAM .............Carthay Circle Pictures & Mgmt.
BLISS, THOMAS........................................Beacon Pictures
BLOOM, JACOB A. ................Bloom Dekom Hergott & Cook
BLOOM, NOEL ..................................Celebrity Home Ent.
BLYE, JEFFREY D. ...............Del, Rubel, Shaw, Mason & Derin
BOBBITT, LEROY ...................................Loeb & Loeb
BOCHCO, STEVEN ................................Bochco Prods., Steven
*BOHBOT, ALLEN J. ...............................Bohbot Entertainment
BOLGER, MICHAEL......................................Royal & Associates, Inc.
BONANN, GREGORY J. ..................Baywatch Production Co.
*BOND, SHERYL ...........................Bank of America, NT&SA
*BONDER, TODD W. ....................Rosenfeld, Meyer & Susman
BONSEIGNEUR, DEBRA........................Freedman, Broder & Co.
*BOONE, GREG .........................Sony Television Entertainment

*BORCHIVER, RICHARD ..................Paragon Entertainment Corp.
BORTMAN, DAVID .......................Bortman, David Attorney At Law
*BORZA, DON .......................Hamilton Entertainment, Inc., Dean
BOS, YVONNE................................................Bank of Montreal
*BOUBEL, RUTH.....................................Cramer Company, The
BOUNDY, JOHN .........................................Lone Star Picts. Intl. Inc.
BOWER, PAUL G. ...............................Gibson, Dunn & Crutcher
BOWMAN, CHUCK.........................Hickox-Bowman Prods., Inc.
*BOWN ZADES, BONNIE ................................Furman Selz Inc.
*BOYANOWSKY, THEA ......................Single Spark Pictures
BOYAR, ROBERT A. ..............................Marsh & McLennan Inc.
*BOYD, JIM.............................................Crown Intl. Pictures
BRADY, JOHN ................................................ITC Ent. Group
BRANCA, JOHN G. ........Ziffren Brittenham Branca & Fischer
BRANCH, DEBORAH .....................................Miramax Films
*BRANDIS, BERNADINE...........Walt Disney Motion Pictures Group
BRAUER, JEFFREY .............................Republic Pictures Corp.
*BRAVERMAN, WARREN...........Cinergi Pictures Entertainment Inc.

BRAY, LARRY E. .........................................Israel & Bray
BRECHEEN, LEIGH C...............Bloom Dekom Hergott & Cook
BREEN, KEVIN ...............Walt Disney Motion Pictures Group
BREIMER, STEPHEN B. ...........Bloom Dekom Hergott & Cook
*BRENNAN, TIMOTHY .........................American Playhouse
BRENNER, STEPHEN .......................................USA Network
*BREWER, FONDA ..................................Hanna-Barbera, Inc.
BRICKER, SEYMOUR ...........Mitchell, Silberberg & Knupp
BRIGGS, JEFFREY C. .................Gibson, Dunn & Crutcher
BRIGHTMAN, KIMBERLY ................Twentieth Century Fox Television
BRINDZE, PAUL ..........Ziffren Brittenham Branca & Fischer
BRINSON, DIANE ..............Near North Insurance Brokerage, Inc.
BRITTENHAM, HARRY.........Ziffren Brittenham Branca & Fischer
BROCCOLI, ALBERT R. ...................................Danjaq Inc.
BROCCOLI, DANA .............................................Danjaq Inc.
BROCK, JAMES .................................Universal Television
*BROCKMAN, MICHAEL ...............Goodson Prods., Mark
*BRODER, JAMIE ...............Paul, Hastings, Janosky & Walker
BRODER, WILLIAM ....................Freedman, Broder & Co.
BRODERICK, LISA A...............Abraham & Company, David
*BROITMAN, JODI ..............................Cramer Company, The
BROKAW, CARY .........................................Avenue Pictures
BROOK, HAROLD ........................................NBC Entertainment
BROOKMAN, STEVEN L. ........Bloom Dekom Hergott & Cook
BROOKMAN, STEWART ........Weissmann, Wolff, Bergman, et al.
BROOKS, BROOKE .................................Davis Entertainment Co.

*BROOKS, MARTIN ....................................Miss Universe Inc.
BROQUIST, W. CHRIS................................World Trade Bank
BROWN, MICHAEL A. ........Zivetz, Schwartz & Saltsman, CPA's
BROWN, NICHOLAS ...............Gelfand, Rennert & Feldman
*BROWN, SHELLEY ...............MGM Worldwide TV Group
BROWN, STEPHEN ...........................Kopelson Prods., Arnold
BROWNING, KENNETH L. ........Browning, Jacobson & Klein
BROWNSTEIN, DAVID K. ....................Mister/SISTER Prods.
BRUEN, CHARLES .......First Entertainment Federal Credit Union
*BRUENELL, DEB. ..........................................Columbia Pictures
BRUSTIN, ARNOLD ...........................De Passe Entertainment
BRYSON, BARBARA ....................................Ledger Domain
BUCHANAN, ESQ., CLAUDIA ....................Lumiere Films Inc.
BUCHTHAL, STANLEY F. ...............Buckeye Communications
BUCKLAND, TERRY ...................Metro-Goldwyn-Mayer Inc.
*BUCKLIN, STEPHEN L. ..................Countryman & McDaniel
*BUNSHAFT, BOB ............................................Pacific Arts
BURES, JOSEPH ........................................NBC Entertainment
*BURG, MARK ...................................Island Pictures Corp.
*BURGER, GEORGE ...............................Alliance Communications
*BURK, JIM ...........................................Universal Pictures
*BURKE, JOHN P. ...................Rosenfeld, Meyer & Susman
BURKE, KEVIN .....................................Wiseman & Burke, Inc.
*BURKON, STEVE ........Ziffren Brittenham Branca & Fischer
*BURRUD, JOHN ...........................Burrud Productions, Bill
*BUSBY, ANN ................................................MCA Inc.
BUSTETTER, PETER ....................................First Charter Bank
*BUTLER, PETER ...........................................Viacom, Inc.
*BYRNES, STACEY M.................Rosenfeld, Meyer & Susman
CALABRESE, ANTHONY ....................Smith Barney Inc.
CALDERA, LAURA .................................Esparza-Katz Prods.
*CALDWELL, LOLA.........................Hickox-Bowman Prods., Inc.
CALHOUN, LAURA ........Bank of America, Ent. & Media Ind. Group
*CALKINS, MARY CRAIG...........Hill Wynne Troop & Meisinger
CALMAN, JEFFREY ...........................Warner Bros. PayTV
*CALUHN, THOMAS E. ...............Mesirow Private Equity
*CAMDESSUS, CHRISTINE ......................Gaumont Television
CAMERON, JAMES.....................Lightstorm Entertainment Inc.
*CAMERON, PAUL .............Olympic Entertainment Group
CAMPBELL, TIMOTHY.....................Orion Pictures Corporation
*CANTERNA, PAUL ............Carthay Circle Pictures & Mgmt.
*CANTON, MARK............Columbia TriStar Motion Picture Companies
CANTROCK, STEVEN L...............Gelfand, Rennert & Feldman
*CAPELL, DAVID ...............................Capell, Coyne & Co.
*CAPLAN LEBOVITS, DIANNE.............Cinergi Pictures Entertainment Inc.

CAPOUCH, STEVE....................First National Bank of Chicago, The
CAREY, ANDRE ...............................TNT/Turner Pictures Inc.
CARLTON, ROSANNE.............................Carlton, Rosanne
*CARLUCCI, NANCY .................................Main Line Pictures
*CARMICHAEL, CARLA .........Cannell Prods. Inc., Stephen J.
CARROLL, ROSEMARY.............................Codikow & Carroll
CARSEY, MARCY ...............................Carsey-Werner Co., The
*CARSON, THOMAS P. ...........Spelling Entertainment Group Inc.
CARSWELL, BARBARA ....................Jaffe Braunstein Films
CASCANTE, GREGORY ..........................August Entertainment
*CASCANTE, GREGORY ...........................Kushner-Locke Co.

| | |
|---|---|
| CASS, DON | Entertainment Brokers International |
| CASS, KATHRYN | MCEG Sterling Ent. |
| *CASTELL, J. RONALD | Blockbuster Entertainment Group |
| *CASTRONOVO, T.J. | Creative Road Corp. |
| *CAVALLERO, RICHARD M. | Entertainment Financiers Inc. |
| *CAVANAUGH, VALERIE | United Paramount Network |
| CAVE, JACK | Entertainment Brokers International |
| CAVELLA, CATHERINE A. | Cavella, Catherine A. |
| CEASE, KAREN | Warner Bros. Television |
| *CHALFIN, ALLAN | Scripps Howard Productions |
| CHAMBERLAIN, ROBERT | Le Studio Canal + (U.S.) |
| CHAMBERLIN, WARD B. | American Playhouse |
| CHAMLIN, MARC | Loeb & Loeb |
| CHAPIN, ANDREW | Cabin Fever Entertainment |
| CHAPMAN, ROBERT | Greenberg Glusker Fields Claman & Machtinger |
| CHAPNICK, GERALD | Gudvi, Chapnick & Oppenheim, Inc. |
| *CHARRET, CHRISTIAN | Gaumont Television |
| CHASIN, BOB | TriStar TV |
| *CHAVEZ, DIANE | Carsey-Werner Co., The |
| CHERNEY, PAMELA | MCA Inc. |
| *CHERNIN, PETER | Fox Filmed Entertainment |
| *CHEYNE, JOHN D. | Hankin & Co. |
| CHICKERING, JOHN | Warner Bros. Intl. TV Distrib. |
| CHIEFFO, VINCENT H. | Gipson Hoffman & Pancione |
| *CHIRAMONTE, DEBORAH | Vision International |
| *CHRISTENSEN, MAREN | Rosenfeld, Meyer & Susman |
| CHRISTIANSON, VICKI | Icon Productions Inc. |
| CHRISTISON, BOB | Carsey-Werner Co., The |
| CHRYSTIE, STEPHEN | Chrystie & Berle |
| *CHU, ALAN | Ixtlan |
| CHUCK, BOB | Clark Prods., Dick |
| CICCONE, MADONNA | Maverick |
| CINGOLANI, LUIGI | Intrazone Inc./Intrazone Interactive Ltd. |
| CLARK, DICK | Clark Prods., Dick |
| CLARK, JAMES P. | Gibson, Dunn & Crutcher |
| *CLARK, JEROME F. | MCA TV Entertainment |
| CLARK, JERRY | MCA TV Entertainment |
| CLARK, ROGER | Bienstock & Clark |
| *CLARKE, AUBREY | Black Entertainment TV |
| *CLARKE, VAUGHN A. | Viacom, Inc. |
| CLEMMER, RONNIE D. | Longbow Prods. |
| *CLIFFORD, GERALD | Maroevich, O'Shea and Coghlan Ins. Brokers |
| CLINE, DENNIS | Behr & Robinson |
| CLINE, KELLY | Twentieth Century Fox Television |
| CLYNE, TIMOTHY | RHI Entertainment |
| COCHI, TONY | Warner Bros. PayTV |
| CODIKOW, DAVID | Codikow & Carroll |
| CODRON, IRVING | Braverman, Codron & Co. |
| COHANNE, POLIN | Hayes, Hume, Petas, Richards & Cohanne |
| COHEN, ALLAN S. | Cohen, Allan S. |
| COHEN, CHARLIE | Metro-Goldwyn-Mayer Inc. |
| COHEN, EVAN | Cohen & Luckenbacher |
| COHEN, GARY | Sidley & Austin |
| *COHEN, JAMEY | Ziffren Brittenham Branca & Fischer |
| COHEN, JOSEPH N. | InterMedia/Film Equities Inc. |
| *COHEN, KATHRYN | Prime Sports |
| COHEN, MARTIN | Cohen & Luckenbacher |
| *COHEN, MERYL | Paramount Domestic TV |
| COHEN, ROBERT | Harmony Gold |
| *COHEN, ROBERT | Twentieth Century Fox Film Corp. |
| COHEN, RON | Near North Insurance Brokerage, Inc. |
| COHEN, VALERIE | Walt Disney Company, The |
| COLBERT, ROBERT | Guild Management Corporation |
| COLDEN, DAVID | Weissmann, Wolff, Bergman, Coleman & Silverman |
| *COLE-FORD, ALAN | Metro-Goldwyn-Mayer Inc. |
| COLEMAN, STAN | Weissmann, Wolff, Bergman, Coleman & Silverman |
| COLEMAN, THOMAS J. | Rocket Pictures |
| COLFIN, BRUCE E. | Jacobson & Colfin, P.C. |
| COLICHMAN, PAUL | IRS Media |
| COLIN, JEFF | Goldman, Sachs & Co. |
| COLLAS, JUAN C. | Imperial Ent. |
| COLLERAN, JOSEPH | Orion Pictures Corporation |
| *COLLIER, THOMAS | Dobson Global Entertainment |
| COLLINS, MARGARET | Metro-Goldwyn-Mayer Inc. |
| COLLISON, EDNA | Stiletto Entertainment |
| *COLVIN, JEFF | Imperial Bank, Ent. Ind. Group |
| COMPTON, MICHAEL | Clark Prods., Dick |
| CONCOFF, GARY | Mitchell, Silberberg & Knupp |
| CONNOLLY, PATTI J. | Warner Bros. Pictures |
| CONRAD ERWIN, JOAN | Shane Co., A |
| *CONROY, TIMOTHY | KCET, Community TV of So. California |
| COOK, MELANIE K. | Bloom Dekom Hergott & Cook |

| | |
|---|---|
| COOKE, GEORGE | HBO (NYC) |
| *COOKE, JOHN | Walt Disney Company, The |
| COOPER, BILL | DIC Entertainment |
| *COOPER, DAVID S. | Dean Witter Reynolds |
| *COOPER, JERRY | Showtime Networks Inc. |
| COOPER, ROBERT | HBO (L.A.) |
| COPLAN, DANIEL J. | Coplan, Daniel J. |
| CORBER, BRIAN LEE | Corber, Brian Lee |
| CORDES, TED | NBC Entertainment |
| *CORMAN, JULIE | Concorde/New Horizons Corp. |
| *CORMAN, ROGER | Concorde/New Horizons Corp. |
| CORT, ROBERT | Interscope Communications Inc. |
| *CORZO, ROBERT | Largo Entertainment |
| *COSTLEY, SUSAN | NBC Inc. |
| COTTON, RICK | NBC Inc. |
| *COTUGNO, JEFF | Taffner Entertainment Ltd. |
| *COUGHLAN, KATHY | Spelling Entertainment Group Inc. |
| COULTER, JULIE | Coulter & Sands, Inc. |
| *COULTER, RONNI | TNT/Turner Pictures Inc. |
| COUNTRYMAN, BYRON C. | Countryman & McDaniel |
| COWAN, GARY | National Lampoon |
| *COWAN, JIM | Pacific Arts |
| COX, CRAIG | Philips Media Electronic Publishing |
| *COYNE, STEPHEN | Capell, Coyne & Co. |
| *CRABBE, MICHAEL | E! Entertainment Television |
| *CRAMER, DOUGLAS S. | Cramer Company, The |
| CRESPO, GLORIA | Actor's Equity Association (A.E.A.) |
| *CROMACK, GERALD H. | Furman Selz Inc. |
| *CRONIN, RICH | Nickelodeon |
| *CROOK, GEORGE D. | Kehr Crook Tovmassian & Fox |
| CRYSTAL, ROBERT | Grundy Prods. Inc., Reg |
| CUCCI, JOHN | Comedy Central |
| CUDDY, CHRISTINE | Mitchell, Silberberg & Knupp |
| *CUNNINGHAM, CHRISTINE | Paramount Domestic TV |
| CUNNINGHAM, KIM | Viewer's Choice |
| CUNNINGHAM, ROBERT | Buena Vista Picts. Distrib. |
| CURRAN, BRIAN | Boz Productions |
| CURRAN, JENNIFER | Island Pictures Corp. |
| CUSTER, BARBARA | Orion Pictures Corporation |
| *CYFFKA, PETER | Twentieth Century Fox Film Corp. |
| D'AMELIO, ANGELO | HBO (NYC) |
| *D'AMICO, KIRK | Videfilm Producers Intl. |
| *D'ONOFRIO, JOSEPH | Armstrong, Hirsch, Jackoway, et al. |
| DA SILVA, LAWRENCE | First Interstate Bank of Calif - Ent. Div. |
| DALY, JED | Movie Group, The |
| *DALY, ROBERT A. | Warner Bros.. |
| *DAMON, MARK | Damon Prods. Worldwide, Mark |
| DANE, KAREN | Walt Disney Motion Pictures Group |
| *DANG, PETER | Saban Entertainment |
| DANTZLER, LARRY | Family Channel, The |
| *DANZIGER, SUSAN | Bohbot Entertainment |
| DASHEV, RONNIE | Maverick |
| DAUGHERTY, DAVID | Polygram Filmed Ent. |
| *DAUMAN, PHILLIPPE P. | Viacom, Inc. |
| *DAVATZES, NICKOLAS | A&E Television Networks |
| DAVEY, BRUCE | Icon Productions Inc. |
| DAVID, PIERRE | Image Organization |
| *DAVIDS, DAN | A&E Television Networks |
| DAVIS, ELIZABETH V. | August Entertainment |
| DAVIS, FRANK | Metro-Goldwyn-Mayer Inc. |
| *DAVIS, GEORGE | Universal Pictures |
| DAVIS, PHILIP | Mitchell, Silberberg & Knupp |
| *DAWANA, FILIP | Castle Rock Entertainment |
| DE FELICE, ALDO | Sullivan Ent. |
| DE LUCA, MICHAEL | New Line Cinema |
| DE MARCO, JOSEPH M. | Twentieth Century Fox Film Corp. |
| DEBITETTO, ROBERT | Walt Disney Motion Pictures Group |
| DEMANN, FREDDY | Maverick |
| *DEMARCO, GUY | AON Entertainment Ltd. Ins. Services |
| *DEVITO, DANNY | Jersey Films |
| DEAN, TOMLINSON | Persky Prods., Lester |
| DEKOM, PETER J. | Bloom Dekom Hergott & Cook |
| DEL, ERNEST | Del, Rubel, Shaw, Mason & Derin |
| *DENENHOLZ, JUDY | Buena Vista Home Video |
| *DENITZ, FRED | Bank of America, NT&SA |
| DENIUS, WOFFORD | Sloane, Owen |
| DENKERT, DARCI | Metro-Goldwyn-Mayer Inc. |
| DERIN, GREG | Del, Rubel, Shaw, Mason & Derin |
| DERN, DIXON Q. | Dern & Vein |
| *DERN, WARREN D. | Dern & Vein |
| DESIDERIO, CARMEN | Paramount Pictures . |
| *DETRES, LOREN A. | Rubenstien & Finch |
| DEVEJIAN, ADAM | InterMedia/Film Equities Inc. |
| DEYHLE, ROLF | Capella Films Inc. |

DEZART, JAMES H. .............................................. Price Waterhouse
DI PIETRA, ROSEMARY ............................ Paramount Pictures .
*DICANIO, GERARD ............................................ NBC Productions

*DIAZ, WENDY ..................................................Chubb Insurance Co.
DICKEY, GARY ......................................................Deloitte & Touche
DIEMER, JOHN D................................ Bloom Dekom Hergott & Cook
DIMBORT, DANNY ......................................................... Nu Image
DIPPLE, EDWARD A. ..................... American Specialty Underwriters (ASU)
DISNEY, ROY E. ....................................... Walt Disney Company, The
DIZENFELD, DAVID ............................................ Stephens & Associates
*DOBSON, ANDREW ...................Dobson Global Entertainment
*DOBSON, BRIDGET........................Dobson Global Entertainment
DOBY, BRENDA ....................................Horwitz Organization, The Lewis
DOCKRY, NANCY ....................................................Dockry Productions
*DOCTOROW, ERIC ............... Paramount Home Video Distribution
DONNENFELD, BERNARD .............. Mitchell, Silberberg & Knupp
DOODAN, MICHAEL ....................Twentieth Century Fox Film Corp.
*DOOLEY, THOMAS E............................................. Viacom, Inc.
*DORAMUS, MARK ........................................... Stephens Inc.
*DORAN, LINDSAY ...................................... Mirage Enterprises
DORSEY, III, ALBERT .................................... O'Hara/Gregg Films
DORT, DENNIS................................. Buena Vista Home Video
DOUGHERTY, CRAIG ...................Union Bank Media Group
*DOUGHERTY, JAY ...................Twentieth Century Fox Film Corp.
DOUGLASS, GARI ANN ............... Paramount Home Video Distribution
DOWNEY, M. PETER ...............................................................PBS
*DOYLE, SEAN ...............................................Laidlaw Holdings Inc.
DRAPKIN, STEVEN G. ..................... Proskauer, Rose, Goetz & Mendelsohn
DUBOW, MYRON ...........................Playboy Entertainment Group Inc.
DUBELKO, BOB ...................................... Carsey-Werner Co., The
*DUDAS, SUSAN ................................... California United Bank
DUDNIK, ROBERT M. ............... Paul, Hastings, Janosky & Walker
*DUFFY, ROBERT E...............................Hill Wynne Troop & Meisinger
DUGGAN, ERVIN ...........................................................PBS
*DUKE, KATHLEEN ....................International Film Guarantors Inc.
DULL, DAVID A. .............................................. Irell & Manella
DUNN, JEFFREY ....................................................... Nickelodeon
DURKIN, RON ...............................................21st Century Film Corp.
*DURNEY, MIKE ............................................... RHI Entertainment
*EATON, DIAN ...............................................Triple-7 Entertainment
EDELL, JEFFREY .......................Duitch, Poteshman, Franklin & Co.
EDELSTEIN, GERALD.........................Edelstein, Laird & Sobel
EDWARDS, LEE .......................Matlen & Associates, C.P.A., H. Roy
EGERTON, ANNE ...............................................NBC Entertainment
*EICHORN, ROBERT ........................Sony Pictures Entertainment
EISEN, BRUCE.....................................................Trimark Holdings Inc.
EISENBERG, ALAN ........................Actor's Equity Association (A.E.A.)
EISENBERG, VIVIANE ...........................................HBO (L.A.)

EISENSTEIN, LOIS ...................................... MTV Networks
EISNER, MICHAEL D. ....................Walt Disney Company, The
ELKINS, FRED ............... Elkins & Elkins, An Accountancy Corp.
ELKINS, GERALD ............... Elkins & Elkins, An Accountancy Corp.
*ELKINS, STEPHEN R. ............ Maroevich, O'Shea and Coghlan Ins. Brokers
ELLIOTT, DOUGLAS F.................................. AmSouth Bank, N.A.
ELMENDORF, RICHARD I.................... First National Bank of Chicago, The
*ELSON, PETER .............................................. Largo Entertainment
ELWAY, PHILIP ....................................................RCS/PMP Films
*EMANUEL, CRAIG ...................Sinclair, Tenenbaum, Olesiuk & Co., Inc.
EMBREE, MEL ................... Gordon, The Law Office Of, Peter D.
*EMILIO, ALISON................... Toronto/Ontario Film Development Corp.
*ENCARNACION, RENE ........................... Bank of Montreal
ENDELSON, RICK ...................................Landsburg Co., The
*ENGEL, CHARLES ...................................Universal Television
EPHRAIM, LIONEL A. ................Percenterprises Completion Bonds, Inc.
*EPSTEIN, ALAN J.... Armstrong, Hirsch, Jackoway, Tyerman & Wertheimer
EPSTEIN, B.L. ...................................Franklin/Waterman Ent.
EPSTEIN, IRA.............Weissmann, Wolff, Bergman, Coleman & Silverman
*ERICKSON, J. GUNNAR.............. Armstrong, Hirsch, Jackoway, et al.
ESKENAZI, BONNIE E. ..... Greenberg Glusker Fields Claman & Machtinger
EVANS, VALERIE J. ...................... American Specialty Underwriters (ASU)
EVANS, ESQ., DAVID J..........................................Evans, David J.
EYRES, JOHN ...............................EGM Film International Inc.
*EYRES, PAUL ...............................EGM Film International Inc.
EZOR, A. EDWARD ...................................Elliott Ent., Lang
FABRICK, HOWARD D. ..... Proskauer, Rose, Goetz & Mendelsohn
FADEM, STEVEN S. .......................................... Viacom Productions
FAGER, CHRISTOPHER ........................ E! Entertainment Television
*FAMULARI, VINCENT ........................Orion Pictures Corporation
FARBERMAN, PAUL ........................................Universal Pictures
FARREN, MERRITT ...................Walt Disney Motion Pictures Group
*FASS, STACY ...............................................Codikow & Carroll
FAST, ADAM .............................................Excelsior Pictures Corp.

FAYNE, STEVEN........................... Rosenfeld, Meyer & Susman
FEDAK, SUZANNE ...............................................In Pictures, Ltd.
FEDERMAN, MARC ............... Near North Insurance Brokerage, Inc.
*FEITSHANS, ERICK ...............Cinergi Pictures Entertainment Inc.
*FELD, KENNETH...............................Pachyderm Entertainment
*FELDGRABER, DON ...................................Warner Bros. Television
*FELDMAN, DAVID B............... Bloom Dekom Hergott & Cook
FELDMAN, LINDSEY ...........................................Sloane, Owen
*FELDMAN, MARK ...............................E! Entertainment Television
FELDMAN, MARTIN ...................Gelfand, Rennert & Feldman

FELDSTEIN, ALAN ...............Hall Dickler Kent Friedman & Wood
FELKER, PATTI C. ......... Nelson, Guggenheim, Felker & Levine
*FELTHEIMER, JON ................Columbia TriStar Television
*FENSTER, FRED ...................................Heenan Blaikie
FERGUSON, KEN ...............................Clark Prods., Dick
FERLEGER, DANIEL ...................Twentieth Century Fox Film Corp.
FERMIN, MARISA ...............................................Twentieth TV
FERN, MARTIN ...................................................Loeb & Loeb
FERRARI, KATHY...............................................Harmony Gold
*FERRELL, GARY ...................KCET, Community TV of So. California
FETTER, TREVOR ...................Metro-Goldwyn-Mayer Inc.
FICKENSCHER, SUE ............... Castle Rock Entertainment
FIELD, TED ............................... Interscope Communications Inc.
FIELDS, BERTRAM............ Greenberg Glusker Fields Claman & Machtinger
FIELDS, FREDDIE ...................................Fields & Hellman Co., The
*FIKE, DAVID...............................................Chubb Insurance Co.
FILLION, JEAN-YVES ...........................................Banque Paribas
*FINCH, ROXANNE T. ...............................Rubenstien & Finch
FINDELLE, STANN ............... Findelle Law & Mgmt., Stann
*FINE, JAKE ...........Padell, Nadell, Fine, Weinberger & Co.
*FINEMAN, THOMAS J.........Myman, Abell, Fineman, Greenspan & Rowan
FINIGAN, CHRIS ...................................Icon Productions Inc.
*FINK, MARTIN ...................................Complete Film Corp.
*FINKEL, HARVEY...................................New World Entertainment
FINKELSTEIN, JEFFREY S. ............... Del, Rubel, Shaw, Mason & Derin
FINKELSTEIN, RICK ...................................Polygram Filmed Ent.
FISCHEL, SHELLEY ...........................................HBO (L.A.)
*FISCHER, JOSEPH A ...................................MCA Inc.
FISCHER, MARTI ............... Ventura Entertainment Group Ltd.
FISCHER, SAMUEL...........Ziffren Brittenham Branca & Fischer
*FISHELMAN, BRUCE C. ............Stanbury, Fishelman & Levy
FISHER, BARBARA ...................................MCA TV Entertainment
FITCHEY, CARY ...................................Sojourn Entertainment
FITZROY, ANNE STEWART ...................FitzRoy, Anne Stewart
FLANAGAN, DAYNA ...................Bochco Prods., Steven
FLEIDERMAN, ARIANE...................Four Point Entertainment
FLEISCHER, MARK O. ................ Manatt, Phelps & Phillips
FLEMING, BOB ....................................................FX Networks
FLICKER, NORMAN ...................................Goldwyn Co., Samuel
FLOCKER, JAMES T....................Program Power Ent. Inc.
FLOYD, CHRIS ...................Walt Disney Motion Pictures Group
FLUGGE, VALERIE ...................................Slaff, Mosk, & Rudman
*FOLTA, CARL D. .............................................. Viacom, Inc.
FORESTER, BURTON N. ...................................Price Waterhouse
FORMAN, RALPH ...................I.N.I. Entertainment Group Inc.

FORTE, DEBORAH ...........................................Scholastic Prods.
FOSSUM, JOHN ...........................................Irell & Manella
FOWKES, RICHARD ...........Paramount Pictures Motion Picture Group
*FOX, DAVID...................................Dog Beach Productions
FOX, DAVID M. ...................Kehr Crook Tovmassian & Fox
*FOX, KAREN...............................................Fox Broadcasting Co.
FOX, LAURA ...................Walt Disney Motion Pictures Group
FOX, MARTIN ............... Bernstein, Fox, Goldberg & Licker
FOX, SAMUEL J. ...........Blanc, Williams, Johnston & Kronstadt
FRANCKE, ROBERT ...................................Austin Prods., Bruce
FRANCO, FRANK ...........Padell, Nadell, Fine, Weinberger & Co.
*FRANK, CHRIS ...................Wood & Freeman Business Management
FRANKENHEIMER, JOHN ...................................Loeb & Loeb
FRANKIE, RICHARD ...................Columbia TriStar TV Distribution
FRANKLIN, JEFF ...................................Franklin/Waterman Ent.
FRANKLIN, LISA A. ...................Walt Disney Motion Pictures Group
FRANKLIN, WARREN ...................................Colossal Pictures
FRANKS, MARTIN ...................................CBS Entertainment
FRASER, HAROLD ............... Paramount Home Video Distribution
FRAZIER, ART ...................Walt Disney Motion Pictures Group
*FREEDMAN, DAVID...........Sinclair, Tenenbaum, Olesiuk & Co., Inc.
FREEMAN, BEVERLY ...........Wood & Freeman Business Management
FREEMAN, STUART ...........Wood & Freeman Business Management
FREIDMAN, GERRY ...................Fox TV Stations Prods.
FRESTON, THOMAS E. ...................................MTV Networks
FREY, STEVEN ...................................*Royal & Associates, Inc.
*FREYDBERG, JAMES ...................................Pachyderm Entertainment

*FRICKLAS, MICHAEL D. .......... Viacom, Inc.
FRIEDMAN, BRIAN P. .......... Furman Selz Inc.
FRIEDMAN, CYNTHIA .......... Orion Pictures Corporation
FRIEDMAN, HAROLD .......... Mitchell, Silberberg & Knupp
*FRIEDMAN, STEPHEN .......... Kings Road Entertainment Inc.
*FRIEDRICKS, LARRY .......... Kushner-Locke Co.
FRIES, CHARLES W. .......... Fries Entertainment
FRIESE, DICK .......... RHH/Albert G. Ruben Ins. Services Inc.
FRISBY, MICHAEL .......... Ashley & Frisby
*FRITH, SARA .......... Katten Muchin Zavis & Weitzman
FRY, RON .......... Reynolds & Reynolds Inc.
FRYMAN, TIMOTHY .......... Squeak Pictures Inc.
FUCHS, MICHAEL .......... HBO (NYC)
*FUELLING, TOM .......... Goldwyn Co., Samuel
*FUNK, JUDD .......... New Line Cinema
FURIE, DAN .......... Warner Bros. Pictures
FURMAN, ROY L. .......... Furman Selz Inc.
*FUTTER, WILLIAM P. .......... Mesirow Private Equity

GABAI, DAVID .......... Check Entertainment
GADNEY, ALAN .......... Film-Video Financial Presentations
GAGLIANO, BOB .......... KPMG Peat Marwick
GALE, RHONDA .......... Orion Pictures Corporation
GALKA, RENEE A. .......... Rosenfeld, Meyer & Susman
*GALKER, ANDREW L. .......... Armstrong, Hirsch, Jackoway, et al.
*GALLOGY, MARTIN .......... Nostalgia Television
*GALLOZZI, SERGIO .......... Castle Rock Entertainment
GARAND, JOHN .......... Walt Disney Company, The
GARIN, MICHAEL N. .......... Furman Selz Inc.
*GARRESI, MARIO .......... First Los Angeles Bank, Ent. Ind. Div.
*GARRETT, ROBERT .......... AdMedia Corporate Advisors Inc.
GARVIN, THOMAS F. R. .......... Ervin, Cohen & Jessup
GARZILLI, RICHARD .......... Le Studio Canal + (U.S.)
GARZILLI, RICHARD .......... Coudert Bros.
GEARY, ROBERT .......... TriStar Pictures
GEFFEN, DAVID .......... Geffen Pictures
*GEFFEN, DAVID .......... Dreamworks/SKG
*GEIBELSON, JEFFREY .......... Savitsky Satin & Geibelson
GELETKO, JUDY .......... Avenue Pictures
GELFAND, CHARLES .......... Gelfand, Newman & Wasserman
GELFAND, MARSHALL M. .......... Gelfand, Rennert & Feldman
GELFAND, TODD E. .......... Gelfand, Rennert & Feldman
GELLEN, ROBERT .......... RHH/Albert G. Ruben Ins. Services Inc.
*GELLES, RICHARD .......... Codikow & Carroll
GEMBALLA, ERIC .......... AON Entertainment Ltd. Ins. Services
GENDLER, MICHAEL .......... Irell & Manella
*GENGA, JOHN M. .......... Hill Wynne Troop & Meisinger
GEOFFRAY, JEFF .......... Blue Rider Pictures
*GEORGE, DANA .......... Castle Rock Entertainment
GERBER, DAVID .......... Gerber ITC Ent. Group, The
GERBER, JEFF .......... American Specialty Underwriters (ASU)
GERSE, STEVEN .......... Walt Disney Motion Pictures Group
*GERSON, ROCHELLE .......... Carsey-Werner Co., The
GERTZ, PAUL .......... Kirschner Prods., David
*GETMAN, ROBERT S. .......... Armstrong, Hirsch, Jackoway, et al.
GETTLESON, HARVEY .......... Ernst & Young
GHALAYINI, SHUKRI .......... Four Point Entertainment
GIACCHETTO, MR. DANA C. .......... Cassandra Group Inc., The
GIBSON, JON .......... TriStar Pictures
GILBERT-LURIE, CLIFFORD .......... Ziffren Brittenham Branca & Fischer
GILLIAM, ANNE .......... Artists Legal & Accounting Assistance
*GILLIN, PHILIP H. .......... Alperin, Esq., Howard K.
GILMARTIN, MAJKEN M. .......... Mister/SISTER Prods.

*GINNANE, ANTONY T. .......... Fries Entertainment
GINSBURG, DANA .......... Icon Productions Inc.
GINSBURG, DAVID R. .......... Citadel Entertainment, L.P.
GIOIA, DINO .......... Spectacor Films
GIRARD, RAYMOND .......... Film Funding Inc.
GLADSTONE, LEON .......... Berger, Kahn, Shafton, Moss, Figler, et al.
GLENN, DAWN WEEKES .......... Blanc, Williams, Johnston & Kronstadt
GLICKMAN, STUART .......... Carsey-Werner Co., The
*GLOTZER, LIZ .......... Castle Rock Entertainment
GLOVER, JEFFREY .......... Goldwyn Co., Samuel
GOCHMAN, MARK .......... Greenberg Glusker Fields Claman & Machtinger
GOEBEL, LARRY .......... Image Organization
GOLD, BERNARD D. .......... Proskauer, Rose, Goetz & Mendelsohn
GOLDBERG, ADA .......... ABC Productions
*GOLDBERG, RALPH .......... King World Prods.
*GOLDBERG, ROBERT .......... Bernstein, Fox, Goldberg & Licker
*GOLDEN, DIANE .......... Mitchell, Silberberg & Knupp
GOLDEN, NATHAN .......... Schlatter Prods., George
GOLDEN, RENEE WAYNE .......... Golden, Renee Wayne
*GOLDEN, ROGER N. .......... Unity Communications, Inc.
*GOLDEN, STAN .......... Saban Entertainment
*GOLDMAN, GERALD .......... Paramount Network TV
GOLDMAN, JOEL .......... Heenan Blaikie
GOLDMAN, STEVEN .......... Paramount Domestic TV
*GOLDSMITH, MICHAEL K. Myman, Abell, Fineman, Greenspan & Rowan
GOLDSMITH, ROBERT .......... Carolco Pictures
GOLDSTEIN, CHARLIE .......... Twentieth Century Fox Television
GOLDSTEIN, DAVID .......... Dancing Asparagus Prods.
*GOLDSTEIN, RON .......... Preferred Investment Group Ltd.
*GOLDWYN, JOHN .......... Paramount Pictures Motion Picture Group
GOLDWYN, JR., SAMUEL .......... Goldwyn Co., Samuel
*GOLIN, STEVE .......... Propaganda Films
*GONG, SANDRA .......... Orion Pictures Corporation
GOODING, STEVE .......... Reynolds & Reynolds Inc.
GOODMAN, DAVID .......... Castle Rock Entertainment
GOODMAN, KATHERINE .......... Katten Muchin Zavis & Weitzman
*GOODNIGHT, MICHAEL .......... Warner Bros. Pictures
*GOODSON, JONATHAN .......... Goodson Prods., Mark
*GORDON, BARRY .......... United Paramount Network
*GORDON, MR. HILLY .......... Duitch, Poteshman, Franklin & Co.
GORDON, PETER .......... Gordon, The Law Office Of, Peter D.
GORENC, NICK .......... Cinetel Films
GOTLIB, MICHELE .......... New Line Cinema
GOTTLIEB, JERRY .......... Jones-David Salzman Ent., Quincy
GOTTLIEB, MEYER .......... Goldwyn Co., Samuel

GOVREAU, LINDA .......... Henson Prods., Jim
*GRABER, DAVID F. .......... Rosenfeld, Meyer & Susman
*GRABER, WILL .......... Second City Entertainment, Inc., The
GRABOFF, MARC J. .......... Hill Wynne Troop & Meisinger
GRAF, LORI .......... California United Bank
GRAHAM, BEVERLY .......... U.S. Film Corp.
*GRAHAM, KARL .......... Padell, Nadell, Fine, Weinberger & Co.
GRAHAM, PETER .......... Ladenburg, Thalmann & Co. Inc.
GRAHAM II, PETER M. .......... Bank of California, The
*GRANA, TONY .......... Universal Pictures
GRANATH, HERBERT A. .......... ABC Cable & Intl. Broadcast Group
GRANT, DAVID .......... Fox Broadcasting Co.
GRAVES, W. REED .......... Price Waterhouse
GRAYSON, MARK .......... Rabbit Ears Prods.
*GRAZIOSI, MASSIMO .......... Castle Rock Entertainment
GREAVES, LAWRENCE H. .......... Bloom Dekom Hergott & Cook
*GREEN, BARBARA .......... Cinergi Pictures Entertainment Inc.
*GREEN, CATHRYN .......... Showtime Networks Inc.
*GREEN, PAUL .......... Propaganda Films
*GREEN, ROBIN .......... Castle Rock Entertainment
GREENBAUM, NORMAN L. .......... Singer Lewak Greenbaum & Goldstein
*GREENBERG, BERNARD .......... Rosenfeld, Meyer & Susman
*GREENBERG, BILL .......... Universal Pictures
*GREENBERG, BLAINE F. .......... Hill Wynne Troop & Meisinger
GREENBERG, JEFF .......... Beldock Levine & Hoffman
*GREENSPAN, ERIC R. .......... Myman, Abell, Fineman, Greenspan & Rowan
GREENSTEIN, SCOTT .......... Miramax Films
GREENWALD, STEPHEN .......... Vision International
GREGOROPOULOS, STEVE .......... Cinetel Films
*GREY, ROBIN .......... Scholastic Prods.
GRIFFITH, JOANNE .......... Paramount Pictures .
GRIFFITH, SHIRLEY .......... RHH/Albert G. Ruben Ins. Services Inc.
*GRIFFITHS, ALLEGRA .......... Bank of Montreal
GRIVETTI, BRUCE .......... HBO (NYC)
*GRODE, JOSH B. .......... Bloom Dekom Hergott & Cook
GRODIN, ALAN .......... Weissmann, Wolff, Bergman, Coleman & Silverman
GRONEMEYER, LYMAN .......... Twentieth Century Fox Film Corp.
GRONICH, DAPHNE .......... Fox TV Stations Prods.
GROSS, RAY .......... Gipson Hoffman & Pancione
GROSS, SUSAN O. .......... TNT/Turner Pictures Inc.
*GROSSI, LEN .......... United Paramount Network
*GROSSMAN, HEATHER .......... Icon Productions Inc.
GROSZ, PHILIP J. .......... Loeb & Loeb
GRUNDY, REG .......... Grundy Prods. Inc., Reg

GUADALUPE, RAFAEL .......... Angelika Films
GUARINO, DOUG .......... Braun Productions, David
*GUARINO, WESCOTT .......... Trimark Holdings Inc.
GUDVI, BERNARD .......... Gudvi, Chapnick & Oppenheim, Inc.
*GUERCIONI, SUSANNE A. .......... Rastar Prods.
GUESSOUS, LORING .......... ING Capital Corporation
GUGGENHEIM, ALFRED KIM .......... Nelson, Guggenheim, Felker & Levine
GUIDO, ANTHONY .......... RHI Entertainment
*GUMPERT, JON .......... Universal Pictures
GUTIERREZ, LOUIS .......... Paramount Pictures .
GUY, PATRICK .......... Lifetime Television (NY)
HABBERSHAW, SUZANNE .......... Carsey-Werner Co., The
*HABER, ROGER .......... Artists Financial Management, Ltd.


©1995, Hollywood Financial Directory No. 3
310-315-4815 or 800-815-0503 outside California

*HAFERKAMP, AL ........ Castle Rock Entertainment
*HAFF, WILT ........ Warner Bros. Television
*HAHN, HELENE ........ Dreamworks/SKG
HAIMOVITZ, JULES ........ ITC Ent. Group
HAINES, GORD ........ Alliance Communications
*HALBERSTADTER, DAVID ........ Hill Wynne Troop & Meisinger
HALDEMAN, E. BARRY ... Greenberg Glusker Fields Claman & Machtinger
HALFON, SHERI ........ Avenue Pictures
HALL, ARSENIO ........ Hall Communications, Arsenio
*HALLAM, KIRK M. ........ Rosenfeld, Meyer & Susman
HALLBERG, KATHLEEN ........ Ziffren Brittenham Branca & Fischer
HALLETT, CANDACE ........ American Specialty Underwriters (ASU)
HALLORAN, NANCY ........ Damon Prods. Worldwide, Mark
*HALLOWAY, LAURA ........ Active Entertainment
HALMI JR., ROBERT ........ RHI Entertainment
HALMI, SR., ROBERT ........ RHI Entertainment
HALPERN, TED ........ Halpern & Mantovani
HAMBY JR., ROBERT E. ........ Multimedia Inc.
*HAMILL, MICHAEL ........ Pacific Arts
*HAMILTON, CAROL ........ RKO Pictures, Inc.
*HAMILTON, DEAN ........ Hamilton Entertainment, Inc., Dean
HAMILTON, DOUGLAS ........ USA Network
*HANDEL, JONATHAN L. ........ Behr & Robinson
HANKIN, ROCK N. ........ Hankin & Co.
HANNA, WILLIAM D. ........ Hanna-Barbera, Inc.
HANSEN, DOUG ........ Banque Paribas
*HANSEN, JOAN ........ Twentieth Century Fox Film Corp.
HANSON, CANDICE S. ........ Bloom Dekom Hergott & Cook
HARBONVILLE, CHRISTOPHER ........ Excelsior Pictures Corp.
HARMON, CAROLE ........ Paramount Domestic TV
*HARNDEN, MISHKA ........ Lauren International
HARPER, WILLIAM L. ........ Gelfand, Rennert & Feldman

*HARPUR, REGINALD G. ........ Warner Bros. Worldwide
HARRAH, VERNA ........ Cinema Line Films Corp.
*HARRELL, RON ........ Castle Rock Entertainment
*HARRIS, JONATHAN ........ TNT/Turner Pictures Inc.
HARRIS, KATHRYN ........ First Entertainment Federal Credit Union
*HARRIS, MEL ........ Sony Television Entertainment
HARRIS, RICHARD S. ........ Katten Muchin Zavis & Weitzman
HARRISON, DANIEL ........ Neila Inc.
*HARSTEDT, ALISON ........ Castle Rock Entertainment
HART, ALISON ........ Hart III Insurance Agency, John William
HART, GARRETT S. ........ Paramount Network TV
*HART, GENO ........ Hart Brothers Ent. Corp.
HART, JOSEPH ........ Weinstein & Hart
HART, LORIANN ........ Hart III Insurance Agency, John William
HART, RUSSELL ........ Hart III Insurance Agency, John William
HART III, JOHN WM. ........ Hart III Insurance Agency, John William
HARTLEY, TED ........ RKO Pictures, Inc.
HASSELHOFF, DAVID ........ Baywatch Production Co.
*HAWKINS, THOMAS W. ........ Blockbuster Entertainment Group
HAWKINS, WILLIAM ........ Paramount Pictures .
HAYES, DANNY ........ Nelson, Guggenheim, Felker & Levine
*HAYNES, DANA L. ........ Hankin & Co.
*HAYUM, GEORGE T. ........ Armstrong, Hirsch, Jackoway, et al.
HAZAN, EDWARD ........ Mruvka Entertainment, Alan
*HEALY, JOHN ........ ABC Cable & Intl. Broadcast Group
HEARST III, WILLIAM R. ........ Longfellow Prods.
HEDSTROM, SCOTTYE ...... Walt Disney Television & Telecommunications
*HEIM, JOHN ........ Nostalgia Television
HEIN, JEAN ........ Rysher Entertainment
HEISS, JERRY ........ RCS/PMP Films
HELFANT, DAVID A. ........ Berger, Kahn, Shafton, Moss, Figler, et al.
HELFANT, MICHAEL ........ Interscope Communications Inc.
*HELFET, TIM ........ Rysher Entertainment
HELLMAN, JEROME ........ Fields & Hellman Co., The
*HEMMERLING, GERALDINE S. ........ Armstrong, Hirsch, Jackoway, et al.
HENDERSON, MARTHA ........ City National Bank - Ent. Div.
*HENDLER, DAVID C. ........ Buena Vista Home Video
HENRY, CAROL ........ Lightstorm Entertainment Inc.
HENRY, JAMES A. ........ NBC Entertainment
HENSON, BRIAN ........ Henson Prods., Jim
HENSON, LISA ........ Columbia Pictures
*HEPPEL, ALAN ........ Paramount Pictures Motion Picture Group
HERGOTT, ALAN S. ........ Bloom Dekom Hergott & Cook

*HERMAN, MICHAEL J. ........ Third Eye Telepictures
*HERNANDEZ, GEORGE ........ Trivision Pictures Inc.
*HERSKER, JOHN ........ Paramount Domestic Distribution
*HERTLEIN, RUDOLPH L. ........ Viacom, Inc.
*HERZ, MICHAEL ........ Troma Inc.
*HERZOG, IRA ........ Padell, Nadell, Fine, Weinberger & Co.
*HESHEJIN, BEHNAM ........ Stone & Asoociates
HESTER, JOHN ........ Orion Pictures Corporation
*HETTRICK, CLYDE M. ........ Hill Wynne Troop & Meisinger
HEVENLY, JUDY ........ British Connection
*HEWITT, ROBIN ........ Neo Motion Pictures, Inc.
HEYWARD, ANDY ........ DIC Entertainment
HICKOX, S. BRYAN ........ Hickox-Bowman Prods., Inc.
HIGGINS, SCOTT ........ MTM
*HIGHTOWER, DENNIS ....... Walt Disney Television & Telecommunications
HIKAWA, CHRISTINE ........ ABC Entertainment
HILL, DENNIS ........ Hill Wynne Troop & Meisinger
HILTON, MEL ........ Diamond Jim Productions
*HINMAN, JOEL ........ Black & White Television, Inc.
HIRSCH, BARRY ...... Armstrong, Hirsch, Jackoway, Tyerman & Wertheimer
HIRSCH, GARY ........ TriStar Pictures
HIRSCH, JAMES G. ........ Papazian-Hirsch Entertainment
HIRSCH, NOAH S. ........ Hirsch, Noah S.
HIRSHLAND, DAVID L. ........ Rosenfeld, Meyer & Susman
HOFFMAN, ELLIOT L. ........ Beldock Levine & Hoffman
HOFFMAN, NATHALIE R. ........ Hoffman, Nathalie R.
*HOFFMAN, RAND ........ PolyGram Video
*HOFMANN, MICKIE ........ Dobson Global Entertainment
*HOGGAN-EGBINGER, ROBIN ........ Castle Rock Entertainment
*HOLDGREIWE, DANIEL ........ Nostalgia Television
HOLENDER, IRV ........ I.N.I. Entertainment Group Inc.
HOLLAND, SALLY ........ MCA TV Entertainment
HOLLANDER, DAVID ........ Morrison & Foerster
*HOLLAR, JOHN C. ........ PBS
*HOLLEY, SUSAN E. ........ Rosenfeld, Meyer & Susman
HOLLIDAY, SUSAN ........ CBS Entertainment
HOLMES, HENRY ........ Weissmann, Wolff, Bergman, Coleman & Silverman
HOLMES, JEFF ........ Skouras Picts. Inc.
*HOLSTEN, TAMI A. ........ Rubenstien & Finch
*HONDROGEN, NICHOLAS ........ About Face Prods.
*HOOPS, KATHLEEN ........ Paramount Pictures .
HOPE, DAVID ........ ITC Ent. Group
HOPE, MICHAEL S. ........ Metro-Goldwyn-Mayer Inc.
HOPKINS, ANNE ........ Rees Assocs., Marian
*HOPP, THOMAS ........ Hopp, Thomas

HORACEK, JOSEPH ........ Manatt, Phelps & Phillips
HORN, ALAN ........ Castle Rock Entertainment
HORNSTEIN, JAMES ........ Greenberg Glusker Fields Claman & Machtinger
HOROVITZ, RACHAEL ........ Longfellow Prods.
HOROWITZ, DR. LAWRENCE ........ O'Hara-Horowitz Productions
HOROWITZ, MARK ........ TriStar Pictures
HORWITZ, LEWIS ........ Horwitz Organization, The Lewis
*HOUSER, CATHERINE ........ Orion Pictures Corporation
HOUSER, CHERYL MILLER ........ Buckeye Communications
HOWARD, ROBERT F. ........ Houlihan Lokey Howard & Zukin
HOWELL, DANIEL P. ........ Mesirow Private Equity
*HOWELLS, JR., TED ........ Sony Pictures Entertainment
*HOWLE, SANDEE ........ AON Entertainment Ltd. Ins. Services
HUANG, RICHARD ........ Fortis Entertainment
*HUBSCH, ANDREW ........ Cannell Prods. Inc., Stephen J.
HUDSON, BILL ........ Vansa Insurance Services
*HULL, TONY ........ King World Prods.
HUME, RICHARD SCOTT ........ Hayes, Hume, Petas, Richards & Cohanne
HUMMEL, ROB ........ Walt Disney TV Animation
HUMPHREY, DAVID ........ Family Channel, The
HUNCKE, JOHN ........ ITC Ent. Group
HUNEGS, CRAIG ........ NBC Entertainment
*HUNG, ASA ........ Walt Disney Motion Pictures Group
HUNTER, THOMAS F. ........ Bloom Dekom Hergott & Cook
HUTCHINSON, DAVID ........ Betzer Films Inc., Just
HYDE, JOHN ........ MCEG Sterling Ent.
IGE-WONG, EILEEN ........ Paramount Network TV
ILITCH, JR., MIKE ........ Prelude Pictures
IMMERMAN, WILLIAM J. ........ Kenoff & Machtinger
INGBER, JEFFREY C. ........ Ingber, Jeffrey C.
INOYUE, RICHARD ........ Cannon Pictures
ISAKOFF, LOU ........ Family Channel, The
ISENBERG, GERALD ........ Hearst Entertainment
ISER, LAWRENCE ........ Greenberg Glusker Fields Claman & Machtinger
ITTNER, MARK ........ Saban Entertainment
*IVERS, JEFF ........ Motion Picture Corp. of America
JACKEL, DAVID ........ Gelfand, Rennert & Feldman
JACKOWAY, JAMES Armstrong, Hirsch, Jackoway, Tyerman & Wertheimer
JACKSON, SARAH ........ Carthay Circle Pictures & Mgmt.
JACOBI, RONALD ........ Sony Pictures Entertainment
*JACOBSEN, LISA ........ Rosenfeld, Meyer & Susman
JACOBSEN, MARK ........ Colossal Pictures
*JACOBSON, ERIC ........ Twentieth TV
JACOBSON, ERIC S. ........ Program Power Ent. Inc.
*JACOBSON, JAKE ........ Paramount Network TV

JACOBSON, JEFFREY E. .... Jacobson & Colfin, P.C.
*JACOBSON, LARRY .... Fox Broadcasting Co.
JACOBSON, WILLIAM P. .... Browning, Jacobson & Klein
JACOBUS, ANN K. .... MCEG Sterling Ent.
*JAHRMARKT, JOHN .... Zenith Entertainment
JAMESON, PAULA .... PBS
*JAMESON, SUSAN .... Sony Pictures Entertainment
*JAMSHIDI, GOLY .... Concorde/New Horizons Corp.
JANKOWSKI, DIANE L. .... JI Business Services
*JANOFSY, LEONARD .... Paul, Hastings, Janosky & Walker
*JASON, ROBERT M. .... Hill Wynne Troop & Meisinger
JENNEY, JOHN A. .... Smith Affiliated Capital Corp.
JENSON, WARREN .... NBC Entertainment
*JENSON, WARREN .... NBC Inc.
JESUELE, ROBERT .... Coudert Bros.
*JHIN, DR. KYO R. .... Sentinel Television Corporation
*JIMIRRO, JAMES P. .... National Lampoon
*JOFFRE, JEAN-FRANCOIS .... Tulchin & Associates, Harris
JOHNS, PAUL A. .... VanDerKloot Film & Television Inc.
*JOHNSON, CHRIS .... Film Capital Corporation
*JOHNSON, DAVID .... Metro-Goldwyn-Mayer Inc.
JOHNSON, FRANKLIN R. .... Price Waterhouse
JOHNSON, KATHLEEN .... Johnson, Kathleen K.
JOHNSON, NEVILLE L. .... Johnson & Assoc., Neville L.
JOHNSON, ROBERT W. .... Walt Disney Motion Pictures Group
*JOHNSON, RUTH .... Berggren, Arthur T.
*JOHNSON, JR., GEORGE D. .... Blockbuster Entertainment Group
*JONES, CAMERON .... Rosenfeld, Meyer & Susman
*JONES, CHRISTOPHER .... Hanna-Barbera, Inc.
JONES, GREG .... Near North Insurance Brokerage, Inc.
JONES, PAUL .... American Business Ins. Brokers LA, Inc./Acordia
JONES, QUINCY .... Jones-David Salzman Ent., Quincy
JONES, WALLACE B. .... Hankin & Co.
*JONES, WILLIAM .... Metro-Goldwyn-Mayer Inc.
JORDAN, CHERYL .... Celebrity Home Ent.
JOSEY, BILL .... Saban Entertainment
*JOSS, ERIS .... Paul, Hastings, Janosky & Walker
JOSTEN, WALTER .... Blue Rider Pictures
JULIEN, JAY .... Julien & Associates Inc.
JUN, JOYCE S. .... Loeb & Loeb
*JUSSIM, JARED .... Sony Pictures Entertainment
*JUSTMAN, JENNIFER .... Mitchell, Silberberg & Knupp
*KACZOROWSKI, JOSEPH C. .... Cannell Prods. Inc., Stephen J.
KACZYNSKI, ADOLPH .... Dockry Productions
*KADEN, ELLEN ORAN .... CBS Entertainment

KAHN, CHUCK .... Berger, Kahn, Shafton, Moss, Figler, Simon & Gladstone
KAHN, TINA J. .... Bloom Dekom Hergott & Cook
KALB, BEN .... JI Business Services
KALB, STEVE .... Esparza-Katz Prods.
*KANE, HARRIS J. .... Rosenfeld, Meyer & Susman
KANE, PETER .... Paramount Domestic TV
KANE-RITSCH, JULIE .... Hanna-Barbera, Inc.
*KANEMOTO, KAREN .... Paramount Domestic TV
*KAPLAN, ANDREW J. .... Columbia TriStar Television
KAPLAN, LAWRENCE .... Buena Vista International
KAPLAN, ROBERT O. .... Kenoff & Machtinger
KAPLAN, WILLIAM .... Mitchell, Silberberg & Knupp
*KARL, DONALD .... Rosenfeld, Meyer & Susman
*KARNES, DAVID A. .... Rosenfeld, Meyer & Susman
KARSCH, ANDREW .... Longfellow Prods.
KARTIGANER, LAWRENCE S. .... Rosenfeld, Meyer & Susman
*KASLOW, HARMON .... Intrazone Inc./Intrazone Interactive Ltd.
KASSAR, MARIO .... Carolco Pictures
KATLEMAN, HARRIS .... Goodson Prods., Mark
KATLEMAN, STEVEN Weissmann, Wolff, Bergman, Coleman & Silverman
*KATZ, MARTIN D. .... Hill Wynne Troop & Meisinger
KATZ, MARVIN S. .... Hearst Entertainment
*KATZ, STEVEN .... Mitchell, Silberberg & Knupp
*KATZENBERG, JEFFREY .... Dreamworks/SKG
*KAUFELT, JONATHAN D. .... Armstrong, Hirsch, Jackoway, et al.
KAUFMAN, KENNETH .... Patchett Kaufman Entertainment
*KAUFMAN, LLOYD .... Troma Inc.
KAUFMAN, PETER L. .... Kaufman Esq., Peter L.
*KAY, JASON .... Berger, Kahn, Shafton, Moss, Figler, Simon & Gladstone
KAYE, JEFFREY .... Gelfand, Rennert & Feldman
KEEGAN, JAMES .... Trimark Holdings Inc.
*KEEGAN, PETER W. .... CBS Entertainment
KEENAN, ROBERT R. .... Price Waterhouse
*KEENAN, WILLIAM .... E! Entertainment Television
KEHR, ROBERT L. .... Kehr Crook Tovmassian & Fox
KEITH, ALAN .... Hanna-Barbera, Inc.
KELLER, MAX .... American First Run Studios
KELLER, MICHELINE .... American First Run Studios
KELLEY, BOB .... MCA TV Entertainment
KELLY, FRANK .... Paramount Domestic TV
KELLY, JAN .... Culver Studios, The
*KELLY, JOSEPH .... Black & White Television, Inc.
KELLY, KEVIN M. .... Irell & Manella
KELTON, BRUCE J. .... Kelton, Law Office of Bruce J.

KEMPER, JULIE .... Magnus Film Group
KENCHELIAN, MARK .... Walt Disney TV Animation
KENOFF, JAY S. .... Kenoff & Machtinger
KENT, CHUCK .... Disney Channel, The
KENT, KURTIS .... Nu Image
*KEPHART, FLOYD .... Ventura Entertainment Group Ltd.
*KERMAN, THEA J. .... Kerman, Law offices of Thea J.
KERN, HAROLD B. .... Kern, Harold B.
*KERR, TOM .... Stanbury, Fishelman & Levy
KERSTETTER, BILL .... Marvel Films
KESHISHIAN, CRAIG .... Sojourn Entertainment
KESKE, LUBA .... Metro-Goldwyn-Mayer Inc.
*KESSEL, SILVIA .... Orion Pictures Corporation
KESSLER, ERIC .... HBO (NYC)
*KESSLER, SUZANNE H. .... Rosenfeld, Meyer & Susman
*KETTLER, C.J. .... Sunbow Prods.
KIEF, GARRY .... Stiletto Entertainment
KIELLEY, MARGARET .... Actor's Equity Association (A.E.A.)
KIJZER, PAUL .... Movicorp Holdings, Inc.
*KINDBERG, ANN .... Patchett Kaufman Entertainment
KING, MARSHA K. .... Warner Bros. Home Video
KING, MICHAEL .... King World Prods.
KING, ROGER .... King World Prods.
KINGMAN, BRIAN .... RHH/Albert G. Ruben Ins. Services Inc.
*KIRATSOULIS, RICHARD .... Damon Prods. Worldwide, Mark
*KIRK, JR., LAWRENCE .... Goldwyn Co., Samuel
KIRMAN, ROGER .... Viacom Productions
KIRSCHNER, DAVID .... Kirschner Prods., David
*KIRSHMAN, CARRIE .... Artists Financial Management, Ltd.
*KIRVEN, CINDY W. .... Mercantile National Bank - Ent. Ind. Div.
*KIVEL, STACEY .... Cinequanon Pictures Intl. Inc.
*KIWITT, SIDNEY .... Lotus Pictures Inc.
*KLAPPER, KAREN .... Bank of Montreal
KLATSKY, GABRIELLE .... Walt Disney Motion Pictures Group
KLEIN, DEBORAH L. .... Bloom Dekom Hergott & Cook
*KLEIN, HERB .... BDO Seidman
KLEIN, PHILIP I. .... Browning, Jacobson & Klein
KLEIN, ROBERT A. .... Smith, Barab, Simpson
KLEIN, WILLIAM B. .... CBS Entertainment
*KLEINBAUM, PAUL .... Capell, Coyne & Co.
KLEINER, STEWART .... LIVE Entertainment Companies
*KLEINMAN, AARON .... Big Sky Entertainment
*KLEINMAN, MATT .... Big Sky Entertainment
KLINE, ROBERT D. .... TransAtlantic Enterprises (TAE) Productions
KLINENBERG, RANDY .... Movie Group, The

*KLUBECK, RICH .... Castle Rock Entertainment
KLUGE, JOHN W. .... Orion Pictures Corporation
*KNIGHT, DAVID .... Stephens Inc.
*KOCH, MARK .... Prelude Pictures
*KOENIG, JOSEPH. Berger, Kahn, Shafton, Moss, Figler, Simon & Gladstone
KOENIG, SALLY .... Johnson & Assoc., Neville L.
KOLOFF, KEVIN .... Paramount Pictures Motion Picture Group
*KONOPKA, KATHLEEN .... Rabbit Ears Prods.
KOPEIKIN, WENDY .... Tisch Co., The Steve
KOPELSON, ANNE .... Kopelson Prods., Arnold
KOPELSON, ARNOLD .... Kopelson Prods., Arnold
KOPLOVITZ, KAY .... USA Network
*KOPPEKIN, STEPHEN .... Paramount Pictures .
*KORAVOS, LORI .... Castle Rock Entertainment
KORCHEK, JEFFREY A. .... Universal Pictures
*KORNBLAU, CRAIG .... Buena Vista Home Video
KOSSOW, DAN .... Bedker, London & Kossow
KOZEE, DEBRA .... Coulter & Sands, Inc.
KRAEMER, JOANNE .... Hickox-Bowman Prods., Inc.
*KRAFT, JOE .... Sony Pictures Entertainment
*KRAMER, JONATHAN M. .... Promark Entertainment Group
KRAMER, MOLLY .... Comedy Central
*KRASK, SYLVIA J. .... Walt Disney Motion Pictures Group
KREEK, ROBERT M. .... Comedy Central
KREIGER, ALAN .... Columbia Pictures
*KRELL, AMI .... Castle Rock Entertainment
KREVOY, BRAD .... Motion Picture Corp. of America
KRICUN, STUART .... Playboy Entertainment Group Inc.
*KRIMMER, MATT .... Disney Channel, The
KRINSKY, MELANIE .... California United Bank
KRISEL, GARY .... Walt Disney TV Animation



©1995, Hollywood Financial Directory No. 3
310-315-4815 or 800-815-0503 outside California

KROELLS, BARBARA ............................... Bochco Prods., Steven
KUGHN, RICHARD ................................................ Longbow Prods.
KUHN, MICHAEL ................................... Polygram Filmed Ent.
KUPERBERG, FREDERICK ................... Disney Channel, The
KUPIETZKY, MOSHE J. ...................................... Sidley & Austin
KURGAN, IRA ............................................ Fox Broadcasting Co.
KURRASCH, ANNE ............................................. NBC Entertainment
*KURTZMAN, HOWARD D. ......... Cannell Prods. Inc., Stephen J.
KUSH JR., HENRY G. ............................... United Jersey Bank
*KUSHNER, DONALD ................................... Kushner-Locke Co.
*KUSHNER, WILLIAM J. .......... Sentinel Television Corporation
LA MAINA, FRANCIS C. .............................. Clark Prods., Dick
LAMORTA, CARLA ................... Turner Broadcasting System
*LAROSE, ROBERT ................................... Wiseman & Burke, Inc.

LAVIOLETTE, JOHN S. ............... Bloom Dekom Hergott & Cook
*LACY, ADENE ....................................... Viacom Productions
*LAI, ANNE ...................................................... RCS/PMP Films
LAIRD, PETER ................................... Edelstein, Laird & Sobel
LAMBERT, PETER .................... Horwitz Organization, The Lewis
*LAMBERT, CHFC, PAUL E. ......... Lambert Financial Services
LANDAU, JULIE ............................... Orion Pictures Corporation
LANDAU, SANDRA E. ....................................... Viewer's Choice
LANDAU, ESQ., PAUL ................................. Fries Entertainment
LANDESMAN, MARK E. ......................... Murphy Prods., Eddie
LANDIS, JOHN ................................... St. Clare Entertainment
LANDSBURG, ALAN ............................... Landsburg Co., The
LANG, MICHAEL C. ................................... ABC Entertainment
LANGBERG, BARRY .............. Langberg, Leslie & Gabriel
LANGBORD, ROY ................................ Showtime Networks Inc.
*LANGDON, DORIAN ............... Hemdale Communications Inc.
*LANGNER, LOLA .............................. Paramount Pictures .
*LANGS, LAWRENCE J. ............ Tulchin & Associates, Harris
*LANSING, SHERRY ........ Paramount Pictures Motion Picture Group
*LANTOS, ROBERT ............................... Alliance Communications
*LAPHAM III, JOHN G. .................... Oppenheimer & Co. Inc.
LARNER, ANDREW ............................ Morgan Creek Prods.
LARSEN, CHARLES ............................................................ MTM
*LAUDE, DAVID ............ Ziffren Brittenham Branca & Fischer
*LAUER, MICHAEL H. ........................................... IRS Media
LAUTANEN, MICHELLE .............. Twentieth Century Fox Television
*LAVAN, KEVIN ......................................... MTV Networks
LAVERY, JR., EMMET G. ............... Taffner Entertainment Ltd.
LAW, LINDSAY ............................... American Playhouse
LAWRENCE, JOANN ............................... Skouras Picts. Inc.
LAYBOURNE, GERALDINE ......................... MTV Networks
*LeMASTERS, KIM ............... Cannell Prods. Inc., Stephen J.
LEAVITT, MARK A. ............... Oppenheimer & Co. Inc.
LEBOWITZ, MARK ............ Sony Television Entertainment
*LEDDING, MARY ............................... Universal Pictures
LEE, BONNIE ......................................................... Geffen Pictures
*LEE, BRYAN ................................................ Columbia Pictures
LEE, PATRICIA E. ........................................... Lee, Patricia E.
*LEE, PATRICK JACK ............... Imperial Bank, Ent. Ind. Group
LEE, SPIKE ............... 40 Acres & A Mule Filmworks Inc.
LEE, STAN ................................................................ Marvel Films
LEGAN, SARAH ............................... Vansa Insurance Services
*LEIGHTON, MICHAEL W. ......... Sentinel Television Corporation
LEINWAND, SHARI ............................... Gibson, Dunn & Crutcher
LEMBERGER, KENNETH ............... Sony Pictures Entertainment

*LEO, THOMAS GLEN ......... Hill Wynne Troop & Meisinger
*LEON, DANIEL ............................................................. Heenan Blaikie
*LEONARD, RICHARD C. ............ Leonard, Dicker & Schreiber
LEPOFF, WAYNE ......................................... Genesis Entertainment
LERNER, AVI ............................................................... Nu Image
LERNER, LAWRENCE ............ Lerner, Lawrence D., A Bus. Mgmt. Corp.
*LESLIE, MICHELLE ............................... Pachyderm Entertainment
LESSER, JOAN .................................................... Irell & Manella
*LESSER, SEYMOUR H. ......................... A&E Television Networks
LEVIN, DAVID ............ Padell, Nadell, Fine, Weinberger & Co.
LEVIN, ERIC ................................................................. HBO (L.A.)
LEVINE, ALAN J. ............................... Sony Pictures Entertainment
LEVINE, JARED E. ............ Nelson, Guggenheim, Felker & Levine
LEVINE, PAUL S. ............................................... Levine, Paul S.
LEVINE, PETER M. ............... Gelfand, Rennert & Feldman
LEVINGSTON, JOHN ............................................. Straightley Films
*LEVINSON, BARRY ............................................ Baltimore Pictures
*LEVINSON, JODI ............................... Warner Bros. Pictures
LEVINSON, KAREN ............................................ HBO (NYC)
LEVINSON, LAWRENCE ................................................ Viacom, Inc.
*LEVITCH, BURT ................... Rosenfeld, Meyer & Susman
*LEVITT, ANDREA ............................................... TriStar Pictures
*LEVY, AVI ............................................... Arama Entertainment

LEVY, HAROLD ............................... Stanbury, Fishelman & Levy
LEVY, JEFFREY ......................... Singer Prods. Inc., Joseph M.
*LEVY, JOHN S. ............................................... TriStar Pictures
LEVY, PHIL S. ............... Hill Wynne Troop & Meisinger
*LEWELLEN, WAYNE ............... Paramount Domestic Distribution
LEWIS, ANDREW ............................... Buena Vista Television
*LEWIS, MEG ............................... Taffner Entertainment Ltd.
LICHNER, MIKE ......................................................... BDO Seidman
LICHTENBERG, MATHEW ............ London & Lichtenberg
LICHTER, ROSALIND ............................... Lichter Esq., Rosalind
LICKER, MARTIN ............ Bernstein, Fox, Goldberg & Licker
*LIEBERMAN, HAL ............................................ Universal Pictures
*LIGHT, JEFFREY TAYLOR .. Myman, Abell, Fineman, Greenspan & Rowan
LILLISTON, BRUCE ST. J. ............ Lilliston, Law Offices of Bruce St. J.
*LINDENBAUM, HOWIE ............................... Island Pictures Corp.
*LINDHEIM, RICHARD ............................... Paramount Network TV
*LIPMAN, PAIGE ........................................... Quince Prods., Inc.
*LIPSKY, MARK D. ............................... Murphy Prods., Eddie
LIPSTONE, HOWARD ............................... Landsburg Co., The
*LISCHAK, WILLIAM ............ First Look Picts./Overseas Filmgroup
LITTLE, CAROLE ............................... Cinema Line Films Corp.
LITTLE, ELLEN ............ First Look Picts./Overseas Filmgroup

LITTLE, ROBERT ............ First Look Picts./Overseas Filmgroup
*LITVACK, SANFORD ................... Walt Disney Company, The
LITWAK, MARK ............... Litwak, Law Offices Of, Mark
*LOCKE, PETER ......................................... Kushner-Locke Co.
LODISE, PETER ............ International Film Resource Group Inc.
LOEVENGUTH, JOHN R. ...................................... Hankin & Co.
LOGIGIAN, JOHN ......................................................... Miramax Films
*LOHMAN, FREDERICK G. .................................... Multimedia Inc.
LOMBARDO, MICHAEL ............................................ HBO (L.A.)
*LONDON, BARRY ......... Paramount Pictures Motion Picture Group
LONDON, EDWIN N. ............ Gelfand, Rennert & Feldman
LOPKER, PATRICK T. ............................... Disney Channel, The
LORINSKY, CLAY ........................................................ TriStar TV
LOUGHERY, DON ............................... Columbia Picts. Television
*LOW, KEN ............................... Castle Rock Entertainment
LOWELL, DOUGLAS ................................... Kushner-Locke Co.
LOWY, JEFFREY ......... Hall Dickler Kent Friedman & Wood
LUCCESHI, JOANNA ............................... California United Bank
*LUCKENBACHER, FRANK ............ Cohen & Luckenbacher
LUDERER, DENNIS ......... Ziffren Brittenham Branca & Fischer
LUDLUM, BARBARA ............................... American Playhouse
*LUELLEN, JACK R. ............................... Sussman, Jerome J.
*LYNCH, JOHN D. .................................................. Lynch Entertainment
LYNCH, THOMAS ............................... Lynch Entertainment
LYNN, RICHARD ........................................................ USA Network
LYNNE, MICHAEL ............................... New Line Cinema
LYTTLE, LAWRENCE ........................... Spelling Television Inc.
MAAS, BRIAN E. ............... Beldock Levine & Hoffman
MACINNIS, TERRI ............ Producers Ent. Group Ltd., The
MACKINNEY, TED ...................................... Propaganda Films
MACKINNON, ROY ............ First Entertainment Federal Credit Union
MACCINI, ROBERT J. ............... Media Services Group Inc.
MACHTINGER, LEONARD S. ............ Kenoff & Machtinger
*MACKINNON, CHRISTINE .............. Orion Pictures Corporation
*MACY, CARLA ................................................................ Jersey Films
*MADOFF, STEVEN ............ Paramount Home Video Distribution
MAGAUDDA, ROBERT ............ Yankee Entertainment Group
*MAGID, KAREN ......... Paramount Pictures Motion Picture Group
*MAHONEY, ED ......................................................... BDO Seidman
MALANGA, THOMAS ............................... MGM Worldwide TV Group
MALO, RENE ............................................... Image Organization
*MALONE ENGEL, COLLEEN ............ Chancellor Entertainment
*MALONEY, MICHAEL ....... Walt Disney Television & Telecommunications
MALTIN, RICHARD A. ........................... Citadel Entertainment, L.P.
MANDABACH, CARYN ............................... Carsey-Werner Co., The

MANDEL, SAM ............ Blanc, Williams, Johnston & Kronstadt
*MANDELBAUM, JAMES C. ............ Armstrong, Hirsch, Jackoway, et al.
MANDELBAUM, RIC ............................................ Resource One Inc.
MANDELL, WALTER ............ Percenterprises Completion Bonds, Inc.
*MANELLA, ARTHUR .................................................... Irell & Manella
*MANNION, PAULA ................................... Chubb Insurance Co.
MANTOVANI, FRANK ............................... Halpern & Mantovani
MARCELLINO, JAMES ......... First Entertainment Federal Credit Union
MARCUCCI, ROBERT P. ............................... Chancellor Entertainment
MARCUS, NORMAN ........................................................ Ernst & Young
MARDEN, SCOTT ............ Philips Media Electronic Publishing
*MARINO-PARK, GABRIELA ............ Carsey-Werner Co., The
*MARINOS, GEORGE ............... Cinequanon Pictures Intl. Inc.
MARK, STEVEN PAUL ............................................ Comedy Central
*MARKOWSKI, LARRY ............................... Magnus Film Group

MARKS, LAURENCE M. .........................Manatt, Phelps & Phillips
MARKS, RICHARD. ............................................ Kushner-Locke Co.
MARKS, ROSALIND........... Walt Disney Television & Telecommunications
MARKS, STEPHEN .................................. Gelfand, Rennert & Feldman
MAROEVICH, VAN .................Maroevich, O'Shea and Coghlan Ins. Brokers
MARQUEZ, PAUL ............................................ Wilshire Court Prods.
*MARSHALL, MICHAEL............................. Arama Entertainment
*MARSHALL, ROBERT F. . Greenberg Glusker Fields Claman & Machtinger
*MARTIN, CLAUDIA .................. Paramount Pictures Motion Picture Group
*MARTIN, SCOTT.......... Paramount Pictures Motion Picture Group
*MARTIN, SUZANNE C. ............................ Cine Grande Corporation
MARTINDALE, LARRY ...........................Martindale, C.P.A., Larry
MASKEY, REBECCA.................. Playboy Entertainment Group Inc.
MASLANSKY, HARRIS ........................................ Savoy Pictures
MASNICA, APRIL ........................... Carolina Barnes Capital Inc.
MASSIS, ALEX ...................................................... Angelika Films
MASTERS, LEE ................................... E! Entertainment Television
*MASTERS, MICHAEL ........................... Paramount Network TV
MASUDA, MEL ..............................................Ernst & Young
*MATALON, DAVID ......................... New Regency Prods. Inc.
MATHER, ANN..................................Buena Vista International
MATLEN, H. ROY...............Matlen & Associates, C.P.A., H. Roy
MATORIN, PETER S. ..................Beldock Levine & Hoffman
MATTHAU, CHARLES ...........................Matthau Company, The
MATTHAU, WALTER ...........................Matthau Company, The
*MAXWELL, ADRIENNE ............................ Maxwell Group, The
MAY, LAWRENCE E. .......................... Kenoff & Machtinger
MAYBERRY, DEL..........................Fox Broadcasting Co.
MAYER, ROGER ................................ TNT/Turner Pictures Inc.

MAYERSON, MICHAEL .................................. Loeb & Loeb
MAYESH, M. JACK...................Shapiro Ent. Inc., Richard & Esther
*MAZZO, JOANNE ............................ Columbia Picts. Television
MAZZOCONE, CARL ................................ Main Line Pictures
MAZZUCA, JOE ................................. Hanna-Barbera, Inc.
MC CLUGGAGE, KERRY ........................ Paramount Network TV
*MCALLISTER, ERIC M. ............. Carolina Barnes Capital Inc.
MCALLISTER, MICHAEL............. RHH/Albert G. Ruben Ins. Services Inc.
MCCAFFREY, TOM ........... RHH/Albert G. Ruben Ins. Services Inc.
*MCCALMONT, TONI ....................Carsey-Werner Co., The
*MCCARTHY, BARBARA J. ..........................Longbow Prods.
*MCCARTHY, GARY ...................................CBS Entertainment
MCCLAIN, KIMBERLY WICK ......................... U.S. Film Corp.
*MCCORMICK, DOUGLAS .................Lifetime Television (NY)
MCCORMICK, SEAN .......................... JI Business Services
MCDANIEL, MICHAEL S. ...................Countryman & McDaniel
*MCDIFFETT, MITCH .................Sony Television Entertainment
*MCELHATTEN, DAVE......................Philips Media Electronic Publishing
MCELHONE, SCOTT ...................................HBO (L.A.)
*MCGARRY, MARK ................................ Phoenician Films
*MCGINNIS, J.R. ...........................Paramount Network TV
MCGRATH, JUDY ......................................MTV Networks
*MCGURK, CHRIS ..........Walt Disney Motion Pictures Group
MCKAY, DEBRA............................ Family Channel, The
MCKENNA, JANICE D. ......... Singer Lewak Greenbaum & Goldstein
MCKEON, DONALD C. ...................Yankee Entertainment Group
*MCLAREN, JENNY .......................... Mirage Enterprises
MCLAUGHLIN, KENT ...................Reynolds & Reynolds Inc.
MCMAHON, KERRY A. ................. Carolina Barnes Capital Inc.
*MCNAMARA, JAMES ...................New World Entertainment
MCNEELY, MILINDA ..........................Paramount Network TV
*MCPHERSON, BRIAN ...............Rosenfeld, Meyer & Susman
MCWETHEY, CINDY ........................... Beacon Pictures
MCGARR, ANITA ...........................Kismet Entertainment Inc.
*MCKVIN, JOEL........... Weissmann, Wolff, Bergman, Coleman & Silverman
*MECHANIC, BILL ........................Fox Filmed Entertainment
MEDANN, ARLYNE ................................ Troubleshooters, Inc.
MEISEL, GARY ............................................. Warner Bros..
*MEISELS, HILLARY.......Berger, Kahn, Shafton, Moss, Figler, et al.
MEISINGER, LOUIS M. ....................Hill Wynne Troop & Meisinger
MELENDEZ, BILL..............................Melendez Prods., Bill
MELOCOTON, ED.............................Spelling Television Inc.
MELTZER, MICHAEL ...................... Le Studio Canal + (U.S.)

MENDELSOHN, MICHAEL ..............................Banque Paribas
MENDEZ, ROBERT G. ...................Paramount Domestic TV
*MENDOZA, MARLENE.............................Film Capital Corporation
MENES, BARRY A. ................................ Menes Law Corp.
MENES, PAUL I. .................................... Menes Law Corp.
MENOSKY, CHRIS ........................Buena Vista Home Video
MENTRE, AGNES ...................................... Miramax Films
MERRILL, DINA ........................................RKO Pictures, Inc.
MERRITT, JR., WILLIAM A. .........Carolina Barnes Capital Inc.
*MESSINEO, MARC ................................ Menes Law Corp.

*METZGER, ROBERT S. .....................Hill Wynne Troop & Meisinger
MEYER, CYNTHIA BERRY ..................Prism Entertainment Corp.
*MEYER, IRWIN ................................ Producers Ent. Group Ltd., The
*MEYER, KEITH .................. Paul, Hastings, Janosky & Walker
MEYER, MARVIN B. ................. Rosenfeld, Meyer & Susman
MICHALSKI, STEPHEN ...................Freedman, Broder & Co.
*MIERCORT, DAVID......................Mitchell, Silberberg & Knupp
*MILCHAN, ARNON ................................ New Regency Prods. Inc.
MILCO, RON ..............................Overseas Financial Services
MILES, BRANDI ...........................................RCS/PMP Films
*MILES, JEFFREY ............................... Peacock Films Inc.
*MILLER, ANDREA ...............................21st Century Film Corp.
*MILLER, ANTHONY .......................................J & M Ent. Ltd.
MILLER, CRAIG ...........................................C.M. Management
*MILLER, DENNIS ....................... Sony Pictures Entertainment
*MILLER, GWEN T. .....Mercantile National Bank - Ent. Ind. Div.
*MILLER, ISABEL ......................................C.M. Management
*MILLER, JAMES ..........................................Savoy Pictures
MILLER, JOHN ...................Chemical Bank, Ent. Ind. Group
MILLER, JULIE .................... Oberman, Tivoli & Miller Ltd.
*MILLER, OVVIE ................... Rosenfeld, Meyer & Susman
MILLER, RICK .................................:...Alliance Communications
MILLER, SARAH ..........................................Comedy Central
*MILLER, TODD A. ......................... Big Sky Entertainment
MILLHAM, J. ERIC .........................................Crestar Bank
MILLITZER, THOMAS E. ...................Abraham & Company, David
MILLS, LAURA ...........................................Rocket Pictures
MILNE, C. SCOTT ............RHH/Albert G. Ruben Ins. Services Inc.
MIMMS, JR., MALCOLM L. ........................ Loeb & Loeb
MITCHEL, RALPH ......................................C.M. Management
MITCHELL, BILL ..........................Chubb Insurance Co.
MITTLEMAN, SHELDON ........................ Universal Television
*MOCCIA, BRUCE .................... Telescene Communications Inc.
MOFFATT, WM. GARY ................First Entertainment Federal Credit Union
MOLITO, THOMAS A. ................. Cabin Fever Entertainment

MONAS, STEPHEN ..........................................Vision International
*MONTGOMERY, JEFFREY A.............Harvey Entertainment Company, The
*MONTGOMERY, MICHAEL ....................... Dreamworks/SKG
MOONVES, JONATHON D. ................... Del, Rubel, Shaw, Mason & Derin
MOONVES, LESLIE .................... Warner Bros. Television
MOORE, A. LE CONTE.............. Marsh & McLennan Inc.
*MOORE, DAVE..........................................Barr Films
*MOORE, ROBERT ..........Walt Disney Motion Pictures Group
*MOORE, TERRY ............................... Di Bona Prods., Vin
*MORACHNICK, TAMI...................... Bohbot Entertainment
MOREA, ANNE .................... Citadel Entertainment, L.P.
MORGAN, ROBERT................. Morgan, C.P.A., Robert F.
MORGAN, TODD .....................Goldman, Sachs & Co.
*MORI, MARK ............................ Single Spark Pictures
*MORI, THORPE ............................ Single Spark Pictures
*MORRIS, GUY ...................................Sojourn Entertainment
MORRIS, KATE ............................... MCEG Sterling Ent.
MORRIS, LARRY ......................................... HKM Films
*MORRIS, LEIGH B. ................Hill Wynne Troop & Meisinger
*MORRIS, MARCY S. Armstrong, Hirsch, Jackoway, Tyerman & Wertheimer
*MORRISON, DEBORAH................... Buena Vista Picts. Distrib.
*MORRISSEY, JOHN ...............................Rastar Prods.
*MORTOFF, LAWRENCE ........................ Kushner-Locke Co.
*MOSES, ROBERT M. ...................Sony Pictures Entertainment
MOSS, IRWIN ................................... Warner Bros. Television
*MOSTAEDI, MANSOUR ...............First Look Picts./Overseas Filmgroup
*MOTT, ROBERT M. ...................... Orion Pictures Corporation
*MRUVKA, ALAN ...................Mruvka Entertainment, Alan
MUELLER, RONI ................................... Warner Bros. Television
MUHL, PHILLIP......................Walt Disney Motion Pictures Group
*MUIR, MARY ............ Hayes, Hume, Petas, Richards & Cohanne
MULLER, LYNN.....................First Entertainment Federal Credit Union
*MUNOZ-RICHARDS, EVA ........................ Rubin, Richards & Co.
*MURAGLIA, SILVIO ............................. Cine Grande Corporation
*MURILLO, RJ..........................Motion Picture Corp. of America
MURPHY, EDDIE ............................Murphy Prods., Eddie
*MURPHY, JAMES M.A. .......... Rosenfeld, Meyer & Susman
MURPHY, LAWRENCE P....................... Walt Disney Company, The
MURPHY, PETER..........................:... Walt Disney Company, The
*MURPHY, PHILLIP ..........................Paramount Domestic TV
*MURRAY, PATRICK..........................InterMedia/Film Equities Inc.
*MURRAY, PATRICK..........................Trans Pacific Films
*MYERS, EDITH E. ..........................InterMedia/Film Equities Inc.
*MYMAN, ROBERT M. ..........Myman, Abell, Fineman, Greenspan & Rowan
NADELL, BRUCE............................. Padell, Nadell, Fine, Weinberger & Co.

*NAGIN, JEFFREY L. ........................ Rosenfeld, Meyer & Susman
*NAMIHISA, OSAMU..........................JVC Entertainment, Inc.

*NANULA, RICHARD D........................Walt Disney Company, The
NAPOLI, LYNN.....................................L.M.N. Enterprises Inc.
NASH, RONALD E. ...................Gelfand, Rennert & Feldman
*NATHANSON, MICHAEL .....................New Regency Prods. Inc.
*NATTER, JANINE ...................................Codikow & Carroll
NAU, ROBERT M. ...........................................U.S. Film Corp.
NEAL, CAROL ..................................Melendez Prods., Bill
NECESSARY, GARY ...........................Schlatter Prods., George
*NEDICK, MITCHELL .............................Warner Bros. Network
NEIDORF, MICHAEL ................................. Perry & Neidorf
NEIDORF, MURRAY ................................. Perry & Neidorf
*NEILSON, JONAS ...............................Persky Prods., Lester
NEIMAND, STEVE .................................Pirromount Pictures
*NELSON, BILL....................................................HBO (NYC)
*NELSON, LENORE ...............................Kushner-Locke Co.
*NELSON, MARK ..................................RCS/PMP Films
NELSON, PETER MARTIN..............Nelson, Guggenheim, Felker & Levine
*NELSON, RONALD ..............................Dreamworks/SKG
NEMSCHOFF, LOUISE ........................ Nemschoff, Louise
NESMITH, MICHAEL .......................................Pacific Arts
NEUENFELDT, JOHN E. ..............................Film Funding Inc.
*NEUFELD, MARJORIE .............................NBC Entertainment
NEUMAN, CPA, HARLEY J. .........Neuman & Associates, C.P.A.s
NEWBERGER, ART.................Hemdale Communications Inc.
NEWBURGER, PATTY .................................. Comedy Central
NEWLON, DAVID ...................................Spectacor Films
NEWMAN, GARY...............Twentieth Century Fox Television
NEWMAN, KAREN S. ............Perlmutter, Sam, Law offices of
NEWMAN, MICHAEL .........Gelfand, Newman & Wasserman
*NEWPORT, BOB ........................................... IRS Media
*NICHOLS, DAVID J. .................................. Hankin & Co.
*NIELSEN, KATHRYN .............Interscope Communications Inc.
NIERS, ROBERT A. ...............Schaefer, Law Offices of Susan G.
NIMMER, DAVID ....................................Irell & Manella
NINE, KELLY.............................. Kismet Entertainment Inc.
NOCHIMSON, DAVID ...........Ziffren Brittenham Branca & Fischer
NOLAN, PETER F. ..................Walt Disney Company, The
NOONAN, JIM ........................................... HBO (L.A.)
NORMAN, MARIA ....................Kopelson Prods., Arnold
NORRIS, BRIAN ............................. Kismet Entertainment Inc.
NORRIS, BUCKLEY..............RHH/Albert G. Ruben Ins. Services Inc.
*NORRIS, RICK E. ..................... Entertainment Financiers Inc.
NORTON, ROBERT ...............................RCS/PMP Films

NORWITZ, ERIC.....................Norwitz Attorney at Law, Eric
NOWAK, EDWARD ......................Walt Disney Company, The
O'CONNELL, KATHLEEN ...........Walt Disney Motion Pictures Group
*O'HANLON, NEIL R. ....................Hill Wynne Troop & Meisinger
O'HARA, MICHAEL..................O'Hara-Horowitz Productions
O'HARE, MARY ....................................... TriStar TV
*O'HARE, MARY ...............Sony Television Entertainment
O'NEAL, WALTER.....Walt Disney Television & Telecommunications
*O'SULLIVAN, MICHAEL ...........Paramount Pictures Motion Picture Group
OBERMAN, ROBERT...................Oberman, Tivoli & Miller Ltd.
*OBLATH, GEOFFRY W. ..........Armstrong, Hirsch, Jackoway, et al.
ODENBERG, CAROL L. .................................. Hankin & Co.
*OFFER, ROBERT D. ...........Bloom Dekom Hergott & Cook
OGLESBY, LARRY ...............Rodeo Drive Financial Mgmt.
OLDAK, MARY ........................................... HBO (L.A.)
*OLESIUK, WALTER ........Sinclair, Tenenbaum, Olesiuk & Co., Inc.
OLESIUK, WALTER W. J. ...........InterMedia/Film Equities Inc.
OLIVER, ANN ...........................................Movie Group, The
*OLSHANSKY, RICHARD ...........Once Upon A Time Films, Ltd.
*ONCIDI, ANTHONY J. ...................Hill Wynne Troop & Meisinger
OPPENHEIM, MICHAEL ...........Gudvi, Chapnick & Oppenheim, Inc.
OPPENHEIM, ESQ., ROBERT L..........Oppenheim Esq., Robert L.
ORSATTI, DOMINIC ................Olympic Entertainment Group
ORSON, MARSHALL ...............Turner Original Productions
*ORTIZ, SANDRA .......................................... Twentieth TV
*OSHER, ROBERT M. ..................TNT/Turner Pictures Inc.
OTTENHOFF, ROBERT .........................................PBS
OVITZ, MARK H. .................................Picturemaker Prods.
OWITZ, KEITH.......................................... HBO (L.A.)
*PACCONE, FRED .................Walt Disney TV Animation
PACE, BILL ..........................................Longbow Prods.
PACE, WAYNE H. ...................Turner Broadcasting System
PACHARES, LIBBY ..................Metro-Goldwyn-Mayer Inc.
PADDOCK, VICTOR ...............................Landsburg Co., The
PADELL, BERT ..............Padell, Nadell, Fine, Weinberger & Co.
PADGETT, DANA ..................................Lumiere Films Inc.
PADNICK, GLENN ...............Castle Rock Entertainment
PAIK, STEPHEN S. ...............................ITB CineGroup
PAINTER, PAUL .................Telescene Communications Inc.
*PALAU, JULIE ................................J & M Ent. Ltd.
PALEOLOGOS, NICHOLAS .......................Zollo Productions

PALLEY, STEPHEN W.........................King World Prods.
PALMER, THOMAS C..................................Crestar Bank
PANDOLFINO, JOHN F. .................Smith Affiliated Capital Corp.

PANITCH, HERSH ...................... Panitch & Co., Inc., Hersh
PAPAZIAN, ROBERT A. ..........Papazian-Hirsch Entertainment
*PARATORE, JAMES .................................Telepictures Prods.
*PARKES, WALTER .............................Amblin Entertainment
*PARKINSON, ERIC .............Hemdale Communications Inc.
PARKINSON, RICHARD.............. AON Entertainment Ltd. Ins. Services
*PARNELL, CHERYL ..............Concorde/New Horizons Pictures
PARRIS, DON .....................Gibson, Dunn & Crutcher
PASAROW, AVERILL C. .........................Pasarow, Averill C.
PASCOTTO, ALVARO ........................Pascotto & Gallavotti
PASICH, KIRK A. ...........Hill Wynne Troop & Meisinger
PATCHETT, TOM ...............Patchett Kaufman Entertainment
*PATERRA, SCOTT ..................................Peacock Films Inc.
PATILLO, TONI ....................... De Passe Entertainment
PATRICK, LOUGENIA ...............Spelling Television Inc.
*PATTON, ROGER L. ...........Bloom Dekom Hergott & Cook
*PAUL, GREG ....................... Castle Rock Entertainment
*PAUL, RANDOLPH ...........Cinergi Pictures Entertainment Inc.
PAYNE, GREG ....................................DIC Entertainment
PEARCE, CHRISTOPHER......................... Cannon Pictures
*PEARSON, NIGEL ...........Sinclair, Tenenbaum, Olesiuk & Co., Inc.
PEASE, ED .................. Gordon, The Law Office Of, Peter D.
*PECKHAM, JENNIFER ...........Cinequanon Pictures Intl. Inc.
PEIKOFF, JODI ....................... Sloss, Law Office P.C.
*PENA, STEVEN .............Twentieth Century Fox Film Corp.
*PENERA, CARLOS ..................................... Universal Pictures
*PERCELAY, DAVID ...............Scripps Howard Productions
*PERELMAN, RONALD ..........................Genesis Entertainment
PEREZ, CARLOS .......................... Castle Rock Entertainment
PERGOLA, CHRIS .......................................... Comedy Central
PERLBERGER, MARTIN ...........Perlberger, Law Offices of Martin
PERLMUTTER, SAM..............Perlmutter, Sam, Law offices of
PERSKY, LESTER .................................Persky Prods., Lester
PETAS, MARK ..........Hayes, Hume, Petas, Richards & Cohanne
*PETERS, JON .......................... Peters Entertainment
*PETRICK, JED .............................Warner Bros. Network
PETRONE, EMIEL .............Philips Media Electronic Publishing
PETRONI, DONALD..............................O'Melveny & Myers
PETRY, GERARD ....................................NBC Entertainment
*PHELAN, MICHAEL .......First National Bank of Chicago, The
PHILLIPS, JOHN R. ..................Gelfand, Rennert & Feldman
PHILLIPS, L.LEE .......................Manatt, Phelps & Phillips
PIASCIK, TRICIA ....................................DIC Entertainment
*PICCININNI, MIKE ........................ Bohbot Entertainment
PIERSON, CINDY .....................................RCS/PMP Films

PIERSON, JANET ...................................Grainy Pictures, Inc.
PIERSON, JOHN ...................................Grainy Pictures, Inc.
*PIRRO, MARK ....................................... Pirromount Pictures
PISANO, A. ROBERT ...........Metro-Goldwyn-Mayer Inc.
PLANCK, PATRICIA ...............Kismet Entertainment Inc.
PLATT, MARC ...........................................TriStar Pictures
PLEPLER, RICHARD...............................................HBO (NYC)
*PLOTKOWSKI, ROBERT J. ........Hill Wynne Troop & Meisinger
*PLUM, STEVEN ...........Paramount Pictures Motion Picture Group
POLK, MIMI .....................................RCS/PMP Films
*POLLACK, ROBERT ...........Pollack & Associates, Robert
POLLEY, LAURA ...................Paragon Entertainment Corp.
POLLOCK, CAMILLE ...............Persky Prods., Lester
POLLOCK, TOM ...........................................MCA Inc.
*POLLOK, STUART .............................Prelude Pictures
*PONGRACIC, ELIZABETH M............Armstrong, Hirsch, Jackoway, et al.
POPE, RON .............................Hart Brothers Ent. Corp.
*PORTERFIELD, CURTIS D..............Hill Wynne Troop & Meisinger
*POSELL, RICHARD E. ......Greenberg Glusker Fields Claman & Machtinger
*POTAMKIN, BUZZ................................Hanna-Barbera, Inc.
POTTASH, BRUCE ....................Paramount Domestic TV
*POTTER, BARR B. ....................... Largo Entertainment
POTTER, BARR B. ....................... JVC Entertainment, Inc.
*POWELL, MARYKAY..................................Rastar Prods.
POWELL, NIK .....................................Scala Prods.
*POWERS, FRANK A. ...........AON Entertainment Ltd. Ins. Services
PRESSER, SHELLEY ....................................Warner Bros..
PRINE, ALICE FAY .................Marsh & McLennan Inc.
*PROBERT, GREG ....................Buena Vista Home Video
*PROKOP, PAUL ................................New Line Cinema
*PROUGH, STEPHEN ............................... Furman Selz Inc.
PURCELL, PATRICK B. ...............Paramount Pictures .
PUTNAM, TOM ...............Vansa Insurance Services
*QUARLES, WILLIAM .......................Hanna-Barbera, Inc.

| | |
|---|---|
| QUATTLEBAUM, JULIAN | Prime Sports |
| QUINN, TRACEY | Marsh & McLennan Inc. |
| RABINOWITZ, LEONARD | Cinema Line Films Corp. |
| *RABINOWITZ, SHELDON | Columbia TriStar Motion Picture Companies |
| *RAINES, SUSAN | First Look Picts./Overseas Filmgroup |
| RAKOW, J. JAY | Paramount Pictures . |
| *RAMSEY, PATRICK | Paul, Hastings, Janosky & Walker |
| RANDALL, GARY | Paragon Entertainment Corp. |
| RANDALL, KAREN | Katten Muchin Zavis & Weitzman |
| *RANDAZZO, JOSEPH | Universal Pictures |
| | |
| *RANKIN, ARTHUR | Rankin/Bass |
| RANSOHOFF, STEVE | Film Finances, Inc. |
| RAPPA, RAYMOND | Creative Road Corp. |
| *RASMUSSEN, JON W. | Hankin & Co. |
| RATNER-GUANCHE, DANIEL | Progressive Asset Mgmt. |
| REAGAN, JOHN J. | Buena Vista Home Video |
| RECTOR, MORGAN | Imperial Bank, Ent. Ind. Group |
| *REDD, MARYLEE H. | Carolina Barnes Capital Inc. |
| *REDDICK III, C.N. | Hill Wynne Troop & Meisinger |
| *REDPATH, JOHN | HBO (NYC) |
| *REDSTONE, SUMNER M. | Viacom, Inc. |
| REDWINE, TOMMIE J. | Warner Bros. Intl. TV Distrib. |
| REED, MARSHA L. | Walt Disney Company, The |
| REES, MARIAN | Rees Assocs., Marian |
| *REID, DONALD R. | Maroevich, O'Shea and Coghlan Ins. Brokers |
| REIFF, DENNIS R. | Reiff & Associates, D.R. |
| *REILLY, JOSEPH | Telepictures Prods. |
| *REILLY, JR., EDWARD | Concorde/New Horizons Corp. |
| REINER, ROB | Castle Rock Entertainment |
| REISS, W. RANDOLPH | Walt Disney Television & Telecommunications |
| REITER, HARRIET NAMIOT | Reiter Management |
| REITER, IRWIN | Miramax Films |
| RELYEA, DOROTHY | Warner Bros. Television |
| *RENDAZZO, DENA | HKM Films |
| RENNERT, IRWIN L. | Gelfand, Rennert & Feldman |
| RESNICK, MARK H. | Twentieth Century Fox Film Corp. |
| *REYNOLDS, RONALD D. | Hill Wynne Troop & Meisinger |
| REYNOLDS, STANLEY J. | Reynolds & Reynolds Inc. |
| RIBEIRO, CHANTAL | Cinema Seven Prods. |
| *RICCI, MICHAEL | I.N.I. Entertainment Group Inc. |
| RICHARDS, PETER C. | Hayes, Hume, Petas, Richards & Cohanne |
| RICHARDS, STEVE | RCS/PMP Films |
| *RICHARDSON, SCOTT | A&E Television Networks |
| *RIGG, JEAN | Lifetime Television (NY) |
| RINGELHEIM, BARRY | Smith Barney Inc. |
| RISHER, SARA | New Line Cinema |
| RITCHIE, MALCOLM | Polygram Filmed Ent. |
| RIVERA, DIANA C. | Buena Vista Home Video |
| *RIVERA, LEE | Turner Original Productions |
| *RIVKIN, CHARLES | Henson Prods., Jim |
| ROACH, JAMES A | Bochco Prods., Steven |
| *ROBBINS, MICHAEL A. | Rosenfeld, Meyer & Susman |
| ROBBINS, RICHARD | Producer & Management Ent. Group |
| ROBBINS, TIM | Havoc |
| *ROBERTS, ALAN | Trivision Pictures Inc. |
| | |
| ROBERTS, ANDREW S. | Roberts, Andrew S. |
| ROBERTS, SUSAN | Kirschner Prods., David |
| ROBERTSON, HUGH DUFF | Maree Jr. & Assocs. Inc., A. Morgan |
| ROBINSON, DAVID M. | Twentieth Century Fox Television |
| ROBINSON, JAMES G. | Morgan Creek Prods. |
| ROBINSON, JOHN | Alliance Communications |
| ROBINSON, PETER | Behr & Robinson |
| ROBINSON, PETER | Robinson/Jeffrey Assoc. Inc. |
| *ROBINSON, RANDY | Avenue Pictures |
| RODDY, JESSICA | Savoy Pictures |
| ROEDIG, PATTEE | Papazian-Hirsch Entertainment |
| ROHNER, FRANKLIN B. | Bochco Prods., Steven |
| ROHRER, SUSAN | NorthStar Ent. Group, Inc. |
| *ROMANO, ED | Warner Bros. |
| ROMANO, EDWARD A. | Warner Bros. Worldwide |
| *RONE, DAVID B. | Walt Disney Motion Pictures Group |
| *ROSE, KELLY | Ernst & Young |
| *ROSE, SHERI | Pollack & Associates, The |
| *ROSE, VICTOR | Capell, Coyne & Co. |
| *ROSELLI, RINA | Paramount Pictures . |
| ROSEN, PHILLIP | New Line Cinema |
| ROSEN, RICHARD | New Dawn Entertainment |
| ROSENBLUM, GAIL | Miss Universe Inc. |
| ROSENFELD, MICHAEL | Rosenfeld, Meyer & Susman |
| *ROSENMAN, SHEP | Browning, Jacobson & Klein |
| ROSENSTEIN, EARL | Prism Entertainment Corp. |
| ROSENTHAL, JIM | New Line Cinema |

| | |
|---|---|
| ROSENTHAL, SOL | Buchalter, Nemer, Fields & Younger |
| ROSENTHAL, STUART M. | Bloom Dekom Hergott & Cook |
| *ROSKIN, WILLIAM A. | Viacom, Inc. |
| ROSS, MICHAEL | ABC Productions |
| ROSS, STANLEY RALPH | Neila Inc. |
| *ROSS, WILLIAM M. | Rosenfeld, Meyer & Susman |
| *ROSSELLINI, VICTORIA | Twentieth Century Fox Film Corp. |
| ROSSET, DANIEL | Metro-Goldwyn-Mayer Inc. |
| ROSSU, ALEX | Fortis Entertainment |
| ROTH, DEBRA | Orion Pictures Corporation |
| ROTH, ROBERT | HBO (L.A.) |
| *ROTH, ROBYN L. | Bloom Dekom Hergott & Cook |
| ROTHENBERG, CHRISTIE | Lancit Media Prods. |
| ROTHMAN, FRANK | Skadden, Arps, Slate, Meagher & Flom |
| ROTHMAN, ESQ., ED | MCA TV Entertainment |
| ROUSSO, CFP, LEON | Entertainment Ind. Financial Strategies Assoc. |
| ROWAN, ALAN | ABC Entertainment |
| *ROWAN, THOMAS P. | Myman, Abell, Fineman, Greenspan & Rowan |
| | |
| *ROYAL, DAVID | Royal & Associates, Inc. |
| ROZELLS, MARK | Walt Disney Company, The |
| RUBEL, MICHAEL | Del, Rubel, Shaw, Mason & Derin |
| *RUBENSTEIN, STEVEN M. | Rubenstien & Finch |
| RUBIN, BARBARA | Spelling Television Inc. |
| RUBIN, JERRY | Kushner-Locke Co. |
| *RUBIN, LAWRENCE M. | Rubin, Richards & Co. |
| RUBIN, ROBERT W. | Universal Pictures |
| RUDKIN, DON | Deloitte & Touche |
| RUDMAN, NORMAN | Slaff, Mosk, & Rudman |
| RUDOLPH, LAWRENCE | Duitch, Poteshman, Franklin & Co. |
| *RUSH, MANDIE | California United Bank |
| RUSSELL, ROBIN | Columbia Pictures |
| RUST, PATRICIA | Rust Prods., Patricia |
| *RUTKOWSKI, LARRY | NBC Inc. |
| RUTLEDGE, MARCIA | RHH/Albert G. Ruben Ins. Services Inc. |
| *RYAN, MICHAEL | J & M Ent. Ltd. |
| RYAN, NORA | Showtime Networks Inc. |
| *RYAN, STEVE | Bank of America, NT&SA |
| SABAN, HAIM | Saban Entertainment |
| *SACKER, NEIL | Miramax Films |
| SACKS, SAMUEL | Sacks, Samuel |
| *SADOFSKY, CHRISTINE | Near North Insurance Brokerage, Inc. |
| SALEH, JOSEPH J.M. | Angelika Films |
| *SALES, DANIEL | Cinequanon Pictures Intl. Inc. |
| *SALHANY, LUCIE | United Paramount Network |
| *SALTER, ROY A. | Houlihan Lokey Howard & Zukin |
| SALTSMAN, MICHAEL D. | Zivetz, Schwartz & Saltsman, CPA's |
| SALZBERG, BUDDY | First Charter Bank |
| SALZMAN, DAVID | Jones-David Salzman Ent., Quincy |
| *SAMAHA, ELIE | Phoenician Films |
| *SAMMS, DAVID H. | Hill Wynne Troop & Meisinger |
| *SAMPLES, KEITH | Rysher Entertainment |
| SANCHINI, RAE | Lightstorm Entertainment Inc. |
| SANDERSON, AURIEL | Wolper Org. Inc., The |
| *SANDLER, ALAN | Goodson Prods., Mark |
| SANTANIELLO, JOSEPH M. | Walt Disney Company, The |
| *SARIEGO, RALPH | Universal Television |
| *SARNOFF, BRET | Carsey-Werner Co., The |
| SATIN, ROBERT | Satin & Company |
| SATRIANO, CPA, THOMAS V. | Satriano & Hilton, Inc. |
| SATTINGER, JACK | Warner Bros. Pictures |
| *SAVIN, ADINA | Rysher Entertainment |
| *SAVITSKY, GEORGE | Savitsky Satin & Geibelson |
| SCALEM, JAMES | PBS |
| | |
| SCALI, LOIS J. | Irell & Manella |
| SCHAEFER, SUSAN G. | Schaefer, Law Offices of Susan G. |
| SCHAEFFER, JAMES | Main Line Pictures |
| *SCHAFFER, HARRY F. | Guild Management Corporation |
| *SCHALBE, SUSAN | New Line Cinema |
| SCHEINMAN, ANDREW | Castle Rock Entertainment |
| *SCHER, DENISE R. | Lambert Financial Services |
| SCHIFF, ESQ., GUNTHER H. | Schiff A Professional Corp., Gunther H. |
| *SCHILLER, ROBERT | Guild Management Corporation |
| SCHIMT, LUCIEN | Albright, Yee & Schimt |
| SCHLESINGER, JEFFREY R. | Warner Bros. Intl. TV Distrib. |
| *SCHLESSEL, PETER | Columbia TriStar Home Video |
| SCHLOSSMANN, COREY P. | Hankin & Co. |
| *SCHLUPP, ANDREA | Tisch Co., The Steve |
| SCHNEIDER, MICHAEL | TransAtlantic Enterprises (TAE) Productions |
| *SCHNEIDER, ROBERT | Budgets By Design |
| SCHNITZER, ROBERT | Movicorp Holdings, Inc. |
| SCHRECK, IRA | Frankfurt, Garbus, Klein & Selz |
| SCHREIBER, JAMES P. | Leonard, Dicker & Schreiber |

©1995, Hollywood Financial Directory No. 3
310-315-4815 or 800-815-0503 outside California

*SCHUBE, PETER ................................................Henson Prods., Jim
*SCHUERMANN, MARTIN.....................Johnson Productions, Don
SCHULBERG, SANDRA.............................. American Playhouse
*SCHULZE, KARL J. ................................................ Hankin & Co.
SCHUSTER, JEREMY G. .................................Schuster & Associates
*SCHWAB III, NELSON ............................ Blockbuster Entertainment Group
SCHWARTZ, DOUG ..........................Baywatch Production Co.
*SCHWARTZ, JEFF.....................Padell, Nadell, Fine, Weinberger & Co.
SCHWARTZ, JOHN ...............................ABC Productions
SCHWARTZ, LESTER J. ...................Zivetz, Schwartz & Saltsman, CPA's
*SCHWARTZ, RUSSELL ......................HBO Independent Prods.
*SCHWARTZ, SANDER ......................Columbia Picts. Television
*SCHWIMER, SCOTT .............................. Crown Intl. Pictures
SCOTT, RIDLEY ........................................RCS/PMP Films
SCOTT, TONY ........................................RCS/PMP Films
*SEAL, JAMES L. .................... Rosenfeld, Meyer & Susman
SEBOLD, MARYELLEN.....................21st Century Film Corp.
SEIBERT, FRED ...........................Hanna-Barbera, Inc.
*SEILER, MARK .............................. Capella Films Inc.
SELDIS, MARK ...................................................... Havoc
*SEMEL, TERRY ................................................ Warner Bros..
*SEVUSH, RALPH ........................Pachyderm Entertainment
SEWARD, AMANDA .............................Hanna-Barbera, Inc.
*SEXTON, JENNIFER ..................................Burrud Productions, Bill
SHADOAN, J.T. ........................................Warner Bros. PayTV
SHAFER, MARTIN .....................Castle Rock Entertainment


*SHAFFER, THOMAS H. .....................First Los Angeles Bank, Ent. Ind. Div.
SHAH, SUNDIP ....................................................Imperial Ent.
SHAH, SUNIL R. ...............................................Imperial Ent.
*SHAMBERG, MICHAEL.........................................Jersey Films
SHANE, ARNOLD ............................ Bochco Prods., Steven
*SHAPIRO, ANDRA .......................................... Nickelodeon
*SHAPIRO, CARL.....................Paul, Hastings, Janosky & Walker
SHAPIRO, CYNTHIA .......................... Bell Associates, Dave
SHAPIRO, ESTHER .....................Shapiro Ent. Inc., Richard & Esther
SHAPIRO, RICHARD .....................Shapiro Ent. Inc., Richard & Esther
SHAW, NINA L. .................... Del, Rubel, Shaw, Mason & Derin
SHAYE, ROBERT ................................ New Line Cinema
SHEEHAN, ROBERT .....................Paramount Domestic TV
SHEINBERG, SIDNEY ........................................MCA Inc.
*SHEPARD, LORNA ........................ New World Entertainment
SHEPHARD, CHARLES ..... Greenberg Glusker Fields Claman & Machtinger
*SHER, STACEY ........................................Jersey Films
SHERMAN, ROGER ....................... Mitchell, Silberberg & Knupp
SHIELDS, WILLIAM A. ................GEL Production/Distribution
SHUGART, GRETCHEN .....................Bank of Montreal
SHUMWAY, JEFFREY L. .....................Rosenfeld, Meyer & Susman
SIEGEL, CLARK ...........................................Loeb & Loeb
*SIFFERMANN, CAROLYN .....................New World Entertainment
*SIGMAN, ROBERT .....................Republic Pictures Corp.
SILBERMAN, JEFF .....................Showtime Networks Inc.
*SILVER, CASEY ....................................Universal Pictures
*SILVERBERG, CHARLES ............ Mitchell, Silberberg & Knupp
*SILVERMAN, GENE ............................ PolyGram Video
*SILVERMAN, ROBIN .....................Bohbot Entertainment
*SILVERMANN, MARSHALL ..................... Warner Bros. Pictures
*SILVERSTEIN, COREY .....................Avenue Pictures
*SIMMONS, JED ....................................Hanna-Barbera, Inc.
SIMON, CRAIG ......Berger, Kahn, Shafton, Moss, Figler, Simon & Gladstone
SIMON, JODY .....................Nelson, Guggenheim, Felker & Levine
*SIMON, SARINA.....................Philips Media Electronic Publishing
SIMON, VANDA .....................40 Acres & A Mule Filmworks Inc.
SIMPSON, LARY C. .....................Bloom Dekom Hergott & Cook
SINCLAIR, NIGEL .....................Sinclair, Tenenbaum, Olesiuk & Co., Inc.
SINCLAIR, NIGEL .....................InterMedia/Film Equities Inc.
SINGER, JOSEPH M. .....................Singer Prods. Inc., Joseph M.
*SINGLAUB, USA (RET.), MAJ. GEN. JOHN K. ........ Sentinel TVCorp.
*SINGLETON, JOHN .....................New Deal Prods., Inc.
SIPOS, THOMAS M. .....................Sipos, Thomas M.
*SIRKOT, DENISE.......................................Gracie Films


SKEGGS, ROY .....................Hammer International
SKOURAS, TOM.....................Skouras Picts. Inc.
SKRZYNIARZ, WILLIAM J.....................Rosenfeld, Meyer & Susman
*SLADEK, DANIEL J. .....................Cine Grande Corporation
SLAN, JON .....................Paragon Entertainment Corp.
SLOANE, OWEN.....................Sloane, Owen
SLOBODIEN, MYRON L. .....................Loeb & Loeb
SLOSS, JOHN.....................Sloss, Law Office P.C.
SMALER, NEAL .....................Fries Entertainment
SMARINSKY, MIKE.....................Metro-Goldwyn-Mayer Inc.
*SMITH, DEBBIE.....................Patchett Kaufman Entertainment
*SMITH, GLEN A. .....................Big Sky Entertainment

*SMITH, JANINE .....................Gipson Hoffman & Pancione
SMITH, JEFF.....................Walt Disney Company, The
SMITH, JEFFREY.....................Lifetime Television (NY)
SMITH, JILL .....................Greenberg Glusker Fields Claman & Machtinger
*SMITH, KELLY.....................Alliance Communications
SMITH, MICHAEL .....................Mesirow Private Equity
*SMITH, PAUL .....................TriStar Pictures
*SMITH JR., GEORGE.....................Viacom, Inc.
SMITH, III, ROBERT G. .....................Smith Affiliated Capital Corp.
*SMITH, JR., HUBERT T. .....................Twentieth TV
SMITH, PH.D, ROBERT G. .....................Smith Affiliated Capital Corp.
*SMOKLER, SANDRA K. .....................Twentieth Century Fox Film Corp.
*SNEED, GREG.....................Twentieth Century Fox Film Corp.
SOAMES, RICHARD .....................Film Finances, Inc.
*SOBEL, WILLIAM .....................Edelstein, Laird & Sobel
SOLAN, AMY .....................Baltimore Pictures
*SOLLIDAY, JR., ROBERT E. .....................Entertainment Financiers Inc.
*SOLOMON, ALAN .....................Telepictures Prods.
*SOLOMON, GENE .....................Mitchell, Silberberg & Knupp
*SOLOMON, JOSEPH .....................Cineworld Pictures, Ltd.
*SOMMER, PAUL .....................Sommer & Bear
*SORRENTINO, EVELYN .....................First Interstate Bank of Calif - Ent. Div.
*SORRENTINO, RALPH .....................Bohbot Entertainment
SOTTNICK, MARK .....................Rabbit Ears Prods.
SPAK, JOANNA .....................Walt Disney Television & Telecommunications
*SPAN, ROBERT .....................Paul, Hastings, Janosky & Walker
SPATT, MICHAEL .....................New Line Cinema
*SPATZ, ALAN B. .....................Hill Wynne Troop & Meisinger
SPEER, JOHN M. .....................First National Bank of Chicago, The
SPELLING, AARON .....................Spelling Television Inc.
*SPELMAN, PETER .....................Rosenfeld, Meyer & Susman
*SPENCER, TARA .....................I.N.I. Entertainment Group Inc.
SPEVAK, ALBERT .....................NBC Productions


*SPIEGELMAN, MARION .....................Film Finances, Inc.
*SPIELBERG, STEVEN.....................Amblin Entertainment
*SPIELBERG, STEVEN.....................Dreamworks/SKG
SPINNER, RICHARD .....................ABC Cable & Intl. Broadcast Group
SPIRA, IMMANUEL .....................Katten Muchin Zavis & Weitzman
SPIRA, STEVEN .....................Warner Bros. Pictures
*SPRINGER, PAUL.....................Paramount Domestic Distribution
SPRY, ROBIN .....................Telescene Communications Inc.
STABLER, STEVEN .....................Motion Picture Corp. of America
STACK, THOMAS .....................Columbia Pictures
STAENBERG, MARC R. .....................Staenberg, The Law Offices of Marc R.
STAGER, PAUL .....................Warner Bros. Television
*STAIKOPOULOS, JOANNE.....................Bohbot Entertainment
STAMLER, GARY .....................Buchalter, Nemer, Fields & Younger
*STANBURY, GEORGE.....................Stanbury, Fishelman & Levy
STANDER, STEPHEN .....................NBC Inc.
STANKEVICH, MARK A....Greenberg Glusker Fields Claman & Machtinger
STARGEL, RANDY .....................Rysher Entertainment
*STARK, RAY .....................Rastar Prods.
STARTZ, JANE .....................Scholastic Prods.
*STASSON, DEBBIE .....................Scripps Howard Productions
STAUB, RUTH .....................Troubleshooters, Inc.
STEELE, DONALD .....................Mitchell, Silberberg & Knupp
*STEELE, GEORGE .....................Pacific Arts
STEELE, SUSAN .....................Cabin Fever Entertainment
STEIN, GARY .....................Lancit Media Prods.
STEIN, MARC .....................Slaff, Mosk, & Rudman
STEIN, ESQ., RICHARD.....................Dancing Asparagus Prods.
*STEINBERG, DAVID.....................First Look Picts./Overseas Filmgroup
STEINBERG, ROBERT H. .....................Gipson Hoffman & Pancione
STEINER, REBEL .....................Loeb & Loeb
STEINHART, TERRAN T. .....................Steinhart, Terran T.
STEINHAUER, PHYLLIS.....................Steinhauer, Phyllis A.
STEINKE, PAUL .....................Walt Disney Motion Pictures Group
*STEPHENS, THERESA.....................Stephens & Associates
*STEPHENS, WARREN A. .....................Stephens Inc.
STERN, ANDREW .....................Celebrity Home Ent.
*STERN, DAVID.....................Twentieth Century Fox Film Corp.
STERN, SANDRA .....................TriStar TV
*STERN, TODD.............Weissmann, Wolff, Bergman, Coleman & Silverman
*STEUBER, SCOTT W. .....................Hill Wynne Troop & Meisinger
*STEVENS, JOE .....................Sony Television Entertainment
STEVENS, PAULINE.....................Morrison & Foerster
STEWART, GARRY D.....................Stewart & Harris
STIFFELMAN, GARY .....................Ziffren Brittenham Branca & Fischer


STIGLIANO, JOAN.....................International Film Guarantors Inc.
STILTS, EVE.....................Near North Insurance Brokerage, Inc.
STODDARD, BRANDON .....................ABC Productions
STODDARD, KENNETH B. .....................United Jersey Bank

| | |
|---|---|
| *STOGEL, LAUREN | Mitchell, Silberberg & Knupp |
| *STOKKE, JON | Elsboy Entertainment |
| STOLNITZ, ART | Warner Bros. Television |
| STONE, DOUGLAS | Mitchell, Silberberg & Knupp |
| STONE, RONALD | Stone & Asoociates |
| *STORMS, STEPHANIE | Viacom Productions |
| STOTT, JEFFREY | Castle Rock Entertainment |
| *STRAUS, SEYMOUR | Padell, Nadell, Fine, Weinberger & Co. |
| STRAUSS, PETER E. | Movie Group, The |
| STRAUSS, ROBERT | Cineville Inc. |
| STREIMER, JAN | Castle Rock Entertainment |
| STRIBLEY, ARTHUR | Horwitz Organization, The Lewis |
| STRUM, NEIL | MTM |
| STUART, JOHN W. | Golden Harvest Films |
| STUBBS, JOHN R. | Price Waterhouse |
| *STULBERG, ROBERT L. | Armstrong, Hirsch, Jackoway, et al. |
| SUBOTNICK, STUART | Orion Pictures Corporation |
| *SULLIVAN, MARY | Mitchell, Silberberg & Knupp |
| *SULLIVAN, MICHAEL | United Paramount Network |
| SULLIVAN, PATRICK | Bank of Montreal |
| *SULLIVAN, REID | Columbia Pictures |
| SUNDERLAND, RONALD B. | ABC Entertainment |
| SUPNIK, PAUL D. | Supnik, Paul D. |
| *SUSAN, TOM | Dean Witter Reynolds |
| SUSMAN, ALLEN E. | Rosenfeld, Meyer & Susman |
| *SUSSMAN, JEROME | Kaufman Esq., Peter L. |
| SUSSMAN, JEROME J. | Sussman, Jerome J. |
| SUTHERLAND, JAMES | Overseas Financial Services |
| *SWANN,, KIM | Hall Communications, Arsenio |
| SWARTZ, KIM | Republic Pictures Corp. |
| SWEENEY, ANNE | FX Networks |
| *SYLVESTER, WARD | Pacific Arts |
| SYMES, JOHN | MGM Worldwide TV Group |
| *TABRIZI, ALEXANDER | Trivision Pictures Inc. |
| *TAFFNER, JR., DON | Taffner Entertainment Ltd. |
| TAKAHASHI, DREW | Colossal Pictures |
| TALLEY, DAVID | Fox Broadcasting Co. |
| TANAKA, JEAN E. | Del, Rubel, Shaw, Mason & Derin |
| TANNEN, KATHY L. | Tannen, Kathy L. |
| TARR, PAMELA | Squeak Pictures Inc. |
| *TARTIKOFF, BRANDON | New World Entertainment |
| TARULLI, JOE | HBO (L.A.) |
| TASHJIAN, H. RICHARD | Tashjian and Tashjian |
| *TATEN, MARY | Katten Muchin Zavis & Weitzman |
| TAUBER, JAMES | Propaganda Films |
| TAYLOR, DONNA | DISC Insurance Services |
| TAYLOR, KAREN | Carolco Pictures |
| TAYLOR, MINNA | Fox Broadcasting Co. |
| TAYLOR, STEPHEN P. | Paramount Picturcs . |
| *TEELE, CYNTHIA | Paramount Domestic TV |
| *TEETOR, JACK | Sojourn Entertainment |
| *TELLEM, NANCY | Warner Bros. Television |
| TEMPLE, MARK S. | Temple, Mark S. |
| TENENBAUM, IRWIN | Sinclair, Tenenbaum, Olesiuk & Co., Inc. |
| TENNISON, DEBORAH | Communication for Transformation |
| TENSER, MARK | Crown Intl. Pictures |
| TENZER, MITCHELL | Ziffren Brittenham Branca & Fischer |
| TESTANI, MARIO | Gelfand, Rennert & Feldman |
| *THAU, ANDREW | Twentieth TV |
| *THAU, ROBERT H. | Rosenfeld, Meyer & Susman |
| THAYER, TOM | Universal Television |
| THOMAS, JEFF | Rysher Entertainment |
| THOMPSON, BRYAN | Clark Prods., Dick |
| THOMPSON, DAVID | Walt Disney Company, The |
| THOMPSON, JANE | Rees Assocs., Marian |
| THOMPSON, LARRY | Thompson Organization, Larry |
| *THOMPSON, RICHARD D. | Bloom Dekom Hergott & Cook |
| THOMSON, JULIE | Pacific Western Prods. |
| THORNBURG, LEE | Lone Star Picts. Intl. Inc. |
| THURLOW, TERRY | Colossal Pictures |
| THURSTON, BARRY | Columbia TriStar TV Distribution |
| TIFFANY, CATHERINE | Tiffany & Associates, Catherine |
| TIMOTHY, RAYMOND J. | Furman Selz Inc. |
| TISCH, STEVE | Tisch Co., The Steve |
| *TITLE, GAIL MIGDAL | Rosenfeld, Meyer & Susman |
| TIVOLI, ALAN | Oberman, Tivoli & Miller Ltd. |
| TOBEY, BRUCE D. | Hill Wynne Troop & Meisinger |
| *TODER, JEFF A. | Hill Wynne Troop & Meisinger |
| *TOLEP, MARTIN B. | Smith Affiliated Capital Corp. |
| TOLL, ROGER | Columbia Pictures |
| TOLLINGER, JANE | Lifetime Television (NY) |
| TOMITSUKA, ISAMU | JVC Entertainment, Inc. |

| | |
|---|---|
| *TON, BRIAN | American First Run Studios |
| *TONAZZI, ESQ., SILVIO | Tulchin & Associates, Harris |
| *TOPPER, NORMAN | Rankin/Bass |
| TORREY, TERESA M. | Travelers Insurance Co. |
| *TOUMASIS, PETE | RCS/PMP Films |
| TOVMASSIAN, HENRY T. | Kehr Crook Tovmassian & Fox |
| *TRAINOR, ED | Paramount Pictures . |
| *TRATTNER, DARREN M. | Rosenfeld, Meyer & Susman |
| TREMAIN, HARRY | Paragon Entertainment Corp. |
| *TRICARICO, CHRISTOPHER | Behr & Robinson |
| *TRIGGS, THOMAS D. | Rosenfeld, Meyer & Susman |
| TROOP, RICHARD | Hill Wynne Troop & Meisinger |
| TROPE, KONRAD L. | Barab, Vaughan & Kline |
| TROSS, ROBERTA LYNN | American Playhouse |
| *TRUNKEY, CHRISTOPHER | Kings Road Entertainment Inc. |
| TRUSS, PAUL | Edelstein, Laird & Sobel |
| TSACALIS, NORMAN A. | Viacom, Inc. |
| TSUDA, KESA | NBC Entertainment |
| *TULCHIN, ESQ., HARRIS E. | Tulchin & Associates, Harris |
| *TULLY, N. LINSEY | Sunbow Prods. |
| TURNER, HANS | Goldwyn Co., Samuel |
| *TURNER, LAWRENCE J. | Turner, Lawrence J. |
| TURNER, RALPH | Turner Accountancy Corp. |
| TURTLE, JON | Rocket Pictures |
| *TUZON, RITA L. | Hill Wynne Troop & Meisinger |
| TYERMAN, BARRY. | Armstrong, Hirsch, Jackoway, Tyerman & Wertheimer |
| ULLOA, RONALD | Hearst Entertainment |
| ULMAN, LARRY | Katten Muchin Zavis & Weitzman |
| *UNDERWOOD, JARED | Imperial Bank, Ent. Ind. Group |
| UNGERMAN, NICOLE | NBC Entertainment |
| *VAJNA, ANDREW | Cinergi Pictures Entertainment Inc. |
| VALLEY, JEFF | Skadden, Arps, Slate, Meagher & Flom |
| *VAN CAMP, LENORE | Intrazone Inc./Intrazone Interactive Ltd. |
| VAN DYKE, ROSE | Truman Van Dyke Co. |
| VAN DYKE, TRUMAN | Truman Van Dyke Co. |
| VAN HOUDT, JAN | First Charter Bank |
| *VAN PATTEN, DENISE | Fox TV Stations Prods. |
| VAN PETTEN, VANCE S. | Twentieth TV |
| VANDERKLOOT, WILLIAM | VanDerKloot Film & Television Inc. |
| *VANCE, MARILYN | Mruvka Entertainment, Alan |
| *VANN, ESQ., BRUCE | Largo Entertainment |
| *VAUGHN, DENNIS | Paul, Hastings, Janosky & Walker |
| VEGLIE, JACQUELINE | Actor's Equity Association (A.E.A.) |
| *VEIN, JON F. | Dern & Vein |
| VERGARA, DOLLY M. | Imperial Ent. |
| VESPERMAN, GARY | Film Funding Inc. |
| *VIEBROCK, MIKE | Sony Television Entertainment |
| VIGMAN, SIOW | Di Bona Prods., Vin |
| VILLARD, DIMITRI | Laidlaw Holdings Inc. |
| VINCENT, E. DUKE | Spelling Television Inc. |
| VIVIANI, ESQ., DOUGLAS D. | Viviani Esq., The Law Office of Douglas D. |
| *VOKULICH, RICHARD | Fox Broadcasting Co. |
| *VOLPE, RAY | Ventura Entertainment Group Ltd. |
| VON ARX, DEBBIE | Beacon Pictures |
| WAGMAN, ROBERT M. | Price Waterhouse |
| WAGNER, ALEX | Lifetime Television (NY) |
| WAGNER, EVE | Greenberg Glusker Fields Claman & Machtinger |
| WAGNER, STEVE | Freedman, Broder & Co. |
| WALCHEK, SCOTT | Sanctuary Woods Multimedia Corp. |
| WALDRON, JAMES | Gerber ITC Ent. Group, The |
| *WALKER, CHARLES | Paul, Hastings, Janosky & Walker |
| WALKER, CHRIS | Intrazone Inc./Intrazone Interactive Ltd. |
| WALKER, DARRELL | Columbia Pictures |
| *WALKER, ROBERT | Paul, Hastings, Janosky & Walker |
| *WALLERSTEIN, ROBERT S. | Armstrong, Hirsch, Jackoway, et al. |
| WALTERS, GARY | Walters, The Law Offices of Gary |
| *WANDER-PERNA, LUCY | Sony Pictures Entertainment |
| *WARD, DAVID | Ventura Entertainment Group Ltd. |
| *WARREN, JOSEPH | A&E Television Networks |
| WASSERMAN, HARMON | Gelfand, Newman & Wasserman |
| WASSERMAN, LEW R. | MCA Inc. |
| WATERMAN, JACK | Paramount Home Video Distribution |
| WATERMAN, STEVE | Franklin/Waterman Ent. |
| *WATERS, TIM | Hemdale Communications Inc. |
| WAX, STEVE | Stiletto Entertainment |
| *WAXMAN, JULIE | Warner Bros. Television |
| WEAKLAND, LEWIS | Carolco Pictures |
| WEATHERSBY, CASSIUS VERNON | Londine Productions |
| WEATHERSBY, NADINE | Londine Productions |
| *WEBB SCHWARZ, WENDOLYN | Harvey Entertainment Company, The |
| *WEBSTER, JOYCE | Columbia TriStar Home Video |
| *WECHSLER, WINIFRED B. | Disney Channel, The |

©1995, Hollywood Financial Directory No. 3
310-315-4815 or 800-815-0503 outside California

WEIER, LARRY .................................................. Universal Pictures
WEINBERGER, AARON ................. Padell, Nadell, Fine, Weinberger & Co.
*WEINER, JON. ................................................ Capell, Coyne & Co.
WEINER, WILLIAM S. ............................... New Regency Prods. Inc.
*WEINMAN, ROSALYN ...................................... NBC Entertainment
WEINSTEIN, BOB ......................................................... Miramax Films
WEINSTEIN, HARVEY ............................................... Miramax Films
WEINSTEIN, JEROME ............................................. Weinstein & Hart
*WEINSTEIN, MARK M. ...................................................... Viacom, Inc.
WEISS, JEFFREY S. ...................................... Genesis Entertainment

WEISS, ROBERT K. ................................... St. Clare Entertainment
WEISSBERGER, KATHI ................... Gerber ITC Ent. Group, The
*WEISSLER, ERIC C. Armstrong, Hirsch, Jackoway, Tyerman & Wertheimer
WEISSMANN, ERIC ..... Weissmann, Wolff, Bergman, Coleman & Silverman
WERNER, KENNETH D. ............................... Buena Vista Television
WERNER, TOM ...................................... Carsey-Werner Co., The
WERNICK, JEFF ............................................... DIC Entertainment
WERTHEIMER, ALAN .................... Armstrong, Hirsch, Jackoway, et al.
WERTHEIMER, THOMAS ................................................. MCA Inc.
*WESLEY, JAMES .............................. Lifetime Television (NY)
WESTBERG, DAVID ................................ Westberg Entertainment
WESTHUSING, ELDEN L. ..................................... Hankin & Co.
WESTMORELAND, PAMELA D. ............... Travelers Insurance Co.
*WEXLER, DAVID D. ..................... Rosenfeld, Meyer & Susman
*WHALEN, MAUREEN ................................... Disney Channel, The
WHELPLEY, ELIZABETH .................... Carsey-Werner Co., The
WHERITY, SCOTT .................................... Miss Universe Inc.
WHITE, LEONARD .......................... Orion Pictures Corporation
*WHITE, PAIGE ............................. Dobson Global Entertainment
WHITEHEAD, GLENN ................................................ HBO (L.A.)
WHITESELL, JOHN .................... Warner Bros. Intl. TV Distrib.
WHITSON, GWEN .......................... Warner Bros. Intl. TV Distrib.
*WILBUR, DAVID E. ........................................... Hankin & Co.
*WILDER, RICHELLE. .......................... Hammer International
WILEY, DAN ............................................................ Wiley, Dan
WILLAIMS, KENNETH ................... Sony Pictures Entertainment
WILLIAMS, HARLEY J. .......... Blanc, Williams, Johnston & Kronstadt
WILLIAMS, JEREMY .............................. Warner Bros. Pictures
WILLIS, CHARLIE. ................. VanDerKloot Film & Television Inc.
*WILSON, ALLISON .......................... NorthStar Ent. Group, Inc.
WILSON, KATHEY ................... Actor's Equity Association (A.E.A.)
WILSON, MICHAEL. ......................................... Danjaq Inc.
WILSON-DELOJE, MOLLY. ................................... HBO (L.A.)
WINDLE, SUSAN B. ................... Zivetz, Schwartz & Saltsman, CPA's
*WINTERINGHAM, TIM ..................................... Hill/Fields Ent.
WISEMAN, BRUCE ................................... Wiseman & Burke, Inc.
WISHIK, GARY ................................ Wishik, Law Offices of Gary S.
WITHEY, RICHARD J. ............................... Price Waterhouse
WITTENBERG, JESS ........................... Castle Rock Entertainment
*WOHL, LINDA ................... Paramount Pictures Motion Picture Group
*WOLF, BRYAN ............................................................ Dern & Vein
WOLF, MARVIN LOUIS ............................... Wolf, Marvin Louis
WOLF, SUSAN ................................................ Kenoff & Machtinger
WOLFE, ELIZABETH. .................................................................. PBS
WOLFEN, WERNER F. ............................................ Irell & Manella

WOLPER, DAVID L. ................................... Wolper Org. Inc., The
WOLPER, MARK M. ................................... Wolper Org. Inc., The
WOLTERS, JOHN ................................................ ABC Entertainment
WOOD, GORDON E. ................... Twentieth Century Fox Television
WOOD, JANET. ......................... Olympic Entertainment Group
WOODBURY, TOM .............................................. HBO (L.A.)
WOODS, MEL ................................................ Saban Entertainment
WOOLLEY, STEPHEN .............................................. Scala Prods.
WOOLNER, KURT .......................................... Film Finances, Inc.
WORKMAN, SUSAN ................................... Universal Television
WULF, MELVIN E. ..................... Beldock Levine & Hoffman
*WYMAN, MARK ................................................ Columbia Pictures
WYNNE, ROBERT J. .................. Hill Wynne Troop & Meisinger
YEE, DEREK ...................................... Albright, Yee & Schimt
YELDELL, ERIC ................................. Fox Broadcasting Co.
YOEL, MARY ........................... City National Bank - Ent. Div.
YOUNG, JAMIE ..................... Ziffren Brittenham Branca & Fischer
*YOUNG, KATHRYN A. ................... Rosenfeld, Meyer & Susman
YOUNG, MELODY .............. Young & Company, M.G., A Bus. Mgmt. Corp
YOUNGBLOOD, JULIETTE ............................... Irell & Manella
*YOUNGER, LAURIE .......... Walt Disney Television & Telecommunications
*YULISH, GREGORY M. ................. Harvey Entertainment Company, The
*YVLOFF, SHARYN .......... First Look Picts./Overseas Filmgroup
ZAPPY, LEAH ....................................................... Brooksfilms, Ltd.
*ZATOLOKIN, JAMES R. ................. Sentinel Television Corporation
*ZEITINGER, JANICE .................. Imperial Bank, Ent. Ind. Group
ZELDOW, EDWARD D. ........................................... Irell & Manella

ZIFFREN, KENNETH .................... Ziffren Brittenham Branca & Fischer
ZIFFREN, LEO G. ................................. Gibson, Dunn & Crutcher
ZIFFREN, LESTER. ............................... Gibson, Dunn & Crutcher
ZILL, STEPHANIE ....................... I.N.I. Entertainment Group Inc.
*ZIMMER, MARY ANN ................... A&E Television Networks
ZIMMERMAN, THOMAS A. ........................ Paramount Pictures .
ZINKIN, BENJAMIN ................................... New Line Cinema
*ZINN, HARRY ................... Paul, Hastings, Janosky & Walker
*ZIONTZ, MEL. ....................... Rosenfeld, Meyer & Susman
ZIPPERMAN, BARBARA ..................... Interscope Communications Inc.
ZISKIN, RON ................................... Four Point Entertainment
*ZOHAR, LIOR Z. ....................... Rosenfeld, Meyer & Susman
*ZOLKE, SCOTT. ................................................ Heenan Blaikie
DE PROSSE, KANDY ................... Matlen & Associates, C.P.A., H. Roy
*VAN DE BUNT, DIRK W. ........................... Carsey-Werner Co., The